T0274975

Atlas of
Dark
Destinations

EXPLORE THE WORLD OF
DARK TOURISM

First published in Great Britain in 2021
by Laurence King Publishing
an imprint of The Orion Publishing Group Ltd
Carmelite House, 50 Victoria Embankment
London EC4Y 0DZ

An Hachette UK Company

3 5 7 9 10 8 6 4 2

Copyright © Text 2021 Peter Hohenhaus
Back cover image © Sean Gallup/Getty Images

The moral right of Peter Hohenhaus to be identified as
the author of this work has been asserted in accordance
with the Copyright, Designs and Patents Act of 1988.

All rights reserved. No part of this publication may be
reproduced, stored in a retrieval system, or transmitted
in any form or by any means, electronic, mechanical,
photocopying, recording, or otherwise, without the
prior permission of both the copyright owner and the
above publisher of this book.

A CIP catalogue record for this book is
available from the British Library.

ISBN 978 1 91394 719 4

Book design: Charlie Smith Design
Commissioning editor: Zara Larcombe
Project editor: Gaynor Sermon
Picture research: Gaynor Sermon and Maria Ranauro
Production: Davina Cheung

Origination by DL Imaging Ltd
Printed in Italy by L.E.G.O Spa

Laurence King Publishing is committed to ethical and sustainable
production. We are proud participants in The Book Chain Project®
bookchainproject.com

FSC   MIX
      Paper
      FSC® C104740

www.laurenceking.com
www.orionbooks.co.uk

Atlas of Dark Destinations

EXPLORE THE WORLD OF DARK TOURISM

Peter Hohenhaus

Laurence King Publishing

Contents

Western & Southwestern Europe

Central Europe

Southern & Southeastern Europe

Introduction

I'm a travel addict, and I've long been interested in modern history – which is of course full of dark chapters. Then I discovered a link between the two: 'dark tourism'. In fact, when I first came across this term, back in 2007 in a newspaper interview with one of the pioneers of the academic study of the subject, I was already a 'dark tourist'. Only the year before I had been on my first trip to Chernobyl (see p220), the year before that I had travelled to North Korea (p314) and in 2003 I had visited Robben Island (p257) in South Africa. All of these trips were extremely memorable.

I can well recall how exciting it felt to enter the Chernobyl Exclusion Zone and stand right in front of the iconic sarcophagus of reactor 4 that I had seen so many times in the media. Actually being there, on the very spot where the disaster had happened, was deeply impressive. I felt connected to history and also to my own biography, because I had keenly watched everything about the disaster and its aftermath on TV. Having made it here felt very rewarding. The trip to North Korea was outstanding in other ways, offering insights into a completely different and utterly unfamiliar world which is both puzzling and crazy but also strangely fascinating. It was great to learn about it firsthand and see it with my own eyes. My visit to Robben Island was very moving because an ex-inmate acted as a guide, so was able to add his own personal story. Given that apartheid (p258) had ended only about a decade before I visited, it felt very fresh and meaningful. On top of the tragic history and grim look of the place it seemed like there was promise of something bright coming out of the darkness.

Having become aware of the concept of dark tourism, I wanted more. In other words, I was immediately hooked. I started reading up on the topic and, more importantly, I increasingly geared my own travelling towards visiting dark destinations. While there was plenty of academic literature about dark tourism, guidance for travellers interested in such places was dearly lacking. So I started my own website – dark-tourism.com – where I give not only practical travel tips but also background information, personal impressions and photo galleries. By now, with many hundreds of such destinations in almost 100 countries under my belt, I've become quite an expert in this. And that is what led to this book.

Sometimes dark tourism receives bad press, with the media overly sensationalizing aspects of it. Maybe one reason for this is that the two words 'dark' and 'tourism' seem to clash, especially when 'dark' is interpreted as something bad while 'tourism' is equated with leisure. But not all travellers simply want escapism. Many seek more than 'getting away from it all' and on the contrary want to engage mindfully with the real world when travelling. Dark tourism is one way of doing that, and for the most part it is perfectly legitimate. Just think about it: if you've ever visited a memorial museum or stood by the grave of a famous person then you, too, have engaged in dark tourism. It might be said that almost everybody is a dark tourist to some degree, at least occasionally. A few dark destinations attract very large numbers of visitors, such as Auschwitz (p170), the largest concentration camp memorial, and Alcatraz, the legendary prison island (p15). These are places where dark tourism and mass tourism overlap.

It should be noted that 'dark tourism', while useful as a cover term, is a rather vague concept. And indeed, what do Auschwitz, Chernobyl or Alcatraz have in common other than that they all have some dark association? Not that much – there are probably more differences between them than commonalities. But the fact that there is such a wide range of different types of dark destinations, in my view, adds to dark tourism's appeal – it just doesn't get boring.

Admittedly, on the fringes of dark tourism (in the broadest sense of the term) there are ethically controversial things, such as 'slum tourism' (viewing ongoing poverty in shanty towns) or travelling to the infamous Aokigahara 'suicide forest' in Japan (with the possibility of discovering a corpse). These extremes are sometimes subsumed under the umbrella of dark tourism but are hardly representative of the majority of dark tourism, and I would personally never partake in them.

Visitor conduct is something that you must carefully consider when going to some of these places. For instance, dark tourism does not go well with taking smiley selfies. Visiting sites of tragedy requires respectful behaviour. Some sites have visitor regulations in place, and these should be observed. Most visitors to sites like Auschwitz and Robben Island do behave appropriately and, when asked their motivation for visiting, answer that they want to learn about history and/or pay their respects to the victims. For some the journey may even be a kind of pilgrimage. Dark tourism may not be uplifting in a purely 'fun' sense, but it is certainly enlightening and broadens one's horizons immensely.

A difficult question relating to dark tourism is this: how much time should have elapsed since a tragedy for a site associated with it to legitimately become a tourist destination? It is generally agreed that going back too soon can be problematic, but how exactly to define 'too soon' is tricky, and there may be borderline cases. For the majority of the destinations included here, however, the dark association is firmly in the past. At the same time, though, this book maintains a focus on modern history and does not relate back much further than the late nineteenth century.

There is a surprisingly widespread misunderstanding about dark tourism: that it is dangerous. Almost all of it is not, with the exception of, say, the possibility of slightly elevated radiation exposure in places like Chernobyl (see Radiation feature on p224), and the physical risks of entering crumbling ghost-town buildings or exploring terrains with volcanic activity. But these are manageable risks. However, travelling to places where you are deliberately putting your life on the line, such as entering active war zones, is something I most definitely would not encourage and I have never done this myself. Hence the selection of places in this book excludes such controversial sites as Aokigahara and war zones. Also not included are destinations that are 'dark' only in a paranormal or fictional sense, so you will not find haunted houses, ghost hunts, UFO sightings or horror movie locations here either.

This book is largely based on my own extensive travel experiences and the research for my website. It is not a digest of that website, though, but has been originally written to provide an overview of the realm of dark travel worldwide, and will hopefully whet your appetite for exploring these places – whether you are an active or armchair traveller. Either way, it is my aim that this book can serve as inspiration for your own adventures as well as an eye-opening atlas of discovery.

Dr. Peter Hohenhaus
Vienna, January 2021

About this book

The main objective of this book is to provide an overview of the most important dark destinations around the globe. Some 300 distinct places have been selected, located in 90 different countries, and include prisons, concentration camps, nuclear test sites, volcanoes, assassination spots, medical museums, ghost towns and more. This is an 'Atlas' insomuch as it is geographically organized, roughly from the northwest to the southeast, starting on the West Coast of North America and ending in the South Pacific. Geography is not the main focus here, however, and simple maps are given at the beginning of each section only for general orientation.

All countries have a short introductory text to provide context to the entries that follow. Note that some of the entries count as both destinations and countries at the same time, in particular some small islands. These include territories that are not fully sovereign states but possessions of other countries, such as the British overseas territories of the Falkland Islands (p66) and Gibraltar (p103). Yet owing to their geographical (and partly political and historical) separateness from their 'mother countries' they are treated here as stand-alone destinations. Also included are a couple of self-declared 'breakaway republics', whose status is, at the time of going to press, contested and which are largely not internationally recognized as independent states, in particular Transnistria (p219) and Nagorno-Karabakh/Artsakh (p268).

Each destination entry includes an indication of its location, what category or categories of dark tourism it represents, and two ratings. The first is a star rating from one to five: this is a general quality assessment, reflecting such criteria as how accessible a place is, how well appointed it is for visitors, whether the interpretation is multilingual or not, and other practicalities relating to the tourist experience. The second rating is a 'dark rating', on a scale of one to ten. This is not intended to weigh up tragedy against tragedy, but rather to indicate how tangible the dark events that took place are to visitors today. Under this system, for example, places with physical reminders of genocide, such as authentic structures and artefacts, are given a higher ranking than places where similarly tragic events are represented by symbolic monuments. Similarly, less grim sites like Colditz (p152) or, say, socialist sculpture parks (which may represent repressive regimes but where nobody came to serious harm directly) are also awarded a lower rating.

There is a mixture of long and short entries in the book, and this reflects the relative significance of the destinations; some places receive only a couple of paragraphs while more important top sites (such as Chernobyl) are spread over as many as four pages. In addition to the ca. 300 destination entries, many more places are mentioned in extra boxes that list similar sites of interest to those on a particular page; for example, the famous Père Lachaise cemetery entry includes a selection of other famous cemeteries to explore, and there are ideas for other Vietnam War-related sites to visit among the main entries for Vietnam. Some of the individual entries in the book have an umbrella function, in particular those about cities and islands, where the text refers to a number of individual sites within these places. Counting all of those sites too brings the total number of places included closer to 800, and the number of countries/territories closer to 130.

Also included in the book are thematic feature boxes providing additional information about topics pertinent to the associated entries, such as nuclear weapons and radiation (p25 and p224) and volcanology (p51), or to provide context to dark chapters in history such as the Rwandan genocide or the Korean War (p250 and p316). There are also a number of additional 'Dark Stats' boxes that give facts and figures relating to some of the entries.

Space comes at a premium in any book, so many of the entries have had to be kept concise. However, for almost all of the places covered in this book, further information, including practical travel considerations, co-ordinates, extra historical background and some more personal observations can be found on my dark-tourism.com website. I have been running this site for over twelve years, so a lot of information and many thousands of photos have accumulated there over time.

This book could be accused of a certain Eurocentrism, as the entries for that continent add up to nearly half of the total page count, but this merely reflects history and how it has been recorded. On the other hand, some of the inclusions and omissions, especially in the Americas, Africa and Asia, reflect this author's own travel history.

I have travelled to the vast majority of the places included in this book and have therefore been able to provide a first-hand account of what it's like to visit them (and many of the photos featured within these pages are my own too). There are, however, a few exceptions – countries I have not yet managed to visit but which I deemed too important to be left unmentioned here, most notably Cuba, Algeria, Australia, or Oceania, where I have so far only been to Hawaii and Easter Island (p339 and p345). There are two countries I had intended to visit in 2020, namely Namibia and Taiwan (p255 and p312), but those trips had to be cancelled due to the global coronavirus pandemic. As I had already done my preparatory research on those places they are still included here.

A note about the coronavirus pandemic: this book was written before the outbreak of Covid-19 in 2020, which brought tourism to an abrupt halt. At the time of this reprint, travel restrictions have largely been lifted, but the situation remains unpredictable. The hope is that the pandemic will eventually be a thing of the past and travel can continue as before. There are, however, voices calling for restraint even when the pandemic is over. Indeed, the environmental impact of tourism has to be taken into account, and this may mean restrictions to tourism in the longer term.

Another unforeseen event at the time of writing was the war in Ukraine (p. 220), which began in February 2022. Since then, several of the sites in this book have become inaccessible for the time being – we can only hope that peace will return soon.

The format of this book means that it does not have to be read from cover to cover but can be dipped into anywhere according to your particular interests; or why not pick a random region of the world and see what this book has to offer for it? It is hoped that this book will serve as inspiration for planning your next adventure, but if real travel is not an option – for whatever reason – then at least it can transport you to far-flung corners of the globe at the turn of a page, and enlighten you as to the wide array of fascinating dark destinations that this world has to offer.

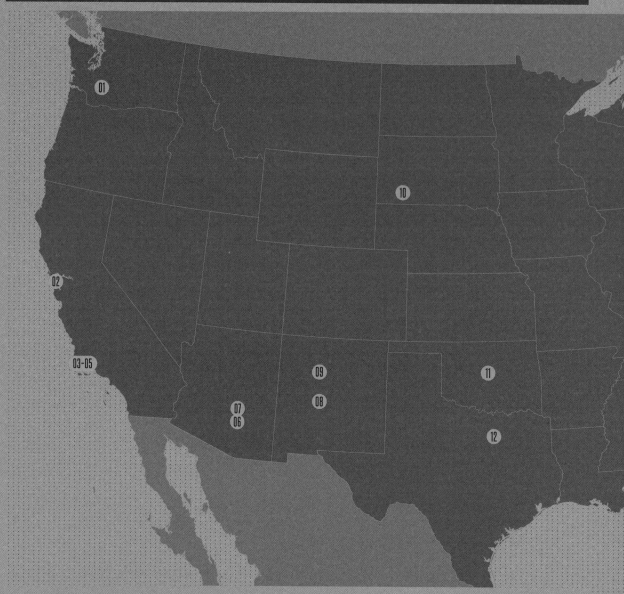

Mount St Helens
Washington State

Alcatraz
San Francisco Bay

Museum of Death
Los Angeles

Holocaust Museum LA
Los Angeles

Museum of Tolerance
Los Angeles

Titan Missile Museum
Arizona

AMARG 'boneyard' and
Pima Air & Space Museum
Arizona

Trinity Site
New Mexico

Museum of Nuclear
Science & History
New Mexico

Wounded Knee
South Dakota

Oklahoma City
National Memorial
Oklahoma

Dealey Plaza
Dallas, Texas

USAF Museum
Dayton, Ohio

West Virginia Penitentiary
West Virginia

Centralia
Pennsylvania

Arlington National Cemetery
Virginia

The Pentagon & 9/11 Memorial
Virginia

US Holocaust
Memorial Museum
Washington D.C.

The National Mall
Washington D.C.

The Enola Gay at
the Smithsonian
Washington D.C.

Mütter Museum
Philadelphia

Eastern State Penitentiary
Philadelphia

National 9/11 Memorial
& Museum
New York

North America

The USA is one of the most rewarding countries for travellers interested in dark destinations. Only a handful of places can be covered here, but among them are noteworthy sites related to the Cold War and nuclear weapons, in addition to some spectacular ex-prisons, natural disaster sites, and the locations of international traumas such as the assassination of President Kennedy and the terrorist attacks of 11 September 2001.

The USA is an ideal destination for road trips and independent travel in general. Rental cars are easily available, and travellers can find motels and chain hotels where pre-booking is rarely necessary almost anywhere other than at particularly popular spots. However, it is a big country, so long distances have to be factored in. It would be pretty much impossible to cover it in its entirety in a single trip; it is best to break it up into several trips and concentrate on specific parts in one visit.

For non-American visitors wanting to explore the 'Land of the Free', the biggest obstacle is getting through immigration. Many nationalities need a visa, and even citizens of those countries that fall under the Visa Waiver Program (including most European countries) must fill in and submit an ESTA (Electronic System for Travel Authorization) form online for which a fee is payable. But once you are in the country, you can move around freely and easily.

Mount St Helens

Washington State • Natural disaster (volcano)

★★★★☆

Dark Rating: 4 ☠

The eruption of Mount St Helens in Washington State in the far northwest of the USA was the biggest volcanic event in the country's history. There had been many warning signs: earthquakes, ash and steam venting and, in particular, a growing bulge on the north slope of the mountain. A state of emergency was declared and access to the area restricted. Only a few scientists and some loggers were allowed in. On 18 May 1980 Mount St Helens blew its top – or rather, its side. The bulge that had been growing for weeks suddenly started moving, creating the largest landslide in recorded history. At the same time, this triggered a lateral blast – a sideways eruption of the volcano.

The mass of hot gas, ash and pulverized rock raced across the land northwards like a gigantic pyroclastic flow (see p51), destroying everything in its path. It reached up to 30km (19 miles) from the crater, some 600 sq km (230 sq miles) were devastated, millions of trees were uprooted and scorched, and the mountain itself lost some 400m (1300ft) in height.

Subsequent lahars (mudflows from volcanic ash) reached as far as 120km (75 miles). The ash plume forming above the volcano rose 25km (15 miles) into the sky. Ash fall affected 11 US states.

In total, 57 people were killed by the eruption, including one scientist, David Johnston, who had positioned himself on a ridge opposite the volcano for observation at what was erroneously deemed a safe distance. Instead, he was right in the middle of the lateral blast's path of destruction and had no chance of survival.

The ridge now bears his name and is the main point of interest for tourists thanks to the visitor centre there, called the Johnston Ridge Observatory. The indoor exhibition provides information about the volcano and how nature is reclaiming the once devastated land. The views over towards Mount St Helens are best from here too; you can see right into the crater and across the pumice plain of total destruction. Near the visitor centre is also a monument dedicated to the victims of the disaster.

Johnston Ridge is reached by Route 504, but only seasonally; the road is closed in winter. The same applies to the roads that lead to the northeastern side of the mountain, from where you get good views of the blow-down zone of forest felled by the eruption, and into Spirit Lake, on the surface of which thousands of dead tree trunks are still floating.

Above
Thousands of trees felled in the eruption in 1980 still float in the lake at the volcano's base.

Left
The north face of Mount St Helens viewed from the Johnston Ridge Observatory. The pumice plain can be seen in the foreground.

Alcatraz

★★★★★

San Francisco Bay, California • Prison

Dark Rating: 5 ☠

This is probably the most (in)famous name of any prison on Earth, the subject of several movies and plenty of stories of escape attempts, revolts and prominent inmates such as Al Capone. Today, it is a very popular tourist destination.

The location, a rocky island in the Bay of San Francisco, California, had originally been a fortified military garrison. It was also already used as a military prison from the late nineteenth century. In the 1930s it was transferred to the Department of Justice and thus became a maximum-security federal penitentiary for the USA's most notorious and dangerous criminals. For that reason, the island attracted the curiosity of ordinary people. Although normal mortals were not allowed to visit the prison island back then, viewing points on the mainland waterfront were set up for those wanting to gaze across the bay through powerful telescopes.

Hollywood played its part in bolstering the almost mystical legacy of Alcatraz, with movies such as *Birdman of Alcatraz* (1962) and *Escape from Alcatraz* (1979). There were indeed several escape attempts, although none were successful. The prison was closed in 1963 and the island abandoned, but in 1969 it was occupied by Native American activists in

Above
The main cell blocks are in the centre of the island with the exercise yard to the rear and ancillary buildings to the left and right.

Below
Looking down a deserted aisle with two levels of prison cells.

an attempt to bring their cause to public attention. By 1971, however, they had abandoned their occupation and a year later the island was given over to the National Park Service.

Since then, Alcatraz has established itself as one of the most popular tourist attractions in the San Francisco region. Visitor numbers are such that it is advisable to book online well ahead (up to 90 days); in high season, tickets may sell out weeks or even months in advance. Tickets are not cheap, but you get a lot for your money. The cost includes the ferry crossing (departing from Pier 33), National Park fees, Park Rangers' talks, an excellent audio-guided tour of the Cellhouse (available in English and ten other languages), and admission to special temporary exhibitions as well as to an introductory historical exhibition by the pier, which also includes the story of the Native American occupation.

The cell blocks are arguably the key attraction here, and the audio-guided tour vividly brings them to life through its narration. This includes the key escape attempts, revolts and other stories. A few cells have been recreated to look as they did when they were occupied, and you can gain an impression of prison life, despite the crowds of visitors.

Other parts of the island can be explored independently, including the exercise yard, gardens and some ancillary buildings, where the throngs thin out. You can also see the administrative block, the lighthouse, the water tower and the prison kitchen and canteen. In total, the recommended visiting time is given as three hours, although you may find that you need longer to explore the island thoroughly. Just make sure not to miss the last ferry back to the mainland!

DARK STATS

Average size of a cell in the main B & C blocks
1.5 X 2.7M (5 X 9FT)

336
Standard cells

In D block (the 'punishment' block), there were
36
segregation cells and
6
solitary confinement cells

Lowest recorded prison population in a given year was
222
and the highest was
302

1545
Prisoners in total

36
Attempted escapes

Average incarceration
8 YEARS

Time as a prison
29 YEARS

Above left
An old warning sign moved into one of the prison island's abandoned buildings.

Museum of Death

★★★☆☆

Hollywood, Los Angeles, California • Death, Murder, Suicide   **Dark Rating: 9** ☻

Los Angeles is primarily known for its association with the entertainment industry, in particular Hollywood. However, not far from the well-known Walk of Fame, at 6031 Hollywood Boulevard, is this highly unusual museum offering a stark contrast to light entertainment. The Museum of Death features one of the most morbid exhibitions in the world. It claims to want to fill a gap in death education, but what you find inside is more often on the gruesome, gory and shocking side.

There is plenty of information, in particular about serial killers and especially about the infamous sect leader Charles Manson. A whole room (called 'Helter Skelter') is devoted to him and the brutal murder of Sharon Tate and friends by the Manson 'Family' in 1969. Other than that, there are graphic photos of other murders, an unofficial photo of the autopsy of JFK (see p28), coffins, body bags and taxidermy. Suicide is covered as a topic too, and exhibits are

included from the Heaven's Gate cult mass suicide of 1997.

Some of the content of the museum is not for the faint-hearted, as the museum duly warns. But for those with enough morbid curiosity, and who think they can stomach it, the museum is certainly worth considering.

Holocaust Museum LA

★★★☆☆

West Hollywood, Los Angeles, California • Holocaust   **Dark Rating: 7** ☻

Formerly known as LAMOTH (standing for Los Angeles Museum of the Holocaust), this has since 2010 been housed in a purpose-built, mostly subterranean structure at Pan Pacific Park in the northwest of the city, just south of Hollywood.

The super-modern permanent exhibition uses audiovisual and interactive elements but also

features original artefacts, such as shoes from Auschwitz (on loan) and the characteristic striped concentration camp clothing. There is also a scale model of the death camp (see p134–5) of Sobibór (p174), made by Thomas Blatt, a prominent survivor of that camp (he passed away only in 2015), who also comments on this topic on a video screen.

The subject of the Holocaust is quite comprehensively covered. The exhibition also touches on related subjects, such as other genocides, including those in Cambodia (p290) and Rwanda (p250).

Museum of Tolerance

★★★☆☆

West Pico Boulevard, Los Angeles, California • Discrimination, Holocaust   **Dark Rating: 7** ☻

This is another museum about the Holocaust in LA, located in the west of the city between Hollywood and Santa Monica; in this case, it is associated with the Simon Wiesenthal Center, a Jewish global human rights organization researching the Holocaust and hate crimes in a historical and contemporary context.

In addition to a didactic 'Tolerancenter', which presses visitors into confronting their own and generally widespread prejudices, the Holocaust Exhibit is at the heart of this institution.

Unlike the more conventional Holocaust Museum LA, the exhibition here is a 'sound-and-light-

guided dramatic presentation', as the museum itself describes it, or rather a prescribed succession of such installations. It is probably aimed more at school groups than adult visitors who may already have a good grasp of the topic, but is still worth seeing.

Titan Missile Museum

Sahuarita, near Tucson, Arizona • Cold War, Nuclear weapons

★★★★☆

Dark Rating: 8 ☠

This is one of the most remarkable sites related to the Cold War in the world. It is much more than a museum: it is a genuine intercontinental ballistic missile (ICBM) silo, complete with a Titan II missile and the associated underground Launch Control Center (LCC). There is a small museum providing background information too, but the real stars here are the ICBM and the LCC.

The Titan II was the USA's largest type of ICBM, and its nine-megaton thermonuclear warhead was the most powerful ever deployed on a missile in the West. In total, 54 of these monsters of the Cold War were in service from 1963 to 1987. They were replaced by simpler-to-service solid-fuel ICBMs.

It was not just the nuclear warhead that made the Titan such a deadly machine; the missile itself was volatile, to say the least.

These were liquid-fuel missiles, and those liquids were extremely toxic and corrosive. The two components together formed a so-called hypergolic fuel, meaning that they spontaneously ignite on contact (so no ignition system was required in the engines).

The two-stage missiles were always on alert fully tanked, so they were ready to be launched in just 58 seconds. All this came at a price: the missiles were difficult to service, requiring spacesuit-like fuel-handling suits; moreover, they were highly accident-prone. This was shown in the Damascus Incident of 1980, when a dropped tool pierced the missile's skin: despite desperate efforts to stabilize the missile, it eventually exploded, blowing off the 760-ton silo lid and propelling the warhead into a ditch by the launch complex's gate. Fortunately it did not go off too.

The Titan Missile Museum site near Tucson, Arizona, is unique – it features the only preserved silo of this type. All the others were destroyed and filled in after decommissioning. The missile inside this sole surviving Titan silo was a training model and does not contain any fuel; nor does it have a real warhead.

There is a square hole on the side of the tip of the missile – apparently this was a requirement of the arms reduction treaties signed by the superpowers around the end of the Cold War. The hole is there to make it verifiable, even by satellite from space, that this is indeed not a working missile. The silo lid, or closure door, is now permanently fixed in a half-open position. The opening is covered by a glass roof so visitors can look inside.

There are a few other items above ground (or 'topside', as the jargon goes), including an original

Left and below
Reinforced underground Launch Control
Center (LCC) with the two desks for the
commander and deputy. They would have
to turn their keys (below) simultaneously
to finalize the launch sequence (having first
entered the correct codes).

Opposite
The 31.5m (103ft) tall training model Titan II
missile in its silo.

Below
The destruction caused in the 1980
Damascus incident when a Titan II exploded
in its silo in Arkansas.

Titan II twin engine, a fuel tanker vehicle and various communications installations.

Guided tours are on offer to get you closer to the missile and into the LCC. The standard one-hour tour takes visitors down into the underground LCC, where a simulated launch sequence is performed. Then the group is walked through the connecting tunnel to the silo for a close-up view of the missile from level two of the silo. The group then goes topside for a look down through the glass roof.

The site also offers a choice of more elaborate tours that allow access to parts the regular tour does not include. For example, on the director's tour (conducted by the museum's director, an actual missileer back in the day), visitors are allowed into the launch duct at level two and can briefly touch the missile (with gloves provided).

Another tour includes visits to the crew quarters and a descent to the bottom of the missile. The most comprehensive option is the 'top-to-bottom' tour, which includes all levels of both the LCC and the silo. You even get to stand at the very bottom, right underneath the actual ICBM in its silo. You cannot experience that anywhere else in the world.

THE COLD WAR

СРЕДИ ЭТОЙ СМЕРТНОЙ ЛЮБВИ.

MEIN GOTT HILF MIR DIESE TÖDLICHE LIEBE ZU ÜBERLEBEN

Left
Urban art on the most famous
symbol of the Cold War, the
Berlin Wall (see p140-141).

After two of the deadliest wars in history, World War One and World War Two, the world entered the Atomic Age from 1945. The two big power blocs, the USA and NATO in the West, and the USSR and the Warsaw Pact in the East, accumulated huge arsenals of nuclear weapons (see p25) directed at each other, enough to destroy the entire world several times over (hence the term 'overkill'). The strategy of deterrence was called MAD (short for 'mutually assured destruction'). Luckily, it never came to nuclear Armageddon: this 'Cold War' never turned hot.

However, there were times when the world came dangerously close to World War Three and thus potential total annihilation. There were several stand-offs in the earlier phases of the Cold War, including in the wake of the construction of the Berlin Wall.

It is usually agreed that the Cuban Missile Crisis of 1962 was one of the most critical phases, when the Soviet Union was preparing to deploy medium-range nuclear missiles on the territory of its Caribbean communist ally Cuba (see p44), within reach of the USA. Fortunately, the crisis was resolved diplomatically.

On other occasions, there were false alarms in the electronic early-warning systems; it was individuals in the military on either side who, on a hunch, did not follow procedures to trigger an all-out retaliatory strike. The world owes these mostly unsung heroes a lot.

The Cold War came to an end during 1989–91 with the Fall of the Berlin Wall, the collapse of the communist regimes all over the Eastern Bloc, and eventually the dissolution of the Soviet Union itself. Americans may think they 'won' the Cold War, although it is probably more accurate to say the USSR 'lost' it by simply giving up, mostly for financial reasons. The cost of the clean-up operations after the 1986 Chernobyl disaster (see p220–23) played a role in this too, according to the USSR's final leader, Mikhail Gorbachev.

While the original Cold War ended peacefully, there is talk these days of a kind of new Cold War emerging, as Russia reasserts its position on the international stage and also militarily, and NATO has at times been challenged, while at the same time new nuclear threats have developed in India, Pakistan and North Korea. Given the size of the arsenals the major atomic powers still have, a nuclear end to human civilization is still a possibility.

AMARG 'Boneyard' and Pima Air & Space Museum

Tucson, Arizona • Aviation, Cold War

★★★★☆

Dark Rating: 4 ☠

The Aerospace Maintenance and Regeneration Group (AMARG), better known as 'The Boneyard', is at Davis-Monthan Air Force Base on a desert plain just outside Tucson. It is the USA's principal storage facility for retired aircraft (mostly military) and missiles. Some are held in reserve, others are brought here to be gutted, broken up and recycled. This is a vast area where hundreds of planes of many dozens of types can be seen, from the Cold War era and beyond.

As this is an active military site, access is restricted, but members of the public can go on tours by bus to see all this from fairly close up (pre-registration online is required, as is ID on the day, and no bags are allowed, but cameras are). For anybody with an interest in military aviation, this is unique and unmissable.

The tours are run from the nearby Pima Air & Space Museum, just south of here. This museum is also worth a visit. It has one of the world's biggest and best aircraft collections (nearly 300) in a large open-air display area as well as inside a few hangars. Included

are icons of both World War Two and the Cold War, such as a B-17, a B-29, a V-1, an SR-71 Blackbird and a B-58 Hustler. The museum also displays three B-52s, the mainstay American bomber in use from the mid-1950s all through the Cold War, heavily used in the Vietnam War (see p294) and still in service today.

Below
Aerial view of part of the 'boneyard', where some 4000 aircraft are spread out over 11 sq km (4¼ sq miles).

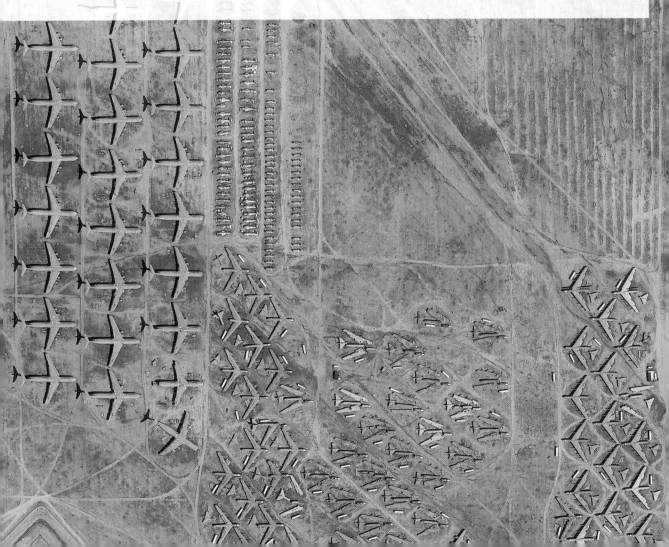

Trinity Site

New Mexico • Nuclear weapons, WW2

★★ ☆ ☆ ☆

Dark Rating: 8 ☠

This is a truly historic site, a place where the world was changed forever: on 16 July 1945, the first ever atomic bomb was detonated here in a test that was code-named Trinity. It was the culmination of the Manhattan Project (see opposite). Thus the Atomic Age had begun. Shortly after the test, a real bomb employing the same design was dropped on Nagasaki (the Hiroshima bomb had been of an untested, cruder design). And so the USA became the first nuclear-armed superpower.

The site, in the middle of the New Mexico desert, is still within a restricted military area, the White Sands Missile Range, but on two days in the year it is made accessible to the public on open house days, usually the first Saturdays of April and October. You have to pass through military checkpoints and are not allowed to leave the prescribed driving route on approach to the site. Once there, you park your car and walk – past stalls selling souvenirs and snacks – to the fenced-off area and along the track

that takes you to ground zero. At the very spot stands a small stone monument with a couple of plaques pointing out its significance. Other than that, there is a trailer with a replica of the Fat Man Nagasaki bomb design, a few information panels attached to a fence and a low structure protecting a patch of original trinitite layer.

The latter is the greenish, glass-like substance that formed when the enormous heat of the atomic fireball melted the desert sand. That layer was later taken away and just this one protected patch was left at the site. People still search the ground and find little bits of trinitite in the soil. You are not allowed to take any with you as a souvenir – the penalties for attempting this are severe – but it is possible to purchase bits from stalls.

While there isn't all that much to see here, it is still one of the most significant spots of dark history on Earth, and thousands of people come every year for the open house days. The military also provides a

shuttle service by bus to the former farm building where the scientists assembled the plutonium core of 'the Gadget', as the Trinity bomb was nicknamed.

Above left
Warning signs attached to the security fence that surrounds the Trinity site in the White Sands Missile Range.

Above
In 1965 US army officials erected an obelisk monument in the desert marking ground zero.

MANHATTAN PROJECT

After the principles of nuclear fission (see p25) were discovered by German scientists in 1938, there were fears that the Nazis might attempt to develop atom bombs. In America, nuclear physicists Leo Szilard (of Hungarian origin) and Albert Einstein (a Jewish refugee who had fled to America) sent a letter to the then president Franklin D. Roosevelt, urging him to initiate a concerted research and development programme by the Allies in order to get there first. This plea was successful, government funding was allocated, and the programme, which became known as the Manhattan Project, was launched in late 1941.

It was a large international co-operation involving notable nuclear physicists, including Enrico Fermi (Italy), Niels Bohr (Denmark), Ernest O. Lawrence (US), Louis Slotin (Canada), Edward Teller (Hungarian-American) and also the Germans Hans Bethe and Klaus Fuchs – the last of whom assumed British citizenship but later proved to have been a Soviet spy supplying vital information for the postwar Soviet development of the A-bomb.

The head of the scientific laboratory operations at the Manhattan Project was J. Robert Oppenheimer, who is therefore usually credited as the 'father of the atom bomb'. The main laboratory was at Los Alamos in New Mexico, a secluded site fit for the secrecy that was required for the running of such a programme. Several other large sites were involved in the production of the necessary nuclear material, including Clinton Engineer Works in Tennessee (also see list on p25).

The programme cost huge sums of money and involved over 100,000 personnel. In July 1945 it culminated in the Trinity Test (see opposite). Shortly afterwards, the bomb was used for real in the nuclear destruction of Hiroshima and Nagasaki in Japan (p322–27). So far, no other nuclear weapons have been

used 'in anger', as the military expression goes, but the threat of nuclear annihilation was a key deterrent during the Cold War (p20).

Some of the physicists involved in the Manhattan Project spoke out against the bombing of Japanese civilians, including Szilard. Several others lobbied against the nuclear arms race that followed the war, including Oppenheimer and Einstein. But the genie was out of the bottle and to this day refuses to be put back inside.

Above
The Manhattan Project culminated in the first ever detonation of a nuclear weapon, which had a yield of about 22 kt.

Left
Control room at Clinton Engineer Works, Oak Ridge, Tennessee, where much of the uranium materials research for the Manhattan Project was carried out.

Museum of Nuclear Science & History

★★★★☆

Albuquerque, New Mexico • Nuclear weapons, Cold War

Dark Rating: 7 ☠

Left and below
The 9-acre heritage park has a variety of decommissioned military aircraft and bombers as well as missiles, such as this Titan II ICBM (left) on display.

This national institution in Albuquerque, New Mexico, east of Kirtland Air Force Base, is the principal museum of all things nuclear in the USA. It covers the history of the science and how, through the Manhattan Project (p23), it led to the development of the atomic bomb. The use of this new weapon of mass destruction on Hiroshima and Nagasaki (p322–27) is covered, as are the ethical dilemmas involved, and the pros and cons of the decision to drop the bomb are fairly weighed up.

The largest part of the museum is devoted to the Cold War era (p20) and its nuclear weaponry (see opposite). Artefacts on display include the smallest atomic weapons ever deployed as well as whole thermonuclear warheads (not real armed ones, of course). Perhaps most interesting is the section on so-called Broken Arrows; that is, accidents involving nuclear weapons. On display here are the bomb casings from the Palomares Incident of 1966, when a USAF B-52 crashed and lost its thermonuclear bombs over Spain, triggering a frantic search and clear-up mission.

The end of the Cold War is celebrated, as is the civilian use of nuclear power, not only in the form of electric power generation, but also in medicine, and in the early naive days of the Atomic Age even in colouring crockery green or red by means of uranium.

The museum has an open-air part where various aircraft are on display, such as a B-52, as well as nuclear (mock-up) bombs and missiles of all sizes, including a Peacekeeper MX and a Titan ICBM (see Titan Missile Museum, p18–19).

NUCLEAR WEAPONS

This is not a physics book, but some rudimentary background information on this topic should be useful. The term 'nuclear' derives from 'nucleus', namely that of an atom. Atoms, the building blocks of all matter, consist of protons, electrons and neutrons. Using the very heaviest naturally occurring element, uranium, it is possible to induce an atom-splitting nuclear chain reaction by firing neutrons at the atoms, which then emit further neutrons, splitting more atoms, and so on, releasing large amounts of energy in the process. This is called fission, and can be done under controlled conditions in a nuclear reactor to generate electricity, or uncontrolled and very rapidly in an atomic bomb.

This discovery led to the Manhattan Project (p23), which eventually came up with two types of bomb. One was the 'gun-type', in which two subcritical amounts of uranium were fired at each other to form a supercritical mass and trigger the explosion. This crude design was used, untested, in the Hiroshima bomb (p322–23). The other design was the plutonium implosion type, tested at Trinity (p22) and then used in the bombing of Nagasaki (p326). In these bombs a spherical core of the artificial element plutonium is compressed into supercriticality by detonating a mantle of conventional explosives around it. This is more complicated, but it is much safer to store and transport, so this became the standard type of A-bomb during the early stages of the Cold War (p20). The USA lost its monopoly on atomic bombs when the USSR also successfully conducted its first nuclear test at the Semipalatinsk Test Site (p276) in 1949. That bomb, called RDS-1, was a more or less exact copy of the American design, obtained by espionage.

The next stage in the development of nuclear weapons was the thermonuclear or hydrogen bomb (H-bomb for short). In these, a two-stage design is used: a fission detonation 'primary' is set off triggering a fusion reaction in the 'secondary' (filled with hydrogen isotopes). This releases significantly more energy than fission alone. Hence it became the standard design for most high-yield nuclear weapons in the later phases of the Cold War and to this day. True two-stage thermonuclear weapons are extremely complicated to make, however, and hence form part of the nuclear arsenals of only the big five nuclear powers – the USA, Russia, China, Great Britain and France.

OTHER NUCLEAR SITES IN THE USA

The three main sites of the Manhattan Project (p23):

- **Los Alamos**, New Mexico, where the main scientific developments were undertaken. Today you can tour the old town where Oppenheimer lived; there is also a dedicated Nuclear Science Museum.
- **Hanford**, Washington State, where the plutonium for the first bombs (and subsequently most of the US nuclear arsenal) was produced in several reactors. Most of Hanford has been decommissioned and levelled, but the first reactor (B Reactor) has been preserved as a National Historic Landmark and can be visited on tours.
- **Oak Ridge National Laboratory**, Tennessee, administrative and military HQ and the largest factory for materials and uranium enrichment. This is still an active site. There are public tours here, but only for US citizens.

Other key nuclear sites of interest include:

- **University of Chicago**, where Enrico Fermi carried out the world's first controlled self-contained nuclear chain reaction in a reactor called Chicago Pile-1. This no longer exists, but there's a monument at the site.
- **Atomic Testing Museum**, Las Vegas, Nevada; mostly about nuclear tests, but also provides insights into nuclear weapons. From here you can go on once-a-month bus tours of the former Nevada Test Site (NTS), where the US conducted most of its land-based atmospheric tests of nuclear weapons until these were banned. Access is restricted and pre-registration far in advance is required.
- **Titan Missile Museum**, Tucson, Arizona (see p18–19)
- **North and South Dakota**; there is a decommissioned Minuteman Missile Silo and associated Launch Control Center (LCC) that is open to the public in South Dakota near Interstate 90. Ex-missileers give tours of the LCC and there is also a small museum. In North Dakota, another Minuteman LCC, Oscar-Zero in Cooperstown, can be visited.
- **Three Mile Island Power Station** near Harrisburg, Pennsylvania, where a reactor suffered a meltdown in 1979. The site is not accessible, but there is a historical marker by the road.

Wounded Knee

Pine Ridge Reservation, South Dakota • Massacre

★★ ★ ★ ★

Dark Rating: 6 ☠

This is a remote and desolate spot, but is of great significance: in the final stages of the so-called Indian Wars, it was here on 29 December 1890 that the US Cavalry massacred some 200–300 Lakota Sioux, including women and children. It was the last 'battle' of the Sioux against the US military, but was preceded by a long string of atrocities perpetrated against the Native American peoples at the hands of the whites. This is a very dark chapter in America's history, but one that was for a long time hardly commemorated properly. It was not until 1990, a full century after the event, that the site of the massacre was declared a National Historic Landmark.

There is not much to see at the original site, which is deep inside the Pine Ridge Reservation in South Dakota between the Badlands National Park and the border with Nebraska. Only a plaque at

the roadside provides some basic historical information. Other than that, there is the cemetery at the location of the original mass grave of the victims. A marker stone within it lists the names of some of the notable figures among the dead, such as Chief Big Foot. The cemetery is still in use, and outside visitors should be discreet, as some Lakota take issue with people going there to take photos. On the other hand, they are quite happy with visitors coming to this remote spot, and some Lakota sell souvenirs, handmade jewellery and crafts, mainly to alleviate the widespread poverty within the reservation.

While visiting the original site is a kind of pilgrimage, an easier and more informative alternative is to visit the Wounded Knee Museum in the little touristy town of Wall. This is right by one of the main east–west traffic arteries of the region, Interstate 90, which runs north of

the Badlands. The museum exhibition covers the whole story of the plight of the Native Americans, concentrating mostly on the details of the events of 29 December 1890 and their aftermath.

Above
The aftermath of the Wounded Knee Massacre. US soldiers survey the debris in the camp. The bodies of four Lakota Sioux wrapped in blankets can clearly be seen in the foreground.

Oklahoma City National Memorial

Oklahoma City, Oklahoma • Terrorism

★★★★★

Dark Rating: 6 ☣

Until 9/11 in 2001, the bombing of the Alfred P. Murrah Federal Building in Oklahoma City on 19 April 1995 was the worst terrorist act committed on American soil. The perpetrator was a US citizen, Timothy McVeigh, a veteran of the Gulf War of 1990–91, who had connections to some underground militia, and was hostile towards the government. The exact motives for the bombing have never been fully unravelled and, since McVeigh was sentenced to death and executed in 2001, they never will be.

The 'bomb' was actually a rental truck, containing a home-made bomb based on two tons of fertilizer, that the attacker parked directly in front of the government building. The device was set off by a time-delay fuse at 9:02 a.m. and the blast caused the whole front of the building to collapse. A total of 168 people were killed, including 20 children in a daycare centre inside the stricken structure.

The ruin was later razed to the ground and replaced by a memorial park. Two large monuments flanking a reflecting pool are the main elements, but there is also a 'Field of Empty Chairs' covering the former footprint of the bombed building, with one symbolic chair for each victim. Nearby, some parts of the building's foundations survive. Most importantly, there is a museum in a neighbouring building, which was also affected by the bombing.

One room has been left in the state it was in after the blast to demonstrate the destruction caused even here. The rest of the expansive exhibition tells the detailed story of the bombing, the rescue operations, police investigations and the trial of the perpetrator. Outside is another, smaller monument and a fence on to which locals and visitors attach little tokens of remembrance. In addition, National Park Rangers give talks at the memorial site.

A 'survivor tree', which miraculously came back to life after being scorched by the explosion, has become a memorial in itself and a symbol of hope and resilience.

Below
View of the Reflecting Pool in the foreground and the western end of the Gates of Time in the background.

Dealey Plaza

Dallas, Texas • Assassination

★★★★☆

Dark Rating: 6 💀

Below
X on the road marks the spot where
President John F. Kennedy was assassinated,
with the Book Depository in the background.

This is probably the best-known and most visited assassination spot in the world. Here, on 22 November 1963, President John F. Kennedy was shot dead as his motorcade passed through. The assassin was Lee Harvey Oswald, who fired the rifle shots from the sixth floor of the then Texas School Book Depository building. That is, at least, the official version. There are countless conspiracy theories that claim otherwise, peddled by numerous freelance 'historians' as well as guides that you can encounter at street level.

The official institution at Dealey Plaza is the Sixth Floor Museum, at the authentic site of the assassin's sniper's nest. The iconic red-brick building is located at the corner of Elm Street and Houston Street. It is

also an incredibly popular museum, arguably the number one visitor attraction in all of Dallas.

The museum includes a mock-up of the assassin's position at the corner window from where he fired the shots. The rest is an exhibition that treads the official line and provides plenty of evidence and background information that leave little room for doubt. Yet the subject of the conspiracy theories is touched upon too. Also included is much of the familiar – and (in)famous – film footage of the assassination, plus countless photos, newspaper cuttings and so forth, but naturally only a few artefacts. These include various cameras of types that would have been in use at the time. Otherwise it is mostly a narrative-based museum.

Other than the Sixth Floor Museum, there is also the John F. Kennedy Memorial Plaza between Main Street and Commerce Street (just behind the 'Old Red' Dallas history museum), which is dominated by a large white concrete monument. More plaques and historical markers can be found either side of Main Street at Dealey Plaza. On Elm Street, little white crosses mark the spots where JFK's car was when the shots were fired. Many visitors want to go to these spots and stand there, probably having their photo taken, but beware: this is still an active traffic intersection, so watch out for cars!

USAF Museum

Dayton, Ohio • WW1 & 2, Cold War, Modern war

★★★★★

Dark Rating: 5 ☣

The United States Air Force Museum is one of the largest and most comprehensive collections of aircraft and missiles in the world. Aviation enthusiasts have much to marvel at here, from the earliest flying machines to the very latest technological developments.

What makes this museum a dark destination is the display of one particular plane: the fully restored *Bockscar*. This was the B-29 bomber that dropped the second atomic bomb on the Japanese city of Nagasaki (p326). The first atomic bomber, *Enola Gay*, which dropped the Hiroshima bomb (p322–23), is on display elsewhere (p36).

The *Bockscar* is celebrated in this museum as the 'plane that ended World War Two', although that interpretation is no longer universally shared among historians: the fact that the USSR entered the war against Japan may have played a greater role. The bombing mission is described in great detail, and there are replica bomb casings of both the Hiroshima bomb, 'Little Boy', and the Nagasaki bomb, 'Fat Man', on display.

Also quite dark are the non-aircraft-dominated sections about the Holocaust (p134–35), the Berlin Wall (p140–41) and prisoners of war. A dark highlight is the vast Cold War section. This has a large collection of military planes on display, including such iconic bombers as the B-52, B-58, B-1 and B-2, plus various replicas/casings of nuclear weapons of all types.

There is a separate section on Intercontinental Ballistic Missiles (ICBMs), with several full-scale examples, including a Titan (see p18–19), a Minuteman and a 'Peacekeeper', the most powerful ICBM ever deployed by the USA (retired in 2005). A model of its warhead with ten nuclear weapons in its Multiple Individually Targetable Re-Entry Vehicle (MIRV) is also on display, as is a mock-up of a Minuteman III Launch Control Center (see p25).

The museum goes beyond the Cold War and up to the present day with displays of stealth aircraft and drones. It is not only American weaponry that can be seen here; several enemy aircraft are also part of the collection, including Nazi German, Soviet and Vietnamese examples.

OTHER COLLECTIONS OF AIRCRAFT & MISSILES

Some particularly interesting collections to look out for in the US (there are many more):

– **Udvar-Hazy Center** at Washington Dulles Airport, Virginia
– **PIMA Air & Space Museum**, Tucson, Arizona (see p21)
– **Strategic Air Command & Aerospace Museum**, Ashland, Nebraska
– **Evergreen Aviation & Space Museum**, McMinnville, Oregon
– **Intrepid Sea, Air & Space Museum**, New York City, New York
– **Museum of Flight**, Seattle, Washington State
– **Wings Over the Rockies**, Denver, Colorado
– **South Dakota Air & Space Museum**, Ellsworth Air Force Base, South Dakota
– **Museum of Aviation**, Warner Robins, Georgia
– **Kansas Cosmosphere**, Hutchinson, Kansas

There are countless similar museums outside the USA too. Here are just a few notable examples:

– **Central Air Force Museum**, Monino, Russia
– **Aviation Museum**, Belgrade, Serbia
– **RAF Cosford**, Great Britain
– **IWM Duxford**, Great Britain
– **Aviation Museum**, Riga, Latvia
– **Oleg Antonov State Aviation Museum**, Kiev, Ukraine

West Virginia Penitentiary

Moundsville, West Virginia • Prison

★★★☆☆

Dark Rating: 7 ☠

Left
The imposing main entrance on Jefferson Avenue; the walls to the left and right are 7.3m (24ft) high and 1.8m (6ft) thick.

Opposite
Cell block where the prison's worst inmates were held.

This former high-security prison in the northwestern corner of West Virginia used to be one of the most notorious and violent of its kind. Construction of the main building began in 1866 and was completed ten years later. It was intended as a 'penitentiary', meaning that inmates should find penitence during their time behind bars here. In this case, the so-called 'Auburn system' was applied, by which inmates were working together during the day only to spend the nights in tiny cage-like single cells, as opposed to the 'Pennsylvania system', where prisoners were held in solitary confinement the whole time – as at the infamous Eastern State Penitentiary (p37).

However, the penitence idea didn't work that well, and it wasn't just the prisoners' fault. For one thing, the cell blocks, originally intended for around 700 inmates in total, soon became overcrowded, housing a prisoner population of up to 2700, so the small cells regularly had to accommodate three or four inmates each. So much for solitary confinement. Moreover, cells on the upper tiers would become baking hot in the summer heat.

The cramped and inadequate conditions sparked aggression; hence many crimes were committed inside the prison walls, both among inmates and against guards. There were also several escape attempts, some successful, and larger-scale riots, especially in 1986, when 12 of the prison personnel were taken hostage by the prisoners in protest against their plight. Eventually, the conditions in this prison were declared 'cruel and unusual punishment' and the whole institution was shut down in 1995.

Since then it has been opened up to the public, and visitors are taken on guided tours through the cell blocks, the inmates' cafeteria, the visitation room, the administration block, the outdoor exercise yards, and the gatehouse in which executions by hanging used to take place. There is also a small museum about the prison. The most remarkable exhibit here is an old electric chair, cynically referred to as 'Old Sparky', which was used for nine executions at this institution in the 1950s.

Above
'Old Sparky', the electric chair that was built by an inmate and used to kill nine prisoners between 1951 and 1959.

OTHER NOTABLE EX-PRISONS TO VISIT

– **Alcatraz**, San Francisco, California (p15)
– **Eastern State Penitentiary**, Philadelphia, Pennsylvania (p37)
– **Missouri State Penitentiary**, Jefferson, Missouri
– **Ohio State Reformatory**, Mansfield, Ohio (right)
– **Old Idaho Penitentiary**, Boise, Idaho

Not prisons, but with a similar look and feel, are former 'lunatic asylums' across the USA, of which the **Trans-Allegheny Lunatic Asylum** in Weston, West Virginia, is probably the most legendary and photogenic; it is also open to the public (unlike many other asylums).

Outside the USA, plenty of former prisons have become popular visitor attractions. These include:

– **Old Melbourne Gaol**, Australia
– **Rommani Nart**, Bangkok, Thailand
– **Museo Penitenciario Argentino**, Buenos Aires, Argentina
– **Crumlin Road Gaol**, Belfast, Northern Ireland
– **Hoa Lo Prison**, Hanoi, Vietnam
– **Presidio Modelo**, Cuba

Above
Cell at the old Ohio State Reformatory, where much of *The Shawshank Redemption* was filmed.

Centralia

★★★★★

Columbia County, Pennsylvania • Underground coal fires, Ghost town

Dark Rating: 5 ☠☠☠

This is a former coal-mining community town in rural Pennsylvania that had to be abandoned after an underground coal seam fire ignited beneath it in 1962. These fires are of the smouldering kind rather than actual flaming fires, but the toxic fumes they emit at the surface and the fact that they can render the ground unstable mean this is a dangerous phenomenon (it is a huge problem in China and India too). Moreover, the fires are almost impossible to put out.

The government encouraged the residents of Centralia to leave their homes through a buyout, but not everybody accepted this; some stayed on until they were practically evicted. Only a small handful resisted eviction and eventually an agreement was reached that allowed them to live out their days in their houses. By 2018, only five

residents were left. Almost all the other buildings were demolished, except for a municipal building, which also served as a fire station, and a wooden Ukrainian Orthodox church, which is allegedly still in use. The rest of the town is only hinted at by the remaining street grid that appears randomly crisscrossing the greenery that has sprung up where the buildings used to be. It is a unique kind of ghost town.

Apart from the eerie non-town and its streets, the main attraction for visitors was the stretch of Route 61 that was closed and blocked off after the underground coal fire caused the tarmac to bend and crack, giving the appearance of having been hit by an earthquake. Some cracks still emitted smoke and steam until recently, but the fires now seem to have died out

here. Over the years, Centralia has attained a kind of mystical allure among fans of abandoned places, particularly the stretch of abandoned road, which attracted ever larger numbers of visitors. The road surface became almost entirely covered in graffiti. Since 2016, 'no trespassing' signs have been erected and apparently police patrol the place at times, yet the allure continues. Then, in April 2020, locals covered most of the old road with dirt and landfill to deter visitors. Tourists today should be discreet, and generally show respect for the people who lost their homes or those who still live here.

Above
Colourful graffiti covering the abandoned stretch of Route 61. Cracks in the road surface caused by the heat of the subterranean fires are clearly visible.

Arlington National Cemetery, Virginia
★★★☆☆

Outside Washington D.C. in Virginia • Cemetery, War graves

Dark Rating: 2 ☠

Right across the Potomac River from Washington D.C., in Arlington, Virginia, lies the USA's principal National Cemetery. Not only are many of the fallen from America's military conflicts around the world interred here, but there are also graves of famous people. Most notable perhaps are those of John F. Kennedy and other members of his family, a monumental Tomb of the Unknown Soldier, plus various memorials, including one commemorating the Space Shuttle Disasters of 1986 and 2003, and one for the victims of the airliner bombing that caused a Pan Am jumbo jet to come down over Lockerbie, Scotland, in 1988. By the main entrance is also a memorial museum dedicated to the Women in Military Service for America.

Adjacent to the cemetery are a few large-scale military monuments,

the most notable being the US Marine Corps War Memorial to the north; its design recalls one of the most famous war photographs of all time, the flag-raising scene on Iwo Jima in the Pacific theatre of World War Two.

Above
The cemetery is the final resting place for more than 400,000 active duty service members, veterans and their families.

The Pentagon & 9/11 memorial
★★☆☆☆

Arlington, Virginia • Terrorism

Dark Rating: 3 ☠

Southeast of Arlington National Cemetery is another icon of American military might: the Pentagon, seat of the US Department of Defense, and the largest office building in the world. It was also one of the targets of the terror attacks of 9/11 (see p38–39). A haunting memorial, consisting of 184 stylized seats (one for each of the victims), has been constructed on the western side of the building.

Left
The symbolic 'seats' bear the names of the victims; whether they were in the building or on the plane is indicated by the seat facing the building or away from it.

US Holocaust Memorial Museum

★★★★★

Washington D.C. • Holocaust

Dark Rating: 8 ☠

Above
The Tower of Faces is a three-floor-high exhibit devoted to the Jews of the Lithuanian town of Eišiškės, massacred by Nazi troops in September 1941. It consists of 1000 reproductions of pre-war photographs.

One of the most significant museums out of Washington's plethora of such sites is this venerable institution, often abbreviated to USHMM. It is one of the leading museums of this kind in the world (perhaps together with Yad Vashem, p262–63). The coverage is vast and the atmosphere suitably sombre (which is also enforced by museum staff). The exhibition includes some especially poignant exhibits, such as a deportation cattle car (you can choose if you want to bypass it or walk through it) and a detailed scale model of one of the gas chambers at Auschwitz (p170–71).

One distinctive feature of the museum is that tickets come with little ID cards of individuals whose particular story you can follow throughout the main exhibition. At the end you'll find out if 'your' person survived the Holocaust.

OTHER HOLOCAUST MUSEUMS IN THE USA

There are many more, smaller-scale Holocaust museums in the USA, for example in New York, Richmond (Virginia), El Paso (Texas), St Louis (Missouri), St Petersburg (Florida) and Los Angeles (California – see p17).

Particularly noteworthy are the Illinois Holocaust Museum in Skokie, just north of Chicago, and the Dallas Holocaust Museum, which is unique in that it concentrates on a single date in 1943 and what happened on that day in different locations, from Poland to the USA.

The National Mall

Washington D.C. • War Memorials

★★☆☆☆

Dark Rating: 4 💀

This is the name under which the band of parks and monuments are commonly subsumed that stretch from the Lincoln Memorial by the Potomac River in the west to the Capitol in the east. The Mall is also lined with many museums (most of them free). Part of this cluster is one of the world's best-known and most visited war memorials, the Vietnam Veterans Memorial, a strikingly designed black marble wall on to which all the names of American servicemen and women who died in this conflict or are 'missing' are etched; nearly 60,000 in total.

There are a few other war memorials in the area, such as the moving Korean War Veterans Memorial, with its 19 shadowy grey sculptures of exhausted and scared-looking soldiers. The World War Two Memorial, on the other hand, is a rather conventional, classically designed affair, located at the eastern end of the Reflecting Pool opposite the Lincoln Memorial and just west of the Washington Monument, which dominates this whole area.

Below
Stainless-steel statues representing a platoon of soldiers on patrol form the core of the monument commemorating the Korean War (see p316).

The *Enola Gay* at the Smithsonian

★★★☆☆

Outside Washington D.C. in Virginia • WW2, Nuclear weapons

Dark Rating: 4 ☢

One of the most famous of the state museums flanking the National Mall is the Smithsonian Air & Space Museum. This has another branch for larger exhibits near Washington's Dulles Airport: the Udvar-Hazy Center. This is significant as a dark destination because among its artefacts is the restored B-29 bomber *Enola Gay*, the one that dropped the atomic bomb on Hiroshima (p322–23) towards the end of World War Two.

Like the USAF Museum (p29), this enormous exhibition of aviation has plenty of other dark connections too, from World War Two to the Vietnam War, and also has a large section on space

exploration, but the *Enola Gay* beats the rest for sheer historic significance.

Above
The US Air Force B-29 bomber that dropped the atomic bomb on Hiroshima in 1945.

Mütter Museum

★★★★☆

Philadelphia, Pennsylvania • Medical museum

Dark Rating: 5 ☢

Part of the College of Physicians of Philadelphia, this is one of the world's most eminent medical museums (see also the Josephinum and the Narrenturm, p160). Its collection of specimens includes shrunken heads from Peru, various conjoined twins, anencephalic or cyclops babies preserved in formaldehyde, a giant colon removed from a man suffering from Hirschsprung's disease, and the utterly bizarre 'Soap Woman': the body of a female who in the nineteenth century had been buried in a kind of soil whose chemical composition turned her body fat into a waxy substance akin to blu-ish-greenish soap.

This place is not for the faint-hearted, and it is no wonder that photography inside the exhibition is strictly prohibited.

Left
Normal, giant and dwarf skeletons – some of the rather less gruesome exhibits in this extraordinary medical museum.

Eastern State Penitentiary

Philadelphia, Pennsylvania • Prison

★★★★☆

Dark Rating: 5 ☠

Often abbreviated to 'ESP', this is a huge, fortress-like, historic former prison. When it was opened in 1829, it was the largest public-sector building in the whole of the USA. Initially, the prisoners were held in total isolation in their cells for 23 hours a day, with only one hour in an equally solitary 'exercise yard'. But this cruel, imposed-silence-and-isolation regime was eroded over the years as the prison became more crowded and imprisonment ethics changed.

One special 'guest' at the ESP in the twentieth century was legendary Mob boss Al Capone. He spent eight months here, in a comparatively plush cell, before being transferred to Alcatraz (p15).

The ESP was finally closed down at the beginning of the 1970s and abandoned. Restoration efforts were started in the 1990s, and this photogenic place has since become a major visitor attraction.

Above
The radial floor plan of the prison was designed to facilitate easy views into all cell block corridors from a single central observation point.

Left
The high, arched ceilings of the cell blocks mimic church architecture and were intended to inspire religious reverence ... and to make prisoners feel small.

National 9/11 Memorial & Museum

Manhattan, New York • Terrorism

★★★★★

Dark Rating: 10 ☻

Left
The footprints of the Twin Towers, here the North Tower's, were turned into large water features that form the core of today's memorial site.

The co-ordinated terrorist attacks of 11 September 2001 ('9/11') were the worst such acts on the USA's territory in history. Almost everybody old enough can tell you where they were when they first became aware of the events. Many saw the second plane flying into the South Tower of the World Trade Center (WTC) in New York City live on TV. Even more witnessed the collapse of the WTC's Twin Towers.

Nearly 3000 people were killed in the attacks, in which four hijacked passenger jets were used as flying suicide bombs. Footage and photos of the events and the immediate aftermath are among the most iconic images in media history. 9/11 caused a national trauma in the USA, and also ongoing health issues for survivors, as well as mass mourning worldwide.

The initial focus immediately after the attacks was on search and rescue, recovery of bodies and clearing away the tremendous amount of debris – a scene that quickly earned the site of the destroyed WTC the nickname 'Ground Zero', in allusion to atomic bomb explosions. Yet it was clear that a historic event of

this magnitude had to be commemorated in some way for posterity. How this was to be done was, and still is, a source of much controversy.

In the end, the footprints of the WTC were converted into large waterfall-sided reflecting pools, the names of all the victims inscribed in metal on the rims of the footprints, and the area between them landscaped to form the 9/11 National Memorial. Also part of this, though largely underground, is the 9/11 Museum. In all, it took ten years to complete and eventually became the most expensive memorial complex ever constructed. It is also one of the most visited.

Various criticisms have been directed at the memorial: the museum's steep admission fee, the fact that there is a commercial gift shop in the museum, some of the symbolism and pathos of the memorial. Yet it cannot be denied that the museum's main topical Historical Exhibition is astounding. It covers every aspect of its subject and goes beyond (for example, in sections about other terrorist acts), from the planning of the attacks to the hijackings and a timeline of

the events as they unfolded, all in minute detail.

Much emphasis is placed on the aftermath, the search for bodies, the investigations and even the emergence of the various conspiracy theories about 9/11, although these don't have much of a chance here, in this context of tremendous accumulation of evidence of all sorts.

There are many artefacts on display, from personal items of the victims and first responders, to plane wreck parts and even a piece of what became termed 'composite': an intangible, compacted mass of material compressed by the thousands of tons of steel that accumulated on top of it from the collapse of the WTC. It has to be assumed that this 'composite' contains pulverized human remains; hence its display being another point of contention.

Outside the Historical Exhibition are other sections, such as the 'In Memoriam' exhibition, which focuses on the victims' stories. Dotted around the halls and passageways underground are large artefacts, such as a damaged fire truck, a section of the antenna that

Below
Displays at the memorial museum include steel girders and other structural elements recovered from the collapsed towers.

stood atop the North Tower, an elevator motor, and a stretch of concrete steps called 'survivor stairs', because hundreds of survivors used it to get from the North Tower to the adjacent street.

Several parts of the bent steel girders and columns of the WTC are on display as well, many vividly illustrating the physical forces that were at play in these events. Especially dramatic is one section from the impact zone between the 93rd and 98th floors of the North Tower, cut in two by the plane that was flown into it.

The largest space is the Foundation Hall, right by the slurry wall (or retaining wall) that was built around the base of the Twin Towers to hold back water from the Hudson River. In the centre of the hall stands the Last Column. This was the final piece of WTC steel to be removed from the site, on which recovery workers, first responders, volunteers and victims' relatives left signatures and mementos.

The National 9/11 Memorial & Museum is not the only institution commemorating the events of that day. There are several other memorial sculptures; the New York City Fire Museum has an exhibition about it, and so does St Paul's Chapel, just round the corner from Ground Zero. Most significantly, there is the 9/11 Tribute Museum, run by the September 11 Families' Association. This features another exhibition of its own, but more importantly offers guided tours around the area led by people who are survivors or relatives of victims or rescue workers, or were in some other way directly involved and affected.

DARK STATS

2753
people killed at the World Trade Center site

1645
of those victims' remains have been identified so far. These efforts are ongoing.

18
survivors rescued from the rubble

Around
400
first responders killed in initial response to the attacks

Time to clear Ground Zero site
9 MONTHS

1.8
million tons of wreckage cleared from Ground Zero

40
victims died when United Airlines Flight 93 was brought down in Shanksville, Pennsylvania

184
victims killed at the Pentagon

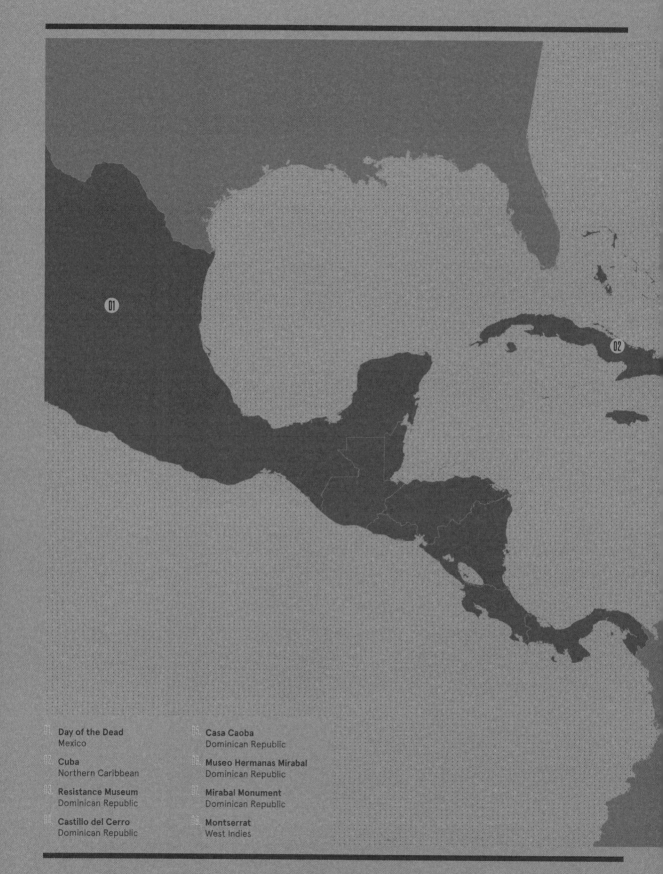

Day of the Dead
Mexico

Cuba
Northern Caribbean

Resistance Museum
Dominican Republic

Castillo del Cerro
Dominican Republic

Casa Caoba
Dominican Republic

Museo Hermanas Mirabal
Dominican Republic

Mirabal Monument
Dominican Republic

Montserrat
West Indies

Central America & the Caribbean

06 07
03 04 05

08

From the big country of Mexico in the northwest, down the thin band of land of smaller Central American countries lined up along the Pacific coast, to the hundreds of islands of the Caribbean, with the West Indies bordering the Atlantic, this is a vast and varied area, although all share a warm tropical climate (except on high mountains, of course).

This climate sometimes gets violent too, with hurricanes becoming increasingly frequent and more destructive. The main hurricane season runs from mid-summer to around November. In addition, there is plenty of volcanic activity here, not just along the Pacific 'Ring of Fire' but also on islands much further east, such as Martinique, Guadeloupe and Montserrat (see p49).

All the places in this section are worthy stand-alone destinations. Combining them in a trip can be tricky, though, as there are often no direct connections between them, so one has to go via other countries or islands. There are direct flights from Europe and the USA to major holiday destinations such as the Dominican Republic, but getting to Montserrat, for example, requires more logistical planning, as there is only a ferry connection and flights by small planes from Antigua. With Cuba, there are political complications to consider, especially for travel from the USA. These have eased in recent years, but the situation could change again.

Mexico

This is a large country to the south of the USA, and in some ways the border is a dark destination in itself. Not only do thousands of impoverished Mexicans risk attempting to cross the border to immigrate illegally into the USA, but also it has become a major political bone of contention – keyword: the Wall.

In many places, the US border fortifications have long included walls or wall-like structures: for example, at the border between El Paso in Texas and Juárez on the Mexican side. If you cross this border, you can see from the graffiti on the Mexican side what they think of this.

Juárez once had the dubious distinction of being the 'murder capital' of the world, but it has now lost that title. Nevertheless, crime, particularly organized crime in the form of drug trafficking, has plagued the country for years. Much of the business of the big drug cartels moved from Colombia to Mexico, closer to where the demand for this trade is (inside the USA).

Day of the Dead

All over Mexico • Festival of death

★★★☆☆

Dark Rating: 3 ☣

Left and opposite
A costumed participant in a carnival, and a cemetery filled with candles and flowers for the Day of the Dead (Día de Muertos) in Janitzio, Mexico.

Below
Mexican artist José Guadalupe Posada's famously macabre skeleton etching depicting the Day of the Dead.

Not a single destination, but an event taking place at several locations all over the country at the same time, is the legendary Día de Muertos (Day of the Dead). This is a celebration of death – or rather a tribute to the dead – held around All Saints' Day (1 November). For that purpose, people gather in cemeteries and decorate the graves, bring photos and mementos and even provide food offerings for the deceased, then eat and drink into the night by candlelight.

Many people dress up for the occasion, and wear elaborate skull-like make-up or skull masks, often in carnival parades. Intricately decorated skulls are made out of sugar too. Many families set up little shrines, also involving stylized skulls, in their homes. It is a very colourful affair overall.

The tradition, which also has roots in other Latin American countries, has spread into global popular culture to a degree, but is still mostly associated with Mexico.

Cuba

★★★☆☆

Northern Caribbean • Revolution, Communism, Cold War

Dark Rating: 4 ☠

Left
Cuban leaders including
Fidel Castro, far left, Ernesto
'Che' Guevara, third from
left, and Spaniard Eloy
Gutiérrez Menoyo, far right,
in 1960.

The largest island of the Caribbean has long been one of the USA's arch-enemies, a socialist thorn in the side of the superpower right in its back yard. The 1950s Cuban revolution under its charismatic leader Fidel Castro (1926–2016) ousted the authoritarian rule of the Batista regime and brought socialist benefits of universal healthcare and a 100 per cent literacy rate, but also media censorship and suppression of freedom of speech. In international political terms, though, it was the Cuban Missile Crisis that was the most dramatic phase in Cuba's history, as it brought the world to the brink of World War Three (see Cold War, p20).

For many years, especially since the easing of tensions between Cuba and the USA during the Obama administration, people have kept saying that Cuba is a country to travel to now, before it changes character and US fast-food chains and modern cars take over. That character is a peculiar mix of Spanish-colonial grand but crumbling architecture, clapped-out ancient American cars, a vibrant Caribbean music scene and the exoticness of an almost closed, old-school socialist country.

In terms of dark destinations to visit, there is no shortage of sites associated with the revolution. In addition, the city of Santa Clara is home to the grand mausoleum of Bolivian revolutionary and Fidel Castro associate Che Guevara.

The Cuban Missile Crisis, among other things, is commemorated in the capital city, Havana, by the Parque Histórico-Militar Morro-Cabaña. Several rockets, or replicas thereof, are on display, including those of the type that the Soviets intended to deploy on Cuba in 1962.

On Cuban soil but under US control is a particularly dark spot on Earth: Guantánamo Bay, the infamous extraterritorial prison camp where the USA holds suspected terrorists, often brought there under dubious circumstances and kept in harsh conditions, even involving elements of torture. Needless to say, the site is out of bounds for ordinary travellers. At best you can catch a glimpse into the enclave from a nearby hilltop.

Off the shores of the main island of Cuba is the smaller Isla de la Juventud, where another prison can be found, this time a historic one. The Presidio Modelo (meaning 'model prison') was built in the 1920s and is now largely a memorial. Fidel Castro himself was imprisoned here at one point. The complex consists of five large circular cell blocks, each with a central watchtower in the middle, now all abandoned, empty and crumbling. There is also a small museum.

Opposite
Rally in Havana, Cuba, during the first year of Castro's government in 1959.

OTHER TROUBLED LATIN AMERICAN COUNTRIES

Colombia
Before Mexico became the unfortunate heartland of drug trafficking and all the associated violent crime, Colombia was the home of the most infamous drug cartels, especially that of the legendary drug boss Pablo Escobar, allegedly once the richest person on Earth. In Medellín, there are even Pablo Escobar-themed guided tours for foreign visitors (these tours, however, are controversial). At the same time, Colombia has had a long-lasting internal guerrilla war. Although in more recent years there have been some negotiating breakthroughs and a 'peace accord', the issue is not yet completely resolved.

Venezuela
Colombia's neighbour descended into chaos and instability with food shortages, violence and hyperinflation after the demise of former socialist leader Hugo Chávez in 2013.

Nicaragua
Here, the neo-socialist government left a significant legacy revolving around the Sandinista of President Daniel Ortega. He had overthrown the previous dictatorship of the Somoza dynasty, in the wake of which the country descended into a brutal civil war (also a USA vs USSR proxy war) with a vicious scorched-earth policy, involving organized death squads, in the 1980s.

El Salvador
This Central American country had a history of violence parallel to Nicaragua in the same period and into the 1990s. A particular lowlight was the El Mozote massacre, in which US-backed right-wing militias burned down an entire village, leaving almost 1000 dead. Today it is a remote memorial site and certainly the darkest destination in the country.

Guatemala
This country became caught up in civil war and outside interference with plenty of violence, including the burning down of the Spanish Embassy in Guatemala City in 1980.

In South America, too, there has been no shortage of brutal military juntas, usually of the right-wing sort. Uruguay, Paraguay and Brazil have all had such phases, but the dictatorships in Chile (p60–61) and Argentina (p62) stand out.

Dominican Republic

Most people associate this Caribbean country with all-inclusive beach holiday resorts rather than anything dark. Yet it had profoundly dark chapters in twentieth-century history. The country's own version of a self-obsessed, megalomaniacal dictator was Rafael Trujillo. He ruled the country (with US backing, because he was anti-communist) with an iron fist from 1930 to 1961, extracting vast riches for himself, his family and his loyal followers while repressing and exploiting the population. He even ordered the genocidal massacre of as many as 20,000 Haitians in 1937.

Trujillo was a racist and a serial rapist. Scores of pretty virgins were picked up all over the country and delivered to his bedroom on a regular basis. Ironically, it was three women, the Mirabal sisters, who became the foremost figures of the resistance against his regime. When he had them murdered in

1960, outside support faded away, and it is assumed that the assassins who finally gunned down Trujillo in 1961 had some assistance from the CIA. It was not the end of dictatorship, though; Trujillo's successor, Joaquín Balaguer, held on to power until 1996. Since then, the country has been on course to democracy, and it is now comparatively stable.

The legacy of Trujillo (p47) is not particularly evident in the contemporary Dominican Republic, although several sites associated with it can be tracked down. The spot where Trujillo was assassinated is marked by a monument, and a car used by the assassins is in theory on display at the Museo Nacional de Historia y Geografía, though this has not had regular opening times for a long while. More sites related to the Trujillo dictatorship are singled out in the following pages.

Resistance Museum

★★★☆☆

Santo Domingo • Dictatorship, Murder, Torture

Dark Rating: 7 ☠

EL LIDERAZGO DE TAVÁREZ JUSTO Y SU FUSILAMIENTO EN "LAS MANACLAS"

This museum in the Dominican Republic's capital city recounts the political history of the country, with a focus on the dictatorship years and the resistance movements in particular. The brutality of the regime is amply illustrated.

There is even a reconstruction of the infamous 'LA 40' torture centre, with an electric chair and graphic images of victims. In the resistance part, the glamorization of Manolo Tavárez (leader of the '14' movement and husband of Minerva Mirabal) is a bit over the top, even featuring an animated Tavárez robot delivering a moving speech. But otherwise this is the best place to learn about the country's dark past.

Above
A star exhibit among the dark artefacts and images is the rather bizarre animatronic Tavárez dummy.

Castillo del Cerro

San Cristobal • Dictatorship

★★☆☆☆

Dark Rating: 6 ☠

The Dominican Republic's megalomaniacal dictator Rafael Trujillo (1891–1961) had many grand mansions constructed for himself; some can still be found and even visited. This one, a modernistic four-storey pile, is in his home town of San Cristobal, but Trujillo did not like it and hence never lived in it. Nevertheless, it provides an insight into the lengths to which his minions would go in order to please their master.

The building is now mostly used as a school for prison guards, and visits can be arranged. Inside you can see a small exhibition and the lavish and garish interior designs fit for an egocentric dictator.

Left
An ornate interior showing elaborate mouldings and chandelier as well as the decorative inlaid floor design.

Casa Caoba

Outside San Cristobal • Dictatorship, Sex crimes

★☆☆☆☆

Dark Rating: 6 ☠

Of the many mansions that dictator Rafael Trujillo had all over the Dominican Republic, this is the one he lived in the most. This means it is also the place where he committed the majority of his sexual crimes. He was fond of putting on lavish feasts and balls, and was infamous for preying on young women – often teenagers. He would 'handpick' them on his visits around the country and his lackeys would later deliver his victims right to his bedroom door, including here at Casa Caoba.

The building is these days a ruin, but access for intrepid explorers can be arranged. It is a decidedly eerie place.

Above
One of the mansion's formerly opulent bedrooms lies derelict.

Museo Hermanas Mirabal

Near Salcedo, Cibao • Dictatorship, Resistance, Murder, Graves

★★☆☆☆

Dark Rating: 2 ☠

This is the former home of the Mirabal sisters, the heroines and martyrs of the Dominican Republic who played a crucial role in the resistance against the Trujillo dictatorship. After Trujillo had three of the sisters murdered (see below), and only six months later was assassinated himself, the surviving fourth sister, Dedé Mirabal, eventually established this museum-cum-shrine. She died in 2014, but the museum is still going strong.

The graves of the three other sisters, as well as that of resistance leader Manolo Tavárez (Minerva Mirabal's husband), are now in the garden outside the house and are a special pilgrimage destination.

Right
In 2000 (the fortieth anniversary of the Mirabal sisters' murder) their remains were moved to the grave site in the museum grounds.

Mirabal Monument

La Cumbre • Murder site

★☆☆☆☆

Dark Rating: 4 ☠

This is the original site where the Mirabal sisters were murdered on Trujillo's orders. Patria, María Teresa and especially the headstrong Minerva Mirabal had long been active in the resistance movement and thus were a thorn in the dictator's side; at some point he must have decided to get rid of them. On 25 November 1960 the Mirabals' car was ambushed on a mountain road as they were driving home from visiting their imprisoned husbands in Fort Felipe in Puerto Plata. The killers bludgeoned the sisters to death and then put them back in the car and rolled it down a hillside to make it look like an accident. Nobody fell for the cover-up.

It was instantly presumed that Trujillo was behind the deaths. It turned out to have been a step too far for Trujillo; he lost whatever outside support he still had, and only six months later he was assassinated himself.

In 1999 the UN designated 25 November International Day for the Elimination of Violence against Women. A monument was erected at the spot where the sisters had been murdered. It is a remote location in the northern mountains down a dirt track branching off a main road (best tackled by a four-wheel-drive vehicle or sturdy bicycle) near La Cumbre village. Other than the monument, there is nothing to see, so it is a real pilgrimage site.

Above
The remote monument for the Mirabals features a bust of each of the three sisters murdered at this site.

Montserrat

★★★☆☆

West Indies, Caribbean • Natural disaster (volcano)

Dark Rating: 8 ☻

This small volcanic island, a British overseas territory in the West Indies in the Caribbean, witnessed some of the most dramatic eruption activity of recent decades. Until 1995 Montserrat was a tropical island paradise just like its better-known neighbours such as Antigua, but then its Soufrière Hills volcano awoke after hundreds of years of inactivity. The island's capital, Plymouth, located at the foot of the mountain to the west, had to be evacuated due to the explosions, pyroclastic flows and ash fall.

By 1997 it was clear that the town would have to be abandoned for good. Subsequent lahars (see p51) have added to the ash cover; today, only the roofs of the higher buildings still poke out of the thick volcanic ash layer. Plymouth has become 'the Pompeii of the Caribbean'.

Nobody was killed by all that destruction in the capital; it was only later that a pyroclastic flow on the other side of the mountain claimed the lives of some farmers who had been tending their lands despite the danger and the warnings.

The volcano expanded the territory of the island. Pyroclastic flows down the eastern slopes of the mountain extended into the sea and created a new coastline hundreds of metres from the old shores. The old airport of Montserrat disappeared under the 'new land'. The whole southern two-thirds of the island have become more or less uninhabitable. Of the once 12,000 inhabitants, only 5000 still live on the island, in the villages and hamlets in the north that are not at immediate risk from the volcano, occasional ash fall notwithstanding.

There are different levels of exclusion zone in the south of the island, which the Montserrat Volcano Observatory (MVO) monitors and sets 'hazard levels' for according to the observed activity. Since 1997 there have been yet more eruptive phases: in 2003 a newly grown lava dome in the crater collapsed (the largest such event ever directly observed), causing massive pyroclastic flows and surges and an ash column above the mountain several miles high.

Below
The Court House in Plymouth is one of the ruins almost completely covered in volcanic debris from the eruptions on Montserrat.

By 2009 a new cycle of dome growth indicated another imminent chapter in this volcanic drama, and indeed it blew its top again in February 2010. After that, things calmed down and some access restrictions could be lifted. But the danger is not over.

As a dark destination, Montserrat offers a unique combination. On the one hand are dramatic volcanic landscapes, ghost-town ruins in and around the ex-capital, Plymouth, and at times spectacular 'live' displays of Mother Nature's wrath. On the other, the island has a relaxed and easy-going Caribbean vibe and, as often found with British overseas territories, a high level of general friendliness (see also St Helena, p70). Locals offer tours, but you can also hire a car to explore the island on your own.

The MVO, sitting on a hill right opposite the volcano, provides the best front-row view of any activity. It also has a small museum about the volcano and its various eruptions, and is thus a must-see destination on the island.

Above
Ash venting and glowing in the dark –
dramatic activity at Soufrière Hills volcano
in early 2010, shortly before the mountain's
latest explosive event.

DARK STATS

19 PEOPLE
killed in 1997

Thickness of the accumulated
ash and mud layer up to
12M (40FT)

7 SQ KM (2.7 SQ MILES)
of land flattened by the
debris and pyroclastic flow in
December 1997

300 YEARS
Since the volcano's
previous eruption

A LITTLE VOLCANOLOGY

Volcanism is the term for phenomena involving magma (molten rock) underneath the Earth's crust coming to the surface, either in flows of lava or in explosive events creating lots of volcanic ash.

The majority of the Earth's volcanoes are located along the edges of tectonic plates – for example, the so-called Pacific Ring of Fire – but there are also volcanoes on isolated hotspots in the Earth's crust far from the edges of tectonic plates. One such hotspot created the island chain of Hawaii (p339).

Volcanoes are usually classified as active (erupting or likely to erupt), dormant (historically active, inactive for a long time, but potentially reactivating, such as Montserrat) or completely extinct.

Volcanoes come in different types. Shield volcanoes are usually created by fluid lava flows, which solidify and slowly build up a mountain that resembles a warrior's shield; that is, their flanks are not very steep. Fluid lava from eruptions can travel long distances, as with, for example, Kilauea on Hawaii (p343–44), thus causing destruction far from the source of the lava. Sometimes lava is also ejected so forcefully that it forms lava fountains.

On Hawaii, lava fountains over 300m (1000ft) high have been observed. Strombolian eruptions (named after the Italian volcanic island of Stromboli) are regular or even constant ejections of red-hot cinder, creating the most photogenic kind of volcanism. Similarly spectacular are the few volcanoes featuring permanent lava lakes (such as Nyiragongo in the DR Congo).

Stratovolcanoes tend to have much steeper slopes and include picture-book-perfect cones such as Mount Fuji in Japan and Mount Mayon in the Philippines. Lava domes often grow in the craters of these volcanoes, as a result of magma pushing upwards. When they collapse, this can create explosive eruptions, ejecting lava bombs rather than liquid lava, and large amounts of volcanic ash, finely ground rock and hot gases. These can rise high into the atmosphere (sometimes disrupting air traffic – since this fine ash is poison for jet engines) and spread over a large area.

Especially large amounts of ash from extreme eruptions can affect the climate around the globe, as was the case when Mount Tambora in Indonesia erupted in 1815. The material that was ejected into the atmosphere caused a 'year without summer', resulting in crop failures and famine.

More immediately dangerous are pyroclastic flows or surges, when super-heated gases mixed with rock and ash travel down a volcano's slope and roll over the surrounding land, scorching everything in their path. Since the heat of the ash acts as an air cushion, pyroclastic flows can reach enormous speeds of several hundred kilometres per hour and are even capable of travelling across water – as was first directly observed in Montserrat. Deposited ash mixed with rainwater can later cause destructive mudflows known as lahars.

There are also volcanic eruptions that come out of the flat land from fissures. The eruption on the Icelandic island of Heimaey (p78) started as such a sudden fissure opening. Fissures are also frequently observed elsewhere, for example on Hawaii or along the East African Rift (for example, Congo). These can form cinder cones or splatter cones, which are also a common feature on Hawaii, Iceland and Fogo (p246).

Underwater volcanoes exist too, for example along the Mid-Atlantic Rift. Lava emitted from these can form round balls of so-called pillow lava. Subglacial volcanoes can melt a glacier's ice in an eruption causing devastating flood waves known as *jökulhlaup* in Icelandic. Finally, there are mud volcanoes, which eject neither lava nor ash; these are not true volcanoes, but rather geothermal phenomena.

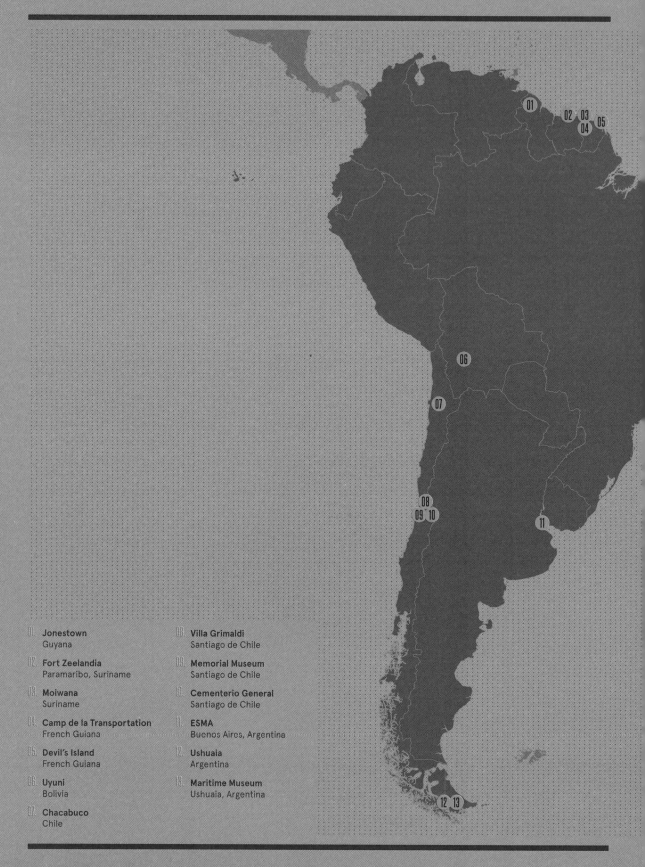

01. **Jonestown**
Guyana

02. **Fort Zeelandia**
Paramaribo, Suriname

03. **Moiwana**
Suriname

04. **Camp de la Transportation**
French Guiana

05. **Devil's Island**
French Guiana

06. **Uyuni**
Bolivia

07. **Chacabuco**
Chile

08. **Villa Grimaldi**
Santiago de Chile

09. **Memorial Museum**
Santiago de Chile

10. **Cementerio General**
Santiago de Chile

11. **ESMA**
Buenos Aires, Argentina

12. **Ushuaia**
Argentina

13. **Maritime Museum**
Ushuaia, Argentina

South America

The Southern Cone of the Americas was mostly 'conquered' by the Spanish; the old Inca and other empires were destroyed and their riches looted. Most South American countries are still Spanish-speaking, with the notable exception of Brazil (Portuguese) and the 'Three Guyanas' in the northeast, which are curious relics of the British, Dutch and French colonial stints on the subcontinent (which in the case of French Guiana still lasts to this day).

The Three Guyanas naturally combine well with each other as travel destinations, but the jungle-covered interior is not so easy to get to and transport can be costly. The other, larger countries dealt with here also combine well with each other, but longer distances have to be covered by plane, though within specific regions, such as Patagonia or the Atacama and Altiplano, overland travel (mostly by sturdy jeeps) is the only option.

In some South American countries, or parts of these, safety can be a concern, most dramatically so currently in Venezuela. But foreign visitors should also take care not to aimlessly wander into slum areas in the large cities such as Buenos Aires.

Guyana

This small country is the only anglophone nation in South America, thanks to it having been a British colony from 1814 until 1966. The sparsely populated interior is home to vast tracts of unspoilt rainforest and savannah. The main reason foreign visitors come to Guyana is for wildlife watching (including giant otters, giant anteaters, jaguars and tapirs) and the spectacular scenery, which includes Kaieteur Falls, the world's largest single-drop waterfall.

There is a major border dispute with neighbouring Venezuela, which claims about half of Guyana's territory, but this has not led to open conflict. Guyana also has one very black spot on its modern history records, one brought to it from the outside: the Jonestown Massacre – see below.

Access to Guyana is mostly by plane, either from neighbouring Suriname or Brazil, or from some of the Caribbean islands, such as Trinidad. The international airport at Guyana's capital, Georgetown, is the usual entry point, but it is also possible to enter Guyana overland from the south via Brazil.

Travel into the interior is also mostly by flying, namely on light propeller-engined planes, providing good views over the endless jungle, as well as the occasional gold-mining operation cutting a toxic gash in the green. Otherwise, travel is by boat on the rivers. Roads are few and they are largely confined to the coast east and west of Georgetown, except for one inland route, which can become impassable in the rainy season.

Jonestown

Near Port Kaituma • Massacre, Mass suicide

★☆☆☆☆

Dark Rating: 8

This was the settlement of the Peoples Temple, a quasi-religious cult led by Jim Jones. It was founded in the USA but moved to a plot of land acquired in Guyana after the organization faced problems at home. In this remote and secluded location in the jungle, Jones hoped the new settlement would provide a sanctuary for his utopian 'apostolic socialism'.

Jonestown became a largely self-sufficient egalitarian commune, yet not everything was as ideal and voluntary as it was nominally supposed to be. Jones employed methods of psychological intimidation, mind control and punishment, as well as the systematic use of drugs. The settlement also had armed guards to patrol the compound and enforce Jones's rule.

In 1978 a US congressman, Leo Ryan, at the request of concerned relatives of Peoples Temple members, started an investigation and flew to Guyana. During his visit, the situation escalated on 18 November. Some Jonestown residents

defected, a few fled and there came a showdown at the Port Kaituma airstrip, where Ryan and several of his entourage were shot dead by Jonestown guards.

Subsequently, in the settlement itself, Jones ordered the 'revolutionary suicide' of the entire commune. This had been on the cards for a while, and there had even been rehearsals of what was called 'white nights'. Now it

Above
Aerial shot showing the aftermath of the mass suicide of the Peoples Temple cult at Jonestown in 1978.

became reality. The cult members were given a concoction of soft-drink mixture laced with cyanide (which gave rise to the phrase 'drinking the Kool-Aid'). While many took the lethal cocktail voluntarily, quite a few others were forced into it (especially youngsters). There was shooting too; Jim Jones himself died from a gunshot wound. In total, 909 people, most of them African Americans, died at Jonestown (918 including those killed at the airstrip).

It was the largest mass suicide event in modern times, although, given that the deaths were not all that voluntary, the incident is more commonly referred to as a massacre.

Of the bodies of the dead, some 400 were interred in a special mass grave in California. At the site of the mass killings itself, however, very little is left. The former settlement has mostly been reclaimed by the jungle and remains largely undeveloped. There is a small memorial stone and a few rusty remnants of vehicles, but you need a local guide and have to machete your way in through the thick undergrowth to reach these. Thus Jonestown is one of the most remote, obscure and difficult dark destinations on Earth.

Above
Hypodermic syringes filled with cyanide and animal tranquillizer were part of the debris of the settlement in 1978.

Left
Very little remains of Jonestown today, just debris and overgrown rusty vehicle wrecks.

Suriname

The former Dutch Guiana gained independence from the Netherlands in 1975 to become the smallest sovereign state on the South American Cone, and the only one where Dutch is the official language.

In its modern history, Suriname has had some dark periods. In 1980 a coup under Dési Bouterse installed a military dictatorship that sparked civil war-like conflict that lasted well into the 1990s. Bouterse's regime soured relations with the former colonial power of the Netherlands, where in 1999 he was tried and, in absentia, sentenced to 11 years in prison on charges of drug smuggling.

Suriname eventually returned to democracy, but in 2010 Bouterse managed to get himself elected president, and he was even re-elected democratically in 2015. In late 2019, however, he was sentenced by a high court in Paramaribo to a long prison term. Bouterse was abroad at the time but returned home and appealed against his conviction. In July 2020 he lost the presidential elections, but he still has a powerful fan base. At the time of writing the appeal case was still not closed. Aside from that, Suriname is a very charming country and the old town of its capital city, Paramaribo, is a World Heritage delight.

Fort Zeelandia

Paramaribo • Murder

★★★☆☆

Dark Rating: 4 ☠

This old Dutch-built fort from colonial times in Suriname's capital city, Paramaribo, was the location of the so-called December murders of 1982, when 15 political opponents of the then military regime – mostly lawyers, union leaders and journalists – were shot dead by dictator Dési Bouterse's soldiers. There are claims that Bouterse took part in the shootings himself, though he has always denied this.

Inside the fort, which opened to the public in 1995, there is a plaque commemorating the incident and its victims. You can still see bullet holes in the wall at the spot where the shootings took place.

Above
The fort stands out as being one of the few stone edifices in the historic centre of Paramaribo, which otherwise consists mostly of wooden buildings.

Moiwana

Main west–east road near Albina • Massacre

★★☆☆☆

Dark Rating: 6 ☠

This little village in the Marowijne district in the east of Suriname was the site of the Moiwana massacre in 1986. It was the home of Ronnie Brunswijk, formerly a bodyguard of dictator Bouterse in the early 1980s. After Brunswijk had fallen out with his ex-boss, he formed the Surinamese Liberation Army, better known as the 'Jungle Commando', which fought for better recognition of Suriname's Maroon minority (descendants of black slaves who had fled into the jungle) and for an end to the military dictatorship.

In the attack on the village, the military burned down Brunswijk's house and killed at least 35 villagers, mostly women and children. Others fled across the border river into French Guiana. In 2005 Suriname was ordered by an international court to pay compensation to the survivors.

Right
The Moiwana memorial complex was inaugurated on 29 November 2007, the 21st anniversary of the massacre.

French Guiana

This small piece of land is the last colony on the South American Cone, an overseas department of France. It is thus part of the EU, French is the official language and the euro is the currency. The country is mostly covered by primeval rainforest, and the vast majority of the inhabitants (about 300,000) live in the capital, Cayenne, or in settlements along the coast.

French Guiana is home to the Kourou space centre, from which the European Space Agency launches its Ariane rockets; since 2011, Russian Soyuz rockets have been launched from here too. The presence of the space centre, and the fact that the country in general relies on French subsidies, means that prices are higher than in neighbouring countries, but standards are higher too.

The country is a dark destination primarily for its history as a penal colony between the mid-nineteenth and mid-twentieth century. The most infamous site of this was Devil's Island, but there were others too, and some are now tourist attractions.

Left
Abandoned ex-prison in Saint-Laurent-du-Maroni, the heart of the former penal colony of French Guiana (see over the page).

Camp de la Transportation

Saint-Laurent-du-Maroni • Prison

★★★☆☆

Dark Rating: 7 ☠

Saint-Laurent, located on the eastern banks of the border river with Suriname, was founded in the mid-nineteenth century as the entry point for convicts sent to the penal colonies of French Guiana, but soon was turned into such a colony itself. The old Camp de la Transportation became essentially a high-security prison, including sections for solitary confinement and 'special treatment'.

The regime was brutal. As a punishment, prisoners were routinely shackled up for days without food, water or any sanitation just for committing small 'crimes' such as making a sound or touching the walls.

The prison remained in operation until just after World War Two. It is now a well-maintained museum site, much more commodified than the old prisons on the Îles du Salut (see below). Guided tours are available (also in English, by arrangement) to take visitors around the sinister compound and relate its grim practices and stories. A highlight is seeing the former cell of Henri Charrière (of *Papillon* fame; see below).

Devil's Island

Off the coast of Kourou • Prisons, Penal colony, Overgrown ruins

★★★★☆

Dark Rating: 8 ☠

Far left
Devil's Island seen from the neighbouring Île Royale.

Left
A bleak corridor inside the prison for French convicts on Île Royale.

The small archipelago of Îles du Salut (Salvation Islands), a few miles from the mainland, is the most infamous of the penal colonies established by France in its South American colony of French Guiana. It was not just criminals who were sent here, but political prisoners too. Their treatment in this tropical hell was brutal.

Internationally, this penal colony is best known for the Dreyfus affair and the book *Papillon*. Alfred Dreyfus was a French army officer who was wrongfully convicted of treason, and sent to Devil's Island in 1895, only to be first pardoned in 1899 and then fully rehabilitated in 1906. *Papillon* is a book by Henri Charrière about his escape from the penal colony – famously turned into a movie starring Steve McQueen and Dustin Hoffman in 1973. In reality, however, Charrière was imprisoned in a different penal colony on the mainland (in Saint-Laurent-du-Maroni; see above), so it is not quite a true story.

The penal colony system was eventually closed down after World War Two. Devil's Island (Île du Diable in French) was the place for political prisoners, while the main penal colony was located on the other two islands of the archipelago, Île Royale and Île Saint-Joseph.

Today, only the latter two can be visited; Devil's Island itself is said to be too dangerous to go to by boat because of strong currents, and thus remains inaccessible for tourists. But there are prison ruins to be seen on both the other islands. On Île Royale you can even stay in the former officers' mess, which has been converted into a hotel and restaurant. Despite their dark history, the islands are popular with both locals and tourists.

On Île Saint-Joseph you are not supposed to enter the prison ruins, but their almost Angkor Wat-like overgrown appeal is hard to resist, and hence many visitors do go there.

Bolivia

This large, landlocked country is the poorest on the Southern Cone of the Americas, and was exploited by outsiders for centuries. Contemporary hopes that Bolivia's rich lithium deposits could bring new fortunes have so far not been fulfilled.

Interestingly, in 2005 the country elected the first president in Latin America who was of native Amerindian descent: Evo Morales, an anti-imperialist socialist and champion of indigenous rights, who was re-elected three times in a row. After the disputed 2019 election, however, he was forced to resign and went into exile, only to return in November 2020, following the overthrow of the right-wing government elected in 2019. Morales remains influential but has not resumed power, as of the time of writing.

For the traveller, however, the country is remarkable mostly for its stunning mountain and Altiplano (high plateau) landscapes, which include bizarrely coloured lagoons and the largest salt pan in the world.

Uyuni ★★★☆☆

In the Altiplano, Andes • Extreme landscape, Mummies, Wrecks   **Dark Rating:** 3 ☠

The little town of Uyuni in the Altiplano of Bolivia is a destination for determined travellers mainly for the nearby Salar de Uyuni, the world's largest salt pan. This vast expanse of white (you have to wear glacier-grade sunglasses) does have otherworldly appeal, especially during the wet season, when a thin layer of water accumulates on the salt surface and turns the Salar into the world's largest mirror of sorts. Yet the salt flat is not without its dangers: in 2008 two jeeps with tourists on board crashed while racing each other, killing 13 people.

Another dark aspect is the sites in the area where you can see mummies. One mummy site at the foot of Tunupa volcano on the northern shores of the salt lake is a common stop on tourist itineraries.

Tourism is currently the principal source of income for this remote region. Uyuni town is characterized by travellers' infrastructure, mostly for the backpacker type of clientele, but there are also more upscale establishments. These include a couple of 'salt hotels', built almost entirely out of blocks of solid salt from the Salar. The larger ones are actually on the shores of the salt lake, but the first and original salt hostel still stands right on the salt flat and is a popular destination for easy excursions on to the Salar.

Another attraction, and a more metaphorical burial place than the mummies' caves, is the so-called train cemetery south of Uyuni town. This is basically a collection of steam engines and carriages simply dumped here to slowly rust away. They do create a strange post-apocalyptic atmosphere all the same. More abandoned old trains and engines can be found in the nearby mining town of Pulacayo.

Top
A rusting locomotive with open steam boiler in the train graveyard at Uyuni.

Above
Bolivian Amerindian mummy with a coin it its eye socket; near Uyuni.

Chile

This long, thin country on the Pacific coast of the South American Cone is still much associated with the military dictatorship of Augusto Pinochet, which started with the violent coup (with CIA support) against the democratically elected neosocialist president Salvador Allende in 1973. This even involved fighter jets attacking the presidential palace. Allende gave a moving farewell speech to his people on the radio before his death in the palace as soldiers stormed it.

Allende's death is presumed to have been suicide, although to what degree he was pressured into it by the military intruders remains controversial. Elsewhere, people were rounded up and held in mass detention centres, including sports stadiums. Other political prison camps were more remote, but even in the heart of the capital city secret prisons and torture centres were set up.

The dictatorship ended in 1990, but its repercussions are still felt today, and politics in the country have often been 'complicated'. Yet Chile is one of the best-developed countries in South America – also in terms of travel infrastructure. It is a prime destination in itself, not least for its varied scenery covering a vast range of climates and topographies, from fjords and glaciers in the south to the world's driest desert, the Atacama, in the north.

Chacabuco ★★★☆☆

Atacama Desert • Concentration camp, Industrial ruins, Ghost town   **Dark Rating: 6** ☠

This remote place in the middle of the Atacama Desert in northern Chile began as a nitrate mining and processing town, which was big business a century ago. Dozens of such *oficinas* were set up at the time. Chacabuco was comparatively late to the game, founded in 1922. It was a model town for some 5000 workers, with excellent infrastructure including a school, sports facilities and even a theatre. Two decades later, however, the nitrate boom was over, and Chacabuco closed and was abandoned.

In 1971 the old ghost town was declared a national monument and some restoration work began. Then came the 1973 military coup and the onset of the Pinochet dictatorship. The junta decided that the conveniently remote location of Chacabuco was ideal for setting up a kind of concentration camp for political prisoners. Chacabuco served that function for about a year until the regime had consolidated itself, and in 1974 the place was abandoned again.

After the end of the dictatorship, restoration work resumed in the 1990s, partly with support from the German Goethe Institute, which was involved in the refurbishment of the old theatre. Two former inmates of the political prison camp returned as caretakers and some information panels were put up. The site is now part of the Rutas Patrimoniales heritage trail, which takes in other former *oficinas* such as Humberstone and Santa Laura. Yet Chacabuco remains an extremely remote destination.

Below
Chacabuco's mostly ghost-town atmosphere adds to its special appeal as a desolate outpost in the middle of nowhere.

Villa Grimaldi

★★★☆☆

Santiago de Chile • Prison, Torture, Murder   **Dark Rating:** 7 ☠

This is the main site in Chile's capital city that is associated with the brutal repression during the Pinochet dictatorship. Villa Grimaldi, formerly a private estate, became a clandestine detention and torture centre shortly after the 1973 coup, and remained so until 1978. Some 4500 political prisoners are believed to have passed through this grim institution, and well over 200 of these were 'disappeared' (murdered and their bodies disposed of, never to be found again). The site is now a national memorial and peace park, featuring monuments as well as a few original structures. A small exhibition room displays evidence of the 'disappeared' salvaged from the sea, including a single shirt button. In this context, such an ordinary little item takes on grim poignancy.

Memorial Museum

★★★★☆

Central Santiago de Chile   **Dark Rating:** 8 ☠
Dictatorship, Torture, Resistance

This large, modern museum, officially called Museo de la Memoria y los Derechos Humanos (Museum of Memory and Human Rights) recounts the years of the military dictatorship and political repression in Chile as well as how this dark era was eventually overcome.

Possibly the grimmest single exhibit here is a rusty bed frame (to which victims would have been tied), together with the sort of electroshock device that was the regime's preferred tool of torture.

DARK STATS

17 YEARS
length of Pinochet's dictatorship

3000
officially recognized cases of disappearances or extra-judicial killings

38,000
cases of torture and political imprisonment

200,000
estimated number of people forced into exile

17 MONTHS
Pinochet held under house arrest in Britain awaiting extradition, 1998–2000

Cementerio General

★★★☆☆

Santiago de Chile • Cemetery, Dictatorship   **Dark Rating:** 5 ☠

This large cemetery in Chile's capital is well worth a look, not only for the imposing Allende family tomb, but especially for the section 'Patio 29' with mostly nameless graves of victims of the early phase of the dictatorship.

Just behind it, at the rear of the cemetery, you can find the grave of Victor Jara, Chile's legendary singer-songwriter, who was tortured and killed in the early days of the coup. At the entrance to the cemetery is a large memorial to those who were executed or 'disappeared'.

Right
Bent metal crosses in 'Patio 29' of the cemetery, where murdered victims of the regime are buried.

Argentina

This large South American country (second largest after Brazil, and eighth largest in the world) is included in this book for very similar reasons as its neighbour Chile. In 1976 a right-wing military dictatorship overthrew the government (with US backing, as in Chile – p60) and embarked on a brutal regime of persecution of liberals, socialists, dissidents, activists; anybody deemed left-wing.

This reign of state terrorism became known as the 'Dirty War'. Of the tens of thousands imprisoned or abducted, between 10,000 and 30,000 'disappeared'. Frequently they were simply tied up, sedated and then thrown into the sea or river estuaries to drown. There were countless clandestine detention and torture centres in the capital city, Buenos Aires, alone. Moreover, several hundred 'children of the disappeared' were given as babies to childless couples within the regime, in some cases to the very people responsible for the disappearance of their biological parents.

In 1982 the military junta, partly in order to distract attention from economic difficulties at home, invaded the Falkland Islands, known in most of Latin America as Las Malvinas, a British oversees territory in the South Atlantic some 480km (300 miles) off the Argentinian coast (p66–67). This move backfired badly. Argentina was defeated in the subsequent war against Britain, and, having lost popular support at home, the military leadership had to step down. New elections were organized, and in 1983 the country returned to democracy.

Coming to terms with the years of human rights violations during the dictatorship proved a difficult and lengthy process and is still ongoing. Commemoration is similarly small-scale, but if you dig below the surface some sites associated with this dark recent history can be found.

ESMA

★★★☆☆

Northern Buenos Aires • Detention and torture centre

Dark Rating: 7 ☠

Above
The neoclassical façade of the former naval academy, later a notorious detention centre.

This former Navy school in the north of Buenos Aires was one of the principal clandestine detention, torture and execution centres during Argentina's 'Dirty War' between 1976 and 1983. An estimated 5000 political prisoners passed through this particular centre, most of them 'disappeared'. During the 1978 Football World Cup, the inmates would have been able to hear the cheers from the nearby River Plate Stadium. Today, ESMA is the key memorial site featuring a museum exhibition with historical documents and victims' testimonies, and guided tours are offered.

To the southeast of ESMA is the Parque de la Memoria, a large landscaped area with sculptures full of symbolism with regard to the 'Dirty War'.

Some of the other former clandestine detention and torture centres, mostly in ex-garages, have become memorials too, such as Garage Olimpo or Virrey Cevallos.

Finally, it is also worth going to Plaza de Mayo, where the 'Mothers (and Grandmothers) of the Disappeared' have marched in silent protest since the years of the dictatorship. Other protests take place there too, including those by veterans of the Falklands/Malvinas War.

Ushuaia

★★☆☆☆

Tierra del Fuego, Patagonia • Extreme landscape, Modern conflict

Dark Rating: 4 ☠

This is the southernmost city on Earth, and as such quite an end-of-the-road destination. Its harbour is also the principal embarkation point for cruises to the Antarctic Peninsula, catering for well over half of all Antarctica tourism (p73). However, the place is included in this book for another reason. Nominally, going by the Argentinian line of argument, Ushuaia would (should) be the administrative capital of the South Atlantic Islands that are claimed by Argentina but remain in British hands; first and foremost the Falklands, known here as Las Malvinas.

In Ushuaia, you can find slogans sprayed on walls that emphasize this claim, and at the harbour gate a large sign proclaims that 'English pirates aren't welcome'. There is also an official Malvinas War memorial, and one section in the local museum is on the topic of that conflict too.

Below
The city of Ushuaia against the backdrop of snow-capped Patagonian mountain peaks.

Maritime Museum

★★★★☆

Ushuaia, Tierra del Fuego • Prison, War

Dark Rating: 5 ☠

The building in which this *museo maritimo* is housed is a particular dark attraction in Ushuaia: it is a large ex-prison complex. This was built at the beginning of the twentieth century, when Ushuaia was a penal colony. By 1920 the prison had five cell blocks with a total of 386 cells. It was closed in 1947 and the premises handed over to the Navy, which established a naval base in Ushuaia in 1950.

It remained a practically closed-off town until after the end of the military dictatorship in 1983. Now the ex-prison and the museum inside it have become the principal tourist attraction down here (other than embarkation for Antarctica cruises). One of the cell-block wings has been preserved in its original state, while the others now house the museum exhibitions. Other than the maritime section, there's also one about the prison (and other prisons around the world; see p31), an Antarctica section, and one about the Falklands War, known here as Conflicto de las Islas Malvinas.

Above
An ancient prison block preserved inside the museum. The prison closed in 1947 and was declared a national historic monument in 1997.

01. **The Falkland Islands**
South Atlantic

02. **South Georgia**
South Atlantic

03. **St Helena**
South Atlantic

04. **Antarctica**

The South Atlantic & Antarctica

Collected in this short section are the vast 'sixth continent' around the South Pole (which is jointly administered by several countries but does not contain any countries as such) and a few islands in the southern ocean north of Antarctica that for various reasons are noteworthy dark places deserving a mention here.

All these destinations are naturally difficult to get to, mostly by boat, although a couple have regular civilian flight connections too (St Helena and the Falklands). All are impossible to get to on a tight budget and can cost serious money, particularly Antarctica. The White Continent's appeal is mainly for the scenery and sheer remoteness, but it has some dark aspects too, not least the tragic stories of early explorers who perished here.

The South Atlantic islands covered here are all British overseas territories, although that is contested in the case of the Falklands in particular, which even led to a modern-era war in 1982. Uncontested St Helena is one of the most isolated inhabited spots on the planet, but it too is well worth a visit for both its (dark) history and its splendid scenery. And while Antarctica and South Georgia are as good as impossible to visit independently, the Falklands and St Helena can be visited by independent travellers. It is extremely rewarding to do so. But because all these islands are very far from mass tourism (an attraction in itself), planning well ahead is essential.

The Falkland Islands

South Atlantic • Modern war

★★★★☆

Dark Rating: 8 ☠

Left
Unexploded landmines are still a danger, but are well marked in the landscape.

Below
Panoramic view of the Port Howard settlement on sparsely populated West Falkland.

This remote and rugged South Atlantic archipelago of sparsely populated islands would not be so well known to the world if not for the Falklands War of 1982, when Argentina invaded this British overseas territory and the UK sent a military Task Force to reclaim and liberate the islands (see p68).

Argentina derives its territorial claim to the islands from a colonial-era deal made between Spain and Portugal, when the two empires divided up their spheres of conquest in the 'New World', by which the Falklands would have become Spanish had Spain seized them, and thus Argentina as a successor state would have inherited them. However, the then still uninhabited islands were first claimed by a British captain and given their English name in the late seventeenth century, long before Argentina even existed.

The first settlers, meanwhile, were from France, in particular from St Malo in Brittany, and they named the islands after their home: *Malouines*. From that derives the name *Las Malvinas*, as the islands are known in Latin America. Over the next century, several countries had a brief stint on the Falklands, including the USA, but nobody made any serious claims to the land until one Luis Vernet tried to establish a commercial enterprise to exploit the islands. This led to the first proper military conflicts between Britain, the USA and the precursor state of what was to become Argentina.

A mutiny of gauchos (horsemen) caused further disruption, during which one British representative was killed, until the UK seriously established British rule in 1834 and invited British settlers to make their home on the islands.

Thus a distinctive community developed. Today, there are about 3000 inhabitants, two-thirds of whom live in the island's capital and only town, Stanley, on East Falkland. Port Howard, the main

Left
Rusting Argentine 105mm gun left behind
on Mt Longdon near Stanley, East Falkland.

Below
The Argentine cemetery at Darwin, close
to Goose Green.

for civilians, and also (more affordable) commercial flights from Chile. More connections may be added in the future. Travel between the islands is mostly by small aircraft operated by FIGAS (Falkland Islands Government Air Service), while overland travel is by jeep.

There is only one full-service hotel, in the capital, Stanley, plus a few B&Bs and guest houses. Outside the town, there are a few full-board lodges as well as self-catering options here and there, even on some of the outlying smaller islands. Planning far ahead of time is essential given the limited tourism infrastructure, and this is not a budget destination.

While most visitors come to the Falklands for wildlife watching, mainly penguins, battlefield tourism is another niche catered for here. A few local guides offer tours of battlefield sites, especially around Stanley, Goose Green and Port Howard. The latter is the main settlement of thinly populated West Falkland; it is from here that some of the more noteworthy sites where fighter aircraft crashed can be visited.

In addition, there are countless memorials, relics of Argentine positions, an Argentine war cemetery and a few local museums (such as those in Port Howard, San Carlos and Stanley). In some areas you can encounter minefield warning signs. Landmines are indeed a controversial vestige of the war, but as long as you obey the warning signs, they pose no risk to visitors.

settlement on West Falkland, in contrast, has fewer than 70 residents. The second-largest village on East Falkland is Goose Green, with about 150 inhabitants. The architecture, especially in Stanley, the red telephone booths and postboxes, the pubs and even the cuisine are all distinctly British, as is the islanders' accent.

The Argentinian claims that there had been an Argentine population that was expelled by the British, or even that there is still now an Argentinian population (speaking Spanish) that is being repressed, are simply not correct. It may seem odd that a territory so far from the UK but so close to Argentina should be British, but that is what history brought about and that is what the islanders want (in a 2013 referendum, 99.8 per cent of the inhabitants voted for retaining the status quo of the Falklands being a British overseas territory).

These days, the islands are largely self-sufficient and self-governed. In the wake of the Falklands War, the islands prospered more than before and the population's average per capita income is now higher than that in Britain. In the aftermath of the war, a large new military base with a proper runway for a permanent stationing of fighter aircraft was established, so the islands are now also better defended than ever before.

For the traveller, this airbase has also made the islands more accessible, because the new runway is suitable for passenger aircraft too. There are flights by the RAF with a number of seats available

THE FALKLANDS WAR

The invasion of the Falklands/Malvinas on 2 April 1982 was a surprise operation begun by the then military junta in Argentina, partly to boost patriotism and partly to distract from an increasingly difficult economic situation at home. The initial landing force of just under 1000 troops quickly took Stanley, which was at the time defended by only about 70 Royal Marines. Being so outnumbered, the governor had to surrender. Up to that point, the invasion went as planned.

What the Argentinians did not expect was the British reaction of deploying a naval Task Force with two aircraft carriers and dozens of other vessels, including landing craft, to sail to the South Atlantic. Since the voyage from the UK to the Falklands took a few weeks, a bombing raid was the first British operation of the war. This was Operation Black Buck and involved scrambling a number of Vulcan bombers from the British base on Ascension Island. This required multiple in-air refuelling manoeuvres. Black Buck was more a symbolic operation, though, as only one bomb hit the airfield at Stanley and the damage was quickly repaired. But it sent a signal.

The first serious engagement at sea came on 2 May, when the Royal Navy submarine HMS *Conqueror* torpedoed and sank the Argentinian cruiser ARA *General Belgrano*. Well over 300 Argentine seamen were killed, the largest loss of lives of any action in this war, accounting for about half the Argentine casualties in the conflict. The sinking of the cruiser was controversial because at the time of the attack it was apparently outside the 'total exclusion zone' that the UK had declared. Britain in turn lost the destroyer HMS *Sheffield* on 4 May after it was attacked by Argentine fighter jets firing anti-ship Exocet missiles. Twenty British seamen perished in that attack.

More losses followed during the British landing operations at San Carlos, Bluff Cove and Fitzroy, when these came under attack from the air. Another destroyer, two frigates and a support cargo ship were sunk. Yet, on 27 May the British were victorious at the Battle of Goose Green, which is widely regarded as the key turning point of the conflict.

The final stage of the war, in June, was the multiple battles for Stanley, the islands' capital, which took place mostly on the mountains around the town, such as Mount Tumbledown, Mount Harriet and Mount Longdon. As the Argentine resistance fell apart, the commanding officer, General Mario Menéndez, surrendered to the British on 14 June.

In the 74 days of conflict, just over 900 lives were lost, more than two-thirds of them on the Argentine side. In contrast to most other modern wars, however, civilian fatalities were limited to just three – the result of friendly fire when a British shell accidentally hit a house in Stanley. Over 11,000 prisoners of war who had been taken by the British were quickly repatriated.

In Argentina, the lost war contributed to the military regime losing its grip on power, and the country returned to democracy in 1983. In Britain, the victory gave a boost to the then prime minister, Margaret Thatcher, who won the next election by a landslide. On the Falklands, peace returned, and eventually also prosperity. The British established a permanent military base and airport at Mount Pleasant, and so far no further military threats have been made against the Falklands, despite occasional propagandistic verbal sabre-rattling by Argentina. Its territorial claim to the Falklands has not been dropped.

Left
The wrecked wing of an Argentine Air Force fighter jet that was shot down by the British during the Falklands conflict.

South Georgia

★ ★ ★ ★ ★

South Atlantic • Extreme landscape, Ghost town, Famous grave

Dark Rating: 6 ☠

Above
Rusty shipwreck of the sealing vessel *Petrel* at the old whaling station in Grytviken.

Right
Shackleton's grave. Because South Georgia had played a key role in his previous expeditions, it was chosen to be his final resting place.

This subantarctic island, together with the neighbouring South Sandwich Islands, forms another remote British overseas territory. Unlike the UK's other South Atlantic outposts, there is no permanent population.

In the past, there were several large whaling stations here. It was one of these that Ernest Shackleton finally managed to reach on his epic escape and rescue journey after the disastrous failure of the *Endurance* expedition to Antarctica (p73) of 1914–17. His grave is at the former Norwegian whaling station Grytviken, now a ghost town. The only visitors he and the island ever get are from cruise ships, which regularly make landings here as part of their exclusive subantarctic journeys.

St Helena

★★★★☆

South Atlantic • Exile, POWs, Slavery, Extreme landscape

Dark Rating: 4 💀

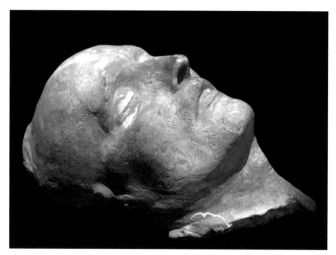

Left
The death mask of Napoleon Bonaparte, which can be viewed at Longwood House, where he lived out his days in exile.

Opposite
The sheer volcanic rock face of the island of St Helena.

St Helena also played a role in the transatlantic slave trade (p244–45), in particular after Britain abolished slavery and the Royal Navy started hunting down other nations' slave ships. Thus thousands of freed slaves were put ashore on St Helena. Recent archaeological digs have revealed a large burial ground for ex-slaves at Rupert's Bay.

The museum in St Helena's small and charming capital, Jamestown, has plenty of information about all that history as well as about general island life then and now. Other than that, places of interest as dark destinations include the Boer POW cemetery and the locations of the camps where they were held; all the Napoleonic sites; and plenty of fortifications from the seventeenth century to the time of World War Two.

This island of volcanic origin in the middle of the South Atlantic, roughly halfway between southern Africa and Brazil, has had a more significant history than might be expected for a place so remote and isolated. Yet it was that very remoteness and isolation that made it ideal as a place of exile.

Being British-owned, it was a favourite place to where the UK would banish those whom it wanted well out of the way. The most famous of those people was Napoleon Bonaparte, who was brought to the island in 1815 after his defeat at Waterloo. A few years earlier, he had escaped his first exile on the Italian island of Elba, so the British wanted to ensure this wouldn't be possible again.

Napoleon died on St Helena in 1821. The exact circumstances of his death were long a matter of controversy and conspiracy theories, but the official line that the ex-emperor died of stomach cancer is now largely accepted. He was initially buried on St Helena too, but his corpse was exhumed and transferred to Paris in 1840. His empty tomb is still a tourist attraction and pilgrimage site, as is the estate where he lived out his final years, Longwood House, which was sold to France and is still under French management. Visitors can tour the restored building, see Napoleon's deathbed and death mask, and learn all the minutiae of his association with St Helena.

There were other exiles on this island too, from Zulu warrior chiefs to Boer prisoners of war. The last ones were three rebel leaders from Bahrain who were incarcerated at Munden's Battery from 1957 to 1961.

Getting to St Helena used to be a time-consuming and rather exclusive affair, namely by Royal Mail ship. But a newly built airport has been in operation since 2017, with weekly flights from South Africa, making this remote spot much more accessible. However, the prices for this, and the relative scarcity of tourism facilities on the island, still make it a niche destination.

While the hopes the islanders had for a tourism boom thanks to the airport proved too high, the upshot is that St Helena retains its unique character – and part of that is a high level of natural friendliness. There is something about remote British overseas territories that must foster this, since the same can be encountered on Montserrat (p49) and the Falklands (p66–67).

St Helena, incidentally, is also the administrative centre of an area that Includes two more remote British-held islands: Ascension Island to the northwest, which is mainly a military airbase, and volcanic Tristan da Cunha to the south. The latter is home to the most isolated small community of people, and visits, although possible in theory, are very difficult to arrange.

Antarctica

★★☆☆☆

Around the South Pole • Extreme landscape, Death

Dark Rating: 6 ☠

Left and below
Archive photo of Scott in his Terra Nova camp at Cape Evans, and the preserved interior of his hut today.

Opposite
The darkly inhospitable landscape of the 'white continent' is one of the deadliest environments on Earth.

The 'white continent' is arguably the ultimate bucket-list travel destination, and the price levels ensure it remains a very exclusive one. There are several cruise ships that head down there, most of them from Ushuaia (p63) in Tierra del Fuego, Argentina. The majority of these, and all those with price tags under the $10,000 mark, only dip into the Antarctic waters; they don't go any further than the Antarctic Peninsula and thus don't even penetrate the Antarctic Circle.

Quite a few of these cruises also combine the trip to the tip of the Antarctic Peninsula with side trips to the Falklands (p66) and South Georgia (p69). These outer Antarctica cruises therefore can make do with regular passenger ships that have been equipped with more or less strengthened hulls to be able to navigate icy waters, whereas for getting deeper into the Antarctic towards the large ice shelves – say, into the Ross Sea – a proper icebreaker can be required.

If you are wondering how the 'white continent' can count as a dark destination, consider this: it is the deadliest, most life-threatening environment on this planet. A few creatures, such as the hardy emperor penguins, manage to live on the edges of Antarctica, but the surface of the inland ice shield, a couple of kilometres thick in places, is completely devoid of life. And despite all that water in frozen form, it is the driest desert on Earth.

Moreover, people have actually died here, in their attempts to conquer the South Pole. The best-known such tragic tale is that of Robert F. Scott, who lost the race to be the first man at the Pole (to Norwegian Roald Amundsen), and whose party perished on the way back in 1912. Scott's expedition's base-camp hut at Cape Evans on Ross Island is still there and has been designated a Historic Site; the same applies to Ernest Shackleton's hut nearby, erected for his unsuccessful 1907–9 South Pole Expedition.

These are the prize dark destinations in Antarctica, but are very rarely visited by any Antarctic programmes, and the few that do include them cost a fortune. The South Pole itself is sometimes included too, by way of flying in by plane. Needless to say, such trips do not come cheap either.

SVALBARD

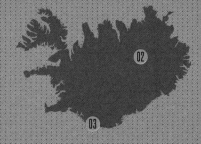

Northern Europe

Beginning in the northwest, this section kicks off outside mainland Europe with islands in the North Atlantic and the Arctic Ocean but that are considered part of Europe politically. While the rest of Scandinavia is connected to the mainland, the British Isles are not: this 'splendid isolation' has had historical consequences, and still impinges on European politics in the present day.

In the high north above the Arctic Circle, the seasons differ to the extreme, with perpetual night during the winter and 24/7 daylight in the summer. For that reason, these places are more rewarding in the summer season, unless it's seeing the Northern Lights that you're after, for which the darkness of the Arctic night is naturally better.

Places that are dark destinations in the figurative sense used here come in the form of Soviet and World War Two relics, as well as natural disaster sites, especially from volcanoes in Iceland. In the rest of Scandinavia and in the British Isles the climate and weather are somewhat less forbidding and the range of dark destinations wider, especially in the UK, from war heritage to recent conflicts and from terrorism to the legacy of the nuclear industry. Note that Scandinavian countries are very expensive destinations, especially so Norway, but the tourism infrastructure is excellent, as it is in all the countries in this section.

Svalbard

This archipelago, also known under the name of its biggest island, Spitsbergen (meaning 'pointed mountains'), is one of the northernmost permanently inhabited places on Earth. Located roughly halfway between mainland Norway and the North Pole, this remote glacial world had only been used on and off by whalers and walrus hunters, but when coal deposits were discovered and mining began around the turn of the twentieth century, the first permanent settlements were established on Spitsbergen.

Disputes about the islands' status and their commercial exploitation were resolved in the 1920 Svalbard Treaty, which recognized Norwegian sovereignty but also laid down certain restrictions – in particular it allowed the signatory nations' citizens the right to reside on Svalbard and have access to mining, fishing and hunting. It also stipulated that the archipelago remain non-militarized. So the unique situation came about that the USSR maintained coal-mining settlements on Spitsbergen, even during the Cold War era, despite Norway being a member of NATO.

Coal mining is still an important industry here, although it has declined since its heyday. Of the Soviet coal-mining settlements, one is still active, now as a Russian exclave, namely Barentsburg, south of the island's only town and administrative centre, Longyearbyen.

Spitsbergen has become the most accessible part of the high Arctic, thanks in particular to the airport of Longyearbyen, opened in 1975, which these days offers daily flights to Norway. As you might expect, it is a rather expensive destination, though worth every penny.

Pyramiden

Spitsbergen • Ghost town, Communism, Soviet legacy

★★★☆☆

Dark Rating: 7 ☠

Formerly the biggest and most significant of the Soviet coal-mining settlements on Spitsbergen, its operations ceased in 1998 and the place was abandoned. In its prime during the Cold War era, Pyramiden was made into a model settlement by the Soviets. Working here was a privilege, with wages much higher than back home, and plenty of amenities. These included a sports centre with a pool, a cultural centre, library, movie theatre, canteen and restaurants. Pyramiden also boasts the world's northernmost Lenin bust and grand piano.

Today, Pyramiden is a time capsule allowing a glimpse into the Soviet past like few other places on Earth. Many structures are well preserved, while others are slowly crumbling away. The town is not totally abandoned – a small Russian workforce lives here year round to look after the site, and more staff join them during the summer season. The town's hotel has been refurbished, so it is possible to stay here overnight, even on full-board basis. Most visitors, however, come on day trips from Longyearbyen, mainly by boat in the summer season.

Tours include a guided walk around the ghost town, during which visitors can see the former Gagarin cultural centre, with its Lenin bust outside, the abandoned works canteen and kitchens as well as the active hotel. The latter also houses a small museum and a bar. The staff and atmosphere are thoroughly Russian, although the guides speak good English. During the tour on foot in the ghost town you are accompanied by guards armed with rifles in case a hungry polar bear should turn up!

Above
Pyramiden's odd name is derived from the pyramid-shaped mountain at whose foot it lies and which contains the old coal mine.

Iceland

This small and famously happy island nation boasts some of the most spectacular scenery on Earth, owed to its latitude just below the Arctic Circle and its volcanism, which also gave the country the epithet 'land of ice and fire'. The volcanic activity is caused by Iceland's position on the Mid-Atlantic Ridge where the Eurasian and North American tectonic plates meet.

While this special geology has created a lot of natural beauty, it is sometimes destructive. Most settlements are a safe distance from volcanic activity, but major events can still be catastrophic. The worst was the Laki eruption of 1783, which devastated agriculture locally, leading to the death of about a quarter of the country's population; it also affected the climate of the entire northern hemisphere. On a much smaller scale, the Eyjafjallajökull eruption of 2010 merely disrupted international air traffic, owing to the ash plumes it spewed into the atmosphere.

Since some of Iceland's volcanoes are located beneath glaciers, an eruption melting the ice can create flash floods (see p51). This happened in 1996 when the Grimsvötn volcano erupted underneath the island's largest glacier, Vatnajökull, creating a flood that washed away the ring road on the southern coast. Most of the time, though, the volcanic landscapes are safe to visit and provide a plethora of spectacular geothermal fields with bubbling mud pools, geysers, hot springs, old lava flows and craters.

The coastal areas can be visited year round, in winter promising the possibility of spotting some Northern Lights, but the spectacular interior is accessible only during the short summer season. There are two inland routes traversing this outlandish moonscape (in fact, NASA used it in the training of the Apollo astronauts for the landings on the Moon); both routes require four-by-four vehicles. The more difficult Sprengisandur route includes frequent fording of rivers, and should only be attempted in convoy, while the more westerly Kjölur route is easier to do independently.

Viti

★★☆☆☆

Central Iceland • Extreme landscape, Volcano

Dark Rating: 4 ☠

Above
Viti explosion crater next to Öskjuvatn, Iceland's deepest lake, contrasts with that cold body of water by being heated through geothermal activity to a balmy 25–30°C (77–86°F) all year round.

A particularly dramatic volcanic site in Iceland is this crater, whose name translates into English as 'hell', deep in the interior highlands at the Askja caldera, a still active volcano that last erupted in 1961 leaving a black lava flow. Viti was created in a violent explosion in the late nineteenth century.

Askja and Viti can be visited, but only in the summer season. You can clamber down to the crater lake at the bottom and take a bath, but it is so sulphurous that you have to go in naked, as any swimsuit would stink of rotten eggs forever afterwards!

To get there you have to brave a very rough inland route, requiring a suitable vehicle, or join one of the organized day tours offered from Myvatn that use a specially adapted high-clearance bus.

Heimaey

★★★★☆

Westman Islands, south of Iceland • Natural disaster (volcano)

Dark Rating: 4 ☣

This is the largest island of the Vestmannaeyjar archipelago (Westman Islands), which lies just off mainland Iceland. It was the scene of the most dramatic volcanic disaster in the country's modern history: in the early hours of 23 January 1973, a fissure eruption (see p51) started without warning and spewed red-hot lava and ash over the island's fishing town. The inhabitants were evacuated that same night, mainly by using the fleet of fishing boats from the harbour to take them to the mainland. Miraculously, there were no fatalities.

On Heimaey, the eruption continued for the next five months. Lava flows and ash covered some 400 houses – about a third of the entire town. Moreover, the lava flow threatened to close off the island's natural harbour, which would have meant an end to any hopes of resurrecting the fishing community. As a countermeasure, sea water was sprayed on to the advancing lava and in the end the flow was halted (although it may have just stopped naturally). It actually improved the sheltered harbour, having formed an additional breakwater.

Soon rebuilding and recovery began, and Heimaey's busy fishing industry resumed. The houses covered by lava were lost, however. Some ruins on the edge of the lava

flow can still be seen today, as can a partly damaged section of the old harbour wall.

Some 40 years after the eruption, work began on excavating some of the buried houses. The project, using the slogan 'Pompeii of the North', eventually gave the Westman Islands the new Eldheimar Museum. This also covers the story of Surtsey, a new island created by an undersea volcanic eruption in 1963; this island is off limits to visitors other than the occasional scientist studying how ecosystems develop on such new islands.

On Heimaey you can explore the new land and climb the volcano cone that the eruption created – named Eldfell, meaning 'fire mountain'. Some parts of the rocky soil inside

the crater are still warm. Heimaey is linked to the mainland by a ferry, although many visitors come by plane from Iceland's capital, Reykjavik, on day tours. Usually these include a boat ride around the island and visiting the cliffs that are the nesting colony of thousands of puffins.

Above
At 13.4 sq km (8.3 sq miles) this is the largest and most populated island off the Icelandic coast.

Below
An excavated house, with the inside left just as it was when the family was evacuated, on display at the Eldheimar Museum.

Norway

This northern Scandinavian country, which includes the northernmost point of mainland Europe, is a travel destination mostly for its mountainscapes and spectacular coastline characterized by fjords. But there are dark places here, for the most part associated with the period when the country was occupied by Nazi Germany during World War Two. Occasionally, even the fjords can have their dark side, as is the case with Tafjord and Lovatnet, where on more than one occasion during the twentieth century catastrophic landslides caused tsunamis that destroyed entire villages and killed well over a hundred people.

World War Two-related dark places in Norway come in different forms. To begin with, there are the military installations that the Nazis left, including coastal gun emplacements. The Norwegian resistance movement against the occupiers is celebrated in several museums: Oslo has one, Narvik another, and Bergen has two. Then there are the places where the Nazis exploited prisoners for forced labour, such as at the Blood Road in the Nordland region. The Falstad Centre not far from Trondheim is the most important such place, at the site of the largest of the Nazi prison camps in Norway.

Kirkenes

In the far northeast of Norway • WW2, Cold War, Iron Curtain

★★★☆☆

Dark Rating: 4 ☠

Above
Russian watchtower on the border with Norway near Kirkenes.

This is Norway's last outpost before the border with Russia. As such, it was of special significance during the Cold War, being the only place in Europe where the Soviet Union directly bordered a NATO member state. The Cold War may be over, but you can still see many vestiges of the Iron Curtain on the Russian side, and the border remains sensitive to this day. A retired Kirkenes border guard was arrested by Russia in late 2017 and convicted of espionage in 2019, but was later pardoned and exchanged for Russian spies.

Before the Cold War, Kirkenes had been a battle-field between Nazi Germany and the USSR and as a consequence almost all of old Kirkenes was destroyed. Today, two places in particular document that grim time – see over the page.

Andersgrotta

★★☆☆☆

Centre of Kirkenes • WW2

Dark Rating: 4 ☠

A cross between a cave and a bunker, this is where the local population took refuge during the many air raids in World War Two. In the 1990s it was opened up for tourists, although visits are by guided tour only. Inside you are shown a film with historical footage from World War Two. There are a few reconstructions of wooden living-quarter sections; otherwise the tunnels are bare and suitably gloomy.

Grenselandmuseet

★★★☆☆

Southern edge of Kirkenes • WW2, Cold War

Dark Rating: 5 ☠

This museum on the edge of town, the name of which translates as 'Borderlands Museum', is the main attraction here. Its permanent exhibition is mainly about the region's sensitive border location and the serious consequences this had during both World War Two and the Cold War; in some ways, it still has repercussions today.

Especially dark are the sections about the aerial bombing of the town when it became a battlefield between Nazi Germany and the USSR. A star exhibit is a refurbished Soviet Ilyushin Il-2 two-seater fighter plane, one of the most produced military aircraft in history, but a rare sight today.

Vemork

★★★★☆

Near Rjukan, Telemark region • WW2, Nuclear weapons

Dark Rating: 3 ☠

The hydroelectric power station of Vemork, in the mountains of southern Norway, was the largest in the world on completion in 1911. It closed 60 years later and was turned into the Norwegian Industrial Workers Museum. This covers the history of unions and workers' movements in Norway as well as that of the associated industries. Yet from its official name you would never guess why this is such a historically significant place with regard to nuclear science.

One of the industries powered by Vemork was a plant where hydrogen was produced through electrolysis (an energy-intensive process). A by-product of this is so-called 'heavy water', which contains larger proportions of the isotope deuterium. In the 1930s it was discovered that highly concentrated heavy water is useful as a neutron moderator in nuclear reactors. When Nazi Germany occupied Norway in 1940, the new heavy-water plant constructed at Vemork also fell into German hands. To thwart any possibility of this contributing to a potential German nuclear development programme that could give Hitler the atomic bomb, British commandos, with the help of the Norwegian resistance, sought to sabotage the plant.

After some failed attempts, they succeeded in blowing up the plant in February 1943; subsequent air strikes added further damage, and the plant was given up by the Germans. Possibly the most significant sabotage act ever, the story was later picked up by Hollywood in the 1960s movie *The Heroes of Telemark*. It is unclear whether the Nazis would actually have successfully pursued a nuclear weapons programme, but the mere thought was frightening enough.

In the end it was the USA that was the first to go through with such a programme (see p23) and use an atomic bomb (p322–23). The museum at Vemork covers this historical angle as well, and is a unique place of interest for any 'nuclear tourist'.

Opposite
This former hydroelectric power station was the target of British/Norwegian sabotage acts in World War Two to prevent Nazi Germany from obtaining heavy water for a possible nuclear programme.

Sweden

Peaceful, neutral Sweden is not normally thought of as a dark place, yet even its beautiful capital city, Stockholm, had its dark sides; for example, when it gave the world the term 'Stockholm syndrome' (after what happened during a bank robbery in 1973, when the hostages taken by the robbers actually bonded with their captors), or when the country's popular then prime minister Olof Palme was assassinated in the street in 1986. Despite its neutrality, Sweden played a role in the Cold War too.

It was a Swedish nuclear power plant (Forsmark) that first picked up elevated radiation levels from the Chernobyl accident (p220–21). However, it is primarily military installations, including some spectacular underground ones, that are of particular interest here. One complex of forts is picked out as an example in the following entry.

Boden fortress

★★★☆☆

Northeastern Sweden, Lapland region • Fortifications, Cold War

Dark Rating: 5 ☠

This is a complex of fortifications around the remote northern town of Boden. Although there is still a military presence here, the forts that had been constructed as a bulwark against Russia in the early twentieth century were all decommissioned by 1998. Most lie abandoned and are nominally off limits to civilians, though intrepid 'urban explorers' can get some access. One of the forts, Rödbergsfortet, has been turned into a museum of sorts and can be visited on official guided tours. These take visitors through the preserved fort, where you can see the soldiers' dorms, the kitchen, infirmary, command centre and ammunitions store. Finally, you ascend some stairs to get to the top of the fort and stand right by the big artillery turrets.

The other forts around Boden are not commodified for tourists and the interiors are locked, but you can still explore some parts of them, in particular the so-called caponier ditches, moat-like deep cuts into the bedrock, some up to 20m (60ft) deep, that surround the central parts of the forts.

Top
Rödbergsfortet viewed from the north. The caponier ditch and the armoured turrets can clearly be seen.

Above
This building was a communications bunker at the time of World War One, and the first radio broadcast in Swedish history was made from here in 1921.

Denmark

Like its northern neighbours, this small Scandinavian country is not normally considered very dark these days, but, like Norway, it was occupied by Nazi Germany during World War Two. The Nazis left behind plenty of relics of fortifications along the North Sea coast, and some are slowly being swallowed up by sand dunes. The country's struggle against the occupation is celebrated in the Museum of the Danish Resistance in Copenhagen. A particularly dark attraction in Denmark is of a very different nature – see below.

Tollund Man

Silkeborg, central Jutland, near Aarhus • Dead on display

★★☆☆☆

Dark Rating: 7 ☠

This is the world's most famous 'bog body', the corpse of a man who had died in the early Iron Age, some 2400 years ago. When he was discovered in 1950 it was initially assumed he might have been a recent murder victim, so well preserved was the body. But carbon dating soon revealed his real age. It is the chemical composition of the peat in which he was submerged that preserved the skin almost perfectly, except for the dark brown tanning.

He is on public display at the small Silkeborg Museum in the town of the same name. It has other artefacts as well, including another bog body, but Tollund Man is the star exhibit. Here you can come face to face, literally, with death and the Iron Age.

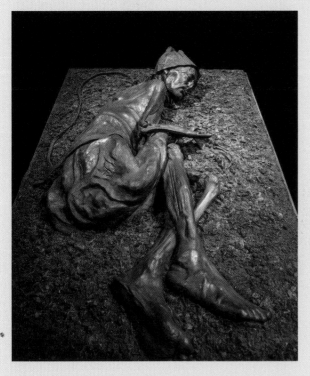

You cannot look him in the eye, because his eyes are closed, almost as if he is merely sleeping, peacefully, even with what appears to be a wry smile on his lips, as if he is dreaming but could wake up and open his eyes any moment.

It is only the head that is original in the displayed body; the rest is a replica. Back in the 1950s, preservation techniques were not advanced enough to save the entire body. Furthermore, sections of his lower body were partly decomposed, and it was deemed too 'macabre' to display him in full. However, extensive examinations of the body revealed some of the mystery surrounding his death.

It is likely that he was a human sacrifice and that he was hanged; a leather noose was found around his neck. Someone must have closed his mouth and eyes and put him in the foetal position before placing him in the bog. This seems too ceremonial for him to have been a common criminal. His age at the time of death is estimated to have been between 30 and 40. But the rest, especially why he was killed, remains a mystery.

Left
The most recent radiocarbon dating of samples from Tollund Man confirms he lived at around the same time as Socrates, 405–380 BCE.

Northern Ireland

When in the 1920s Ireland finally attained independence as a Republic (see p88) after centuries of domination by England, this came at the price of partition. The northeastern six counties of the province of Ulster, which unlike the rest of the island were predominantly Protestant rather than Catholic, remained with the UK. But since Northern Ireland is not part of Great Britain, it is treated as a separate entity here.

The religious divide runs parallel to the politics with (predominantly Catholic) nationalists/republicans, who would rather see a united Ireland, and (mostly Protestant) loyalists/unionists, who are loyal to the United Kingdom and do not want to be part of the Republic of Ireland. This divide, coupled with repressive politics to the disadvantage of Catholic communities, gave rise to what has become known as the Troubles, markedly from the 1960s onwards.

This escalated into three decades of sectarian murders and terrorist bombings, and heavy-handed operations by the Royal Ulster Constabulary (RUC) and British military – including massacres such as Bloody Sunday (see opposite), detention without trial and even torture. Underground organizations such as the IRA (Irish Republican Army) also carried the Troubles outside Northern Ireland, with bombings in London, Birmingham and Manchester, the latter as late as 1996.

However, the 1990s also brought progress on the negotiating front, culminating in the Good Friday Agreement of 1998, which gave Northern Ireland a multi-party devolved government and newly set out the country's relations with both the Republic of Ireland and Great Britain.

This Peace Process was not welcomed by everybody, and a radical splinter group of the IRA calling itself the 'Real IRA' carried out the worst bombing of the Troubles only a few months after the accords had been signed. This was the Omagh bombing, resulting in the death of 29 civilians. Overall, however, progress has been remarkable: the Troubles have been regarded as over since the start of the millennium, yet underlying resentment remains on both sides.

Since 2016 fears have returned that the Peace Process might be adversely affected by developments connected to the UK's exit from the European Union. What the future will bring remains to be seen, but up to the time of writing, Northern Ireland has come a long way in both stability and economic progress; that also includes opening up to tourism rather than terrorism.

Above
An injured protester is carried past British soldiers on the streets of Derry/Londonderry on Bloody Sunday, January 1972.

Derry/Londonderry

★★★☆☆

In the far northwest of Northern Ireland • Division, Repression, Atrocity

Dark Rating: 7 ☹

What's in a name? Well, in the case of Northern Ireland's second city, quite a lot. To begin with: it has two names. The difference between them is directly linked to the political and sectarian divide at the heart of the Troubles, with republicans preferring the shorter 'Derry' and unionists the longer name that alludes to the British capital. To maintain neutrality, both names are used here.

Left
First painted in 1969, this famous slogan in the Bogside refers to the self-declared autonomous Irish nationalist district.

Below
The *Hands Across the Divide* sculpture was unveiled in 1992, twenty years after Bloody Sunday.

Derry/Londonderry is regarded as the place where the Troubles really started, when working-class Catholic citizens, feeling unfairly disadvantaged compared to the Protestants (even though in this city Catholics were actually in the majority), took to the streets in protest, especially in the district of the Bogside, just northwest of the centre. The marches led to confrontations with loyalists and with the police, and in August 1969 the so-called Battle of the Bogside saw riots lasting for three days.

Eventually, Britain sent in the army, which in turn became a target for the IRA. Then, on 30 January 1972, what has become known as Bloody Sunday happened. In response to a peaceful demonstration, British soldiers fired live ammunition into the crowd of unarmed protestors and 14 were shot dead. Subsequently, draconian security measures were introduced and the region became one of the most militarized in Europe, with roadblocks, armoured vehicles, curfews, arrests and yet more casualties on both sides. The city has come a long way since then, especially since the Peace Process led to the Good Friday Agreement after the official IRA laid down its arms.

A few reminders of the dark past remain, such as the old mural proclaiming 'You are now entering Free Derry' in the Bogside. There are monuments and murals, many more recent ones on themes of peace and reconciliation, although more aggressive, confrontational ones can still be found too. There is evidence of the division between unionist and republican quarters: in some places painted kerbs in either Irish or British colours make it clear whose turf you are on. In the cemetery above the Bogside, memorials celebrating IRA fighters jar with the peaceful image that the city otherwise tries to project, whereas the sculpture *Hands Across the Divide* at the southern entrance to the old town centre is its most optimistic symbol of reconciliation.

Museum of Free Derry

★★★★☆

Bogside district, Derry/Londonderry • Repression, Atrocity

Dark Rating: 7 ☠

DARK STATS

Sectarian violence
killed around
3600 PEOPLE
between 1968 and 1998;
MORE THAN 36,000
were injured

Republicans were
responsible for about
60 PER CENT
of the killings;
loyalists for around
30 PER CENT
and British soldiers around
10 PER CENT

The deadliest year of the
Troubles was 1972, when
467 PEOPLE
were killed, including
321 CIVILIANS

14 PROTESTERS
shot dead by British
soldiers during a peaceful
demonstration on
Bloody Sunday

Above
Artefacts from the Battle of the Bogside,
including posters, banners, truncheons and
tear-gas canisters on display at the museum.

Informally known as the Bloody Sunday Museum, this museum also covers the wider context of the Northern Ireland conflict and the special status the Bogside district had in it. The exhibition features some poignant artefacts, such as bloodied bandages and clothes that some of the victims were wearing, on which you can clearly see the holes torn by the bullets. Some bullets are on display too, as are gas masks, petrol bombs fashioned from milk bottles, and so on.

With substantial state funding, the museum was updated and expanded, and reopened in 2017 twice its previous size. It has become one of the major attractions in the city. For anybody travelling to this part of the world looking to understand this decades-long conflict better, this museum is a must-see.

Belfast

★★★★☆

In the east of Northern Ireland • Shipwreck, Repression, Terrorism

Dark Rating: 6 ☠

Two 'T's dominate the dark sides of the capital city of Northern Ireland: the *Titanic* and the Troubles. The former is because this ship, whose maiden voyage ended in tragedy in 1912, was built at the Harland & Wolff shipyards in Belfast. For almost a century after the *Titanic* disaster, this wasn't talked about much here; it was seen as an embarrassment. But with the centenary of this most media-covered shipwreck of all time, it became a core element of the touristification of the city.

Today there is the Titanic Belfast Experience, featuring a hi-tech, immersive exhibition about all aspects of the *Titanic*. Parts of the old shipyards have also been developed for visitors, such as the Thompson Graving Dock, in which the *Titanic* was outfitted after her launch. The landmarks otherwise dominating the area's skyline are the two huge yellow gantry cranes of the shipyard, called Samson and Goliath.

Street names such as Falls Road and Shankill Road became bywords for the confrontations between the Catholic and Protestant communities in West Belfast during the Troubles. Since the official end of the conflict, some of these places have become tourist attractions. This started small, with the legendary Black Taxi Tours, local taxi drivers taking visitors interested in this dark past to those places on private tours. It has developed into a well-oiled tourism industry, with coach tours and large groups, although the small tours by taxi still exist.

You get to see many of the (in)famous murals, some new, some old and very political and confrontational. A usual stop is by the so-called Peace Wall, constructed to segregate the two sides. The name seems a bit of a misnomer: if there was genuine peace, no such wall would still need to be here, nor would the gates be locked at night. You can also still see

houses standing directly by this wall shielded by bars and wire mesh over the windows to protect them from objects thrown over the wall.

Below
A mural on the Peace Wall between Falls Road and Shankill Road, West Belfast, both a potent reminder of the past and a symbol of the present.

Republic of Ireland

Widely known as the Emerald Isle, this island nation on the Atlantic edge of Europe has had a long dark history, especially in the form of repression by its big neighbour Britain (or rather, England). For centuries Ireland was treated like a colony: exploited and downtrodden. A particularly infamous episode was the so-called Potato Famine in the nineteenth century.

This was more than just a crop failure; the reason for the mass starvation, and consequent mass emigration, had more to do with land ownership, political power, goods distribution and in general ignoring the plight of the poor Irish peasant population. There is a poignant Famine Memorial in Dublin. Nearby is a replica of one of the sailing ships, the *Jeanie Johnston*, that took emigrants across the Atlantic to America, known as 'coffin ships' due to the cramped conditions on board.

The Irish eventually rebelled, gaining momentum in the early twentieth century. A noteworthy event was the Easter Rising of 1916. The rebels marched into Dublin, took control of strategic positions and declared a Republic. Yet the British brutally crushed this rebellion. You can still see bullet holes in some walls and in a female figure that forms part of the O'Connell Monument.

By executing 15 of the rebels, the British made martyrs out of them. This would backfire, as it gave the independence movement an additional boost. This led to a short War of Independence after World War One, at the end of which a Treaty was tabled. As this made Northern Ireland a part of the UK, the Pro- and Anti-Treaty controversy split society and led to civil war. In the end Ireland did become independent in the 1920s, although it was only in 1948 that it formally left the Commonwealth and became a Republic, albeit minus Northern Ireland (p84).

The Republic of Ireland long remained one of the poorer countries in Europe. Yet in 1973 it joined the EEC (now EU), and two decades on it experienced an economic boom that lent it the epithet 'Celtic Tiger'. Ireland today is a modern, well-developed country and also a popular tourist destination, including its capital city, Dublin.

Above
Memorial on Dublin's dockside commemorating the Great Famine, when over a million people died and two million more were forced to emigrate.

Kilmainham Gaol

West of Dublin city centre • Prison, Repression, Executions

★★★★☆

Dark Rating: 7 ☠

The principal dark attraction in Dublin is undoubtedly this old jail. It was constructed in the late eighteenth century and was initially intended for regular criminals. Soon political prisoners were incarcerated here, including many of the rebels against English rule in Ireland. After a brief closure in 1910, the prison was back in service after the Easter Rising of 1916 to house those arrested in the crushing of the rebellion. It was here, in the courtyard of Kilmainham Gaol, that 15 of the Rising's leaders were executed.

Following the civil war and Irish independence, the prison was closed for good, abandoned, and fell into disrepair. Efforts to save the structure began in the 1960s, and it became a museum in 1986. In more recent years, further refurbishments have improved the site; you can go on guided tours of the cell blocks, and two modern museum exhibitions have been added. These not only tell the story of the prison but also give the whole historical background and context of the Irish struggle for independence, and are full of remarkable artefacts.

Above
The grim interior has been the set for many films, notably *The Italian Job*, *In the Name of the Father* and *Michael Collins*.

Below
The cross marks the place of execution by firing squad of leaders of the 1916 Easter Rising.

Great Britain

This is England, Wales and Scotland together, which occupy the largest of the British Isles, hence the 'Great'. Britain's history includes lots that could be considered 'great' as well, although it also contains plenty of dark chapters. Britannia once ruled not only the waves but also a vast global empire, built on exploration, exploitation, repression, military (especially naval) superiority and slavery. Britain was a key player in the transatlantic slave trade, yet it was also at the forefront of the movement that led to the abolition of slavery (p244–45).

Dark places to visit in Britain mostly relate to war – particularly World War Two, but also the Cold War.

The nuclear industry added a couple of dark spots too, as did part man-made, part natural disasters.

Even though recent political developments have brought much uncertainty and a deep division in British society, as a travel destination these lands remain a treasure trove of marvellous landscapes, from green rolling hills to the rugged coastlines of Cornwall, Wales and (especially western) Scotland, as well as modern cities. Moreover, there is a wealth of industrial heritage sites – after all, the Industrial Revolution started here.

Out of the plethora of dark places in Britain, the following are just a few major examples.

Dounreay

★★☆☆☆

North coast of Caithness, Scotland • Nuclear site

Dark Rating: 6 ☠

After Sellafield (see opposite), this is probably Britain's second most historically significant nuclear site, located in a remote spot in the far north of Scotland. The most iconic element here is the fast breeder reactor sphere. Apart from that experimental reactor, the complex also included a reprocessing plant and the 'Vulcan' site, where the reactors for Britain's fleet of nuclear-powered submarines were developed and tested.

Like Sellafield, Dounreay is undergoing decommissioning and lost its visitor centre a while ago, although there is a viewpoint from where you can get a distant impression of the site. A museum in nearby Thurso, called Caithness Horizons, inherited some of the contents and put the old control room from one of the plant's early reactors on display. The museum had to close in 2019 for financial reasons. Thankfully, it has since reopened

under new management and a new name: North Coast Visitor Centre. Fortunately, the Dounreay exhibition inside has survived.

Below
The reactor was surrounded by a steel sphere, which for the time being remains a prominent feature in the landscape.

Scotland's Secret Nuclear Bunker

County of Fife, near St Andrews • Cold War

★★★★☆

Dark Rating: 5 ☣

Strictly speaking, we should say 'formerly secret', since this is now a tourist attraction. The fact that there are road signs directing visitors to it with the word 'secret' on them makes many people giggle. But seriously, this is a major Cold War-era relic, a former 'regional government relocation facility' in the event of nuclear war. Some 300 people – government and military personnel and support staff – could be accommodated here, 30m (100ft) underground, to 'take control' of the crisis situation. But you have to ask yourself what they could have done and what kind of world they would have resurfaced into after air and food supplies had run out.

The bunker was decommissioned in 1993 and opened to the public. Plenty of Cold War-era military hardware is on open-air display outside, including some of Soviet origin. You step inside an inconspicuous-looking farm cottage above ground and from there enter a tunnel system leading to the bunker proper. It is on two levels, and includes dormitories, switchboards, various operations rooms (not only the government's but also one for the Royal Observer Corps) and an RAF radar room, all full of vintage electronic equipment. There is a section about nuclear disarmament campaigns, and films related to the topic are also shown.

There are many other such facilities across Britain. A few have been turned into 'museums' and are open to the public, including Hack Green in Cheshire and Kelvedon Hatch in Essex.

Sellafield

Cumbria, northwestern England • Nuclear (accident) site

★★☆☆☆

Dark Rating: 6 ☣

Left
The Sellafield site is being decommissioned, but many buildings still stand, including those for storage of irradiated nuclear waste, as well as the reprocessing plant.

Britain's most significant nuclear site, historically speaking, was originally constructed to supply plutonium for the UK's atomic weapons programme shortly after World War Two. It was also the place where the world's first commercial nuclear power plant, Calder Hall, started supplying electricity for the population in 1956. An accident in 1957 known as the Windscale fire (after the name of one of the military reactor plants) still stands as the worst in British history.

Later, Sellafield also became a reprocessing facility. Repeated leaks of radioactivity have ensured that the site remained controversial, even to this day. Most of the complex is undergoing decommissioning, and several parts have been demolished (such as the iconic cooling towers of Calder Hall), but it will be a long time before the site can be declared properly cleaned up.

Visits to what remains of the actual plant are virtually impossible for most people, and the site's visitor centre closed down more than a decade ago. However, the Beacon Museum in the nearby town of Whitehaven includes an exhibition called 'The Sellafield Story': this covers the history not only of that plant itself but also of the whole topic of nuclear power and weaponry. The Windscale fire of 1957 gets a mention, but overall the tone of the exhibition is rather celebratory.

Coventry Cathedral

West Midlands • WW2 aerial bombing

★★★★☆

Dark Rating: 4 ☠

Actually, this is two cathedrals: a ruined old one and a new, modern one. The former is Britain's best-known ruin from World War Two. It fell victim to one of the first massive air raids by the German Luftwaffe, involving some 500 planes, aimed at destroying a civilian city rather than hitting any military targets. This attack became a blueprint for later such air raids, including those subsequently flown by the RAF to destroy German cities (see p129 and p153).

After the war, the ruins of the old cathedral were kept as a memorial while a new one, with a highly modernistic design, was erected directly adjacent. The ruins form an open-air memorial park and contain a sculpture called 'Reconciliation'. That's also the motto of the new cathedral, which contains several items on the same theme, including a 'peace bell' which came from Germany.

Below
Winston Churchill walking through the ruins of Coventry Cathedral. The air raid on the city left hundreds dead or injured.

Bletchley Park

Near Milton Keynes, Buckinghamshire • WW2, Secret intelligence

★★★★★

Dark Rating: 2 ☠

Left
Recreation of Turing's workstation
at Bletchley Park.

Below
A replica of a code-breaking
Bombe machine on display.

Once 'Britain's best-kept secret', now a unique visitor attraction, Bletchley Park and its manor house were where mathematician and cryptologist Alan Turing and his team, building on groundwork provided by Polish colleagues, managed to break the infamous Nazi German 'Enigma' code during World War Two. This was done mainly using the so-called Bombe machine, a mechanical precursor of the computer, designed by Turing. It may have had more far-reaching consequences for the course of the war than any single military operation.

These heroes remained largely unsung for many decades; during the war this was a top-secret site, and it remained so through the Cold War. Nobody was allowed to discuss it. Only since 1990 has the place received proper recognition – and it was eventually turned into today's state-of-the-art museum, which opened in 2014. Housed in several refurbished original buildings, set in sprawling grounds, it is so chock-full of information and artefacts that you need more than a day to take it all in (fortunately tickets are valid for two days).

The coverage of the museum is vast and the detail so rich that those not mathematically minded will find that a good proportion of it goes over their heads. But even so, all the cryptological complexity is balanced by the personal stories of the men and women involved, which are fascinating (especially Alan Turing's, which ended in tragedy). The offices in the manor house, as well as the workplaces in the various huts and bungalows, have been faithfully restored.

Adjacent to Bletchley Park is the National Museum of Computing, where a reconstructed 'Colossus' computer, the culmination of the code-breakers' achievements, can be seen in operation. Colossus is generally regarded as the world's first real, electronic computer – and, true to its name, it is a giant. The rest of the museum covers the post-World War Two history of computing and has a few other remarkable artefacts, such as an original WITCH computer from an early British nuclear power station, said to be the world's oldest original computer still in working order.

Above
The three-rotor, wooden-boxed Enigma
model used by the German army in the early
stages of the war.

Aberfan

★☆☆☆☆

Near Merthyr Tydfil, southern Wales • Disaster (landslide)

Dark Rating: 5 ☠

Left
Two days after the soil slip, as townsfolk, rescue teams and volunteers tried to come to terms with the tragedy.

This small community in one of the old coal-mining areas in Wales was the site of the deadliest disaster on British soil in the twentieth century. On 21 October 1966 a landslide engulfed parts of the village and in particular Pentglass Junior School, where, at 9:15 a.m., lessons had just begun. Five teachers and 109 schoolchildren perished, plus another 30 children and adults in surrounding buildings. This was not a natural disaster, though.

The landslide was actually a wall of slurry that had formed when a coal-mine spoils tip on a neighbouring hillside collapsed after heavy rain. However, the spoils tip had been placed on unsuitable land from the beginning, and the blame was ultimately put squarely on the National Coal Board. Yet nobody was prosecuted, and only after lengthy campaigning were similar potentially dangerous spoil heaps near Aberfan removed. The trauma suffered by the community, where an entire generation had been wiped out, is a lasting one. It is still palpable today, even though no signs of the destruction or its causes are still visible.

The disaster is commemorated by a memorial garden where the school once stood, and the paths and flowerbeds subtly recreate its floor plan. In the local cemetery a section was set aside for the children lost in the disaster. It consists of two rows of white marble monuments, of a uniform arch design, rather than traditional headstones. There is an extra memorial space next to it with a small garden and benches. All this is more for the local community. Aberfan is not, and clearly does not want to be, a tourist destination, and there is no tourism infrastructure. Outsiders intending to make a brief pilgrimage here should be discreet and on their best respectful behaviour.

Below
The rows of white arches in Aberfan's Bryntaf Cemetery for the children killed in the disaster.

Churchill War Rooms

Whitehall, London • WW2

★★★★☆

Dark Rating: 4 ☠

This formerly hidden site, right in the heart of London, was the original bunker headquarters of the prime minister Winston Churchill and his war cabinet during World War Two. The old cabinet rooms, bedrooms, offices and military operations rooms have been recreated and opened to the public. They are peopled by dummies in period clothing/uniforms, including a replica Churchill mannequin on the phone to the US president. A separate add-on exhibition provides in-depth coverage of the life of Churchill, also pre- and postwar. The site is one of the branches of the Imperial War Museum (see below).

Right
The main Cabinet War Room, constructed by converting a storage basement in Whitehall.

Imperial War Museum

Lambeth Road, London • WW1, WW2, Cold War, Modern wars

★★★★★

Dark Rating: 7 ☠

Left
The museum is housed in what was the Bethlem Royal Hospital. Since 1968 two 38mm (15 inch) gun barrels from World War One battleships have been displayed outside.

This is the 'mother' of all war museums in the UK, and one of the leading institutions of its type worldwide. Its main branch was given a major overhaul for the centenary of the outbreak of World War One, during which it had originally first been conceived.

Today's scope of the permanent exhibitions goes far beyond the two world wars, though, and includes later conflicts, such as the Falklands War (p68) and the two Iraq wars in which Britain sided with the USA. Another particularly dark section is the Holocaust exhibition.

The museum, usually abbreviated to 'IWM', has other branches, including outposts in Manchester and Duxford as well as one more site in London: the HMS *Belfast* cruiser, moored as a museum ship opposite the Tower of London.

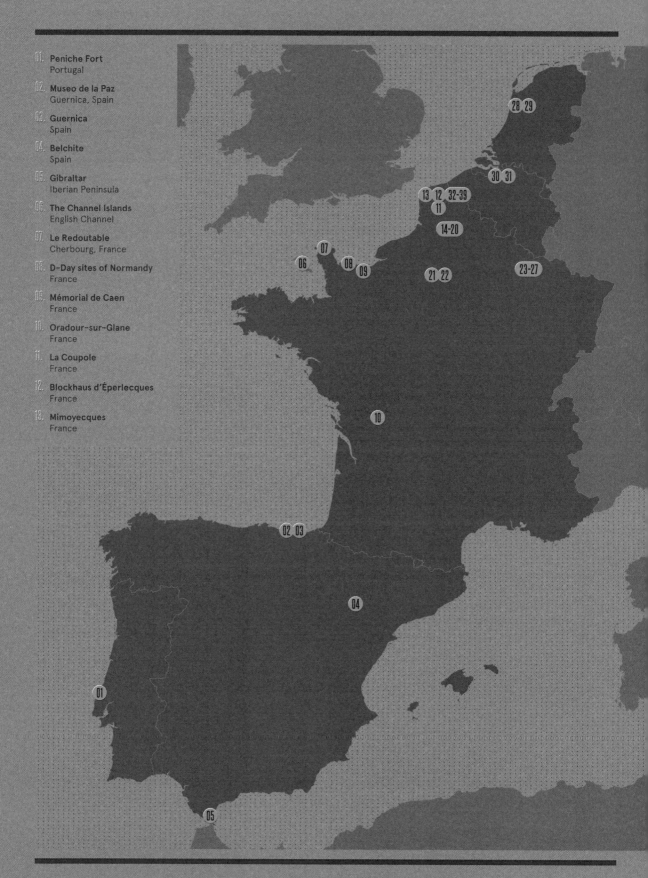

01. **Peniche Fort**
    Portugal

02. **Museo de la Paz**
    Guernica, Spain

03. **Guernica**
    Spain

04. **Belchite**
    Spain

05. **Gibraltar**
    Iberian Peninsula

06. **The Channel Islands**
    English Channel

07. **Le Redoutable**
    Cherbourg, France

08. **D-Day sites of Normandy**
    France

09. **Mémorial de Caen**
    France

10. **Oradour-sur-Glane**
    France

11. **La Coupole**
    France

12. **Blockhaus d'Éperlecques**
    France

13. **Mimoyecques**
    France

Western & Southwestern Europe

This section covers the Iberian peninsula, France and the Benelux countries, as well as two British overseas territories, Gibraltar and the Channel Islands. Portugal and Spain are of dark significance for their dictatorial regimes that lasted until the 1970s, which in the case of Spain came about through a well-documented, bitterly fought Civil War. All of this is currently becoming better commemorated than in previous times.

In the sections covering France and Belgium, World War One is represented in what might appear to be disproportionate depth, but it was here that the Western Front changed the nature of warfare and world history forever, and hence this focus is justifiable. It also goes to show just how localized this war against the German Empire was here (the latter also fought a parallel war with Russia in the east until 1917). Today, the Western Front sites can in theory be covered in a single, intense war history trip. And this is indeed one of the few areas in dark tourism where organized themed package tours are available.

France, Belgium and the Netherlands were all occupied by Nazi Germany during World War Two, and this has left some significant heritage sites. In France there is one unique attraction associated with the Cold War – a nuclear submarine.

Travellers to all the countries in this section will benefit from excellent road and rail networks that make independent travel easy and pleasant.

Portugal

This small country on the western edge of mainland Europe has a great seafaring legacy and was one of the first to reach for riches beyond Europe. It was often Portuguese colonizers who grabbed new lands first; some were later lost (the biggest became Brazil), but some it clung on to into the second half of the twentieth century – for example, Cape Verde (p246) and East Timor (p304).

The end of colonialism finally came with the fall of the dictatorship at home, when the so-called Carnation Revolution in 1974 brought down the Estado Novo ('new state'), the dictatorial regime that had been in power since the early 1930s. It also ended the dark era of repression by the secret police (PIDE), during which many political opponents were incarcerated and tortured. Coming to terms with this dark legacy has been slow in Portugal, but recently serious efforts for a commemoration have been made.

Portugal's capital city, Lisbon, has a few dark attractions, such as the ruins of the Igreja do Carmo, which was destroyed in the devastating earthquake of 1755 and left in its ruined state as a memorial. The church site and its museum are by the top of the famous Elevador de Santa Justa in the Chiado district.

A fairly recent (2015) small museum on the edge of the famous Alfama district is dedicated to the dark years of political repression as well as the resistance and fight for freedom. It is called Museu do Aljube and is housed in a former prison of that name on Rua de Augusto Rosa. The headquarters of the infamous PIDE secret police, on the other hand, has been converted into luxury apartments.

Peniche Fort

★★★☆☆

North of Lisbon • Prison, Torture, Repression

Dark Rating: 7 ☠

Left
The sixteenth-century fortress has seen many uses: as a garrison, to house refugees and to incarcerate political prisoners.

The most promising recent development in terms of commemorating Portugal's dictatorship and repression from the early 1930s up to 1974 is this site about 80km (50 miles) north of Lisbon. The fort, originally a military bastion whose construction began in the late sixteenth century, used to be one of the main sites where political prisoners were incarcerated by the regime of António de Oliveira Salazar. After years of slow repairs to the structure, the fort is now being turned into a National Museum of Resistance and Freedom. This has the potential of becoming Portugal's most important dark place of them all.

Spain

Portugal's larger neighbour is also primarily a travel destination for sunseekers, but it too has had a dark history partly in parallel with Portugal's. Both were ruled by right-wing regimes until the mid-1970s, and only since then have opened up to the rest of Europe.

Spain's darkest period was the Spanish Civil War, 1936–39, which is well known abroad partly because of the amount of international participation in it. It is also claimed to be the most studied war in history. Here, the very briefest of summaries must suffice. The conflict was essentially between right-wing nationalists and left-wing republicans. It started when, following an election victory by the leftist Popular Front, some nationalist military generals launched a coup. Led by Francisco Franco, the nationalists advanced from the southwest, but initially the left was able to defend its strongholds in the large cities (in particular Barcelona and the capital, Madrid) as well as the eastern and northern parts of the country.

Gradually, though, the military superiority of the nationalists – crucially bolstered by support from Fascist Italy and Nazi Germany with their then much more advanced air forces – prevailed, and the republicans lost. Their last-ditch offensive in the Ebro region in the northeast failed, ending in a collapse of the resistance and a mass exodus of republicans fleeing to France. The left also suffered from fragmentation and infighting, especially as support from the Soviet Union was sought. As a result of the Soviet involvement, the non-Stalinist factions within the republican camp came under pressure. In its early days, the leftist utopia created in Barcelona probably came closest to their promised ideals, but ultimately the alliance between anarchists and various socialist/communist groupings broke up in 1937.

The story is linked with the English writer George Orwell, who had joined the republicans and saw some battle action, but became a victim of the Stalinist intervention and had to flee (an experience that inspired his later novels *Animal Farm* and *1984*). After the defeat of the republicans, Franco established himself as a ruthless dictator who would stay in power until his death in 1975.

The wounds of this period have never quite healed. Instead, Spain followed an approach of amnesia and amnesty after the end of the dictatorship and the return of democracy. Only in recent years have more efforts been made at a proper commemoration and at coming to terms with those long dark decades. Interestingly, in terms of tourism, this was pioneered by foreigners, in particular Brits, who had come to live in Spain and have for years catered for the interest of foreign visitors in the Spanish Civil War legacy, with specialist guided tours on the theme in Barcelona and Madrid.

Museo de la Paz

Centre of Guernica • Spanish Civil War, War crime, Atrocity

★★★★★

Dark Rating: 6 ☹

The dark legacy of the bombing of Guernica (see over the page) is naturally the main theme of this local museum, including an emotional sound and light installation, but it also goes beyond and covers the wider context of the Spanish Civil War, as well as topics such as conflict resolution, human rights and peace in general. It is well laid out, although it occasionally drifts off into a somewhat 'poetic' kind of narrative before finding its factual feet again. Texts are in Basque and Spanish only, but you can borrow a folder containing English translations.

Left
As part of the exhibition, visitors literally walk over the rubble from the bombing, which is on display beneath glass plates set into the floor.

Guernica

★★★ ☆ ☆

Basque country, northern Spain • War crime, Atrocity

Dark Rating: 5 ☠

The name of this town is forever associated with the horrors of war brought about through aerial bombardment of civilians. It was not the very first such aerial bombing of civilians – nearby Durango had already been targeted, for example – but the way the attack on Guernica on 26 April 1937 was orchestrated was the first instance of what was soon to become a blueprint for air raids on cities throughout World War Two.

The Guernica operation was conducted by the Nazi German Legion Condor squadron. It lasted for three hours and consisted of a first wave of bombers dropping heavy high-explosive bombs to 'crack open' buildings, followed by waves of planes dropping masses of lightweight incendiary bombs causing an inferno – a dastardly technique of causing maximum destruction in the most 'economical' way.

This test run at Guernica was such a 'success' that it was later applied in Germany's attacks on Britain in World War Two – the bombing of Coventry (p92) followed the same pattern. But it would come to haunt Germany, namely when the Allies applied it on a much larger scale in their bombings of cities such as Hamburg (p129) and Dresden (p153).

The exact death toll of the bombing of Guernica is contested, as initially reported figures in excess of 1500 may have been inflated. Still, for such a small town, the losses were massive. Moreover, about 85 per cent of the town's buildings were destroyed. The horrors of Guernica are most famously depicted in the painting of the same name by Pablo Picasso; his *Guernica* is one of the most recognizable works of art of the modern era. Reproductions of it can be found all over the rebuilt town today (the original is on display in Madrid).

Near the station is a surviving air-raid shelter that has been restored and is open to the public. Otherwise, modern Guernica is a quiet but pleasant little town steeped in Basque culture. Here and there you can still find little references in graffiti and flags to ETA, the Basque separatist terrorist organization that used to have its home ground here.

Above
The smouldering centre of the town after the bombing raids carried out by Franco's German allies of the Legion Condor.

Belchite

★★★☆☆

In Aragon, south of Zaragoza • Ghost town, Spanish Civil War

Dark Rating: 8 ☠️

Left and below
Today, Belchite still looks like a war zone, with piles of rubble and ruined buildings pockmarked with bullet holes.

This town in northeastern Spain found itself in the middle of a fierce battle in the Spanish Civil War in August 1937, after the republicans launched an offensive to halt the advance that the nationalist forces were making in the area at the time. The republicans managed to take Belchite by 7 September, but in the process it was more or less completely destroyed.

In the end it was for nothing, as the offensive was a failure overall: the main goal of taking the region's capital, Zaragoza, was not achieved. In fact, the battle was a turning point for the Francoists, who soon afterwards were gaining ground again and moved forward towards the Ebro (see over the page).

General Franco grasped the propagandistic value of the ruined town and ordered it to be preserved as a memorial – the message being 'See, this is what communists do!' A new town was built next to the old one to provide replacement housing. Old Belchite, meanwhile, has become one of the most visually stunning war relics that can be visited today. Walking the streets lined by ruins and shell-scarred church spires, it almost looks as if the war had ended only yesterday.

In the past you were free to roam around independently, but these days there is a fence around the site and visits are by guided tour only (possibly in response to repeated vandalism – you can still spot graffiti from both camps). Tours are in Spanish but an English-language audio guide is offered at no extra cost. It has lots of information (maybe too much), but the main thing is the visual impression.

OTHER PLACES RELATED TO THE SPANISH CIVIL WAR

There are numerous individual sites with a connection to this conflict; this is just a selection, by region.

Barcelona

English-language walking tours take in various places where important moments of the era played out, and you can see scars still visible on buildings from aerial bombing or sites that are related to George Orwell's time in the city. There was a campaign for the creation of a proper Civil War Museum here too, but nothing has come of it so far. Another museum project has been proposed in Teruel, but whether that will ever open is anybody's guess.

Madrid

Spanish Civil War-themed tours are offered in and around Madrid. The most controversial site is the Valle de los Caídos ('valley of the fallen') in the mountains northwest of Madrid. Started in the 1940s on General Franco's order to commemorate the 'martyrs' on his side (while using political prisoners in the construction), it is a pompous affair with a giant cross above a vast underground basilica. Infamously, Franco was buried here after his death in 1975, which subsequently made the place a pilgrimage site for old Francoists. After a long campaign and court hearings, Franco's remains were finally removed for reburial elsewhere in October 2019.

Ebro

A wide range of Spanish Civil War sites can be found in the Ebro region in Catalonia, where the final battles of the war raged. Many of the individual small museums are in Spanish and/or Catalan only, but a few also cater for English-speaking visitors. One example is the independent Historical Museum in Gandesa. A range of other sites is managed under the banner of Consorci Memorial dels Espais de la Batalla de l'Ebre and includes the excellent 115 Days Interpretation Centre in Corbera d'Ebre (which also features a ruined ghost town similar to Belchite) and the engaging 'Internationals in Ebro' exhibition in La Fatarella (about the International Brigades).

For other sites, such as the specialist Blood Hospitals interpretation centre, about the medical side of the war in Batea, or the large artefact collection in the Museo Batalla del Ebro in Fayón, you may need a guide/translator. There are countless outdoor sites of the battles, including excavated and restored trenches and other fortifications as well as yet more memorials, but you will need a guide to explore those properly.

Above
The 150m-high (500ft) cross at the Valle de los Caídos is the tallest in the world, and is visible for 32km (20 miles).

Gibraltar

★ ★ ★ ★ ☆

Iberian Peninsula • WW2, Underground tunnels

Dark Rating: 4 ☠

A geological and political oddity at the southern tip of the Iberian peninsula, this limestone promontory jutting up to 436m (1400ft) above sea level has always been of special strategic significance, overlooking the strait between Europe and North Africa at the western end of the Mediterranean. It has been under British control since the early eighteenth century and is still a British overseas territory, although this status has long been contested by Spain.

During the Franco dictatorship, the border with Spain was closed and Gibraltar isolated. Only since Spain joined the EC (EU) in 1986 has the border become more easily penetrable, although at times Spanish border checks slowed crossings down. More recently, the 2016 Brexit referendum in the UK (in which Gibraltar voted overwhelmingly against leaving the EU) brought back anxiety about border uncertainties. What Brexit will mean for Gibraltar remains to be seen.

Over three centuries, Gibraltar has repeatedly come under military attack, most notably in the Great Siege of 1779–83, when Spain and France tried to capture 'the Rock' but ultimately failed. After the opening of the Suez Canal in 1869, Gibraltar's strategic role became even more important; hence additional fortifications were built, including the installation of two massive 100-ton coastal guns.

During World War Two, the entire civilian population was evacuated from Gibraltar and the military dug miles of underground tunnels and chambers into the rock for storage of fuel, ammunition and other supplies. In July 1943 Poland's prime minister in exile, General Władysław Sikorski, died when his plane crashed shortly after taking off from Gibraltar. The incident has been the subject of conspiracy theories ever since, up to the suggestion that it was sabotage on the part of the British or the Soviets to get rid of Sikorski. The case remains unsolved.

Today, many vestiges of Gibraltar's military history can be visited, including the Great Siege Tunnels at the northern end of the Rock, as well as the World War Two tunnels deeper inside the mountain. The former have been equipped with replica historic guns and dummies in period uniforms, while the latter are more authentic but can be visited only on guided tours. In addition, the O'Hara's Battery atop the crest towards the southern end of the Rock has been opened up for visitors, as has the one remaining 100-ton gun. At Europa Point, the southernmost spot in Gibraltar, another gun emplacement can be visited and there is a Sikorski monument commemorating the plane crash.

Above
Great Siege tunnel hewn into the raw rock. At various points there are openings from where cannons were fired down.

Left
Lord Airey's Battery seen from O'Hara's Battery atop The Rock, high above Europa Point.

The Channel Islands

★★★★☆

English Channel between Normandy and Brittany • WW2

Dark Rating: 5 ☠

This group of islands is closer to France than to Britain, yet it is an offshore British territory, in this case with the status of so-called Crown Dependencies that are not part of the UK. They are very English in character, despite some palpable French influences and place names. In World War Two, these islands were the only British territory occupied by Nazi Germany. There were even concentration camps on Alderney, of which hardly anything remains today – there is no proper commemoration. This is the cause of an ongoing controversy between local authorities and historians, as is the fact that the topics of collaboration and the deportation of the islands' Jewish population are under-acknowledged across the Channel Islands.

In contrast, the many military installations and fortifications constructed by the Nazis during the occupation are well developed for visitors and promoted by the local tourism industry. There are some large bunkers to explore, and a few sites contain museum exhibitions, such as the La Vallette Underground Military Museum on Guernsey. A major visitor attraction is the Jersey War Tunnels, aka German Underground Hospital, inside an uncompleted subterranean structure from the war years on the archipelago's biggest island. There are also specialist tour operators offering deeper insights into all this military heritage.

Below
A German observation tower in the northwest of Jersey at Battery Moltke, which formed part of the Nazis' 'Atlantic Wall' coastal defences.

France

The *Grande Nation*, as it likes to call itself, has had such a rich and multifaceted history that there is no shortage of dark aspects and associated places. Many of these are related to wars, in particular the two world wars, and for dedicated war history buffs the fortifications left by the Nazis during their occupation of France are major attractions.

Collectively known as the Atlantic Wall, many of these are found along the northern coast. Especially noteworthy are the submarine (U-boat) pens inside massive concrete bunkers in port cities such as Lorient, St-Nazaire or La Rochelle along the Bay of Biscay. The French Resistance is celebrated in a dedicated Musée de la Résistance in Lyon, which also covers the topic of the deportation of French citizens by the Nazis during that time. The deportation of Jews from France during the Holocaust is the topic of the Drancy memorial on the edge of Paris, at the site of a former collection and transit camp.

In the Alsace region, which belongs to France (it has swapped between Germany and France several times), there is the only full-blown concentration camp memorial on French soil: Natzweiler-Struthof (see p134–5).

Le Redoutable

Cherbourg, Normandy • Cold War, Nuclear weapons

★★★★☆

Dark Rating: 7 ☣

France's first nuclear-powered submarine carrying nuclear-warhead ballistic missiles gave the French Force de Frappe (strike force) the third element of the nuclear triad of sea-, air- and land-based atomic weapons. Over time, SLBMs (submarine-launched ballistic missiles) became ever more important, and today they are the main part of the nation's nuclear deterrent. *Le Redoutable* was laid down in 1964 and entered service in 1971, carrying 16 missiles. The latest missiles each had a one-megaton warhead – a mighty weapons system.

This sub was decommissioned in the early 1990s and later converted into a museum ship placed in a purpose-built dry dock. The section with the nuclear reactor was cut out. Needless to say, the nuclear-armed missiles were removed too, so there is no risk of radiation to today's visitors. It is a unique visitor attraction: the largest and only (ex-) nuclear SLBM submarine open to the public in the world.

Even from the outside, the 128m-long (420ft) submarine is something to behold, but the real treat is that you can explore the inside too, including the 'bridge'/command post and the section with the SLBM silo tubes, as well as the officers' mess, the galley and eventually the torpedo compartment inside the bow.

Le Redoutable is part of the Cité de la Mer museum complex, located in the harbour of Cherbourg in the north of Normandy. It is by far the biggest exhibit, but there are more parts with a dark connection – in particular that on the *Titanic* (see p87), which is here because Cherbourg was one of the last places from which the ill-fated ship picked up passengers.

Above
The bridge, or command centre, is lit up in red, as if under alert/combat conditions, which gives it an eerie appearance.

D-Day sites in Normandy

Between the Cotentin peninsula and Ouistreham • WW2, Cemeteries

★☆☆☆☆ – ★★★★☆

Dark Rating: 2–7 ☠

Left
German artillery bunkers at Pointe du Hoc, overlooking Utah Beach to the west and Omaha Beach to the east.

The Allied invasion of Nazi-occupied France in June 1944 was the largest military operation of its kind in history. It was code-named Operation Overlord, but the main part of it, the amphibious landings on a series of beaches in Normandy, with airborne support, is more commonly referred to as 'D-Day'.

Although it was costly in terms of casualties, and there were logistical complications, D-Day was deemed a success as it gave the Allies a foothold in enemy territory from where they would begin to recapture France and advance into Germany. D-Day may not have been the beginning of the end for the German war effort

(that, arguably, was Stalingrad – see p237), but it was the biggest nail in its coffin, as now there was a western front too, and the mighty military machine of the USA joined the land operations. Yet there was desperate defence and resistance, and it was almost another year before the Third Reich was finally defeated.

This significant stretch of Normandy coast boasts scores of memorials, relics of fortifications, specialist museums, and several war cemeteries. It is impossible to provide a halfway complete list here, so only a few examples are picked out. Among the war cemeteries, the most visited is the American Cemetery near Omaha Beach (where US troops landed). It also features a visitor centre with a museum. At Omaha Beach itself is one of the most moving of the many monuments in the area: a sculpture depicting a US soldier dragging along a wounded comrade.

Also at Omaha Beach, remains of coastal fortifications and gun emplacements can be seen, especially at Pointe du Hoc, where the land above the beach and cliffs still shows signs of the shelling in the form of bomb craters and pockmarked concrete. More bunkers and gun positions stretch along the entire coastline. At Longues-sur-Mer there is a gun battery with the coastal guns still in place. Relics of the Allies' hardware used in the operations include the pontoons that were part of the artificial harbour constructed at Arromanches. Several of these still lie rusting on the beach.

Above
US casualty on Omaha Beach on D-Day, 6 June 1944. Crossed rifles in the sand are a comrade's tribute to a fallen soldier.

Mémorial de Caen

Northwestern edge of Caen, Normandy • WW2, Cold War

★★★★★

Dark Rating: 6 ☠

Of the many museums covering (aspects of) the Normandy Landings, this one has to be picked out especially. Located in the city from which it takes its name, this museum covers not only the landings in detail, but also the whole context, from the beginnings of Nazism in Germany and the run-up to World War Two all the way to its end and beyond, including a section about the Cold War and how this came to its end. Also incorporated is a separate bunker section. The museum also offers its own guided tours to parts of the D-Day beaches.

Left
Part of the museum shows what life was like for civilians in Vichy France, with depictions of their everyday lives and stories of repression and resistance.

Oradour-sur-Glane

Near Limoges, central France • Ghost town, WW2, Massacre

★★★★☆

Dark Rating: 8 ☠

On 10 June 1944 an SS unit entered this village and, apparently in reprisal for some increased activity by the French Resistance in the wake of the Allied D-Day landings (see opposite), massacred nearly the entire population. The men were shot while the women and children were locked in the village church, which was then set on fire. The total death toll was 642. After the war, a new village was built next to the old one, which was preserved in its ruined state and turned into one of the most remarkable memorials in the country. A Memorial Centre with a modern exhibition about the tragic events was added later.

Below
After the war it was decided by then president Charles de Gaulle that the ruined town should be preserved in that condition as a permanent memorial.

La Coupole

Near Saint-Omer, Pas-de-Calais • WW2, Terror weapons

★★★★★

Dark Rating: 7 ☠

This gigantic concrete dome was part of a complex built in 1943–44, intended to become an assembly, storage and launch site for V2 missiles. These were to be aimed at London and the south of England. However, the site was never completed and so never fired a missile. This was prevented by heavy bombing raids disrupting construction work; then, in September 1944, the complex was captured by Allied troops. The derelict site lay

abandoned for five decades before it was converted into a museum, which opened in 1997.

After passing through the visitor centre at the foot of the hill you enter the main approach tunnel, one surviving part of a whole network of underground structures. Some side chambers now contain extra exhibitions, including coverage of World War One (which seems a little out of place here), as well as aspects of World War Two,

such as the development of tank warfare or the role of cryptology (see also p93). The history of La Coupole itself is also explained.

A lift takes visitors into the concrete dome, where the main permanent exhibition is housed. This is on two levels: the upper part concentrates on the development of the V1 and V2, including the history of Peenemünde (p137) and Mittelbau-Dora (p152), as well as the postwar exploitation of German missile technology expertise in the 'space race' up to the Moon landings. The second part is about France under Nazi German occupation. The presentation is all state of the art, varied and illuminating. This is one of the top war history sites in France.

Above
The enormous bunker was originally designed to launch V2 rockets on an industrial scale.

Blockhaus d'Éperlecques

Near Saint-Omer, Pas-de-Calais • WW2, Terror weapons

★★★☆☆

Dark Rating: 4 ☠

Blockhaus, or 'blockhouse', is a term used for bunkers that are constructed mostly above ground. This is another former V2 launching complex, also in the Pas-de-Calais region. The site is a private museum these days. The main item is a large rectangular bunker, partly in ruins from Allied bombing. Various military hardware is on display, including a complete launch ramp for V1 flying bombs. The main bunker is partly accessible; inside is a full-size silhouette of a V2 and a replica 'tallboy' bomb.

Above
Despite its impressive scale, the Blockhaus is only a third of the size it was originally intended to be.

Mimoyecques

Landrethun-le-Nord, Pas-de-Calais • WW2, Terror weapons

★★★☆☆

Dark Rating: 7 ☠

This is an absolutely unique site. It was supposed to be the next stage in Nazi Germany's so-called *Vergeltungswaffen*, or 'retaliation weapons'. This was the euphemism for what were essentially pure terror weapons, such as the V1 and V2, targeting cities to cause indiscriminate damage and kill civilians. At this underground site, a new type of 'wonder weapon' was to be installed: the V3, a multiple-charged 'super-gun' with barrels over 100m (350ft) long and capable of accelerating a projectile to such a muzzle velocity that it could travel more than 160km (100 miles), bringing London within range of this site.

Five clusters of five such super-guns were planned, able to fire ten shots a minute, making it a total of 600 rounds every hour, meaning that these V3s would have been showering London with shells continuously. However, and luckily for Britain, the design was fraught with technical problems and never went beyond a prototype version. Also, the site had already been targeted by the Allies; eventually it was so severely damaged by deep-penetration 'tallboy' bombs that it was given up. It was seized by Allied troops in September 1944 and further demolished. Yet parts of the tunnels survived and the site was reopened as a kind of memorial,

since 2010 under the management of La Coupole (see opposite).

The main thing to see here is the tunnel system. A replica of a section of a V3 can be seen at the end of one tunnel. Multilingual information panels provide historical and technical background.

Above
The eerie, dank and dimly lit tunnel system at the secret underground base for the V3 super-gun.

THE SOMME

The region along the upper reaches of the Somme River as well as further north towards Arras was one of the main battlefields of World War One on the Western Front. It saw an international involvement of foreign powers joining forces against Imperial Germany, in particular the British, as well as Commonwealth nations such as Canada and South Africa, alongside the French.

The designation of this part of World War One derives from the river of the same name, but is generally applied to the whole region in this section of northeastern France. The four-and-a-half-months-long Battle of the Somme of 1916 stands like few others (but also see Ypres, p122, and Verdun, p116) for the horrors and futility of the 'Great War'. In terms of casualties it was one of the bloodiest battles in history. Yet a mere 10km (6 miles) were gained into German-held territory. The general stalemate more or less remained. Another campaign was the Battle of Arras in 1917, in which more of an advance was made, but again the result was a stalemate.

Today there are numerous reminders of the war all over the region along and behind the former front line. In particular, the many large war cemeteries highlight the sheer scale of the slaughter. In addition, a plethora of memorial monuments have been constructed and there are several museums, some big and 'official', others private collections of war relics. There are too many of these to be covered comprehensively here, so a few select places of interest are presented.

Below
British soldiers of the Wiltshire Regiment near the Albert–Bapaume road at Ovillers-la-Boisselle in northern France, 1916.

DARK STATS

141 DAYS
total duration of the battle
(1 July–18 November 1916)

On the first day, the British army suffered their highest ever casualties in a single day,

57,470
in total, of which

19,240
were killed

300,000
deaths and more than

1 MILLION
casualties over the
full course of the battle

72,000
British and Commonwealth soldiers killed during the battle have no known grave

Notre-Dame-de-Lorette ★★★☆☆

Southwest of Lens, Pas-de-Calais • WW1, Cemetery **Dark Rating: 5** ☠

This site north of Arras is the French National Necropolis, a large military cemetery with 42,000 graves. Adjacent to it is a Ring of Remembrance monument on which are etched the names of over half a million soldiers who fell in northern France. Nearby is one of the newest additions to the museums about this war, the Mémorial 14–18, a design-heavy exhibition that opened in 2015.

Right
The central church on this hilltop location sits within a sea of crosses in this largest of all French military cemeteries.

Vimy ★★★★☆

Between Lens and Arras, Pas-de-Calais • WWI **Dark Rating: 6** ☠

Vimy Ridge was an important location in the Battle of Arras, in which four divisions of the Canadian Corps captured the ridge from the German army in April 1917. Towering atop the ridge today is a major landmark of the region: the Canadian National Vimy Memorial. In addition to a tall monument and a Canadian war cemetery, there is a small museum and some trench reconstructions, as well as a section of underground tunnels that can be visited on guided tours, providing an insight into the subterranean aspects of the war.

Parts of the former battlefields are still littered with unexploded ordnance (UXO) and are therefore not safe to walk around in, as red warning signs point out.

Left
Reconstruction of part of the extensive network of trenches and tunnels at Vimy Ridge.

Somme 1916 Trench Museum

Centre of Albert • WW1

★★★☆☆

Dark Rating: 7 ☠

This is one of the stand-alone museums in the Somme region that deserves a special mention here. It's located right in the heart of the town of Albert and, unusually, is housed in an underground passage some 250m (800ft) long, so you emerge in a different location from the entrance. The exhibition inside is rather old-school and has a plethora of artefacts from the war on display, including guns, shells and soldiers' personal items.

What makes the museum stand out are the many life-size dioramas of scenes from the trenches, peopled by dummies in uniforms (from all sides), being on watch, playing cards and so on. These detailed and occasionally quite graphic depictions offer an insight into the everyday lives of soldiers in the war. Particularly gruesome is a field hospital scene showing a soldier undergoing surgery. A large museum shop sells war relics as well as scores of old shells featuring more or less elaborate decorative engravings.

Right
An exhibit showing a soldier at his watch post in the museum's recreation of trench warfare at the Somme.

Historial de la Grande Guerre

Centre of Péronne • WW1

★★★☆☆

Dark Rating: 5 ☠

Housed in the Château de Péronne, this is a large and modern museum. It features not only lots of war artefacts, but also multimedia elements and some grim art reflecting on the horrors of the war, as well as remarkable examples of the propaganda on both sides. In particular it looks at the lives of civilians and how they were affected, so this is not just a military museum.

Right
Displays of images and authentic artefacts from military and civilian life during the war of 1914–1918.

Auchonvillers

★★☆☆☆

Between Mailly-Maillet and Beaumont-Hamel, north of Albert • WW1

Dark Rating: 3 ☠

The André Coilliot collection in this small village is a noteworthy private museum. It is mainly an assortment of World War One artefacts, but also covers some of World War Two, making it the only military collection on the Somme battlefields that comprises artefacts from both world wars. The museum is associated with the British-run 'Ocean Villas' tea rooms and guest house next door (named after the typical English mispronunciation of the village's name).

This place is an excellent base from which to explore the Somme region, and right behind the guest house some restored original trenches can be seen. During the war these would have led straight to the front line at nearby Beaumont-Hamel. At that place, just to the southeast of Auchonvillers, are various war cemeteries as well as the Newfoundland Memorial adjacent to a large section of land still carved through by remnants of trenches, some of which you can walk in.

Right
Excavated trenches running behind the restored farmhouse.

Thiepval

★★★☆☆

North of Albert, near Authuille • WW1, Cemetery

Dark Rating: 4 ☠

The Thiepval Memorial is the largest monument in the region. It is dedicated to the 72,000 missing British and South African soldiers of the Battle of the Somme (see p110). Next to the monument is an Anglo-French war cemetery. A more recent addition is a visitor centre with a small but modern museum exhibition, which is a branch of the larger World War One museum in Péronne (see opposite).

Left
The Thiepval monument, standing 43m (140ft) tall, is regarded as one of the greatest British pieces of monumental architecture.

The Paris Catacombs

Beneath Paris • Subterranean ossuary

★★★★

Dark Rating: 6 ☠

This is one of the best-known and longest-established dark-tourism sites in the world. This ossuary of bones stacked high along underground passages is a macabre feast for the eyes, so famous it has even made its way into literature (for example, Victor Hugo's *Les Misérables*).

The catacombs owe their existence first to the fact that the ground beneath France's capital city has been used as a quarry for two millennia, so it's like a Swiss cheese – a network of tunnels covering about 300km (200 miles). Second, as Paris grew and its cemeteries became overcrowded, it was decreed in the late eighteenth century that the remains be exhumed and transferred to these underground spaces.

The bones and skulls were artfully arranged and embellished and became quite a sensation. Still today it is one of the most visited dark attractions in Europe. Only a relatively small proportion is open to the public, but there are so-called cataphiles too, Parisians who infiltrate parts not legally open and even have underground (literally!) parties down there.

DARK STATS

1786

the year Paris's cemeteries began to be emptied; the last bones were moved in 1860

The remains of over

6 MILLION

bodies were removed and stored in the catacombs

1200 YEARS

estimated age of the oldest remains

20M (65FT)

average depth below ground of the publicly accessible catacombs

Left
The bones of over six million people are reportedly layered here, including the remains of revolutionaries Robespierre and Danton (although exactly where, nobody knows).

Père Lachaise

20th arrondissement, Paris • Cemetery

★★★★☆

Dark Rating: 4 ☠️

As one of the world's most fabled cemeteries, Père Lachaise receives possibly the largest number of tourists. It was established in 1804 as one of the 'new' cemeteries on what was then the outskirts of Paris, after inner-city cemeteries were banned (and remains removed to underground catacombs – see opposite).

Of the individual graves, one of the most visited is that of the American rock star Jim Morrison, who died suddenly, aged only 27, in Paris in 1971. Morrison had been known for his wild personality and lifestyle, so his rather bland tomb can be a bit of a letdown. Another anglophone superstar also known for his flamboyant lifestyle as well as his works and now to be found buried here is Oscar Wilde. His bizarre tomb matches its occupant's reputation much more than does Morrison's. It is clearly a pilgrimage destination too, going by the graffiti signatures and countless lipstick kiss marks that visitors left on the stone until a glass barrier was installed (now the marks are left on the glass).

Among the famous French people buried here are Claude Chabrol, Édith Piaf, Frédéric Chopin and Honoré de Balzac. Often it is the less well-known names' tombs that are visually the most unusual. It

Above
This is a marvellous example of a park-like cemetery with lots of Gothic elements and remarkable sepulchral art.

is certainly worth taking some time to explore, looking out for marvels of sepulchral art. In addition to graves, there are several memorial monuments, including a row of sculptures commemorating concentration camps of the Third Reich (p134–35 and p143).

OTHER FAMOUS CEMETERIES TO VISIT

In addition to those included in this book, there are countless other cemeteries in the world worth mentioning. Here is a selection of noteworthy examples:

- **Montmartre** and **Montparnasse**, also in Paris, are worth seeing too.
- **Ohlsdorf Cemetery**, Hamburg, Germany, is the largest cemetery in Europe and is like a vast garden.
- **Mirogoj Cemetery** in Croatia's capital, Zagreb, is also of a great size and features many remarkable tombs and monuments.
- **Recoleta Cemetery**, Buenos Aires, Argentina, has monumental tombs, including the grave of Evita Perón.
- **The Glasgow Necropolis**, Scotland, occupies a wonderful vantage position on a hill.
- **Waverley Cemetery**, Sydney, Australia, is located on a cliff overlooking the sea.
- **Montjuïc Cemetery**, Barcelona, Spain, is of significance in the context of the Spanish Civil War.

- **Novodevichy Cemetery**, Moscow, Russia, is full of graves of famous Soviet and post-Soviet figures.
- **Kerepesi Cemetery**, Budapest, Hungary, contains enchanted tombs and a socialist-era monument.
- **Antakalnis Cemetery**, Vilnius, Lithuania, includes graves of victims of the 13 January 1991 uprising against Soviet rule (p214].
- **Okopowa Street Cemetery**, Warsaw, Poland, has one of the largest Jewish sections in the world and some Holocaust-related monuments.
- **The Old Jewish Cemetery**, Prague, Czech Republic, is a crowded jumble of headstones, probably making it the most densely 'populated' cemetery.
- **Wadi-us-Salaam**, Najaf, Iraq, is the world's largest cemetery by absolute 'body count', containing tens of millions of bodies.
- **Calvary Cemetery**, Queens, New York City, USA, is probably the largest cemetery by number of burials (around three million) in the Western world.

VERDUN

The Battle of Verdun was the longest and one of the bloodiest of World War One. It lasted from February to December 1916 and cost over 300,000 lives on both sides (and wounded around twice as many more). It also demonstrated the industrialization of warfare, with ever more and ever bigger modern artillery dominating the battle. The constant shelling not only killed and maimed, but also altered the landscape. Moreover, many of those soldiers who survived in the muddy trenches amid all this carnage suffered severe psychological damage, which gave the world the term 'shell-shocked'.

The battle began as a German offensive with the aim not only of inflicting mass casualties on the enemy but also of capturing a series of fortifications atop a ridge to the northeast of the town of Verdun. At the centre of this was Fort Douaumont. The Germans did manage to take the forts, but with the beginning of the Battle of the Somme (p110) Germany moved some of the artillery there, thus reducing their strength at Verdun. Eventually the forts and lost territory were regained by the French. Neither side had really 'won'; it was just that the stalemate was reinstated, albeit at a terrible human cost.

However, for Germany it was still in a way a defeat – the objectives set out for starting the battle were not achieved, so the losses were all for nothing. In German, the brutal nature of the battle is often summed up as *die Hölle von Verdun* ('the hell of Verdun'). For the French it was more of a victory, as they managed to stand their ground, so there is often a good dose of patriotism involved in the French commemoration of Verdun. However, it is universally agreed that Verdun marked a turning point for humanity, even a fall from grace. The 'war to end all wars' had in fact created a whole new era of industrialized warfare with mechanized mass slaughter.

Ossuary of Douaumont

Verdun • WW1, Ossuary, Cemetery

★★★★☆

Dark Rating: 8 ☠

Above
At the top of the tower is a rotating red-and-white 'lantern of the dead', which shines like a beacon above the battlefields at night.

This grand structure is at the heart of today's battlefield memorial complex of Verdun. Here a large oblong building holds the remains of around 130,000 unidentified soldiers. On the outside walls are small openings at the base of the ossuary where you can look in and see the mass of bones and skulls. Above the skeleton-filled basement is a cloister, a long hall with inscriptions on the walls and an eternal flame. At the centre stands a 46m-high (151ft) tower, which you can climb, offering commanding views of the former battlefields; inside is a small exhibition. In front of the ossuary extends a formal war cemetery – a sea of white crosses.

Fort Douaumont

Verdun • WW1

★★★★☆

Dark Rating: 5 💀

The moonscape that the ferocious shelling created is these days covered by grass and trees, although there are sections where you can still clearly recognize the craters from the mass bombardments. In some places vestiges of trenches can be seen, while others have been partially reconstructed. The biggest war relics, however, are the forts, first and foremost Fort Douaumont, a mostly underground structure covered with earth, except where gun positions poke out. You can go inside and explore the dark, damp passages, and climb into the inside of one of the gun turrets. The relatively intact Fort de Vaux, to the southeast, can also be visited.

Mémorial de Verdun

Verdun • WW1

★★★★★

Dark Rating: 8 💀

By the road towards Douaumont is this main museum about the battle and the Great War in general. The permanent exhibition inside is modern and visually the most impressive of all the Great War museums in France. The recreation of the battlefield ground is quite graphic, including semi-decomposed corpse replicas lying in the fake mud. Its informational coverage is also broad, concentrating not just on the military side of the battle but also going beyond, such as looking at personal angles, including the food soldiers had to make do with, the friendships that were formed, and the grim medical aspects.

The latter include not only obvious wounds and disfigurement caused by shells and gunfire, but also the infamous 'trench foot', a kind of gangrene resulting from prolonged wearing of boots in the damp and unsanitary trenches. The psychological damage inflicted on soldiers, simply known as 'shell shock' at the time, is also covered.

Camp Marguerre

To the northeast of Verdun • WW1, Bunkers

★★★☆☆

Dark Rating: 4 💀

A remarkable set of bunkers and other World War One relics can be found at this little-visited special site in a secluded forested area behind the former front line. Despite the French-sounding name this was actually a German camp, which took its name from an engineer from Berlin who specialized in pioneering concrete bunker constructions. Somewhat ironically, the site was later used by the French Resistance to hide from the Germans during World War Two. Some of the buildings are semi-collapsed, others still relatively intact, and most are atmospherically overgrown.

Trilingual (French, German, English) information panels have been erected that provide background information about the various components of the site, together with historical photos for comparison.

Above
Here and there in the camp, remnants of German inscriptions can still be seen on these World War One bunkers.

The Netherlands

The northernmost of the three Benelux countries between northern France and Germany has a history much grander than the small size of its home territory would suggest. It was once one of the main colonial powers, with a global empire reaching all the way to Southeast Asia to include what is today Indonesia (see p299).

In World War Two, the country was occupied by Nazi Germany, which brought with it the Holocaust, when Dutch Jews, as well as German Jews who had fled to the Netherlands to escape persecution, were interned in various concentration camps/transit camps (see p134–35 and p143) and deported to the east.

Anne Frank House

★★★★☆

Prinsengracht 263–267, Amsterdam • Holocaust

Dark Rating: 5 ☻

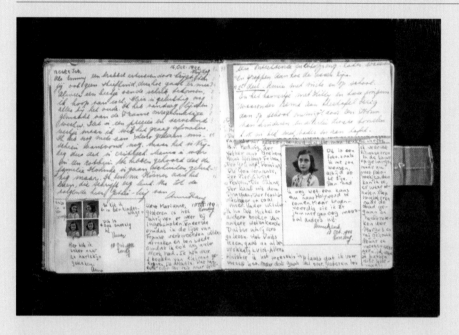

Left
The diary of Anne Frank, from the collection of the Anne Frank House Museum.

One of the world's most visited dark destinations, the story the Anne Frank House tells is possibly also the best-known of the Holocaust. This is thanks to the best-selling book *Anne Frank's Diary* (also the most translated Dutch book of all time). In brief: after the Nazis occupied the Netherlands and the repression of Jews increased, Anne's father, Otto Frank, decided to take the family into hiding instead of risking deportation.

They took refuge in a hidden annexe in their merchant house, and were secretly supplied with food and information by non-Jewish office staff. They had held out for just over two years when they were captured in an SS raid in August 1944. Clearly they must have been betrayed, but by whom is still a mystery.

The family were sent to the Westerbork transit camp and then deported to Auschwitz (p170–71). Anne and her older sister Margot were later 'evacuated' to the Bergen-Belsen concentration camp. That's where they died from typhus shortly before the end of the war. Anne was just 15 years old.

Otto Frank, the sole survivor of the family, discovered Anne's diary on his return to Amsterdam. He first published it in 1947 (after some initial bowdlerization of the sexual thoughts the teenage girl had entrusted to her diary). Since then the book has seen countless editions in numerous languages. As it is especially suitable for a younger audience, having been written by a teenager, it is often the first (and possibly only) book about the Holocaust that many young people encounter. So its significance cannot be overstated.

The Franks' house on Prinsengracht was eventually turned into a museum. It first opened its doors in 1960, but has been much modernized since. These days it is one of the key tourist attractions in Amsterdam and receives well over a million visitors annually. The circuit through the building is enhanced by general historical information panels and suchlike, but the main feature is entering the formerly secret annexe. It is mostly bare, as all the furniture has been removed. But it's still quite emotional for many visitors to step into these historic chambers. Given its popularity, it is best to order tickets in advance online.

Above left
Bronze commemorative sculpture of Anne close to the Anne Frank House.

Above right
The revolving bookcase on the landing that concealed the entrance to the secret annexe.

Dutch Resistance Museum

★★★★☆

Plantage district, Amsterdam • WW2, Holocaust, Resistance

Dark Rating: 5 ☠

Known in Dutch as Verzetsmuseum, this is another museum in Amsterdam about the time of the Nazi occupation. It thus perfectly complements a visit to the Anne Frank House, as it provides an insight into the wider context of the Holocaust and the various forms of resistance against the Nazis during World War Two. It is also far less crowded.

Right
The museum recreates the atmosphere of Amsterdam during German occupation through films, posters and original artefacts.

Belgium

This is a small country of more varied landscapes than its Benelux neighbours, from the beaches of the North Sea to the wooded hills of the Ardennes, plus some very pretty cities (Bruges and Ghent are only the best-known examples). Today its capital, Brussels, is the seat of some of the most important institutions of the European Union. Domestic politics are notoriously complicated by the fact that Belgium is culturally and linguistically more like two countries: the francophone south (Wallonia) and the Flemish (Dutch) north.

Belgium has some older dark history too. It had a stint at colonialism in Africa, even if it got on the bandwagon rather late. Still, it left a gruesome legacy, especially in the Congo, and also laid some of the groundwork for later atrocities to unfold in Rwanda (see p250).

At home, however, the dark chapters of Belgian history in the twentieth century were ones of victimhood, first in World War One (see Ypres, p122) and again in World War Two, when Belgium, like its neighbours, was overrun and occupied by Nazi Germany.

Fort Breendonk

★★★☆☆

South of Antwerp • WW2, Holocaust, Prison, Transit camp

Dark Rating: 7 ☠

This is one of the many forts that were constructed all over Europe before World War One, in this case in 1909. During the Nazi German occupation of Belgium in World War Two, the fort was requisitioned and used for incarcerating political prisoners. Moreover, the place was also turned into a transit camp for Belgian Jews, who were then deported to the death camps in the east during the Holocaust.

As early as 1947, the fort became a memorial, which has since been expanded and modernized, and features an informative exhibition. But it is the gloomy interior of the fort as such that exudes an especially dark atmosphere.

Above
The prison's gallows, built by the Nazis, are preserved along with some cells and a torture chamber.

Left
Between September 1940 and September 1944, around 3500 prisoners passed through Breendonk's gates.

HALT!
Wer weiter geht wird erschossen!
Wie verder gaat wordt doodgeschoten!
Qui dépasse cette limite sera fusillé!

Kazerne Dossin

Mechelen • WW2, Holocaust, Repression, Genocide

★★★★☆

Dark Rating: 7

During the occupation of Belgium in World War Two, the Nazis used the former army barracks of Dossin in this Flemish city as a 'collection camp' for Belgian Jews before their deportation to Auschwitz (p170–71) between 1941 and 1944. The barracks have since been turned into housing, although a section of the basement still serves as a memorial.

Just across the road, however, an all-new purpose-built memorial museum was opened in 2012. It is home to a modern exhibition that doesn't have many artefacts (an original Zyklon B gas canister is a particularly grim one) but is rich in documents, images and multimedia elements. It is spread over several floors and additionally covers topics beyond the Holocaust itself, such

as the nature of prejudice leading to ostracism and worse. Other genocides are also discussed here, especially those in Rwanda (p250) and Cambodia (p290).

Below
Archive photograph showing Belgian Jews in the courtyard of the barracks in 1942.

Above
Original letters and photographs are part of thousands of documents in the collection.

Top
Photographs of deportees from Dossin lining a wall inside the museum.

YPRES

Also spelled *Ieper* in Flemish, this place in the north-west of Belgium is, like Flanders – the name of the region it is in – forever associated with the horrors of World War One. It saw battles all through 1914–18, beginning with the First Battle of Ypres between German forces and French and British Expeditionary Force troops clashing in what is known as the 'war of movement'. That soon gave way to digging in and trench warfare in which the front line barely moved. In 1915 a German offensive (the Second Battle of Ypres) failed to take the city, which nonetheless suffered severely from shelling.

More than two years later, the Allies went on the offensive (the Third Battle of Ypres), and the front line was pushed forward under atrocious conditions and huge losses up to the village of Passchendaele. Then, in early 1918, the Germans were on the advance again, reclaiming the lost ground. But the German war effort had run its course. Spent and suffering from battle fatigue, they were swept back by counter-attacking Allies between August and October. The front line now gone, the old battlefields were a wasteland littered with the countless unclaimed bodies of the fallen.

In the end, more than 150 war cemeteries were created in the region. Countless monuments and museums commemorate the war; some are small private affairs, others larger and more official. It is impossible to include everything here, but some of the most significant sites are featured. The pretty reconstructed town of Ypres makes an ideal base for exploring the region independently. Alternatively, there are plenty of tour operators offering Western Front-themed guided packages.

Below
Soldiers survey no man's land – once a forest in 'Flanders's Fields'– after four years as a battleground, 1919.

In Flanders Fields Museum

Ypres • WW1

★★★★★

Dark Rating: 7 ☠

This is the principal museum about World War One in the region. The name is a reference to the famous war poem by Canadian poet John McCrae, who served as a surgeon at Ypres.

On entering the museum visitors receive a 'Poppy Bracelet' containing a microchip which activates the language for the audio guide. The state-of-the-art exhibition is comprehensive and includes many sobering elements; for example, the section on the use of poison gas. The end of the exhibition has large panels suspended from the ceiling on which all the conflicts around the world since the Great War are listed, making the hackneyed phrase 'Never again!' look rather empty.

Above
The museum is housed in the rebuilt grand Cloth Hall in the very centre of Ypres.

Menin Gate

Ypres • WW1

★★★☆☆

Dark Rating: 5 ☠

Also located in the town itself, this is the largest and best-known World War One monument of the region. It is dedicated to the British and Commonwealth fallen soldiers who remained missing; that is, they have no grave. It was unveiled in 1927. Since then, every evening at 8 p.m., a 'Last Post' ceremony has been held here, where the bugle call is played and wreaths or crosses with red poppies attached are laid by visitors. Despite the crowds that often gather for the ceremony, it is a very sombre occasion every time.

Right
The names of over 54,000 Commonwealth soldiers lost in Ypres are listed on the walls.

Tyne Cot

★★★☆☆

Between Zonnebeke and Passchendaele • WW1, Cemetery

Dark Rating: 4 ☠

Of the many war cemeteries in the region, this is one to pick out, partly because it is the most visited of all. Moreover, it is the largest Commonwealth war cemetery in the world, with nearly 12,000 graves, well over 8000 of them nameless. There is a small exhibition in the visitor centre that provides background information about the battles in this area.

Right
In addition to the sea of white gravestones, an adjacent memorial wall lists the names of some 35,000 missing soldiers.

Memorial Museum Passchendaele 1917

★★★★☆

Zonnebeke • WW1

Dark Rating: 7 ☠

Left
Ordinary objects including buttons, safety pins and items from a soldier's mess kit are evocative artefacts on display.

After the main museum in Ypres itself, this is probably the second-most important one in the region. The main permanent exhibition, housed in an old chateau, has a broad coverage, although the focus is naturally on the battle that gives the museum its name. The displays are varied and full of original artefacts. An especially noteworthy part is the station where you can sniff the smells of four different types of poison gas that were used in the battles here, including mustard gas and phosgene.

The museum also includes a convincing reconstruction of a dugout tunnel system. You can walk through this dimly lit, claustrophobic maze to get a 'real life' impression of the cramped conditions in these subterranean shelters. Outside in the open-air part you can walk through some trench reconstructions.

Hooge Crater

★★★☆☆

East of Ypres • WW1

Dark Rating: 4 ☠

This is a cluster of several sites. One is the private Hooge Crater museum, housed in a former chapel. It contains collections of battlefield artefacts such a shells, helmets, rifles and gas masks as well as a large-scale model of the red triplane of the 'Red Baron', the famous German fighter pilot ace.

Across the road is a Commonwealth war cemetery also named after Hooge Crater. This derives from deep underground mine explosions (the work of tunnelling companies) that left huge craters. Of these a couple are now lakes just east of the museum. Around them is a small open-air museum with trench remnants, old bunkers and lots of rusty battlefield relics.

Left
Archive photo shows New Zealand officers watching a bombardment at Hooge Crater.

Sanctuary Wood

★★☆☆☆

South of Hooge • WW1

Dark Rating: 3 ☠

Like Hooge, this is a cluster of several sites. There is a private museum, which also goes by the name of Hill 62, with an indoor exhibition of war relics. Outside is a wooded area full of part-preserved/reconstructed trenches, a long, dark tunnel and rusty battlefield relics. Further south at the end of the road is the Hill 62/ Sanctuary Wood Canadian Memorial.

Right
Preserved trenches, which visitors may walk freely among, at the Sanctuary Wood Hill 62 museum.

Bayernwald

★★☆☆☆

Between Voormezele and Wijtschate • WW1

Dark Rating: 4 ☠

A German site worth mentioning in the context of Ypres is this one, whose name means 'Bavaria Forest'. It is mainly a system of trenches, shafts and bunkers that has been meticulously restored by volunteers.

But it also has a connection to later history: in 1914–15, a young Adolf Hitler apparently served here.

The site is a little tricky to access and not always open. Moreover, you have to obtain a ticket from the

Heuvelland Tourist Office in the village of Kemmel several miles to the southwest, where you will be given a code to open the automatic gate in the fence around the trench site.

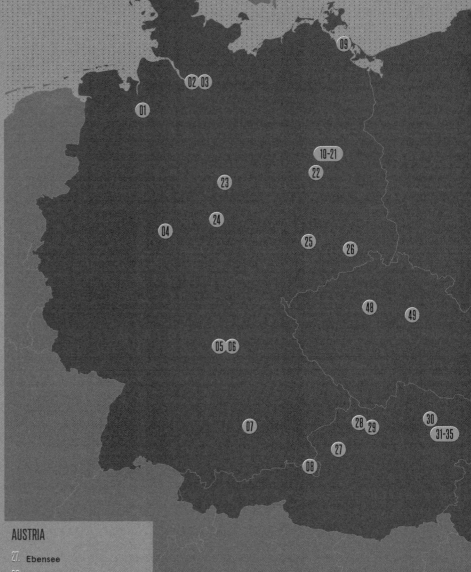

GERMANY

01. **Bunker Valentin**
    Bremen

02. **Nikolaikirche memorial**
    Hamburg

03. **Bullenhuser Damm Memorial**
    Hamburg

04. **Sepulchral Museum**
    Kassel

05. **Memorium Nuremberg Trials**

06. **Nazi Party Rallying Grounds**
    Nuremberg

07. **Dachau**
    Near Munich

08. **Eagle's Nest & Obersalzberg**
    Berchtesgaden

09. **Peenemünde**
    Usedom

10. **Berlin**

11. **The Berlin Wall**
    Berlin

12. **Holocaust Memorial Berlin**
    Berlin

13. **Topography of Terror,** Berlin

14. **Berlin Story Bunker,** Berlin

15. **German Resistance**
    Memorial Centre
    Berlin

16. **Spy Museum**
    Berlin

17. **Stasi Museum**
    Berlin

18. **Hohenschönhausen**
    Berlin

19. **Teufelsberg**
    Berlin

20. **Allied Museum**
    Berlin

21. **German-Russian Museum**
    Berlin

22. **Beelitz Heilstätten**

23. **Hötensleben**

24. **Mittelbau-Dora**

25. **Colditz**

26. **Military History Museum**
    Dresden

AUSTRIA

27. **Ebensee**

28. **Hartheim**

29. **Mauthausen**

30. **Zwentendorf**

31. **Vienna**

32. **Flak Towers**
    Vienna

33. **Josephinum & Narrenturm**
    Vienna

34. **Museum of Military History**
    Vienna

35. **Funeral Museum &**
    Central Cemetery
    Vienna

POLAND

36. **Westerplatte**
    Gdańsk

37. **European Solidarity Centre**
    Gdańsk

38. **Museum of the**
    Second World War
    Gdańsk

39. **Wolfsschanze**

40. **Warsaw**

41. **Warsaw Uprising Museum**

42. **Kraków**

43. **Auschwitz**

44. **Majdanek**

45. **Treblinka**

46. **Sobibór**

47. **Bełżec**

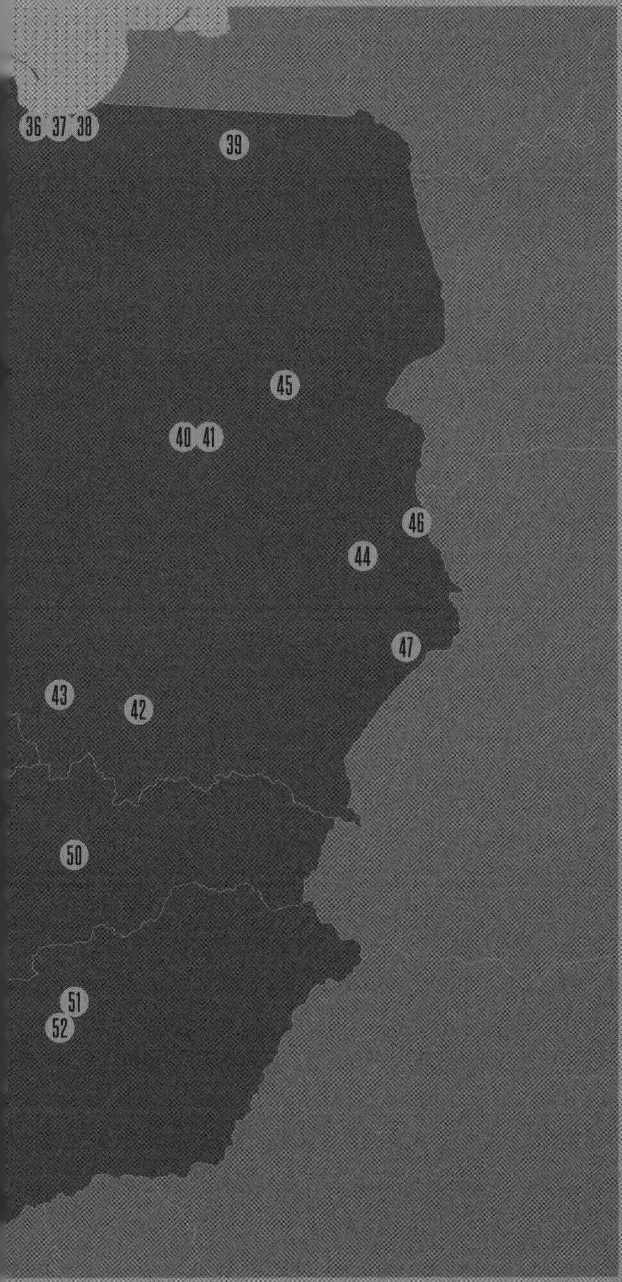

Central Europe

This section covers the big Central European power that is Germany and its smaller southern neighbour Austria, as well as Hungary, Slovakia, the Czech Republic and Poland. The latter four could also have been classed as Eastern Europe, but in this book that classification is, for practical reasons, reserved for the former Soviet states.

Germany and Austria offer a wide array of dark destinations of quite different types, and both are easy to travel around in thanks to decent public transport and excellent road networks. The more eastern states are not too complicated to explore either. In these countries the dark destinations have mostly to do with World War Two, Nazism and the Holocaust, or with the communist period that followed and how that was overcome.

During the Cold War, the Iron Curtain sliced right through the middle of Germany, separating the FRG (West Germany), a NATO member, from the GDR (East Germany), a Warsaw Pact member, and continued all along neutral Austria's northern and eastern borders. (There were also stretches of the Iron Curtain in Norway – see p79 – and Finland on their borders with Russia, and along Turkey's border with the Caucasus.) Few relics remain of what was once the most sophisticated border fortification system ever constructed, but those that still exist are a unique sight.

CZECH REPUBLIC

Lidice

Sedlec Ossuary

SLOVAKIA

Múzeum SNP
Banská Bystrica

HUNGARY

House of Terror
Budapest

Memento Park
Budapest

Germany

This is a country with plenty of dark history: in the twentieth century it started with the first genocide of the era, in the then German colony of what is today Namibia (p255), against the Herero people. At home, growing militarism within Imperial Germany contributed to the outbreak of World War One, and defeat in this war led to the end of the monarchy and severe reparations in the newly formed Weimar Republic. It was a chaotic and unstable time, and only 15 years later Hitler and the Nazis seized power, leading to dictatorship, renewed militarism and World War Two.

This turned into the deadliest war of all time, and the Nazis committed what will probably stand as the worst ever crime against humanity: the Holocaust, the systematic murder of six million European Jews. In the end, the Allies defeated Germany again, and the whole country suffered from intense bombing campaigns that left most of Germany's larger cities in ruins. Immediately after World War Two, the Cold War loomed and Germany was divided into two states: the Federal Republic of Germany (FRG), formed with the support of the Western Allies, particularly the USA, in the west, and the Soviet-supported socialist German Democratic Republic (GDR) in the east.

The Iron Curtain between the two power blocs, NATO in the west and the Warsaw Pact in the east, ran through the heart of Germany and became the most sophisticated border fortification ever. This applied even more to the divided city of Berlin, when the Berlin Wall was built. The Allies kept the western part divided into sectors of their own, giving West Berlin a special status of a still 'occupied' exclave, while East Berlin became the capital of the GDR and the FRG established a new capital in Bonn.

Germany would have been the most likely battleground if a nuclear World War Three had broken out, and that would probably have annihilated the entire country. Instead there came the peaceful revolution of 1989 in the east, which culminated in the Fall of the Berlin Wall (it was a bit more complicated than that, but that is the event that has come to stand for this period). As the rest of the Eastern Bloc was falling apart, Germany became reunited. This brought its own problems, which still have repercussions today, yet Germany has established itself as a powerful member of the EU.

Germany is unique in how it eventually tackled coming to terms with its dark past, in particular the Nazi era and the Holocaust. In fact, German has a special word for this: *Vergangenheitsbewältigung*, and Germany has established an elaborate commemoration culture that leads the world. You could fill a whole separate book with the memorials and other dark places in Germany. For this book, though, a rigorously selective approach had to be adopted. Germany has more entries in this book than any other country, but this simply reflects the fact that it is the country with the highest concentration of dark places in the world.

Below
Civilians walking through the ruins of the southwestern German city of Ulm after Allied aerial bombing, in ca. 1944.

Bunker Valentin

★★★★☆

Rekum, northwestern edge of Bremen • WW2, Forced labour

Dark Rating: 4 ☠

This gargantuan U-boat bunker was intended for the serial production of submarines for the Kriegsmarine, the Nazi German navy. Construction began in 1943, utilizing slave labour by POWs and concentration camp inmates, as was usual in the large-scale building projects in the Third Reich. Several thousand POWs did not survive. However, not a single submarine was ever laid down here. Shortly before the bunker was completed in 1945 it was attacked by the Allies using 'Grand Slam' and 'Tallboy' heavy bombs. They caused enough damage for the Nazis to relinquish the site, although most of the bunker remained standing.

After the war the bunker became a storage facility for the new West German military. They left in 2010 and the site was converted into a memorial. It is visually stunning, and the museum exhibition provides plenty of historical insights.

Above
The huge concrete bunker is over 400m (1,400ft) long, about 30m (100ft) high and nearly 100m (325ft) wide.

Nikolaikirche memorial

★★★☆☆

Hamburg city centre • WW2 aerial bombing

Dark Rating: 5 ☠

In July 1943 Allied bombing raids destroyed large parts of the north German port city of Hamburg in what was code-named Operation Gomorrah. The incendiary bombs created a firestorm on a hitherto unprecedented scale, and an estimated 35,000 people, mostly civilians, lost their lives. Many were incinerated in the flames; others were asphyxiated as the tornado of fire sucked out all the oxygen from makeshift air-raid shelters in cellars.

In the city centre, the neo-Gothic spire of the Nikolaikirche served to guide the bombers. The church was hit by bombs too and the nave was largely destroyed. The rubble was removed after the war but the spire remained standing and was declared a *Mahnmal* (translated as 'memorial', although that doesn't capture the element of *mahnen*, meaning 'to warn').

There is a museum in the crypt of the former church underneath the open space where the nave used to be. Its exhibition not only covers the history of the site itself and the bombing of Hamburg (explaining, for example, the physics of the firestorm in the process) but also puts it into context, and points out that German air raids on cities such as Coventry in England (see p92) preceded the Allied bombing campaigns.

Above
The remains of the spire and a sculpture dedicated to the memory of prisoners who died at the POW camp Sandbostel.

Bullenhuser Damm Memorial

★★★☆☆

In the southeast of Hamburg • Atrocities, Murder

Dark Rating: 7 💀

The large school building at Bullenhuser Damm in the Rothenburgsort district of Hamburg had in 1944 been turned into a satellite camp of Neuengamme. That concentration camp was 'evacuated' in April 1945 as Allied forces were advancing and the Third Reich was about to collapse. Twenty children, on whom an SS doctor had been performing medical experiments at that camp, were taken to the basement of the former school building and executed there (by hanging, one after the other) in an attempt to cover up the medical crimes. The case was largely forgotten until it was uncovered by a journalist in the 1970s. A rose garden commemorating the children was then planted in the schoolyard. Further investigations since then have made it one of the best-researched Nazi crimes of this kind. The identities of most of the children could be established, and since 2011 a proper memorial exhibition has been housed in the original basement rooms. Numerically it may seem a small case compared to the millions who died in the Holocaust, but it is perhaps precisely because it is a story of just a few young individuals that it is so very moving in comparison with big statistical numbers elsewhere.

Above
The inscription in the Rose Garden at Bullenhuser Damm reads: 'Here you stand in silence, but when you turn to leave, be silent no more.'

Sepulchral Museum

★★★☆☆

Kassel, Hesse • Funeral culture

Dark Rating: 4 💀

This museum focuses on funeral culture (see also p162). It also goes beyond that, looking at how different societies have dealt with death in various ways through the ages. This includes some perhaps unexpectedly lighter sides of death, such as the flamboyant 'fantasy coffins' from Ghana or black-humoured cartoons on the subject of death.

In addition to the permanent exhibition, the museum features regularly changing temporary ones on related topics (for example, capital punishment, forensics and mummies).

Above
Elaborately decorated coffins on display at the museum.

Memorium Nuremberg Trials

West of Nuremberg city centre • War crimes tribunal

★★★★☆

Dark Rating: 4 ☠☠

Above
The defendants, surrounded by American military police, include Hermann Göring, Rudolf Hess, Joachim von Ribbentrop and Albert Speer.

The Nuremberg Trials were a milestone in international law: the first time that war criminals were held accountable before a court. The Nazis at the very top responsible for these crimes committed suicide to evade justice, so Hitler, Himmler and Goebbels could not be tried. Of the top dogs it was only Hermann Göring who was put in the dock in Nuremberg. He was sentenced to death but the night before his execution he took a cyanide pill in his cell (how he had obtained the poison has never been clarified).

Other high-ranking Nazis such as Ernst Kaltenbrunner and Joachim von Ribbentrop were sentenced to death and executed by hanging. Some others, including Albert Speer and Rudolf Hess, received long prison sentences. The hall in which the trials were held later returned to serving as a regular courtroom. It fulfilled that function until early 2020 and up to then could be viewed only when no proceedings were taking place, but now that court hearings in this room have been discontinued altogether it should be accessible all the time during normal opening hours.

Next door, a museum exhibition was set up that covers the trials and their context, before and after, in quite some depth. The exhibition is short on authentic artefacts, although it includes a couple of the original defendants' benches. Out of context these would be unremarkable, but when you know who once sat on them they take on a very dark aura.

DARK STATS

In the main trial of top-ranking Nazis there were

24 DEFENDANTS; 22 RECEIVED SENTENCES
(one had committed suicide, one was held unfit for trial)

Of those 22,

12

were sentenced to death by hanging,

3

were acquitted,

4

were imprisoned for 10–20 years, and

3

were imprisoned for life

216 COURT SESSIONS
were held

4 COUNTRIES
provided judges for the trials: the USA, USSR, Great Britain and France

Subsequent trials were held to prosecute other Nazi officials. In total, there were

199 DEFENDANTS, 161 OF WHOM WERE CONVICTED

Nazi Party Rallying Grounds

On the southeastern edge of Nuremberg • Nazi legacy

★★★★☆

Dark Rating: 7

It was here that Hitler's Nazi Party held its mass gatherings from 1933 after coming to power in Germany. These events were not so much party rallies – no tabling of motions, no discussions, no voting – but pure propaganda shows, designed to enthuse the party's followers and intimidate everyone else. In 1935 a pompous grandstand was erected to designs by Hitler's favourite architect, Albert Speer, featuring rows of classical columns, flying hundreds of Nazi flags, and a central rostrum from where the Führer would address his followers.

The field below had space for some 100,000 spectators and participants. Seating for 70,000 more spectators ringed the complex. To add to the spectacle was the 'Cathedral of Light', where over 150 powerful anti-aircraft searchlights pointed their beams vertically into

the sky. It was certainly a jaw-dropper. For many participants, these gatherings also had the character of a funfair, fuelled by beer and a sense of camaraderie.

All this seductive propaganda and show staging is the topic of a documentation centre that was set up in a nearby giant Nazi-era building, the unfinished Congress Hall, at the northern end of the former rallying grounds. The main exhibition, entitled 'Fascination and Terror', provides the full context and explains the exploitative and delusional psychology involved in these events.

At the original Zeppelin Field site, the grandstand is still there, although somewhat diminished. The giant swastika that used to sit atop the central part was blown up by the Americans after the end of the war. The colonnades were

demolished later. But the main central part, with Hitler's rostrum and the seating to either side, are still there. The field in front hosts concerts, festivals and racing events or is otherwise used for car parking. When there are no big events on, skaters scoot about and people use the high rear walls of the grandstand for tennis practice. So in a way, the combination of light-hearted fun and a sinister background is still there too.

Above
The remains of Speer's Zeppelin Field grandstand. In 2019 the Mayor of Nuremberg announced that the grounds would be preserved and made accessible for educational purposes.

Dachau

Just north of Munich • Concentration camp

★ ★ ★ ★ ★

Dark Rating: 8 ☠

This is probably the best-known of all the concentration camps in Germany. It was also the very first one, established shortly after Hitler seized power, and, since it wasn't liberated until just before the end of the war, it was the one in operation the longest.

It was initially intended primarily for political prisoners and other 'undesirables'. Jews were sent there too, but Dachau was not an extermination camp like Auschwitz; here, no gas chambers were used for systematic mass murder, only for disinfecting clothes. It was still a deadly place, and of the 200,000 people who were sent to Dachau more than 40,000 died there, but about four-fifths of the inmates survived, albeit psychologically and often also physically damaged.

Dachau is today one of the most visited memorial sites of this kind and is particularly geared towards an international audience. Furthermore, it is relatively easy to reach, even by public transport from Munich. Of the original camp, the gatehouse, the crematorium, the arrest block (the prison inside the prison) and some other buildings are still there, and the watchtowers and fence have been restored. The main part of the camp is an almost empty space, since none of the former rows of wooden barracks survive, although two have been reconstructed. The locations of all the others are now indicated by rectangular spaces filled with gravel.

One of the larger buildings houses an excellent in-depth museum exhibition that covers the entire history of the camp as well as its wider historical context. Guided tours around the compound (also in English) are offered too.

Above
One of the original crematoria ovens used to dispose of the dead at Dachau.

Left
Watchtowers overlook what was once rows of barracks.

CONCENTRATION CAMPS, DEATH CAMPS & EXTERMINATION CAMPS

There is often some degree of confusion with regard to this set of terms. They are conceptually different, although there is some overlap. Concentration camps are internment camps set up to hold large numbers of particular types of prisoners in one 'concentrated' place. Contrary to what many think, it was not originally a German idea, but was first systematically implemented on a large scale by the British during the Second Boer War in South Africa in 1900–02. Tens of thousands of mostly civilians, especially women and children, were forcibly moved into such camps, where living conditions were terrible, sanitation poor, food supplies meagre and disease rife. Around 30,000 prisoners died.

The Nazis later 'perfected' the concept of concentration camps, called *Konzentrationslager* or 'KZ'

for short, and took the inhumanity of these camps to unimaginable new levels. The first camps were set up soon after Hitler had come to power, with Dachau (see p133) founded as early as March 1933. Several others (see p143) followed in the years before World War Two, all within German territory.

These camps were primarily intended for political opponents and other 'undesirables'. Later, such prisoners were systematically exploited for forced labour on an ever-increasing scale. During the war, POWs, in particular Soviet ones, became concentration camp inmates and slave workers too, and were usually treated even worse. Jews also formed a sizeable proportion of the concentration camp populations and had to do forced labour too, but it is important within the context of the Holocaust to distinguish these camps from those further east that were set up primarily for the systematic murder of Jews through gassing in what has become known as 'the Final Solution'. This euphemism was used at the Wannsee Conference in Berlin in January 1942, where the implementation of the *Endlösung der Judenfrage* or 'final solution to the Jewish question' was discussed at a meeting of high-ranking Nazis, chaired by Reinhard Heydrich. The method of gassing, already used in the euthanasia centres (p155), was adopted and new, special camps for this purpose were commissioned.

This phase of the Holocaust was code-named *Aktion Reinhard* or Operation Reinhard (after Heydrich). Three death camps or *Todeslager* were constructed for this: Bełżec, Sobibór and Treblinka (p173–75). These were relatively small camps in secluded locations far in the east of the occupied territories in Poland, and were pure killing factories. Inmates arrived by cattle train and were usually gassed within a couple of hours, using engine exhaust fumes (carbon monoxide). Only small contingents of slave labour *Sonderkommandos* or 'special commandos' were housed in the camp. These were forced to do the dirtiest work imaginable: emptying the gas chambers and burying or cremating the corpses.

So death camps and concentration camps are very distinct concepts. However, the distinction is blurred by the fact that the most infamous of all camps, Auschwitz,

Opposite
A cattle carriage of the type used to transport millions of victims to the camps. Openings were often covered with barbed wire.

Left
Jewish families being transported to Auschwitz-Birkenau concentration camp in 1944.

had a dual role of both forced-labour concentration camp and death camp, especially from 1942 onwards. It was also at Auschwitz that the poison Zyklon B was used in the gas chambers (also at Majdanek, p172).

The third term here, extermination camp – from the German *Vernichtungslager* – is the least clear. It is sometimes used interchangeably with 'death camp', but since the Nazis also pursued the strategy of *Vernichtung durch Arbeit* – 'extermination through work' – other camps used primarily for slave labour can sometimes also be referred to as extermination camps, such as Mauthausen in Austria (see p156). One particularly mixed case is that of Maly Trostenets, the camp outside Minsk (p217), which was initially set up as a concentration camp but was soon transformed into a place whose primary function was the murdering of local Jews. It has to be noted, though, that while Jews were the prime target of the Nazis' extermination policy, it also included other groups such as Roma and Sinti.

The imagery associated with concentration camps is certainly among the most powerful and grimmest in world history: those endless rows of wooden barracks with the bunk beds inside, the watchtowers, the electrified barbed-wire fences, the inmates' striped clothing, and so forth – and not least the slogan *Arbeit macht frei* ('work sets you free') that featured on many concentration camp gates (but not at the death camps).

In addition to these two or three types of camp, or mixed-type camps, there were also the transit camps called *Durchgangslager* or *Sammellager*, especially in France, Belgium and the Netherlands, where mostly Jewish victims were assembled and held before being deported to the camps in the east.

Most of the main concentration camps also had satellite camps, or *Außenlager*, in the regions around them, at places where slave labour was exploited. Many of the POW camps set up by the Nazis, in particular those for the hundreds of thousands of captured Soviet soldiers, closely resembled concentration camps as well.

DARK STATS

AROUND 6 MILLION
Jews murdered in the Holocaust between 1940 and 1945, which accounted for approximately

TWO-THIRDS
of the Jews in Europe in 1939

1 MILLION
Jews are estimated to have been murdered at Auschwitz–Birkenau alone

Of other camp populations, up to

250,000
Sinti and Roma and

70,000
people described as 'repeat criminal offenders and asocials', including homosexuals and political activists, are estimated to have been murdered

In total there were more than

20 CONCENTRATION CAMPS
plus thousands of associated satellite camps, transit camps, POW camps and other detention centres within Germany and its occupied territories (see p143)

Eagle's Nest & Obersalzberg

★★★★☆

Near Berchtesgaden, southern Bavaria • Nazi legacy, Bunkers

Dark Rating: 8 ☻

This area in the scenic Alpine Berchtesgadener Land in southern Bavaria was Adolf Hitler's favourite place. It was here that the private Hitler relaxed, although he also received political guests. There is some famous historical film footage of this place, shot by Eva Braun, that shows high-ranking Nazis and their families and especially the Führer himself with his dog Blondi. This footage was taken at the Berghof, Hitler's private residence here, but there were other buildings too: private houses for other prominent Nazis, a large guest house called Platterhof, and SS barracks and bunkers. Obersalzberg is the collective name for all this.

'Eagle's Nest' is actually called Kehlsteinhaus; this mountaintop house was a gift for Hitler's 50th birthday. The construction of the building at such an extreme location was an engineering feat – and an expensive one (it cost an estimated 180 million US dollars in today's money). However, Hitler visited it only a few times.

As the war's fortunes turned against Nazi Germany with the advances of the Allies, the Obersalzberg area was fortified and large underground bunker complexes constructed. It did not become the

'last redoubt' as the Allies at some point assumed – instead Hitler breathed his last not here but in Berlin (p144). Yet the RAF carried out a massive air raid on Obersalzberg in April 1945. It caused significant damage, including at the Berghof (whose ruins were later blown up and bulldozed), but the Kehlsteinhaus survived unscathed.

During the Cold War era, the Americans used the complex as a military recreation centre. It was only after the US military left following Germany's reunification in 1990 that the area was opened to the public. The Kehlsteinhaus is now a popular tourist attraction during the summer season. Inside is a traditional Bavarian restaurant.

Many people come here simply to enjoy the views, but the place's association with Hitler has an undeniably strong allure, particularly for anglophone tourists. This explains why, even though the site is in Germany, the guided historical tours of the place and the region are predominantly offered in English.

Complementing the Eagle's Nest is the Dokumentation Obersalzberg, a memorial museum at the site of a former guest house in the Nazis' compound, and incorporating parts of the underground bunkers. The centre provides important historical context and explains the Nazi propaganda associated with this place. At the time of writing, the centre was undergoing an expansion programme that will quadruple the available exhibition space.

Above
The so-called Eagle's Nest sits at an elevation of 1,834m (6,017ft) on the Kehlstein mountain high above the town of Berchtesgaden.

Left
Part of the underground tunnels and bunkers at Obersalzberg.

Peenemünde

Northwestern end of the island of Usedom
WW2, Terror weapons, Ruins

★★★★★

Dark Rating: 6 ☠

This is a site of massive ambivalence: on the one hand it is arguably the place where the 'Space Age' began, with the legendary V2 rocket performing the first flight into space in history. On the other hand, the V2 was developed not for space-exploration glory but as a terror weapon for Nazi Germany in World War Two. Like its precursor, the V1 (the world's first cruise missile), the V2 was fired at London and other enemy targets for indiscriminate destruction. Moreover, the Peenemünde research facility also made use of slave labour by concentration camp inmates.

The head of the facility was the legendary Wernher von Braun, who defected to the Americans at the end of the war. He was transferred to the USA and first helped kick-start the American intercontinental ballistic missile programme in the early phases of the Cold War; he later became the glamorous head of NASA's development of the Saturn rockets for the Apollo missions. The Americans may have turned a blind eye to his Nazi roots, but for a more complete historical picture these should not be forgotten.

After World War Two, the site was long occupied by the East German military and has become more accessible only since German reunification. Today, the former power station of the complex houses an excellent Historical Technical Museum about the rocket development but also its Nazi context. A few of the other original sites are also accessible to varying degrees. Some relics of the forced labour camps can still be found, and there is a memorial monument to the victims at nearby Karlshagen, both freely accessible. The remnants of the original test launch sites are in a restricted part of the island, but some can be visited on guided tours. The largest ruin is the old oxygen plant, which is still standing but is threatened. Whether it can be saved and ideally incorporated into the museum complex remains to be seen.

Above
Full-scale model of the V2 rocket on display in the grounds of the power station.

Below
Former site of the Army Research Institute and the Peenemünde power plant.

Berlin

★★★★★

In the centre of eastern Germany
WW2, Nazis, Cold War, Iron Curtain, Communism

Dark Rating: 10 ☠

Left
The Reichstag building remained largely unused until after German reunification; it was restored by Norman Foster Architects and since 1999 has housed the Bundestag.

Opposite
The Nazi-era Tempelhof airport remained in service until 2008; the plane seen in this photo is a 'candy bomber' from the Berlin Airlift.

This great city, the capital of reunified Germany, can also be considered the capital of dark tourism. Berlin was the power centre of imperial Germany, the Weimar Republic, the Third Reich and the GDR. During the Cold War, West Berlin was the focal point of tensions between the two power blocs. It was also here that the Iron Curtain, in the form of the Berlin Wall, was opened in November 1989, heralding the collapse of the Eastern Bloc.

Berlin has embraced its dark legacy like few other cities. Here, dark tourism and mainstream tourism frequently merge seamlessly. The famous Brandenburg Gate is not only a major tourist attraction but also once stood for the division of Germany, located right on the east–west border and off limits for decades. The city's most conspicuous landmark, the iconic TV Tower at Alexanderplatz, is the most visible of all GDR-era sights.

Over the following pages some of the most significant dark places in Berlin are presented. There are many more, though. Here follows a short overview.

An icon of Berlin is the Reichstag, the old parliament building that burned in 1933, giving Hitler a pretext for hammering through repressive legislation; after reunification it was brought back to life and now houses the Bundestag, the FRG's parliament. You can visit and go up the glass dome.

A huge relic of the Nazi era is the Olympic Stadium, built for the controversial 1936 Games. The old Tempelhof airport terminal building is the biggest relic of Nazi architecture. The airport made history during the Berlin Airlift of 1948–49 and was closed in 2008. The empty building can be visited on guided tours, including sections formerly occupied by the US military.

A large war ruin is the Kaiser Wilhelm-Gedächtnis-Kirche, the shell of a church tower. At ground level is a small exhibition.

A very sobering memorial site is the House of the Wannsee Conference on the city's southwesternmost edge, which is where the Nazis discussed the 'Final Solution' (see p134–35).

The Anti-War Museum, originally founded in response to the horrors of World War One, closed down by the Nazis, but later re-established, is small, but also covers World War Two and the nuclear threat during the Cold War.

A cluster of small museums can be found on Rosenthaler Straße in Mitte. The 'Silent Heroes' exhibition is about underground resistance during the Nazi era; next door, the Otto Weidt Workshop for the Blind is dedicated to one particular such case, and the nearby Anne Frank Centre is a branch of the more famous Anne Frank House museum in Amsterdam (p118–19).

Berlin has three Soviet war memorials. The most central is near the Brandenburg Gate; another is at Schönholzer Heide in the northeast, and the most dramatic, largest and most Soviet in style is in Treptower Park. One of the largest preserved ensembles of Stalinist-era architecture can be found along Karl-Marx-Allee.

The so-called Palace of Tears is another place that commemorates the division of the city and Germany: this was one of the main GDR border crossing points because it was at Friedrichstraße

station, which was on East Berlin territory but was used by West Berlin trains, the only such point of direct contact. All other stations in the East that Western trains still passed through were sealed and became ghost stations. At Nordbahnhof there is a small exhibition about this peculiar phenomenon of Berlin at the time.

Another famous point on the border is Glienicke Bridge, near Potsdam. It became one of the symbols of the Cold War when on several occasions the bridge was used for exchanging spies who had been captured on the respective other side.

Featuring a particular East German focus are the GDR Museum near Alexanderplatz, and the Life in the GDR Museum in Prenzlauer Berg.

Not to be confused with 'Berlin Story' (see p144), the 'Story of Berlin' on Kurfürstendamm is a 'visual experience' kind of modern history exhibition. As a bonus there are tours from here to an adjacent former nuclear fallout shelter from the Cold War era.

The German Museum of Technology at Gleisdreieck also has many dark elements, including World War Two and covering the Nazi era, especially the role of the railways in the Holocaust.

Easily reachable from Berlin is Potsdam, where the post-World War Two order in Europe was laid down by the Allies at the Potsdam Conference in Cecilienhof. Today it houses a memorial museum about these momentous events. Also in Potsdam is an old KGB prison as well as the former Stasi prison on Lindenstraße, both now impressive memorial sites.

Left
The *Olympiastadion* from the 1936 Games has been modernized, and remains the largest stadium in Germany, but its façade clearly still bears the hallmarks of Nazi-era aesthetics.

The Berlin Wall

Formerly running right through Berlin • Iron Curtain, GDR legacy

★☆☆☆☆ – ★★★★★

Dark Rating: 1–5 ☠

Left
At Bernauer Straße, a reconstruction of part of the fortification looks like a slice of border wedged between two high steel walls.

The Berlin Wall was the most sophisticated border fortification in history. Here the Iron Curtain of the Cold War era was at its most impenetrable. Still, people did try to cross it: some were successful, while at least 140 were killed in their attempts.

When it was first erected in 1961, it was just a wall and a bit of barbed wire. By the mid-1970s, it consisted of an outer wall made of concrete segments with a tube-like top. This was the so-called *Mauer feindwärts*, the wall facing the 'enemy' – that is, the West – and ran along the actual borderline. Behind it was the *Todesstreifen*, or 'death strip', consisting of watchtowers, signal wires, floodlights, a sand strip and a patrol track for border security guards. Finally came the *Hinterlandmauer*, another wall, facing the East.

This border strip ran through the middle of Berlin roughly north to south for more than 42km (25 miles). The rest of West Berlin was surrounded by a similar border, in total about 155km (100 miles) long. It is hard to imagine today what a menacing aura this border strip exuded. Historical photos can only partly capture this.

After the euphoria following the opening of the border on 9 November 1989, the Berlin Wall was dismantled in frenzied haste, so only a few small sections remained. The most important one is Bernauer Straße. Here, a stretch of the outer wall has been preserved. Moreover, it is home to the official Berlin Wall Memorial, which includes a visitor centre and exhibition, as well as a short stretch of reconstructed border strip complete

with a shortened watchtower and a *Hinterlandmauer*. It cannot quite convey what the real border strip looked like, but it is the closest you can get in Berlin (see also Hötensleben, p151).

Another stretch of Wall can be found at the Topography of Terror (see p142), and a small section still stands near a railway bridge on Liesenstraße. Of the *Hinterlandmauer*, more relics still survive, for example at the Invalidenfriedhof, a cemetery in Mitte by the Berlin–Spandau Canal.

Perhaps the most visited Berlin Wall section is the East Side Gallery. This is a stretch of Wall almost 1.2km (0.75 miles) long and famous for the many paintings that originally were the result of an artists' initiative in 1990, but have been repeatedly restored and

Left
Photo from 1981 clearly shows the border fortifications, including the outer wall (facing West Berlin), barriers, sand strip, patrol track, floodlights, signal-wire fence and rear wall (facing East Berlin).

Bottom
A heavily graffitied stretch of the Wall along Bernauer Straße in the Mitte district.

altered since. At the southeastern end of the East Side Gallery, the Wall Museum (a private venture) was established featuring a visual type of exhibition.

Of the once over 300 watch-towers that stood along the Wall only a few survive; for example, at Kieler Eck and Schlesischer Busch. Of the former border crossing points, the one at Born-holmer Straße is the most signifi-cant historically, as it was here that the border was first opened on 9 November 1989. The site is now an open-air memorial with monu-ments and information panels.

The most legendary of all Berlin's border crossing spots is Checkpoint Charlie. It was here that one of the most dramatic moments of the Cold War played out when it came to a stand-off between US and Soviet tanks directly facing each other during the Berlin Crisis of October 1961. The site today is completely changed, and still in flux, although a replica check-point booth in the middle of the street is a popular spot for selfies, and the whole area is full of tour-isty souvenir shops. Also here is the Mauermuseum – Museum Haus am Checkpoint Charlie, or simply Checkpoint Charlie Museum for short, which has some remarkable original artefacts.

Those who want to explore the former course of the Wall can follow the official Berlin Wall Trail, best done by bicycle and spread over several days. You can also down-load a free app that provides details (in English) and historical photos along the way.

Below
Checkpoint Charlie, the famous border crossing point in the US sector.

Holocaust Memorial Berlin

★★★★★

South of the Brandenburg Gate in Mitte • Holocaust

Dark Rating: 7 ☠

This much-discussed large-scale memorial, officially called 'Memorial to the Murdered Jews of Europe', is the result of years of campaigning and was finally realized and inaugurated in 2005. The design is unique: a large field of grey concrete blocks of different heights separated by a maze of passageways which you can walk and get lost in. There is an exhibition beneath the monument, not especially large but very sombre and primarily focused on a select number of individual stories from the Holocaust.

Above
The monument consists of 2711 concrete slabs, or 'stelae', in a grid pattern across a vast field.

Topography of Terror

★★★★★

Centre of Berlin • Nazi legacy, Atrocities, Repression

Dark Rating: 6 ☠

Left
The archaeological open-air exhibition includes remnants of the foundations of the old Gestapo HQ.

This was formerly the nerve centre of the Nazi reign of terror, in particular the headquarters of the infamous Gestapo – short for *geheime Staatspolizei* or 'secret state police'. After World War Two the heavily bombed area ended up right by the new border between East and West Berlin and was hence long left undeveloped. Since German reunification, the site has been turned into a remarkable memorial centre.

The focus of the main exhibition is on the Nazi apparatus of repression, from propaganda to torture, massacres and the Holocaust. The outdoor exhibition includes the remains of the Gestapo HQ, and, bordering Niederkirchnerstraße to the north, one of the last three remaining stretches of the Berlin Wall (p140–41). This one is badly battered from the chiselling done by the so-called wall woodpeckers – people hacking away at the wall after the opening of the border.

CONCENTRATION CAMP MEMORIAL SITES

Left
Gatehouse of the former
Natzweiler–Struthof
concentration camp.

The system of Nazi concentration camps (see p134–35) comprised many more than just those few well-known sites such as Dachau (p133) or Auschwitz (p170–71). Within and close to Germany are also the following:

- **Sachsenhausen**: just outside Berlin and one of the first camps established, as early as 1936.
- **Ravensbrück**: the main camp for women, located north of Berlin.
- **Buchenwald**: one of the largest and best known of the main camps, this vast complex near Weimar was set up in 1937.
- **Neuengamme**: a very large former camp near Hamburg (p130).
- **Bergen-Belsen**: one of the last camps to be set up, mainly to house the many inmates 'evacuated' from camps in the east.
- **Flossenbürg**: perhaps the least known of all the major camps, set up in 1938 to house forced labourers who had to work in a nearby quarry.
- **Natzweiler-Struthof**: Alsace region, now in France.
- **Groß-Rosen**: a major camp near Wrocław, the former Breslau, now in Poland.
- **Stutthof**: near Gdańsk, now also in Poland.
- **Theresienstadt**: north of Prague in today's Czech Republic (p176), also called Terezin in Czech, this was supposed to be a 'model camp', infamously used in Nazi propaganda to try to convince the Red Cross that these camps weren't so bad after all.

Austria (see p154), from 1938 annexed by Nazi Germany, also had camps, the main one being **Mauthausen** (p156). A former satellite of this later became a full-size concentration camp too, **Gusen**.

Within the German-occupied parts of Poland during World War Two, the very largest of the camps was established: **Auschwitz** (p170–71). Not so much a concentration camp but more a small site with an 'experimental' function was Chełmno not far from Łodz. Here the method of murdering victims in 'gas vans' by carbon monoxide was pioneered, a technique later adopted in the three Operation Reinhard camps of **Treblinka**, **Sobibór** and **Bełżec** (p173–75).

Moreover, there were other camps further afield, such as those outside Minsk, Belarus (p217) and Riga, Latvia (p210). There were also various transit camps in France (including **Drancy**, on the edge of Paris), Belgium (p121) and the Netherlands, with **Westerbork**, **Amersfoort** and **Vught** being the names that stand out and where substantial memorials can be found today.

Berlin Story bunker

☆☆☆☆☆

Anhalter Bahnhof, central Berlin • Bunker, WW2, Nazi legacy   **Dark Rating: 7** ☠

Over the past couple of decades, this museum has gone from humble beginnings as a small exhibition tagged on to a bookshop to this highly acclaimed, elaborate incarnation spread over several levels and dozens of rooms inside a former air-raid bunker from World War Two. It features two exhibitions. The first is a general one about the history of Berlin; the second is a special exhibition entitled 'Hitler – how did it happen?'

This uses the thread of Hitler's biography to cover the whole Nazi regime and how it functioned. The end point of it all was famously depicted in the 2004 movie *Downfall*, culminating in Hitler's suicide in the *Führerbunker*. A model of that bunker, props from the film and a complete life-size recreation of Hitler's study inside it have been integrated into the exhibition.

The authentic site of the *Führerbunker* is famously a 'non-site': it ended up in the border strip between East and West and remained inaccessible and sealed. The area was built over with nondescript housing. After the Fall of the Wall, it was investigated and opened up again,

or rather what little was left of it. There were calls for turning the place into some kind of memorial, but this was rejected in order to avoid it becoming a pilgrimage site for neo-Nazis. Instead it was sealed up again, and today there is a car park over it. A single information panel was placed there to mark the location and at least provide some essential background information.

Above
Recreation of the room in the Führerbunker where Hitler spent his final days.

German Resistance Memorial Centre ★★☆☆☆

Bendlerblock, near Tiergarten • Nazi era, Resistance　　　**Dark Rating:** 4 ☠

The various forms of resistance against the Nazi regime are little known internationally, so the prevailing picture, especially outside Germany, is that virtually all Germans blindly followed the Führer. The only well-known exceptions are the failed 20 July 1944 plot by the German officer Claus von Stauffenberg at the Wolfsschanze (p166, Poland) and perhaps the White Rose underground student movement in Munich. But there were many more, including the assassination attempt on Hitler by Georg Elser as early as November 1939, at the very beginning of World War Two.

This exhibition is quite text-heavy and demanding, but it closes an important gap. The location is historically significant and linked to the centre's topic: the Bendlerblock is where the July 1944 conspirators hatched their plot; it was also in the courtyard that Stauffenberg and some of his co-conspirators were summarily shot after their assassination attempt had failed.

Above
The site of Stauffenberg's execution by firing squad is marked with a commemorative plaque and wreath.

Spy Museum ★★★★☆

Leipziger Platz, Mitte • Espionage, Murder, WW2, Cold War and beyond　　　**Dark Rating:** 5 ☠

A relatively recent addition to Berlin's vast portfolio of museums, this is an extremely hi-tech affair with lots of innovative interactive elements that make it true 'edutainment'. Following an introductory section on the ground floor that covers the history of espionage from ancient times to just before World War One, the main part is upstairs and covers mostly the twentieth century. The cryptology achievements in World War Two (see Bletchley Park, p93) are one focus, as are the surveillance techniques of the Stasi in the GDR.

International espionage during the Cold War is another big focus. One particularly remarkable incident from that time is picked out: the 'umbrella murder' of a Bulgarian dissident by means of a poisoned umbrella tip on Westminster Bridge in London. More modern cases are covered too, such as the murder of Russian ex-KGB man Alexander Litvinenko by means of poisoning with the highly radioactive element polonium, which also happened in London, in 2006.

The section on whistle-blower Edward Snowden and the topic of data security in the digital age could not be more contemporary, while the large add-on section about the fictional agent hero James Bond, with various props from Bond movies on display, is more nostalgic.

Above
The infamous poisoned umbrella used in the murder of a Bulgarian dissident in 1978.

Stasi Museum

★★★★☆

Normannenstraße, Lichtenberg
Communism, Surveillance, Repression, Resistance

Dark Rating: 6 ☠

'Stasi' is an acronym for *Staatssicherheit*, the name of the former secret 'security' police organization and intelligence network in the GDR. In proportion to the state's total population, this was the largest such organization in history, with some 180,000 staff formally employed and countless more unofficial collaborators: *inoffizielle Mitarbeiter*, or IMs for short. These were 'recruited' – often by means of psychological threats – from among the general public to spy on colleagues, friends and even family members. No wonder the Stasi was much feared. Its main headquarters was at this place in East Berlin.

When it became clear during the peaceful revolution in the GDR that the very existence of the state was threatened, and hence that of the Stasi too, staff began destroying the masses of files they had accumulated. Protesters intervened by storming various regional seats of the Stasi, and also the HQ in Berlin. The files that survived fill whole libraries; the question of what to do with them remains a highly charged political issue in reunified Germany.

Part of the main former Stasi HQ complex has been turned into a memorial, including the Stasi Museum, which covers the history of the Stasi and the repressive regime in the GDR in general, as well as resistance and the eventual demise of the GDR in 1989–90. The centrepiece is the most remarkable relic here: the original rooms of the then GDR minister responsible for the Stasi, Erich Mielke. The furniture has a typical 1970s design.

The surveillance technology exposed in the exhibition includes all manner of bugs, a letter-opening device and a buttonhole camera. Perhaps the most poignant exhibit is a specimen of the 'scent samples' that were collected during interrogations: pieces of cloth strapped on to chairs on which the 'suspects' had to sit. These pieces of cloth were then put into labelled lab jars so that they could later be used by sniffer dogs if necessary – chilling evidence of the Stasi's officiousness and efficiency.

DARK STATS

The Stasi had files on around

6 MILLION

citizens – at a time when the population of the GDR was about

17 MILLION

180,000

Approximate number of official Stasi employees

Estimates of the number of the Stasi's unofficial informers vary between

500,000 AND
2 MILLION

The files in the Stasi archives stretched out over

164KM (102 MILES)

In 1991 a law was passed allowing people to view their Stasi files; about

2 MILLION

people have chosen to do so

Above
The forbidding façade of the Stasi HQ, now housing the memorial museum.

Hohenschönhausen

Lichtenberg district in eastern Berlin • Prison, Repression

★★★★☆

Dark Rating: 9 ☠

Above
A grim view of a cell block where 'suspects' would await interrogation by the secret police.

This was the main remand prison for political 'offenders' in the GDR run by the infamous Stasi (see opposite) in East Berlin. Usually 'suspects' were brought here for interrogation prior to their trial. The prison was within a restricted, gated and guarded district and thus invisible to the public.

Today this is one of the most important memorial sites related to the legacy of the Stasi. In one building, a special exhibition has been set up about not just Hohenschönhausen but the whole system of political repression in the GDR. The actual prison, however, is accessible only by guided tour. Some of these are especially interesting if the guide is a former inmate, which is usually the case for the tours conducted in German, as you then get to hear details of a particular individual's case. There are also tours conducted in English.

Tours include the garage where prisoners arrived in special arrest vans, interrogation rooms, and of course the cell blocks. The latter come in different forms. The grimmest are the basement cells in the oldest part of the complex that were already in place when the site was run by the Soviet NKVD (the predecessor of the KGB) before it was handed over to the Stasi in the early 1950s. The more modern cell tracts in the newer buildings are somewhat less basic, but still quite depressing. Occasionally, the tours feature a peek inside a special railway carriage that was used for transporting inmates to other prisons.

OTHER STASI SITES & PRISONS

- **Lindenstraße Stasi prison**, Potsdam
- **Stasi prison Bautzner Straße**, Dresden
- **Bautzen**, the main 'proper' prison for the GDR's convicted political prisoners
- **Runde Ecke**, Leipzig, a former regional headquarters of the Stasi
- **Stasi bunker Machern**, a 'relocation facility' in the event of a crisis or war
- **Mielke-Bunker**, a larger 'relocation facility' for the Minister for State Security

More GDR prisons and other Stasi-related sites turned into memorials can also be found in Schwerin, Rostock, Cottbus and Halle/Saale.

Teufelsberg

Grunewald, western Berlin • Cold War, Spying

★ ★ ★ ☆ ☆

Dark Rating: 4 ☠

The name of this place translates as Devil's Mountain. It is one of Berlin's *Trümmerberge*, an artificial hill, some 120m (400ft) high, made from the heaps of rubble left from the bombing damage that Berlin sustained during World War Two. During the Cold War, the US and British military established a 'Field Station' up here to spy on Soviet and Warsaw Pact communications, exploiting the fact that West Berlin was an 'island' within an Eastern Bloc state, the GDR.

After the end of the Cold War, the site was used for air-traffic control for a while, but was then abandoned. For years it was one of the favourite places in Berlin for urban explorers and fans of Cold War relics, but the days of 'wild' access to the site are over; it is now fenced and accessible only on guided tours. The inside of most buildings is still off limits. At the time of writing, what was once the highlight of the tours, going up the main radome tower, has been suspended too, apparently for health and safety reasons. It may be resumed in the future.

The somewhat tattered radome spheres are visually intriguing, and the acoustics inside the top radome are legendary. The rest of the complex is also a kind of open-air gallery of graffiti, some by renowned international street artists who were specially invited to contribute, so there is a certain underground-culture vibe about too.

Below
The view of Germany's capital from this former US 'listening station', perched high on a hill of rubble, is breathtaking.

Allied Museum

Dahlem, southwest Berlin • WW2, Cold War, Espionage

★★★★☆

Dark Rating: 2 ☠

West Berlin was divided into four 'occupation sectors' by the Allies after World War Two. While the Soviet sector became the new capital of the GDR in 1949, the Western sectors remained under the control of the British, French and US military. The Western presence proved crucial during the Berlin Blockade by the USSR in 1948–49, for which the legendary Berlin Airlift operation was formed. The Allies left Berlin after Germany's reunification in 1990, and this museum commemorates their special role for the city. It is located in what used to be the American sector, and incorporates a former US cinema.

The permanent exhibition covers the end of World War Two, the Berlin Airlift, tension between East and West, propaganda items and a restored section of a 'spy tunnel' constructed by the British in 1953 to tap Soviet communications in East Berlin. Outside, the original border booth from Checkpoint Charlie can be seen, as well as a GDR watchtower and pieces of the Berlin Wall (p140–41).

German–Russian Museum

Karlshorst, eastern Berlin • WW2, Atrocities, POWs, Soviet era

★★★★☆

Dark Rating: 5 ☠

A truly historic location, this was the building where the unconditional surrender of Nazi Germany to the Allies was signed, which officially ended World War Two in Europe. At the Soviets' insistence, a ceremony was held in Berlin on 8 May, despite the fact that the German high command had already basically surrendered on 7 May in Reims, France, but without anyone from the Red Army present. Because the signing in Berlin took place late in the evening, when in Moscow it was already 9 May, that is the date when the end of the war has always been celebrated in Russia, whereas 'VE Day' in the West is 8 May.

The main exhibition concentrates largely on World War Two and on German atrocities committed on the Eastern Front, the Leningrad Blockade (see p232) and the fate of Soviet POWs in the Third Reich. The postwar commemoration of the conflict is another topic. One highlight is the preserved study of Marshal Zhukov, the commander of the Red Army that liberated Berlin; he remained as supreme commander of the Soviet forces in Germany after the war for about a year.

Above right
The hall where the surrender signing took place has been restored and is the centrepiece of the museum.

Right
Chief of the German Armed Forces High Command Wilhelm Keitel signing the ratified surrender terms, 8/9 May 1945.

Beelitz Heilstätten

★★★☆☆

Southwest of Berlin
Abandoned buildings, Ruins, Medical, Soviet legacy

Dark Rating: 6 ☻

This former sanatorium was built at the beginning of the twentieth century as a place to cure tuberculosis, a widespread disease at the time. During World War One, it was used as a military hospital; a young Adolf Hitler was a patient here. Following World War Two, the site was taken over by the Soviets and became their largest military hospital in the GDR until the troops were withdrawn in the 1990s upon German reunification. After that, the buildings became a playground for urban explorers, one of the most fabled complexes of atmospheric abandoned buildings in Germany.

Today, access is controlled and visits regulated. In addition, there are guided tours of some of the more dilapidated buildings. Because the place is so photogenic, there are also special tours for photography enthusiasts, some of which allow access to otherwise off-limits parts.

Top
A treetop-level walkway was constructed that provides good views into a couple of the ruins.

Above
The atmospheric interior of the former sanatorium.

Hötensleben

Near Helmstedt, between Salzgitter and Magdeburg
Iron Curtain, GDR legacy

★★★☆☆

Dark Rating: 7 ☠

OTHER MEMORIALS OF THE FORMER INNER GERMAN BORDER

- **Marienborn**, a preserved former GDR border checkpoint on one of the main transit routes that connected West Berlin with the FRG
- **Mödlareuth**, another border stretch featuring a wall as in Berlin, plus a museum with border guard equipment and GDR memorabilia
- **Schifflersgrund**, a stretch of 'regular' border strip that has been preserved: one where the outer border is marked by a metal mesh fence. There is also a museum with large open-air exhibits such as military helicopters and border patrol vehicles
- **Point Alpha**, not only parts of the GDR border fortifications, including a complete watchtower, but also a US military observation point from the Cold War era in the so-called Fulda Gap, where the border bent deep into the East and was therefore expected to be a first point of attack had the East ever launched one

More border museums featuring preserved authentic Iron Curtain fortifications include the open-air museum at Behrungen and the Borderlands Museum Eichsfeld. There are also countless smaller, private border museums and isolated relics.

Those who want to get an impression of what the infamous Berlin Wall really looked like should head here, rather than to Berlin. While in the capital only a few battered and/or heavily altered sections of the Wall survive, here in provincial Hötensleben the then mayor had the foresight of saving a section of the suddenly redundant border fortifications when the Wall came down in 1989–90.

Moreover, at this point along the former FRG–GDR border it involved the same kind of wall as in Berlin, because the village on the eastern side was so close to the border that the GDR deemed it necessary to block the view across the border and install extra security measures. Hence here you get a mini Berlin Wall together with tank barriers, sand strip, patrol track, barbed-wire fences, lamp posts, dog tracks, *Hinterlandmauer* and a couple of watchtowers (see p140–41).

Viewed from the right angles it looks as if nothing has changed and the border is still there – except no border guards are patrolling or aiming their rifles at visitors, and these days a road leads straight across the ex-border right next to the monument. Further up along the borderline, the wall gives way to the more typical metal border fence, of which a stretch has also been preserved.

Above
Here you can see a stretch of Berlin Wall-like border that is over 350m (¼ mile) long.

Mittelbau-Dora
★★★★☆

Near Nordhausen in Thuringia • Concentration camp, WW2, Missiles   **Dark Rating: 10** ☠☠

One of the last Nazi concentration camps established during the Third Reich, in mid-1943, this was originally a satellite camp of Buchenwald (see p143), but from October 1944 it became a camp in its own right, with its own independent administration. The purpose of the camp was the production of V1 and V2 missiles in underground tunnels dug deep into a mountain to be safe from Allied bombing.

Working and living conditions underground were atrocious and about a third of all inmates died. The camp was liberated in April 1945; the Soviets subsequently blew up the entrance tunnels to the underground site. Of the above-ground facilities most were

Above
A rusting V2 rocket engine inside the eerie tunnels.

demolished, except for the camp crematorium. During the GDR era this formed part of a memorial.

After German reunification this memorial was reworked and expanded, and in 2006 a purpose-built visitor centre with a special exhibition about the camp's history and its association with Peenemünde (p137) was opened. The foundations of the camp buildings have also been cleared and information panels added.

In 1995, the underground production tunnels were opened up again. A new access tunnel has been constructed and now visitors can see the inside of the mountain on guided tours. Most tunnels made accessible are full of debris (you can identify parts of V1s!), but a metal walkway leads safely through this dark, dank labyrinthine system. Tours end at a two-storey tunnel whose lower level is flooded. Going any deeper would require extreme caving and is not possible for ordinary visitors.

Even so, the tunnels that can be seen are impressive. You have to remind yourself of the sinister sides of the forced labour and what the missiles produced here were for: pure terror weapons. At the cavern where the new access tunnel meets the first section of the original part, an old, rusty V2 rocket engine has been put on display. Next to it a 3D model of the tunnel system conveys a rough idea of how extensive it was.

Colditz
★★★★☆

Halfway between Leipzig and Chemnitz • WW2, Prison, Escapes   **Dark Rating: 1** ☠

Colditz Castle had been requisitioned by the Nazis in World War Two to house high-ranking Allied POWs. The conditions they were held in were infinitely better than in regular POW camps, and the officers on both sides evidently had respect for each other. The escape attempts by inmates have become legendary owing to their ingenuity and bravado. One successful escapee, Pat Reid, wrote a popular book about his escape and the 1955 movie based on it ensured that Colditz became a household name.

Since the place had ended up deep in the East after the war, it had long been inaccessible to Westerners. In the wake of Germany's reunification the site has seen much development, and archaeological investigations are ongoing. It has also become an attraction for visitors – almost exclusively anglophone ones. For these, guided tours in English are on offer, and there is a museum exhibition in the castle as well.

Above
The preserved entrance of a tunnel through which an (unsuccessful) escape was attempted.

Military History Museum Dresden

Neustadt, north of the Elbe • War, Militarism, Terrorism

★★★★★

Dark Rating: 7 ☠

This might be the boldest, most daring military museum in the world. While such institutions typically concentrate on the presentation of military hardware and past glories – often in overly celebratory fashion – this museum looks at the topic of war from a wide range of angles, including the grimmest and darkest aspects.

There are two distinct parts. One is more traditional and organized roughly chronologically, covering the two world wars and going up to more or less the present day, including joint NATO operations and the fight against terrorism. But it is the other, more modern, part that is more fascinating overall. This begins with the architecture, the work of the internationally renowned Daniel Libeskind – also famous for his design of the Jewish Museum in Berlin. He designed a wedge of metal and glass that seems to be driven right through the middle of the west wing of the old building. Inside, the exhibition is subdivided into themes, including

unexpected ones such as 'war and fashion', 'war and play', 'music and the military' and 'war and language'. The grimmest part, naturally, is the section 'war and death'. This has a separate entrance with a sign warning that there are graphic exhibits inside, so visitors can decide whether they want to skip it.

Since this museum is located in Dresden, the catastrophic aerial bombing of the city by the Allies in February 1945 is taken as the starting point of the modern exhibition in the new wing, right at the top of the metal lattice 'wedge' structure that pokes out of the building. Inside, a part of the firestorm-scorched pavement of Dresden forms the key exhibit. As you go deeper, there are also some interesting visual arrangements; for example, the display of all sorts of missiles suspended from the ceiling on wires as if they are showering down on you in parallel.

Above
The museum is housed in a former military arsenal in the Albertstadt district, which was once the largest garrison in Germany.

DARK STATS

Approximately

800

bombers from British Bomber Command took part in the attack on 13 February 1945. Around

500

bombers from the US Eighth Air Force continued the attack over the following two days

2700 TONS

of bombs were dropped on the first night

The attacks continued over the next two days;

3900 TONS

of bombs were dropped overall

An estimated

25,000–35,000

civilians were killed, although the figure may have been higher due to the presence of undocumented refugees

Around

6.5 SQ KM
(2.5 SQ MILES)

of the city centre were destroyed

Austria

This small country occupying the eastern Alpine region and the northern end of the Pannonian Basin was once at the heart of a great empire, dominated by the Habsburg monarchy. But after the Austro-Hungarian Empire initiated and lost World War One (see p194–95 and p189), the empire consequently fell apart and Austria became a republic.

The troubled interwar years brought much instability and political extremism, including 'Austro-Fascism', but it was the annexation of Austria by Nazi Germany in 1938, proclaimed by Adolf Hitler (an Austrian by birth) as the *Anschluß* or 'incorporation' into the German Reich, that ushered in the darkest period of Austrian twentieth-century history.

With the Third Reich's defeat in World War Two, Austria was divided into occupied zones, just like Germany, between the victorious Allies. This lasted until 1955, when, under the guarantee of remaining militarily neutral, Austria was released into independence again. The new state bordered the Eastern Bloc in the east and northeast, and socialist Yugoslavia in the southeast, and thus had one of the longest stretches of the Iron Curtain surrounding its eastern half. On the one hand this brought a certain isolation from the West, with which the country was politically aligned, but on the other it gave Austria a 'middleman' role, as a crossroads between East and West.

When the Eastern Bloc collapsed, this suddenly became an advantageous position, and Austria benefited a great deal both economically and politically from the opening up of the east. Eventually integrated into the EU, it is a largely stable and prosperous member state, even though at times the return of the political far right to prominence and even government office has given the outside world some headaches.

Many dark sites in Austria, especially outside Vienna, have to do with its Third Reich Nazi legacy, but there are also more contemporary dark issues. One is global warming, which affects Austria's Alpine glaciers. The largest glacier, Pasterze, has shrunk to a fraction of its former size.

Ebensee ★★☆☆☆

Near Traunsee, east of Salzburg
Concentration camp, WW2, Underground tunnels

Dark Rating: 7 ☠

Of the many satellite camps of Austria's main concentration camp, Mauthausen (p156), the one at Ebensee is remarkable in that a dramatic relic can still be seen. The camp was completely dismantled after the war and a new village built at the site, so only a memorial cemetery marks the place now. However, the camp was for forced labourers working on the construction of a nearby underground tunnel system intended to become an arms-industry production facility similar to Mittelbau-Dora (p152).

The site was still unfinished when it was seized by the US Army in May 1945, but one nearly completed main tunnel can be visited. Inside is a small exhibition of historical photos and documents.

Above
Visitors are able to peek into unfinished tunnels of raw rock that branch off the main tunnel.

Hartheim

Outside Alkoven, near Linz, Upper Austria
Euthanasia centre, Nazi legacy

★★★★☆

Dark Rating: 8 ☠

Possibly the darkest element of the Third Reich after the Holocaust was the euthanasia programme code-named *Aktion T4* – 'Operation T4'. The name derives from the address Tiergartenstraße No. 4 in Berlin, which was the administrative headquarters of the programme. The terms are all euphemisms for the systematic murder of people with disabilities, who were deemed *lebensunwert*, 'unworthy of life', and a burden on society as 'useless eaters', in particular the mentally ill.

Once Hitler had signed the document authorizing doctors to grant such patients what he called *den Gnadentod*, 'mercy killing', six euthanasia centres were established. The one at Castle Hartheim in Austria became the deadliest: at least 30,000 names of patients killed here are known. The method employed for the killings was a precursor to that later used in the Holocaust (see p134–35): gassing by carbon monoxide, in specially installed gas chambers. Some of the personnel who committed these atrocities at Hartheim later moved on to oversee the industrial mass murder in the death camps.

It took a long time for these crimes to be properly commemorated, but Castle Hartheim has been a memorial since 2003. This includes an extensive exhibition, which also traces the roots of the ideology of eugenics that formed the basis of the euthanasia idea. This ideology of eugenics was by no means limited to Germany but also had proponents in, for example, the USA.

Above
Part of the memorial is the castle's basement, in the original rooms used in the murders.

OTHER T4 EUTHANASIA CENTRES

Six 'euthanasia' centres were set up in Nazi Germany. In addition to Hartheim these were:

- **Hadamar**, Hesse: here, in addition to an extensive exhibition, a wooden garage has been restored where the infamous grey buses arrived that were used to transport the victims to the killing centres. It is the only such structure surviving.
- **Bernburg**, Saxony-Anhalt: features the authentic gas chamber and gas ducts in the basement, making it an especially gruesome place.
- **Grafeneck**, Baden-Württemberg: a remote, rural location now used as a Samaritan care home. A new documentation centre about the 'euthanasia' programme has been added in recent years (German language only).
- **Pirna-Sonnenstein** in Saxony: this was long an almost forgotten site, but more commemoration efforts have been made since the 1990s. Some original rooms are still in situ and a documentation centre has been established.
- **Brandenburg/Havel**, in Brandenburg: this was the first of the six T4 centres; in 2012 a new documentation centre was established here, making this one of the best such memorials today.

Mauthausen

★★★★★

Near Linz, Upper Austria • Concentration camp, Forced labour

Dark Rating: 9 ☠

This was the only full-scale, autonomous Nazi concentration camp (p134–35) on Austrian soil during the Third Reich, although there were many satellite camps, some quite sizeable. Forced labour was carried out in the adjacent stone quarry (to produce building material for the Nazis' monumental architecture projects), and SS guards would often push inmates over the edge of the quarry's vertical cliff just to see them fall to their death. They cynically called it *Fallschirmspringerwand* ('parachute jump wall').

Exhausted inmates, laden with heavy rocks, often fell down the steep 186-step stairway to the bottom of the quarry; hence this became known as *Todeststiege* or 'death stairs'. There was a gas chamber at Mauthausen, although this was not a systematic 'extermination camp'. Yet of the 200,000 inmates who passed through this camp only about half survived. The camp was liberated by US troops on 5 May 1945, immediately before the end of the war, and was handed over to the Soviets, in whose occupation zone the site fell. It was given back to Austrian administration and a memorial was set up as early as 1949.

Several monuments were added over the years and a first exhibition opened in 1970. Since then, the site has undergone much modernization: a new visitor centre was built just outside the main gate in 2003,

Left
Prisoners forced to carry granite up the 186 'death stairs' at Mauthausen quarry.

Below
The main camp consisted of 32 wooden barracks surrounded by barbed wire and high stone walls.

and an all-new state-of-the-art main permanent exhibition inside the camp opened in 2013.

What sets Mauthausen apart from other such sites is that so many of its original structures have survived, having been built from the quarry's sturdy granite. Thus, the fortress-like outer wall and the imposing gate and watchtowers are more or less unchanged. Some original wooden barracks are still in place too. The reworked exhibitions are now fully bilingual, so international visitors are much better catered for than in the past.

Outside the camp itself and past the cluster of memorial monuments, you can also walk the path towards the top of the old quarry. You could even walk down the infamous 'death stairs' – and back up.

Zwentendorf

On the Danube, near Tulln • Disused nuclear power station

★★★★★

Dark Rating: 7 ☷

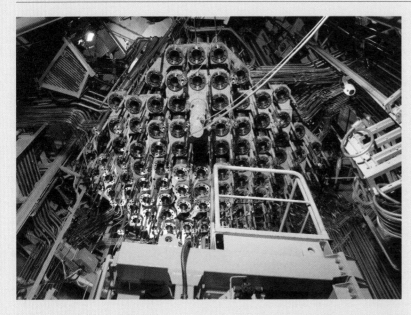

Left
Control-rod mechanism on the bottom of the reactor pressure vessel at the power plant.

The 1970s were an important decade for Austria: it gained more international recognition, the United Nations set up a European headquarters in Vienna, and a forward-looking government decided to catch up with the rest of Western Europe in the civilian use of nuclear power. The nuclear power plant (NPP) at Zwentendorf was commissioned in 1971, and construction began the following year. By the second half of the decade, however, the public's attitude to nuclear power had changed, and an anti-nuclear-power movement was gaining momentum. So just before the NPP was ready to start operating, it was decided to hold a referendum on Zwentendorf's future.

The margin of the vote on 5 November 1978 was very narrow, but to the government's surprise and embarrassment it came out as just over 50 per cent voting against nuclear power. So the country had a brand-new, ready-to-use NPP that it had to abandon. The fuel rods had already been delivered but not yet inserted into the reactor. This also means that the site never saw any radioactivity, so is sometimes dubbed 'the safest NPP on Earth'. This would prove an advantage for this unique industrial 'ruin', as it presented the possibility of using it as a safety training facility for NPP staff from elsewhere. It has been used as a film set too – all without any risk of radiation exposure.

There are guided tours for the general public on which you get the chance to enter parts of an NPP that are completely out of bounds to outsiders everywhere else, stand right beneath the control-rod inserting mechanism underneath the reactor, peek down into the reactor core from above, and step inside the steel containment vessel. Unfortunately, these tours run only once a week and are booked up almost the minute they become available, so you need luck and persistence to get a place. Otherwise the only way of getting inside is to pay for a specially arranged group tour (very expensive, unless you have a group of twenty people to share the cost).

Above
A 1970s electronics panel in the control room.

Vienna

On the Danube in eastern Austria • Cemeteries, Crypts, WW2   **Dark Rating: 9** ☣

Modern Austria is a federal state, but it is rather centralist. Its capital, Vienna, even though located far in the east, is very much the centre of gravity politically, economically and culturally; it is also a premier dark travel destination.

The city has a special relationship with the black-humoured and morbid, reflected in the famous line *Der Tod muss ein Wiener sein*, 'death must be a Viennese'. This even applies to the top echelons: the mortal remains of the Habsburg emperors and their family members can be visited in not one but three separate places. The bodies are lined up in grand sarcophagi in the Kaisergruft, the 'Imperial Crypt', while the hearts are stored separately in a small crypt called the Herzgrüftl in the Augustinian Church in the Hofburg palace. The intestines, meanwhile, are stored in urns within the catacombs of St Stephen's Cathedral.

The latter also includes an underground maze of tunnels and chambers filled with skeletal remains of bodies relocated here when the inner city's cemeteries were closed in the eighteenth century for sanitary reasons. Regular guided tours are conducted with plenty of morbid tongue-in-cheek remarks.

More bodies, some of them semi-mummified, can be seen in the crypt of St Michael's. Right on the eastern edge of the city there is the Friedhof der Namenlosen, or 'cemetery of the nameless'. Here, corpses washed up on the banks of the Danube were given a burial place. Since the identity of many of these was unknown it gave the cemetery its designation, even though not all graves are nameless. There is even one of a child marked as '*ertrunken von fremder Hand*' (murdered by drowning).

Those looking for famous graves may be searching for Mozart's, and

therefore head for St Marx cemetery. However, Mozart was buried in an unmarked mass grave whose location within the cemetery is not known. Therefore, the city set up a mock grave-cum-monument in the composer's honour in order to give tourists a place to which to make their pilgrimage.

Also in this cemetery some tombstones can be found that are pockmarked with bullet holes from the battle of Vienna in World War Two, when the Soviet Red Army took the city in April 1945.

Above
The crypt beneath the church of St Michael, where many mummified bodies and skeletal remains can be viewed.

Flak Towers

Three locations in Vienna • WW2 relics, Nazi legacy

★★☆☆☆

Dark Rating: 2 ☻

Three cities of the Third Reich – Berlin, Hamburg and Vienna – were equipped with flak towers, or *Flaktürme*, during World War Two. *Flak* is short for *Flugabwehrkanone*, 'anti-aircraft gun'. The towers came in pairs: the *Gefechtsturm*, or 'battle tower', with the guns at the top, and a smaller *Leitturm*, or 'guidance tower', with early forms of radar and distance measurement equipment to aid the guns' aim. As weapons these systems proved ineffective during Allied air raids, although the bunker towers did provide shelter for the civilian population.

As so often with such massive construction projects, forced labour by POWs and concentration camp inmates was used in the creation of these brutes of concrete.

After the war, the towers in Berlin were all destroyed. In Hamburg the *Leittürme* were demolished and the *Gefechtstürme* converted for other uses. In Vienna, the situation is mixed: one is used as a museum storage facility; one still contains a government relocation bunker; the *Leitturm* in Esterhazy Park has been turned into an aquarium and city zoo (called *Haus des Meeres*), and now also houses a small museum exhibition about these bunkers and their dark history. The remaining bunkers have no function today.

Visually most impressive is the pair in Augarten Park, which still stand abandoned and unused. However, they are free-standing, without any neighbouring buildings, giving the best impression of their overwhelming size. The larger *Gefechtsturm* in Augarten

is damaged at the top, apparently from a postwar explosion of ammunition that was left behind.

The inside of the bunkers is not normally accessible and the entrances are sealed. What the future may hold for these towers is uncertain. Opinions range from 'demolish them' (easier said than done) to 'turn them into proper memorials'. There are no signs informing passers-by about the nature of these huge grey monsters, so they often generate puzzled looks on the part of people who encounter them for the first time.

Right
The brooding concrete monster that is the giant *Gefechtsturm* in Vienna's Augarten Park.

Josephinum & Narrenturm

On the university campus at Alsergrund • Medical collections

★★★★★

Dark Rating: 6 ☣

These are two exhibitions associated with Vienna's Medical University, one of the world's oldest such institutions. The Josephinum was founded in 1785 during the reign of the 'enlightened' emperor Joseph II, and named after him. It consists primarily of a collection of anatomical wax models, inspired by those he had seen in Italy. These were initially intended for teaching medicine, although the collection was also accessible to the general public from early on.

The models, some whole bodies, others body parts, illustrate various functions and also diseases or complications, for example during childbirth. In fact, the obstetric section is a key component of the collection. To the layperson, many of these models appear gruesome, although they are also educational. For the more medically minded visitor, they are marvels – medical works of art. (After a long period of refurbishment, the exhibition reopened in September 2022.)

The nearby Narrenturm was originally built as a lunatic asylum (*Narr* means 'fool' or 'idiot'), also during the reign of Joseph II. It was intended to reform the treatment of the mentally ill, though from a contemporary perspective it was still a harsh regime. Inside, 28 cells branch off the circular corridors on each floor.

From 1866, it ceased its original function and first became lodging space for nurses. Since the early 1970s, it has housed the Medical University's pathological 'study collection', and part of it is on public display today. The main permanent exhibition features various specimens of a wide range of diseases and deformities, some in the form of skeletons, others floating in jars of formaldehyde. One especially touching exhibit is the 'Devil of Korneuburg', a rather angelic-looking anencephalic (meaning born 'without a brain', or rather with a severely underdeveloped brain and open skull). The exhibition has the subtitle: *Faszination und Ekel*, 'fascination and repulsion', and that sums it up rather well.

Above left
The Narrenturm is a fortress-like five-storey tower now housing medical collections.

Above right
A wax anatomical model on display at the Josephinum.

OTHER MEDICAL EXHIBITIONS

There are numerous medical museums around the world, and many medical universities and/or hospital complexes have exhibitions open to the public. There are too many to list in full, but here is a selection of noteworthy examples:

- **Palazzo Poggi**, Bologna, Italy
- **Charité Museum of Medical History**, Berlin, Germany
- **Mütter Museum** (p36), Philadelphia, USA
- **Kunstkamera**, St Petersburg, Russia
- **Paul Stradins Museum of the History of Medicine**, Riga, Latvia
- **Meguro Parasitological Museum**, Tokyo, Japan

Museum of Military History

In the former Arsenal, 3rd district • WW1, WW2, Nazi era, Cold War

★★★★★

Dark Rating: 5 ☠

Left
The museum is housed in a grand Byzantine-style building that was once part of the Vienna Arsenal.

Below
The open-top car in which Franz Ferdinand was assassinated – you can see a bullet hole to the rear next to the back seat.

This is one of the world's oldest military museums, first opened in 1856. Originally a celebration of imperial military glory, this institution has evolved over time and now champions the thematic slogan *Kriege gehören ins Museum* – 'wars belong in museums' – to underscore its contemporary peace-promoting approach.

While the museum also covers older history, the most significant parts in dark terms begin with the World War One section. This was completely overhauled and modernized for the centenary of the outbreak of the Great War and is now one of the best exhibitions on the subject worldwide.

A star exhibit is the car in which Archduke Franz Ferdinand was assassinated in Sarajevo (p194–95) in 1914, which became the 'starting gun' for the war. Not only can you see the bullet hole in the car, but also the Archduke's bloodied uniform is on display. The main part of this section looks at all aspects of the slaughter that was World War One, including medical and

propaganda aspects. Among the artefacts, a really big brute stands out: a gigantic Austrian-built 38-cm (15-in) howitzer weighing 80 tons.

The more modern sections deal with the interwar years, including the display of the bloodstained settee on which Chancellor Engelbert Dollfuss died in the 1934 assassination. The Nazi period is represented by some remarkable

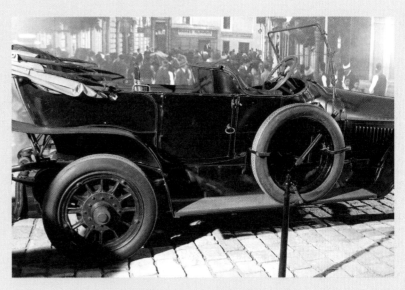

artefacts too, and is immediately and seamlessly followed by the postwar period and the Allied occupation of Austria. A relatively new exhibition focuses specifically on the years from 1955 to the end of the Cold War.

Funeral Museum & Central Cemetery

★★★★☆

Southeastern edge of Vienna · Funeral culture, Cemetery

Dark Rating: 4 ☠

Founded in 1967, Vienna's Bestattungsmuseum was the first of its kind in the world. Much altered and more recently relocated to Vienna's largest cemetery, it is a jewel in Vienna's morbid crown. The exhibition explores the very Viennese notion of the *schöne Leich* – literally, 'beautiful corpse', but figuratively referring to the most elaborate, even pompous, funeral ceremonies that were once an important part of the upper class showing off, even in death.

Among the exhibits is a 'recyclable' coffin design, from the period of 'reformer' Emperor Joseph II, with a bottom hatch for dropping the corpse into the grave, after which the coffin could be reused. Despite the practical merits, the idea did not catch on. Another exhibit is a 'heart dagger', a stiletto blade intended for making sure the deceased was really dead – a procedure you could request in your will in Austria. It stems from a time when there was much fear of being buried alive.

The setting of the museum is ideal for combining it with an exploration of one of the world's largest cemeteries, the Zentralfriedhof, or 'Central Cemetery' – so called not for its central location in the city (it is anything but) but rather because it 'centralized' funerals, whereas the inner city before had countless small cemeteries (which were closed for health reasons).

Among the 300,000 graves today are many prominent names, from classical composers to Falco, Austria's biggest pop-music export. The most poignant area is the western section with the old Jewish part, which is mostly overgrown and deserted, a silent testimony to the lasting legacy of the Holocaust.

Above
The so-called economy coffin, introduced in 1785 by Emperor Joseph II.

Top
The museum gives insights into the funeral and cemetery culture of the past and present.

Poland

This country has been kicked about by its bigger, more powerful neighbours to the east and west for centuries. In 1939 it became the first victim of Nazi German aggression, which quickly turned into World War Two. At the same time, the Molotov–Ribbentrop Pact, aka the Hitler–Stalin Pact, allowed the Soviets to swallow up parts of eastern Poland, until the Nazis also invaded the USSR in 1941.

During the Third Reich's occupation of Poland, it committed many of its worst crimes here, in particular the 'Final Solution' part of the Holocaust (see p134–35). After World War Two, Poland was left in the lurch by its Western Allies when they allowed Stalin to keep Poland in the Soviet sphere of influence. Poland was communist and a member of the Warsaw Pact throughout the Cold War era. It was also in Poland, however, that communist rule was first challenged to such a degree that cracks appeared in the regime's grip on power.

Thanks in particular to the efforts of the independent trade union network Solidarność, 'solidarity', in the 1980s, communist rule was overcome by the end of the decade and a Solidarność member eventually became president. In fact, the struggle against communism in Poland was an inspiration for similar movements in other socialist countries, and is hence seen as the beginning of the end of that era and the Cold War period.

Westerplatte

North of the harbour of Gdańsk • WW2

★★★☆☆

Dark Rating: 4 ☠

In the interwar years, the region of East Prussia was a German enclave within Poland along a stretch of Baltic coast. The city of Gdańsk and the area around it were just west of that region. Then known by its German name, Danzig, it was given special status as a 'Free City' by the League of Nations, and Poland was granted access to the sea via the Vistula River, which has its estuary here. Hence there were also Polish institutions, including a military transit depot at the promontory known as Westerplatte.

When on 1 September 1939 Nazi Germany launched its attack on Poland (the first military action of World War Two), the very first shots were fired at Westerplatte, namely by the German battleship *Schleswig-Holstein*, which began shelling the Polish garrison. This made the location so historically significant that several memorials were later erected here. The biggest of them is the 25m-tall (82ft) stone monument from the socialist era that towers over the peninsula. In addition, there are various smaller ones, as well as remnants of fortifications from the period before World War Two.

Housed in one of the preserved bunkers is a small museum about the attack on Westerplatte. Nearby, a heavily damaged ruin of one of the concrete buildings shelled in the attack has been made accessible by walkways. All around, information panels provide plenty of historical background. At the time of writing, proposals were on the table for further commodification, which is seen as controversial by some. It remains to be seen what will develop.

Above
Visitors can access one of the heavily shelled concrete buildings and view the damage up close.

European Solidarity Centre

★★★★★

Old shipyards in Gdańsk • Communism, Repression, Resistance

Dark Rating: 3 ☠️

This is the latest of a string of institutions commemorating the momentous years of the Solidarność movement, its repression and how resistance and protest eventually ended the communist era in Poland. The current exhibition is housed in a new purpose-built edifice that vaguely resembles a ship under construction, clad in plates of rusty steel. The location is significant, being right by the main gates to the former Gdańsk shipyards, where the movement began.

On the square in front of the gates stands a landmark monument that commemorates earlier protests by shipyard workers. The main exhibition inside the Centre is comprehensive and modern, featuring plenty of artefacts and some impressive life-size, walk-through dioramas. Just a few steps from the main museum is the old Sala BHP building, where on 31 August 1980 the Polish government met the Interfactory Strike Committee's '21 demands' and signed an agreement

leading to the creation of Solidarność. Today, there is another exhibition inside, less elaborate than the big neighbouring one, but with the added bonus of place authenticity.

Behind this building, some parts of the formerly off-limits shipyard premises have been opened up to the public.

Above
The rusty steel building of the museum with the Monument to the Fallen Shipyard Workers of 1970 in the foreground and the historic Gate Number 2 of the shipyard to the right.

Below
One life-size exhibit shows an original police truck and broken-down gates.

Museum of the Second World War

★★★★★

Northeast of the Old Town of Gdańsk • WW2, Atrocities, Holocaust

Dark Rating: 8 ☠

This large state-of-the-art museum, housed in a striking piece of modern architecture, is the newest addition to Gdańsk's dark attractions portfolio, and has to be regarded as one of the most significant war museums in Europe. It has, however, been in the media a fair bit in the context of the politicization of the commemoration of World War Two. When the museum opened in 2017, Polish nationalists apparently criticized the main exhibition for not being 'patriotic' enough.

The original director was sacked and replaced by someone who altered the narrative by adding more emphasis on 'Polish heroes'. The original finale (which reflected on conflicts since World War Two, up to the present day) was removed and a more glorifying projection provided instead. While these changes have attracted some criticism, it has to be stressed that most of the exhibition's content remains unchanged – and is excellent. There is understandably a focus on the war within Poland and how Polish people were affected by it, so there is comparatively less on other theatres of World War Two, such as the Pacific and Africa (although they are not omitted altogether).

The museum does not shy away from exposing the darkest aspects of the realities of war, such as the aerial bombing of civilian targets, mistreatment of POWs, massacres and the Holocaust. Instances of Poles being not just victims but also perpetrators are not swept under the rug, but are given due consideration, most notably the Jedwabne pogrom. In between the traditional text-and-photo panels, smaller artefacts and countless interactive screens, there are some walk-through dioramas: for example, a pre-war Polish street and a street scene after the ravages of war. Those seeking displays of big military hardware may be disappointed; this museum keeps such artefacts to a minimum and instead concentrates on the human aspects of the war – something about which many other war museums are less eloquent.

Above
A German propaganda poster from 1939 showing the 'Polish Corridor' and the 'Free City of Danzig'.

Left
A recreated scene complete with a real Soviet tank with the word 'Stalin' painted on its side.

Wolfsschanze

Masurian region of northern Poland • Nazi legacy, WW2

★★★☆☆

Dark Rating: 7 ☠

Also known as 'Wolf's Lair' in English (and *Wilczy Szaniec* in Polish), this was Adolf Hitler's main headquarters in the East: a complex of massive bunkers where the Nazi top brass basically dug in as the war progressed. The sheer size of the concrete blocks in which the inner circle of the Nazi leadership sought refuge is testament to their growing fear of attack. Not only was the physical protection through concrete extreme, but also security at this site was generally the highest possible.

Yet it was right here that one assassination attempt on Hitler got the closest to succeeding. On 20 July 1944 Claus Schenk von Stauffenberg, an army officer who had access to briefings with Hitler, had plotted with some other high-ranking members of the military to kill the Führer in order to save Germany from total annihilation by the Allies.

Stauffenberg managed to place a bomb hidden in a briefcase near Hitler, but through unfortunate circumstances it was not close enough to him when it went off. While it killed several people who were in the room, Hitler himself survived with only minor injuries. In the wake of the failed plot, a campaign of revenge caused additional terror in Germany and the plotters were rounded up and executed (see p145).

The Wolfsschanze bunkers were blown up by the Nazis as they retreated from the advancing Red Army later in 1944, but they proved too massive to be destroyed completely. Today, these more or less broken monsters of concrete still stand as silent relics.

There is a memorial monument to Stauffenberg too, and a small exhibition room.

Nearby, yet more Nazi-era bunkers can be found that were not blown up, especially at a site called Mauerwald, or Mamerki in Polish, a few miles northeast.

Above
Hitler spent more than 800 days at the Wolfsschanze HQ, over a period of three and a half years.

Warsaw

★★★★☆

Centre of eastern Poland
WW2, Holocaust, Atrocities, Resistance, Communism

Dark Rating: 7 ☠

Poland's capital suffered more than others in World War Two: first came air raids by Nazi Germany, then brutal repression during the city's occupation. The Jewish population was targeted in particular, and in Warsaw the largest of the Jewish ghettos enforced by the Nazis was established. Life inside it was horrendous, but worse was to come when the ghetto was 'liquidated' and deportations, mostly to the death camp of Treblinka (p173), began.

In April 1943 this led to the Ghetto Uprising, which was brutally crushed by mid-May, with some 13,000 Jews shot dead or burned alive as the Nazis torched the ghetto and then razed it to the ground. In the summer of 1944 a general uprising ended in even more destruction. Hopes that the Soviet Red Army, which had by then reached parts of Warsaw on the other side of the river, would intervene to help the inhabitants in their struggle against the Nazis proved wrong. Initially the uprising went well, but the unhindered retaliation of the Nazis was relentless and ended with the razing of about half of all buildings that were still standing and the killing of around 200,000 Poles.

When the Nazis finally had to retreat, about 85 per cent of Warsaw lay in ruins. Rebuilding after the war included many quick-to-construct residential blocks, also over the site of the ghetto, but the Old Town kernel was reconstructed faithfully in the 1950s. Showpiece communist architecture was added, especially along the grand Marszałkowska Boulevard. The most iconic building from communist times is the love-it-or-hate-it Palace of Science and Culture, a typical Stalinist skyscraper and a 'gift' from the Soviet Union. It is still a major landmark and tours are available.

The dark days of World War Two are commemorated at a number of sites, including the basement of the former Pawiak prison and the Szucha Gestapo prison. The area of the former Jewish ghetto has a series of memorials, in particular the central monument, erected in 1948 in front of the more recent Jewish museum (see p236).

The city's largest monument is the Warsaw Uprising Monument just outside the Old Town. Next to it is a small Insurgents Museum. Another more recent large memorial is the dramatic Monument to the Fallen and Murdered in the East. Smaller in scale but much adored is the Little Insurgent statue of a child soldier that stands by the Old Town ramparts. The Katyń Museum in the old Citadel north of the Old Town commemorates the great tragedy of 1940 when the Soviets massacred a large part of the Polish military officer class and intelligentsia in the woods near Smolensk.

The socialist era is commemorated in the Life under Communism Museum. Of historical importance is also the Pałac Namiestnikowski, now the presidential palace, where the Warsaw Pact was signed in 1955 and where the crucial Round Table Talks between the government and Solidarność were held in 1989. Nearby is Piłsudski Square, where there is a soldier-guarded eternal flame and a number of monuments, including one commemorating the 2010 Smolensk plane crash in which then president Lech Kaczyński was killed.

Left
Photo from 1942 shows the wooden footbridge built by the Nazis over Chłodna Street, dividing the Warsaw Ghetto. The bridge allowed ghetto inhabitants to cross without setting foot on the 'Aryan' road.

Warsaw Uprising Museum

West of Towarowa Boulevard • WW2, Resistance, Atrocities

★★★★★

Dark Rating: 6 ☠

Regarded as one of the best museums in Poland, this covers the uprising in minute detail and its presentation is state of the art. Among the artefacts are some impressively large ones, such as a replica of a B-24 plane with RAF markings that hangs in the central hall. Another life-size exhibit is a reconstruction of a stretch of sewers that you can walk through – the Polish resistance fighters used Warsaw's sewers to move around below street level, out of the Nazis' firing line.

Thankfully, this sewer reconstruction does not come with an olfactory element, although an audio installation recreates the sound of running water. The museum is housed in a former power station and parts of the boilers can still be seen, adding an industrial heritage appeal. There is also a small open-air exhibition with a mock-up of a Kubuś, an improvised armoured vehicle used by the insurgents in the uprising.

Above
The museum has thousands of artefacts on display, including submachine guns and rifles from the 1944 Warsaw Uprising.

Right
Portrait of Władysław Szpilman on display in the museum, the Polish pianist and composer widely known from the film *The Pianist*.

Kraków

★★★★☆

Centre of the south of Poland · Holocaust, WW2, Communism

Dark Rating: 5 💀

Sometimes called Poland's 'secret capital', this city is a popular gem. Since it was chosen by the Nazis in World War Two as their administrative centre for the so-called General Government, a euphemism for the German-occupied central Polish territories, the city suffered far less destruction than Warsaw or Gdańsk. But that does not mean the populace escaped Nazi brutality. As in other cities, a Jewish ghetto was established, and Kraków had its own concentration camp on the outskirts of the city at Płaszów. The latter is associated with the blockbuster Hollywood movie *Schindler's List*, directed by Steven Spielberg. Another association of Kraków with the film industry is the fact that the famous Polish director Roman Polanski was born here and actually survived the Kraków ghetto as a small boy.

As a dark travel destination today, Kraków features various sites of its own, but it also serves as the main base for tours to Auschwitz (see p170–71). Within Kraków, the old Jewish quarter of Kazimierz is worth visiting. Also in this district is the Galicia Jewish Museum, which is more a photo exhibition about the suffering of the Jewish people and all the places that have been lost.

Further south, across the river in Podgórze, remnants of the Jewish ghetto can be found, in particular a stretch of the original old ghetto wall. Nearby is the Apteka pod Orłem museum, which is about the ghetto, and in the square in front a peculiar monument consisting of rows of steel chairs, symbolizing the Nazis' practice of throwing furniture out of the windows when they raided Jewish houses and took the occupants away.

Further east across the railway line, the old Oskar Schindler Enamel Factory, familiar from the movie, has been converted into a museum too. Of the Płaszów concentration camp almost nothing remains. A notable exception is the surviving 'Grey House' (not open to the public), which was where camp commandant Amon Göth had his office and from where he personally shot at inmates of the camp, as depicted in *Schindler's List*. His residence is nearby, but is unmarked and privately owned, and hence inaccessible too. Within the former camp's grounds only a few monuments can be found, including a large stone one from the communist era.

The adjacent Liban quarry, now overgrown and derelict, was used by Steven Spielberg as a film set for the camp, and some props remained for a long time, blurring the authentic with the fictional.

The period after World War Two and the socialist era are covered by the Communism Tours on offer in Kraków, which use vintage vehicles and primarily head to the suburb of Nowa Huta in the east of the city, next to the old giant steelworks, which was also a hotbed of the Solidarność movement. Also in Nowa Huta, two Cold War-era underground nuclear shelters can be visited.

Above
The desk at which Oskar Schindler's original list was compiled. This office reconstruction is an exhibit in the museum at the old Schindler Enamel Factory.

Left
A 12m-long (40ft) fragment of the old ghetto wall at Lwowska Street.

Auschwitz

Between Katowice and Kraków • Holocaust

★★★★★

Dark Rating: 10 ☠

Nothing stands for the horrors of the Holocaust as much as Auschwitz. It was the biggest, deadliest and most notorious of all the concentration camps the Nazis established during the Third Reich. What also sets it apart from (almost) all other camps is the fact that it was both a concentration camp and a death camp (see p134–35). In the former function it housed political prisoners and other 'undesirables' who had to do forced labour. But increasingly Auschwitz became the largest place to which Jews were deported, mostly to be murdered.

It was at Auschwitz that the systematic mass murder became the most 'industrialized'. Large gas chambers were built, alongside specially designed high-capacity crematoria. The poison gas used at Auschwitz was Zyklon B, originally produced as a pesticide. SS men would pour the deadly crystals down shafts in the gas chambers and a reaction with air released poison gas (the gas chambers may have been disguised as shower rooms, but the gas did not seep through over-head showerheads, as is erroneously believed by many).

After the hundreds of victims had died an agonizing death, *Sonderkommandos*, specially selected groups of inmates, had the gruesome task of emptying the gas chambers of the contorted mass of bodies, cleaning the chambers and burning the corpses. *Sonderkommandos* usually lasted only a few months before being gassed themselves. As deportations escalated and more and more trains full of victims arrived, these were unloaded at a special ramp. Here, the SS officers and doctors would perform the 'selection', i.e. decide who was useful and fit for forced labour, while the rest were sent straight to the gas chambers. It is estimated that the total death toll at Auschwitz was well over a million, the vast majority of them Jewish.

Even though the systematic killing had been brought to the attention of the Allies,

Auschwitz continued to operate until January 1945, when it was 'evacuated' by the SS before the Soviet Red Army arrived to liberate the camp.

The first memorial was set up at the site in 1947. Since then it has evolved considerably and become one of the best-known and most visited memorials on Earth. Visiting Auschwitz has also been called 'the epitome of dark tourism'. A large proportion of visitors come on organized trips, many of them school classes or study groups, but day tours to Auschwitz are also the top tourist activity offered in Kraków (p169).

Visitor numbers have exceeded two million annually in recent years. This means that, in high season, crowd-control measures have become necessary and group tours with a guide compulsory; tickets have to be prearranged online. Off-season you can roam freely and free of charge, but guided tours incur fees. You need plenty of time here, a minimum of half a day, better a whole day or even two to see everything. The short tours on offer provide at best a limited introduction.

Auschwitz is actually three sites. The original *Stammlager* of Auschwitz I was a former barracks that was converted into a prison camp. It is here that you find that infamous gate with

Opposite, top
The Auschwitz-Birkenau State Museum's collection includes 110,000 pairs of shoes that belonged to victims of the camp.

Opposite, bottom
The iconic gatehouse of Auschwitz II-Birkenau, where the railway line terminated.

the sign reading *Arbeit macht frei* ('work sets you free'). This is also where the main parts of the museum exhibition are, as well as country-specific memorial exhibitions housed in some of the brick barracks.

The second and much larger site is Auschwitz II-Birkenau, a few miles to the northwest of the *Stammlager*. It was at Birkenau that the endless rows of wooden barracks, the gas chambers and the crematoria were located. The 'selection ramp', initially just outside the camp, was later moved into the camp grounds when railway sidings were built beyond the main gate. This sprawling complex is characterized by a set of brick buildings southwest of the main gatehouse and a row of wooden barracks to the north. The electrified barbed-wire fence around the compound and the wooden watchtowers all add to a profoundly eerie atmosphere. At the back are the ruins of the gas chambers and crematoria, blown up by the Nazis as they abandoned the camp. Additional exhibitions have also been set up in some of the Birkenau buildings.

In contrast, the third site, Auschwitz III-Monowitz, remains largely uncommodified. This was to the east of the town now known under its Polish name, Oświęcim, at a huge chemical industrial complex where the Nazis produced synthetic fuels. The industrial plant is still there and in use, hence off limits to visitors. Only a small monument nearby acknowledges Auschwitz III.

Above
The main gate of Auschwitz I. The infamous inscription above it is now a replica, since the original was stolen in 2009.

Below
Hungarian Jews from the Tét Ghetto undergoing selection on arrival at the ramp of Auschwitz-Birkenau in 1944.

Majdanek

Southeastern edge of Lublin • Holocaust

★★★★☆

Dark Rating: 10 ☠

Right
The crematoria building. Owing to the hasty evacuation of the camp, Majdanek is now the best-preserved such site of them all.

Below
Rows of wooden barracks and watchtowers remain in much the same condition as they were in 1944.

This former concentration camp in southeastern Poland is less well known than Auschwitz but bears similarities to it. Although smaller than Auschwitz, Majdanek is generally assumed to have had an equivalent dual function, namely that of regular concentration camp on the one hand, and special extermination camp on the other (see p170–71 and p134–35). It also started out as a place of incarceration for political prisoners, POWs and Jews. It was primarily a labour camp, but during Operation Reinhard it became the site of systematic mass killings as well.

The poison gas Zyklon B was used here, as it was at Auschwitz. Majdanek was the first camp to be liberated by the Allies, more precisely the Red Army, and that as early as in the summer of 1944. Moreover, the SS command evacuated the camp hastily and without the systematic destruction of incriminating evidence that was practised elsewhere. Thus the camp fell into Soviet hands more or less intact. It was the first real insight the Allies, and the world at large, gained into the true nature of these camps and the Nazis' crimes. The total death toll was initially overestimated, and at the Nuremberg Trials was claimed to be many hundreds of thousands. A more conservative consensus now places the number of victims at Majdanek at around 80,000.

The site was turned into a memorial before World War Two was completely over. Two rows of wooden barracks can be seen, plus a row of workshop barracks. The crematorium and gas chambers are fully intact, and there is even a stack of Zyklon B gas canisters on display. In one of the barracks, victims' shoes have been amassed in wire-mesh cages, providing further evidence of the scale of death at this camp.

A gigantic concrete monument in typical oversized socialist style stands closer to the main road. Next to this is the site's museum building. Majdanek is not quite as vast a site as Auschwitz, and the museum is not as polished or modern as at some camp memorials in Germany, but it is still one of the most significant for its intactness and authenticity. It also sees only a fraction of the visitor numbers that Auschwitz has to cope with.

Treblinka

Northeast of Warsaw • Holocaust

★★☆☆☆

Dark Rating: 9 ☠

This was one of the three purpose-built Operation Reinhard death camps (see p134–35), a centre for the industrialized mass murder of Jews (around 2000 Roma were murdered here too, but 99 per cent of the victims were Jewish). It was a relatively small camp; there were no long rows of wooden barracks to house inmates, because almost all the victims were immediately 'processed' for gassing on arrival.

At the ramp, men and women and children were separated. On the pretext of having to take a shower before being deported onwards, they had to undress and move along a bent, fenced pathway called the *Schlauch*, or 'hose', that led straight to the gas chambers. Here they were killed by carbon monoxide, which took a torturous 20–25 minutes for each 'batch' of victims. Ten gas chambers were installed, 'processing' up to 5000 people at the same time. At peak times, up to 17,000 people were murdered in a single day.

All of this was overseen by just two dozen SS men assisted by approximately 120 Trawniki guards

(mostly Ukrainians), plus so-called *Sonderkommandos*, or 'special commandos', prisoners who had the grisly task of emptying the gas chambers and burying the corpses in mass graves.

Operations started in July 1942 and finished in October 1943. In that time, around 800,000 victims were gassed. This makes Treblinka the most deadly spot on Earth – more victims died at Auschwitz in absolute numbers, but over a much longer span of time. In relative terms, measured against the time it was in operation as a place of industrial mass murder, Treblinka holds a terrible record.

The numbers are so inconceivable that they feel somewhat abstract. But one individual case has become well known for its touching humanity: that of Janusz Korczak, a pedagogue and author of children's books who had run a Jewish orphanage in Warsaw. When the Nazis came to round up the orphans, Korczak was offered freedom (because of his prominent name), but he refused and went with 'his' children into the gas

chambers and stayed with them to the bitter end. A special memorial stone is dedicated to him at the site.

As operations were nearing completion, there was a revolt at Treblinka on 2 August 1943, when the *Sonderkommando* inmates managed to steal some weapons from the SS, set buildings on fire and tried to escape in the ensuing chaos. Many were machine-gunned down, but several dozen made it to freedom and survived.

It is thanks to these survivors that the story of Treblinka could be told. No traces were left at the site itself. After operations ended, the mass graves were exhumed and the corpses burned on pyres, all buildings were demolished and the whole site ploughed over and replaced with a make-believe 'farm', with one of the former guards acting as farmer to complete the cover-up.

Today's memorial (created in the 1960s) is a little abstract but still very moving. An approach path leads past a symbolic rendition of the railway ramp with sleepers made of concrete. The main memorial consists of one large stone monument and a field of broken stones around it, many bearing the names of places where the victims had come from. Rectangular patches of black tar symbolize the pyres. A few information panels provide the essential historical context. There is a small museum at the site, but only a few artefacts are on display. Some original relics of the nearby labour camp Treblinka I (the death camp was officially Treblinka II) and its quarry can still be seen today.

Above
The camp was destroyed by the Nazis, and today the site is covered with a field of memorial stones.

Sobibór

★★★☆☆

Eastern Poland, near the border with Ukraine • Holocaust

Dark Rating: 8 ☠

As another of the three Operation Reinhard death camps (see p134–35), Sobibór operated in much the same way as Treblinka (see p173). In total, around 200,000 victims were gassed here between May 1942 and October 1943. The closing of the camp followed a revolt, led by a Soviet POW officer, which culminated in the mass escape of some 300 prisoners. Many were shot or recaptured and executed, but some 50–60 got away and survived the war. Among them was Thomas Blatt, one of the key campaigners for commemoration and justice after the war (see also p17).

Awareness of Sobibór was also raised by a couple of films that were made about the revolt and escape. As a memorial site, however, Sobibór had long been neglected, and its remote location meant that it was visited only by a few dedicated pilgrims. All that could be seen there was a couple of memorial stones and a large circular monument containing a mound of ashes. In recent years the site has undergone substantial changes, archaeological investigations were undertaken and a new museum constructed. Work was completed

and the site again opened to the public in October 2020.

Top
The old station sign by the railway sidings at Sobibór.

Above
The large circular enclosure contains ashes and crushed bones of the victims, collected at the site.

Bełżec

Southeastern corner of Poland • Holocaust

★★★★☆

Dark Rating: 9 ☠

This was the first of the three Operation Reinhard Nazi death camps (p134–35) to start operating, in March 1942, and the first to finish its gruesome task, in July 1943. Like Sobibór and Treblinka, it was an industrial killing factory where victims, again mostly Jews, were systematically murdered in gas chambers. Here, too, all traces of the operations were covered up afterwards. The corpses were burned on pyres fashioned from railway tracks and the whole site was ploughed over and disguised as a farm.

The total death toll at Bełżec is second only to Treblinka and Auschwitz: estimates range from 430,000 to over 600,000. Unlike at the other two Operation Reinhard camps, there were no revolts here

and hardly any survivors (only two are known and only one testified after the war). In that sense, Bełżec was the most 'efficient' of these killing centres: nearly 100 per cent. It was long almost forgotten, marked only by a poorly maintained, small memorial. At the end of the Cold War, when Western visitors could reach the site, a new memorialization concept was devised. The present memorial and modern museum opened in 2004.

The museum is small but illuminating. It is, however, the main monumental memorial design that is the most striking thing here. The camp perimeter on a shallow slope has a concrete ring around it into which are set the names of the places victims had come from. The sloping field inside is filled with

crushed blocks of cinder. From the entrance, a path is carved into the slope, flanked by rusty metal bits poking out like symbolic fences.

As you walk in, the sides rise until they are some 6m (20ft) high, before ending at a polished marble wall. This design emulates the *Schlauch* into the gas chambers (see Treblinka, p173), and the effect is psychologically oppressive – really a very ingenious design that is fitting for such an extremely dark site.

Below
The cinder field fills the perimeter of the former camp, and the path/corridor running through the middle symbolizes the *Schlauch* approach to the gas chambers.

Czech Republic

This country was the northwestern half of the Czechoslovak Socialist Republic (CSSR), which after the fall of communism split in two (Slovakia being the other half – see p178), basically doing the opposite of what Germany did (p128). Just as in Germany, the end of communism in the CSSR was brought about peacefully, in a 'Velvet Revolution'. But an earlier attempt at reforms, the 'Prague Spring', ended in a brutal crushing by Soviet and Warsaw Pact troops in 1968.

An even darker period was the German annexation and occupation from before World War Two, beginning with the takeover of the Sudetenland, which was sanctioned by France and Britain in the Munich Agreement of 1938, hailed as 'peace for our time' by the then British prime minister Neville Chamberlain. That did not stop the war, and the period of German repression was particularly bitter for the Czechs.

Today, the Czech Republic is peaceful and welcoming to visitors, who flock there in droves, in particular to the capital, Prague. In dark terms the city offers several attractions, including a Museum of Communism, a KGB Museum and a nuclear bunker that can be visited on guided tours. The world-famous Jewish quarter also has its tragic elements. One of the most notable dark sites outside Prague is the Vojna Memorial, a well-preserved former forced labour camp mainly for political prisoners from the early communist era.

Lidice

Northwest of Prague • Massacre, WW2

Dark Rating: 7 ☠

Left
Memorial to the Children Victims of the War, a bronze sculpture commemorating the 82 children of Lidice gassed at Chełmno in 1942.

On 27 May 1942 Czech resistance fighters, with help from British intelligence, assassinated Reinhard Heydrich in Operation Anthropoid. Heydrich was the so-called Deputy Reich Protector of Bohemia and Moravia, and head of the RSHA (*Reichssicherheitshauptamt*, 'Reich state security office', which included the feared Gestapo). He was the highest-ranking Nazi ever to be successfully targeted in such a way. But the price the Czechs had to pay for this was high. In their wrath, the Nazis launched a ruthless campaign of arrests and retaliation, and the worst affected was the village of Lidice.

After some rather tenuous connections with the assassination were made, the Nazis descended on Lidice, assembled all the men living there and executed them. The women and children, meanwhile, had been herded into a school building. The women were then sent to the concentration camp at Ravensbrück (p143) as 'political prisoners', and most of the children were deported to the death camp at Chełmno for gassing, but a handful of very young ones were instead handed to Nazi families for 'adoption' and 'Germanization'. The village was razed to the ground.

After the war, a new village was built next to the vanished old one, and a memorial complex was established that includes some excavated foundations of old village buildings, a small museum and various monuments. Of these, the children's monument is perhaps the most touching.

Sedlec Ossuary

★★★★☆

Kutná Hora, east of Prague • Skeletal remains on display

Dark Rating: 5 ☠

Left
The huge chandelier is allegedly made from all the bones in the human body.

This is possibly the world's most celebrated bone chapel, or 'ossuary'. It goes back to a Cistercian monastery, where some soil from the Holy Land was scattered on a cemetery in the thirteenth century. As a result, burials in this graveyard became very popular and eventually it was overcrowded. Consequently, the skeletal remains of some 30,000 to 40,000 bodies were dug up and transferred to the crypt of a new chapel, where in 1870 they were arranged by a local artist in the sculptural and decorative way we see today.

There are strings of skulls throwing atmospheric shadows on to the ceiling, a bone chandelier, a 'bone bird' with spread wings, and a coat of arms made from bones within which a little bird made from bones seems to be picking at a skull's eye socket. In the central arrangements, little cherubs contrast with the skulls and bones, lightening the macabre atmosphere.

OTHER NOTABLE OSSUARIES

There are many more such places, also known as 'charnel houses', including others in the Czech Republic; Italy has several, as do neighbouring countries, but they can also be found outside Europe. Here are just a few examples worth visiting:

- **Capela dos Ossos**, Évora, Portugal
- **The Skull Chapel, St Bartholomew's Church**, Lower Silesia, Poland
- **San Bernardino alle Ossa**, Milan, Italy
- **Santa Maria della Concezione dei Cappuccini**, Rome, Italy

- **Capuchin Catacombs**, Palermo, Sicily, where you can also see some remarkable mummies
- **Eggenburg Charnel**, Eggenburg, Austria
- **Beinhaus**, Hallstatt, Austria, with its painted skulls
- **St Leonard's Church**, Hythe, England
- **Monastery of San Francisco**, Lima, Peru

Slovakia

The other, eastern half of the former CSSR is off most tourists' radar, but deserves to be better known. It has plenty to offer in terms of dark places. There are countless memorials all over the country relating to the dark times when Slovakia was a de facto protectorate of Nazi Germany during World War Two, and in particular to the Slovak National Uprising (SNP) against Nazi rule in 1944 (see below), as well as to the victims of the subsequent Nazi reprisals, for example at Nemecká and Kalište.

The communist era also left its relics; for instance, in the form of the grand Slavín monument in the capital, Bratislava. Traces of the Iron Curtain can be seen right on the edge of Bratislava by the border with Austria. The capital also offers some 'urban exploration' opportunities and a few superb examples of socialist-era architecture, such as the iconic Most SNP, a bridge across the Danube River that is topped by a flying saucer-like disc containing a restaurant and bar.

Múzeum SNP

★★★☆☆

Banská Bystrica, central Slovakia • WW2, Resistance, Atrocities

Dark Rating: 5 ☠

Right
The museum is housed in a futuristic 1960s building, two asymmetric reinforced-concrete monuments joined by a bridge.

The main site commemorating the Slovak National Uprising (*Slovenské národné povstanie* in Slovak, hence the abbreviation 'SNP') is not well known outside the country, but this rebellion is regarded as the largest operation of the resistance against the Nazis and became a defining element of Slovak national identity after the war.

In late August 1944 the resistance had about 50,000 troops. As the Red Army closed in from the east, the rebels launched their offensive and took the town of Banská Bystrica and made it their headquarters. The hope for assistance from the Soviets, however, evaporated quickly – the Soviet leaders mistrusted the Slovak resistance, because it was not entirely communist but a motley collection of different factions, so they held back their support (see also Warsaw, p167). Hence the resistance was unable to withstand the massive counteroffensive the Nazis then launched, in which they effectively occupied the country and meted out vicious reprisals. Dozens of villages were destroyed and countless atrocities committed. It was not until early 1945 that the Nazis retreated.

The main permanent exhibition here, which originally painted the uprising as a purely communist act of heroism, was updated in 2004 to offer a more balanced representation. In addition there are open-air exhibits of tanks, planes and artillery.

Hungary

Once part of the Austro-Hungarian Empire, the country was much reduced in size and significance after its defeat in World War One. After living through difficult times in the interwar years, Hungary sided with the Axis Powers and hence the Nazis in World War Two from 1941. Following signs that the country might seek a peace deal with the Allies, Germany invaded and occupied Hungary in March 1944. This was bad news for the Hungarian Jewish population, who had up to that point been safe from the grip of the Nazis. Now they were rounded up, with the help of Hungary's own nationalist movement, the 'Arrow Cross'. Almost half a million Hungarian Jews were systematically deported, mostly to Auschwitz (p170–71), and thus became late victims of the largest mass murder in history.

After World War Two, Hungary became a member of the Soviet-dominated Eastern Bloc. A large-scale nationwide uprising in 1956 was crushed by the Red Army; thousands were killed and even more arrested. Later Hungary developed a softer type of reformed socialism that was often referred to as 'goulash communism' (after the best-known Hungarian dish). In 1989 Hungary was at the forefront of the process that would soon end the communist era altogether. It was at the Hungarian border with Austria that the Iron Curtain was first opened.

Thousands of East German citizens took advantage of this and fled to the West via Hungary, before their own revolution swept their communist regime, and in the end the whole state, away. Hungary transformed dramatically, becoming a member of both NATO and the EU, but in recent years it has seen a significant rise in right-wing nationalism, which has become a worry for some other EU members.

Below
Soviet tanks in the streets of Budapest during the brutally crushed uprising of 1956.

House of Terror

★★★★☆

Central Budapest • Nazi terror, WW2, Communism, Repression

Dark Rating: 6 ☠

Called *Terror Háza* in Hungarian, this museum is quite overtly a dark attraction, made clear even by the external design. The building in which the museum is housed was the headquarters first of the Arrow Cross and then of the Hungarian secret police. Today, the façade is painted a stark dark grey, and at the top a black overhanging installation with stencilled letters allows the sunlight to project the word 'TERROR' on to the walls or the street outside.

The exhibition is comprehensive and concentrates more on the repression under communism than Nazism, although this is covered too. Former interrogation cells can be seen and various Stalinist relics are on display. The largest exhibit is a whole T-54 tank in the atrium, a type used in the Soviet crushing of the Hungarian Uprising of 1956.

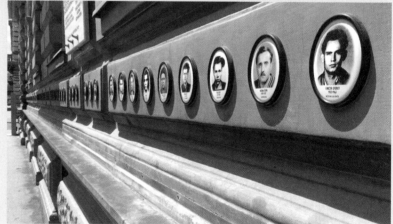

Top
Depending on the position of the sun, the word 'Terror' is projected on to the building façade or street at different times of the day.

Above
Portraits of victims of the regime are mounted on the exterior of the museum.

Above
Russian tank in front of the memorial wall
at the House of Terror, commemorating
Hungarian victims of the communist regime.

Memento Park

Southern edge of Budapest • Communism, Cult of personality

★★★☆☆

Dark Rating: 2 ☠

Above
The largest and most flamboyant of the communist-era statues on display here.

Also known by the Hungarian name *Szoborpark*, this is a collection of communist-era statues and sculptures. As the socialist regimes of the Eastern Bloc disintegrated in 1989–91, their icons were also removed, especially in countries that had felt under the thumb of the Soviet Union, as Hungary certainly did.

In most of these countries, all those Lenin statues and other communist idols were removed and destroyed or dumped out of view. Here in Budapest, somebody saved these works of socialist art and put them together in a small open-air exhibition. Now they form an unlikely motley crew of heroic workers, partisans, soldiers and of course stoic-looking Marx and Engels figures, as well as the unavoidable Lenins. The Hungarian Uprising of 1956 that was crushed by the Soviets is one of the topics in a supplementary exhibition entitled 'Witness Square'.

01 **Vajont Dam**
Italy

02 **Cimitero Monumentale**
Milan, Italy

03 **Ustica Memorial**
Bologna, Italy

04 **Villa Torlonia & bunker**
Rome, Italy

05 **Malta**

06 **Kobarid & the Isonzo Front**
Slovenia

07 **Goli Otok**
Croatia

08 **Željava**
Croatia

09 **Vukovar**
Croatia

10 **Sarajevo**
Bosnia & Herzegovina

11 **Srebrenica**
Bosnia & Herzegovina

12 **Belgrade**
Serbia

13 **Skopje**
North Macedonia

14 **Tirana**
Albania

15 **Bucharest**
Romania

16 **Buzludzha**
Bulgaria

17 **Gyaros & Makronisos**
Greece

18 **Gallipoli**
Turkey

19 **The Green Line**
Cyprus

Southern & South-eastern Europe

The countries collected in this section cover a large area geographically and are a bit of a mixed bag. Italy, Malta and Greece have histories going back to antiquity and today are classic mainstream holiday destinations. But they all had their dark chapters in modern history too. The sites associated with those dark periods, however, are often rather off the beaten track and not easily accessible, even though in general the travel infrastructure is good.

Of the Balkan countries that emerged following the break-up of the former Yugoslavia, EU members Slovenia and Croatia are also easy travel destinations, whereas it can get a little rougher, but still doable, further south and east. The Yugoslav wars of the 1990s brought full-on military conflict and atrocities to Europe for the first time since World War Two, and these left a number of especially grim sites to visit today. Albania, Romania and Bulgaria are also all ex-communist states. The latter in particular struggles with its communist heritage, although there are specialist guided tours for foreign visitors on that theme.

The European part of Turkey and especially the island of Cyprus are on the very edge of the continent but relatively straightforward to visit – except where there are military restrictions (e.g. in the no man's land on Cyprus between the Greek and Turkish Cypriot parts).

Italy

Italy has long been one of the world's foremost travel destinations and is arguably also the birthplace of what has become known as cultural travel or 'heritage tourism'. It began two and a half centuries ago with the so-called Grand Tour of privileged young Europeans travelling to Italy to lap up its ancient culture.

Thus, Pompeii near Naples became an early dark tourism destination. This ancient Roman town was famously destroyed by an eruption of Mount Vesuvius in 79 CE. Discovered under the layer of volcanic ash from pyroclastic flows (see p51) were not only culturally valuable mosaics and suchlike, but also hollow spaces left by the decayed bodies of those killed in the disaster. These were later filled with plaster, creating vivid 3D models of the victims. They are still one of the key attractions of Pompeii today.

Another top sight from the ancient Roman period that has attracted attention as a dark site is the Colosseum in Rome, the iconic giant arena where bloody games, including gladiator fights and throwing convicts to the lions, took place in front of a baying crowd. However, since this book concentrates on dark destinations of the modern era, none of those old sites is included here.

And it's not as if twentieth-century Italy doesn't offer enough contemporary darkness. Not only was Italy a player in World War One, in the interwar years it saw the first rise of Fascism, under Benito Mussolini, even before the Nazis came to power in Germany, with whom Mussolini then aligned Italy in World War Two. There are several relics of the Fascist days, such as the Foro Italico in Rome, and at the Mussolini family crypt in Predappio in the Emilia-Romagna region you can see plenty of evidence that the reverence for the former dictator hasn't all gone away. It is therefore an especially controversial site. After Mussolini was deposed in 1943 and Italy surrendered to the Allies, who had meanwhile invaded Sicily, Nazi Germany intervened and occupied northern Italy.

These events also brought the Holocaust to Italy. This wasn't commemorated much in Italy for many years, and sites such as the former concentration camp of Fossoli near Carpi (also in Emilia-Romagna) are still underdeveloped. However, there is now an elaborate Shoah Memorial in Milan, and the memorial at the Risiera di San Sabba, a former rice mill in Trieste used as a concentration camp by the Nazis, has seen significant modernization in recent years too.

Vajont Dam

★★★☆☆

Near Longarone, northern Italy • Man-made/natural disaster

Dark Rating: 6 ☻

The Vajont Dam was a hydro-electric power generation project, the main part of which was a tall re-inforced concrete dam. When it was completed in 1959, it was the tallest such structure in the world at 262m (860ft). As such, it was a remarkable engineering feat. However, the mountains to the side of the reservoir that was formed by the dam were unstable. Smaller landslides had been warning signs, but they were not heeded. This is why today the disaster that soon unfolded is regarded as partly man-made. It could have been prevented, but wasn't.

On the night of 9 October 1963, the side of Mount Toc collapsed into the artificial lake, displacing millions of tons of water. The enormous wall of water overtopped the dam's crest and surged down the valley, washing away everything in its path, including villages and the small town of Longarone. The disaster claimed the lives of some 2000 people. The dam itself, remarkably, survived almost intact and so still stands today, without a purpose other than to serve as a grim reminder of the tragedy of 1963. The partly filled-in reservoir and the power-generation station were given up after the disaster.

The views down the rear of the dam and into the steep, rocky gorge behind it are truly spectacular. In addition, there is a memorial chapel, and various plaques, and further up the valley in the village of Erto is a visitor centre with a small exhibition about the Vajont Dam and the disaster of 1963.

Opposite
A metal walkway has been constructed along the crest of the dam, and visitors can cross it on guided tours in the summer season.

Cimitero Monumentale

North of the centre of Milan • Cemetery

★★★★☆

Dark Rating: 3 ☠

Above
The cemetery is home to a plethora of extraordinary and often very expressive statuary.

Italy has several impressive cemeteries, and this one in Milan is one of the best in terms of creativity in the designs of the tombs. This is sepulchral art at its highest level, surpassing even the more famous Père Lachaise cemetery in Paris (p115). Here it is less about famous graves and more about the nature of the graves themselves. In addition to a wide range of fantastically designed tombs with expressive sculptures, there is also a memorial to Italians who died in Nazi concentration camps. The large columbarium (for the storage of urns) near the grand main gate is worth visiting, and there is a small funeral culture museum too.

Ustica Memorial

North of the centre of Bologna • Plane crash, Atrocity

★★★☆☆

Dark Rating: 8 ☠

The Ustica disaster is named after an island north of Palermo, Sicily: it was here that on 27 June 1980 a DC-9 passenger plane, Itavia flight 870, crashed into the sea, killing all on board. What sets this plane crash apart from others is the mystery that surrounds the cause of the disaster. A technical fault or accident was ruled out, as was the possibility of a terrorist bomb. Many years later, however, it was established that the plane had actually been shot down by an air-to-air missile; that is, by a military plane.

Whose military would have done this and why remains unclear and is the subject of numerous conspiracy theories. For instance, there was a NATO exercise in the area at that time, and apparently a plane carrying Libya's Colonel Gaddafi was also in the airspace. Maybe it was a botched attempt to shoot him down, but the fighter jets got the planes confused. The case remains shrouded in mystery, but in 2007 the Ustica Memorial museum

opened in Bologna, the city from where the plane had taken off. Its principal exhibit is the reassembled wreck of the plane itself. Surrounding the display of the wreck are some artful installations, such as lights suspended from the ceiling, one for each victim, that flash on and off at roughly the speed of breathing. Next to the plane are black boxes, which allegedly contain personal belongings of the

passengers. It is very moving and eerie, although those who are afraid of flying should probably not visit!

Above
The reassembled plane wreckage is the result of a forensic investigation in Rome after the debris had been salvaged from the sea.

Villa Torlonia & bunker

Northeast of central Rome • WW2, Fascism, Bunker

★★★☆☆

Dark Rating: 6 ☣

Left
Mussolini rented the neoclassical villa from a wealthy admirer for a nominal one lira per year.

Because Benito Mussolini aspired to become Italy's *Duce*, or 'leader', he had to move from his native northern Italy to the capital, Rome, where a wealthy admirer let him reside in the stately Villa Torlonia set in the park of the same name. Here Mussolini lived with his family and frequently held court in grand style. However, as Italy entered World War Two, he became increasingly concerned about Allied air raids reaching Rome or even targeting him personally, so he had an air-raid shelter constructed in the cellar of the villa, where his family could seek refuge during bombing raids on Rome. Later this was augmented by a proper reinforced-concrete bunker connected to the house by an underground tunnel. Yet Mussolini would never use this bunker. Before it was finished, he was deposed and arrested in 1943. (He was freed by the Nazis, but partisans recaptured and executed him in April 1945.)

Villa Torlonia was never hit by bombs, and after the liberation of Rome in 1944 the Allied High Command occupied the building until 1947. Later it fell into neglect and the underground bunkers were almost forgotten. In recent years, the villa was refurbished, and now it serves mainly as an art gallery. The bunker was restored, and since 2014 has been accessible to the public on guided tours.

Left
Eerie underground shelter constructed for Mussolini to seek refuge in during air raids.

Malta

★★★★☆

In the Mediterranean, south of Sicily
WW1, WW2, Cold War, Air-raid shelters

Dark Rating: 5 ☠

This island nation was part of the British Empire from around 1800 until the country gained independence in 1964. It had always been heavily fortified, but in the run-up to World War One this increased and included two 100-ton guns, one of which survives today (the only other one is in Gibraltar, p103). The island did not see any battle action in that war but became home to a large military hospital (especially for casualties from Gallipoli, p203), which gained it the epithet 'Nurse of the Mediterranean'.

In World War Two, Malta became the target of Italian and later Nazi German air raids, and it is claimed that it was the most bombed place of the entire war. During this time the civilian population had to hold out in the numerous underground air-raid shelters that were dug into the soft rock. In the later phases of World War Two, the Allies launched the invasion of Sicily from Malta. After the war, Malta was the main Mediterranean HQ for NATO, until the island became independent, the Royal Navy left its base and the young nation assumed a path of neutrality. It did, however, join the EU in 2004 and the eurozone in 2008.

In October 2017 Malta's international reputation suffered a major blow when the investigative journalist Daphne Caruana Galizia was assassinated, Mafia-style, by a bomb planted in her car, after she had been looking into Maltese politicians' involvement in murky dealings (the Panama Papers) and corruption. The

Above
Injured soldiers disembarking at Malta's harbour during World War One.

case has, at the time of writing, not been fully solved, although at the end of 2019 several high-ranking politicians resigned because of it.

Most of Malta's dark sites are related to its military role. Several air-raid shelters have been preserved and made accessible to the public. Some are private, such as the Mgarr World War Two shelter, while the more official Malta at War Museum in Vittoriosa (aka Birgu) also features extensive shelters. More can be found in Mosta and Rabat. Under the auspices of the Malta Heritage Foundation, Wirt Artna, are Fort Rinella, with its 100-ton gun, as well as the Saluting Battery that overlooks Valletta harbour and where every day, at noon and again at 4 p.m., a vintage cannon is fired.

The main war-related site in Valletta is the Lascaris War Rooms, the underground headquarters of the Allies during World War Two and the invasion of Sicily, which has been faithfully restored and opened to the public. Visitable only by guided tour is the War HQ Tunnels, the underground complex that served as the British and NATO headquarters in the Cold War era and that was abandoned after the Royal Navy left for good in the late 1970s.

Left
The map used for Operation Husky, the Allied invasion of Sicily in 1943, in the Lascaris War Rooms.

Slovenia

This small country at the crossroads of Central Europe and the Balkans was the first part to break away from the socialist federation of Yugoslavia in 1991. This triggered a ten-day war with the Yugoslav military that cost a small number of lives, but that was nothing compared to what would later happen in Croatia and Bosnia (see p190–96). In January 1992 Slovenia was recognized by the European Community as a sovereign state, and it formally joined the EU in 2004.

The war and subsequent developments are covered in the Museum of Contemporary History in the country's charming capital, Ljubljana, and are also touched upon in the general History Museum at Ljubljana Castle. But the country features in this book for a different reason, which has to do with World War One, as Slovenia had been part of the Austro-Hungarian Empire until the end of that conflict.

Kobarid & the Isonzo Front

★★★★★

Western Slovenia, on the border with Italy • WW1

Dark Rating: 4 ☠

When people think of World War One they usually first think of the Western Front, especially Ypres (p122) and the Somme (p110), but what is largely forgotten is the fact that this brutal war also raged in the Alps, in particular between Italian and Austro-Hungarian forces. Here, too, the war was fought in trenches and by means of heavy artillery, and it was no less deadly. Italy is believed to have suffered about half its total war dead, around 300,000, in this conflict along the Isonzo Front in successive battles between 1915 and 1917. There were around 200,000 dead on the other side too, making it half a million altogether, significantly more than even at Verdun (p116).

Kobarid was a village that found itself in the midst of the fighting and was largely destroyed in the process. Today it is home to the best museum about the Isonzo Front, the Kobariški musej. Also in Kobarid is a large Italian Charnel House, containing the remains of some 7000 Italian soldiers. The site in distinctly Fascist architectural style was even unveiled by Mussolini himself in 1938.

Kobarid is on the so-called Walk of Peace, a 250-km (140-mile) route along the former front line in the mountains where various relics of the battles can still be found, some restored and some supplemented by interpretative panels and suchlike, both on the Slovenian and on the Italian side of the present-day border. Some parts require proper mountaineering, but there are also easily accessible sites. A good example is not far from Kobarid on a mountain called Kolovrat. Here a network of trenches and underground shelters has been restored to give an impression of trench warfare in this Alpine territory.

Left
The charnel house at Kobarid was built in the interwar years when this part of Slovenia belonged to Italy.

Croatia

A small country with a big dark heritage, Croatia became a Nazi puppet state during World War Two under its leader, Ante Pavelić, whose Ustashe regime not only helped Hitler in the Holocaust, but also set up their own concentration camps for incarcerating mainly ethnic Serbs and Jews. In Croatia, World War Two ended with the partisans gaining the upper hand under their Croat-born leader, Josip Broz Tito, and subsequently it became one of the constituent parts of the socialist Yugoslav federation. In 1991 Croatia was among the first (together with Slovenia; see p189) to break away from Yugoslavia.

The Yugoslav military reacted violently. With the battle of Vukovar (see p193), full-on war returned to Europe for the first time since 1945. The capital, Zagreb, came under attack twice, by air strikes and missiles. The war ended in 1995, with Croatia regaining most of its lost territory, except Eastern Slavonia, which was returned only after a UN-supervised three-year transition period. Since then Croatia has made much progress and joined NATO (in 2009) and the EU (in 2013).

All this history left several dark sites that can be visited today. The most infamous of the Ustashe concentration camps was Jasenovac, where today there is a striking monument and a small documentation centre. Villa Rebar, the former home of Pavelić in the north of Zagreb, is only a ruin, but urban explorers can find the old escape tunnel underneath it. Various memorial monuments celebrate the Croatian resistance by the partisans; perhaps the grandest of these was Petrova Gora, south of Zagreb. Today it is only a shadow of its former self, heavily vandalized, but another top attraction for urban explorers.

Such tourists also head for the abandoned ruin of one of Tito's many grand mansions, Villa Izvor, in the mountains above the Plitvice Lakes (Croatia's top mainstream tourism attraction). Tito's premier summer residence on the island of Brioni is still intact. You can even stay at his former guest house, where he used to entertain not only other world leaders but also Hollywood stars such as Richard Burton and Liz Taylor. There is a Tito museum on Brioni too.

The 'Homeland War', as the Croatian part of the Yugoslav wars is known here, is commemorated in various places, not just in Vukovar but also, for instance, in a museum in Karlovac. In Zagreb there is a small memorial centre about the aerial attacks the city endured in 1991 and 1995.

Goli Otok   ★★☆☆☆

In the Adriatic, between Rab and the mainland • Prison, Ghost town, Ruins   **Dark Rating: 8** ☠

Sometimes referred to as the 'Croatian Alcatraz', this island was used as a penal colony, initially established to incarcerate political prisoners during the early phases of the Socialist Federal Republic of Yugoslavia, and hence also known by the epithet 'Tito's Gulag'. Later 'regular' criminals were held here too. Inmates had to do forced labour in quarries and various workshops and there are many stories of cruel mistreatment, so it is certainly one of the darkest places related to Yugoslav history.

The prison closed in the late 1980s and the island has since been largely abandoned. Farmers graze sheep on the island, but otherwise it is uninhabited. However, in the summer season, boat tours from neighbouring Rab (one of Croatia's many beach-holiday destinations) go to Goli Otok, and one of those tourist 'trains' makes a circuit around the old prison complexes. Those who prefer to experience this highly atmospheric ghost-town island without such touristy hullabaloo should go off-season, hiring a boat or a skipper with a boat and exploring the island alone.

From the small harbour a road leads uphill beyond a gatehouse and past various empty former workshops to the central plateau. Further inland is the former infirmary as well as the block with isolation cells for the punishment of recalcitrant prisoners. Around the Bay of Vela Draga is the complex of administrative buildings and housing for the prison guards. North of the landing stage yet more buildings can be found, including garages, a former cinema and some bunkers, as well as one of the main quarries.

Opposite
Prison cell blocks, workshops, guards' accommodation and administrative buildings have all slowly fallen into dereliction.

Željava

★★☆☆☆

South of Plitvice, west of Bihać • Abandoned underground airbase

Dark Rating: 7 ☻

Left
A floodlit image of the otherwise pitch-black interior of one of the tunnels of this huge underground airbase inside a mountain.

This highly unusual site is a military relic from the Yugoslav era: an airfield and underground tunnels inside a mountain in which MiG-21 fighter jets used to be based safely behind massive blast doors in caverns equipped with everything needed to keep the planes combat-ready and to support all the staff required for this. The top-secret site was used in the Yugoslav wars too, although it is not clear in exactly what ways. But the Homeland War Museum in Karlovac has wreck pieces of a MiG-21 labelled as being from Željava.

The Yugoslav air force had given up the airbase by the end of 1991, and the runways were partly destroyed by explosives. The base then fell into the hands of the self-declared Serbian 'Republic of Krajina', which set off additional detonations inside the tunnels. You can still see the blast damage today. After the Yugoslav wars, the site ended up right on the border between Croatia and Bosnia, which is why this is still a sensitive area. On the hillsides there are still land-mines, as warning signs clearly indicate. In theory you could explore the place independently, but you should not accidentally cross the border illegally. Guards patrol the area and if you get caught you may face interrogation. However, there are guided tours to Željava from Zagreb, which co-ordinate with the border forces, so that everything is legitimate.

Inside the tunnels you need good torches, otherwise you won't see much (tours provide them). Deeper inside the tunnel system it is totally dark. Watch your step too, as many objects lie strewn about.

Below
Close by the former airbase an old Douglas C-47 'Dakota' plane lies abandoned.

Vukovar

Eastern Slavonia, on the Danube • Modern war, Ruins, Cemetery

★★★☆☆

Dark Rating: 7 ☠

As the first cracks appeared in the federation that was Yugoslavia, Vukovar became the scene of clashes between Croats and the large resident Serb community in the second half of 1991. After a number of skirmishes and attacks on the police, the Serb-dominated Yugoslav Army intervened. An 87-day siege and battle ensued. In the end, the defending Croat forces were overwhelmed and the town fell into Serbian hands. It was a proper military conflict, costing the lives of 2000 combatants and more than 1000 civilians.

In excess of 20,000 former inhabitants were displaced. The town centre was almost completely reduced to rubble. Not all civilians managed to escape, and some became the victims of atrocities of the sort that tragically came to characterize the Balkans conflicts of the 1990s: 'ethnic cleansing', improvised concentration camps, massacres. Things later got much worse in Bosnia and Herzegovina (see p194), but it was here in Vukovar that it all started.

Today, Vukovar still has many war scars, and only about half the number of inhabitants it had before the war. The Old Town centre and much of the salient infrastructure have been largely rebuilt and people are trying to get on with their lives, but tensions remain.

The horrors of 1991 are commemorated at several memorial sites. Of these, the recreation of the cellar rooms at the hospital, where hundreds sought refuge during the battle, is perhaps the most poignant.

Another sombre memorial can be found at Ovčara, south of Vukovar. Here 200 of those who had held out at the hospital were eventually taken by Serbian paramilitary forces and massacred. Nearby is a mass grave. A section of Vukovar's main cemetery on the eastern edge of the town also has war graves and a memorial. The military aspects of the conflict are covered at the Homeland War Memorial Centre, which consists of a vast open-air display of tanks, artillery and other military hardware, as well as two topical indoor exhibitions.

War ruins can still be spotted all over the town. The most iconic is the shelled water tower, which has become the official symbol of Vukovar and is now being converted into yet another memorial site. A cluster of raw war ruins can be found to the north of the centre, at the Borovo shoe factory. This once huge complex, which had 20,000 employees, now operates in one refurbished building with a workforce of around 500. The rest of the ruined factory lies abandoned, but some parts can be accessed by intrepid urban explorers.

Below
The old railway station has been left in its ruined state, yet a new sign has been mounted on the front façade.

Bosnia & Herzegovina

Another constituent part of the federation of Yugoslavia until it fell apart, this is where that break-up was more violent than anywhere else. That is partly because of the complex ethnic and religious make-up of the population. Muslim Bosniaks, Catholic Croats and Orthodox Serbs lived together peacefully until the social cohesion in Yugoslavia dissolved and gave way to increasing ethnic tension. Open conflict had already erupted in Croatia, but here in Bosnia & Herzegovina (often abbreviated 'BiH') it escalated to unprecedented levels.

The long siege of Sarajevo and the Srebrenica massacre (see p196) were only the most noted atrocities. The conflict raged elsewhere too. In Mostar, for instance, Croats and Bosniaks clashed and the world-famous iconic medieval bridge was destroyed – later reconstructed, but still a symbol of the war. Rebuilding has progressed in Mostar, but some war ruins are still in evidence.

All over the countryside you can see ruins of abandoned family homes, whose inhabitants either fled or became victims of the conflict. International intervention and the Dayton Accords of 1995 put an end to the war, but the resultant independent state of BiH is still fragile. It is in fact a construct of three entities: in addition to the Federation of Bosnia and Herzegovina there is also the Republika Srpska, an 'entity' inhabited mostly by ethnic Serbs, partly as a result of internal displacement (or even 'ethnic cleansing' – a euphemism that came to prominence in the media through the reporting on the Bosnian war). Its administrative centre is in Banja Luka, but it wraps around the edges of BiH's capital, Sarajevo, too. You can see from the graffiti on road signs (in Cyrillic once you're in Serb territory) that the tensions continue, even if it is without open violence these days.

Sarajevo

★★★★☆

In the centre of southern Bosnia • WW1, Modern war, Atrocities, Ruins   **Dark Rating: 8** ☻

The capital city of Bosnia & Herzegovina suffered the longest siege in modern history during the Bosnian war of the 1990s: nearly four whole years, from 1992 to 1996. Serbian forces shelled the inner city from the surrounding hills and snipers targeted people running for shelter. In total, over 10,000 Sarajevans were killed and the living conditions in the city were atrocious, yet the inhabitants carried on.

The citizens were helped by a tunnel that was dug underneath the airport to supply the city from the outside. This Sarajevo War Tunnel, aka 'Tunnel of Hope', south of the runway, has been partly preserved and today forms one of the prime tourist attractions in the city. There is also a small exhibition at the southern entrance to the tunnel, and the house there still bears pockmarks from the war. There are now various war-themed tours on offer

Above
Part of the 'Tunnel of Hope', which once ran 340m (nearly ¼ mile) beneath the Sarajevo airport runway.

in Sarajevo, some of which include the tunnel. Other stops are the so-called sniper alley in the west of the city, cemeteries of victims, the refurbished parliament building and the remaining war ruins.

There has been a lot of reconstruction since 1996, but you can still spot high-rises scarred by shelling and the heavily shelled ruin of a retirement home that was under construction at the time (located by the main road, Džemala Bijedića). Further out of town are the remnants of the bobsled track from the 1984 Winter Olympics in the hills south of the city centre, now easy to get to by a new cable car.

There are a few war-themed museum exhibitions in town, such as the Sarajevo Siege section in the History Museum, the more recent Museum of Crimes Against Humanity and Genocide, and the War Childhood Museum. All over the city centre you can see the so-called Sarajevo Roses – shell scars in the pavement where people were killed that have been filled with red resin so that they look like splattered blood.

Finally, Sarajevo had a place in dark history long before the Yugoslav wars. It was here that the Austrian Archduke Franz Ferdinand and his wife were assassinated in 1914, which is widely regarded as having been the trigger that sparked World War One. At the site at the northern end of the Latin Bridge in the city centre is a small museum about the assassination and Sarajevo during the Austro-Hungarian era.

Above
Battle-scarred tower blocks can still be seen in the south of the city.

Below
The bridge where Austria's Archduke Franz Ferdinand was assassinated in 1914 by Bosnian Serb Gavrilo Princip.

Srebrenica

★★☆☆☆

Northeast of Sarajevo • Massacre, Genocide

Dark Rating: 9 ☠

This place name has come to stand for the blackest spot in the dark history of the region. It was here, or rather just outside the village of Srebrenica, at the Potocari industrial site, that Bosnian Serbs under General Ratko Mladić murdered over 8000 male Bosniaks in July 1995. Srebrenica had been a Muslim enclave within the Republika Srpska and the Serbs 're-claimed' the place: it was one of the starkest acts of 'ethnic cleansing' of the whole Balkans war period. In fact, it is often classed as genocide, since

the victims were targeted solely on the basis of their ethnicity.

What was particularly painful for the outside world was that the place in which these victims had sought refuge, an old battery factory, had been declared a 'UN safe area', but the small contingent of Dutch UN soldiers were unable to prevent or stop the massacre. This failure contributed to the decision for NATO to intervene more forcefully to stop the war. Today, there is a large cemetery for the victims. It is still growing as more corpses

are identified by DNA analysis and buried alongside the existing graves. In addition to the cemetery there is a memorial hall and photo exhibition in the former factory complex across the road.

Below
The cemetery now numbers around 7000 graves of victims of the Srebrenica massacre.

DARK STATS

The death toll of the 1992–95 Bosnian war is estimated at

100,000
The population was around 4 million at the time

The largest proportion of victims, about

80 PER CENT
were Bosniaks

2 MILLION
people were displaced as a result of the war

OVER 8000
men and boys murdered in Srebrenica, the largest massacre in Europe since the Holocaust

Serbia

This central Balkan country was the largest constituent part of the former Yugoslavia and, together with Montenegro, held on to that country name until 2003, when it was changed to Serbia & Montenegro. The two-part union was dissolved peacefully in 2006, and since then Serbia has been going it alone. At the break-up of the former socialist state, Serbs intervened militarily in the republics that split off first, especially in Croatia (p190) and Bosnia & Herzegovina (p194) in the 1990s Yugoslav wars, and again in the Kosovo conflict.

Around the turn of the millennium, Serbia was something like the prime pariah state within Europe. Although some Serbs still feel that their country was treated unfairly by the outside world in those troubled years, much has changed since. A course of reconciliation was begun with the West, which slowly lifted the sanctions it had imposed on Serbia, and the country is currently aspiring to join the EU.

Belgrade
★★★★☆

Confluence of the Danube and the Sava • WW2, Modern war, Holocaust   **Dark Rating: 6** ☠

Serbia's capital is one of the grand old cities of Southeastern Europe and offers a range of dark sites. The Military Museum inside the Kalemegdan Fortress in the Old City covers Serbian history from before World Wars One and Two, through the Yugoslav socialist era, up to recent Yugoslav wars and NATO bombing. The latter section portrays Serbia as the victim of Western intervention. Displays include a cluster bomb – a banned weapon – and ammunition with depleted uranium tips used by the Americans.

The futuristic building of the Aviation Museum by the airport also has wreckage of US fighter planes and drones shot down by Serbian forces. Damage done by the NATO bombing of 1999 during the Kosovo war can still be seen in Belgrade along Kneza Miloša and in the bombed-out shell of the former TV centre next to Tašmajdan Park.

A relic of the socialist era is the grand Tito mausoleum, where the cult of personality around Yugoslavia's former leader is still very much in evidence. The neighbouring Museum of Yugoslavia, on the other hand, has changed dramatically, and at the time of writing was closed for a complete overhaul. The dark years of Nazi occupation during World War Two and the Holocaust are documented in a small museum commemorating the Banjica concentration camp at an old military barracks in the south of Belgrade.

The even bigger Sajmište concentration camp at the requisitioned fairground just across the Sava River in the Zemun district is commemorated only by a modest monument by the river, while the dilapidated original structures are abandoned or used in other ways.

Below
Government buildings bombed in 1999 remain in a state of ruin to serve as a memorial.

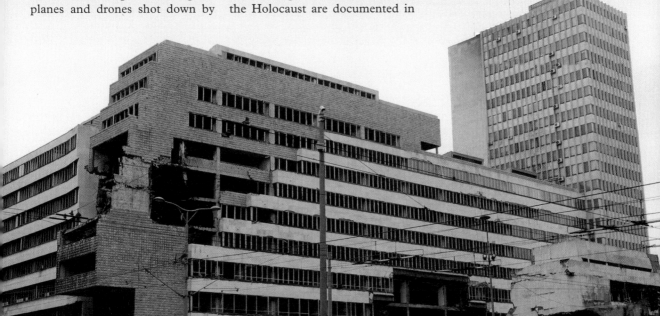

North Macedonia

This is the new name for the country that until early 2019 had the unwieldy official designation 'former Yugoslav Republic of Macedonia' (FYROM). The reason for this was that Greece to the south has a province called Macedonia and therefore objected to the same name being used for its northern neighbour. Simply adding the 'North' descriptor was an acceptable compromise.

The country emerged from the break-up of Yugoslavia in 1991, but without the violence that befell its northern neighbours. There have, however, been problems with its western neighbour Albania and Kosovo to the north. Looking back further, in World War Two Macedonia, like Greece, became a victim of the Holocaust, when about 98 per cent of Macedonian Jews were deported by the Nazis (in this case to Treblinka, p173).

Today, the country is peaceful and welcoming to visitors. The main attractions are not of a dark nature but rather involve scenery and old architecture. Lake Ohrid is often called the 'pearl of the Balkans' and is certainly picturesque. The dark element is to be found in the capital, Skopje.

Skopje ★★★☆☆

In the north of North Macedonia • Natural disaster (earthquake), Holocaust   **Dark Rating: 3** ☠

The city was tragically hit by a major earthquake on 26 July 1963. The epicentre was right underneath the main square. More than half the city's buildings were destroyed, over 1000 inhabitants killed and thousands more made homeless. Today, the semi-ruin of the old railway station is a visible reminder of the disaster. The intact wing of the ex-station houses the City Museum, which has a small section about the earthquake.

Also of interest is the Holocaust Memorial Centre for the Jews of Macedonia just south of the Kale Fortress on the north bank of the river. To the northeast of this is Skopje's Old Town, a warren of little alleyways that looks more Turkish than European, while the city centre south of the river has undergone dramatic changes in modern times.

After the devastating earthquake, the city was rebuilt in a modernist, brutalist style, according to a 'master plan' in which the Japanese star architect Kenzo Tange played an important role. The futuristic concrete structure of the central post office is a prime example. Many others, however, have recently fallen victim to a government programme of hiding this modernist architectural legacy behind faux-classical façades and mock-Greek columns to create a fake historical look for the city.

Left
The station clock is forever stopped at 5:17 – the time the tremors hit on the morning of the earthquake.

Albania

For a long time, this little country in the southern Balkans was the biggest enigma in Europe: a closed communist country ruled by the paranoid ultra-Stalinist autocrat Enver Hoxha, who fell out with the Soviet Union and later China to go it alone. When Hoxha died in 1985, having ruled with an iron fist for more than four decades, the country initially stayed communist but began introducing reforms. Yet it was not until 1992, after the collapse of the communist regimes in Eastern Europe and the USSR, that Albania followed suit.

After a period of semi-anarchic chaos and organized crime, the country evolved into a parliamentary democracy, though one still plagued by corruption. It became a member of NATO in 2009 and is aspiring to join the EU. For many years, the dark periods of the Hoxha regime were simply not mentioned and commemoration was scant at best. More recently, however, things have begun to change. A few Hoxha-related sites have opened up in the capital. A couple of the former political prisons and labour camps have become memorial sites too, such as the infamous political prison at Spaç.

Still visible all over the country are countless pillbox bunkers. Hoxha had thousands of these built in his paranoid fear of the outside world, and many survive, either empty and abandoned or having found new functions (for example, as bars). The enigma of Albania is still partly there, but now you can go and explore it.

Tirana ★★★☆☆

Centre of Albania • Communism, Cult of personality

Dark Rating: 5 ☠

The capital city of Albania struggles to win visitors over. At first glance, it seems to consist largely of drab residential prefab blocks, and even the post-communist attempts at brightening them up by painting them in garish colours don't quite do the trick. If you look closer, though, the city does have its quirky charms, and much of this is thanks to its dark ultra-communist past.

The National History Museum, whose front façade is adorned with a huge socialist-realist mosaic, features a section about 'communist persecution' during the Hoxha years. Right by the central boulevard used to be the largest relic related to the former dictator: the 'Hoxha Pyramid'. This was to be a museum glorifying the deceased leader, but it closed in 1991. Much vandalized and largely derelict for a long time, the structure is now being converted into a mixed-use space with an IT education centre, cafes and shops.

Enver Hoxha's mansion, in the formerly closed district of Blloku, has been preserved as it was when he died but has long remained closed. Now there is talk of possibly opening it up to the public. Already open are two bunker complexes from the Hoxha years, run under the name Bunk'Art 1 and 2, featuring not only original furnishings but also exhibitions about the history of the places, the system of repression by the feared secret police Sigurimi, and other dark aspects.

Another new addition to Tirana's portfolio of dark sites is the Museum of Secret Surveillance in the 'House of Leaves', the former headquarters of the Sigurimi.

Below
The pyramid-shaped building was co-designed by Hoxha's architect daughter and opened in 1988, only to be shut down again in 1991.

Romania

Many people associate this country, and in particular the Transylvania region, with Count Dracula or vampires in general. The local tourism industry certainly milks this – especially so at Bran Castle, which is touted as 'Dracula's Castle', even though the connection could hardly be more tenuous. The historical fifteenth-century figure of Vlad Țepeș 'the Impaler', upon whom the Dracula myth is loosely based, may have stayed at Bran for a few days once, so it's not really 'his' castle – although that doesn't stop today's tourists. There are also vampire-themed hotels, bars and restaurants.

In the modern world, however, Romania was ruled for decades by a real-life baddie in the form of Nicolae Ceaușescu, who came to power in the communist era and took the nepotism and cult of personality associated with most communist regimes to new levels of bizarreness. As he opposed the Soviet Union on a number of issues (such as the crushing of the Prague Spring in the CSSR in 1968), he was seen more benignly in the West, but at home he was increasingly feared and loathed. When one after the other the communist regimes of the Eastern Bloc collapsed, the same thing happened in Romania, but in the least peaceful way of any of these 'revolutions'.

As protests and violence escalated, Ceaușescu and his influential wife, Elena, fled the capital but were eventually captured, court-martialled and executed on Christmas Day 1989. The place where this happened, in Târgoviște, has been turned into a museum of sorts. A memorial to the victims of the Ceaușescus' repressive regime can be found at the former political prison of Sighet in northern Romania.

Bucharest

★★★☆☆

In southern Romania • Communism, Repression, Revolution

Dark Rating: 5 ☠

The Romanian capital was once one of the grand metropolises of the East, but suffered badly during the Ceaușescu regime. Allegedly inspired by a visit to North Korea's capital, Pyongyang (p315), the dictator had a large part of Bucharest bulldozed to make way for socialist high-rises, especially along a new boulevard in the centre, at the top of which the most megalomaniacal of all Ceaușescu's construction projects was erected: the grandiose Palace of Parliament.

This orgy of marble, crystal chandeliers and gold fittings cost billions and crippled Romania's economy. When the 1989 revolution came, the building was 90 per cent finished. It never served its intended purpose, but does now house some branches of government and is otherwise used as a conference centre. Tourists can go on guided tours of the interior.

A place associated with the 1989 revolution is the aptly renamed Piața Revoluției Square. Here, at the former Central Committee building, Ceaușescu gave his final speeches until he was booed off and had to flee by helicopter as protesters stormed the building. You can still see bullet holes on the façade from the street fighting during the revolution. Standing just to the north, the former HQ of the feared secret security organization Securitate was partly destroyed at the time, but has since been converted into offices and a bar. At the city's Ghencea cemetery you can find the graves of Nicolae and Elena Ceaușescu.

Above
When it was built, the Palace of Parliament was the second largest building in the world by floor space, after the Pentagon.

Bulgaria

This country on the southeastern edge of Europe with a stretch of coast on the Black Sea was part of the Eastern Bloc and so close to the USSR that it was sometimes regarded as a kind of 16th Soviet republic. It couldn't be more different now. With Bulgaria a NATO and EU member and thus looking much more west than east, fierce anti-communist regulations are in force that even outlaw the public display of communist symbols.

However, there are relics to be found even in the capital, Sofia: for example, at the Museum of Socialist Art or in the Military Museum. At the house museum of Bulgaria's communist leader of 35 years, Todor Zhivkov, in Pravets outside Sofia, the (comparatively mild) cult of personality still lingers, and gifts from other countries' leaders are on display. One of Zhivkov's residences in Arbanasi near Veliko Tarnovo has been converted into an upscale boutique hotel, but you can visit the ex-dictator's former study. You can even go on communism-themed tours of Sofia and Bulgaria at large; just be careful not to wave any red flags in public.

Buzludzha ★★★★★

Balkan mountains, central Bulgaria • Communism, Cult of personality   **Dark Rating: 8** ☠

Left
The grand symbolism-filled auditorium in the central hall.

The grandest of all communism-era monuments in Bulgaria, this futuristic, UFO-shaped structure high on a mountaintop was originally designed as a celebration of socialism, to serve as a kind of party museum and gathering place. It was built in the late 1970s and inaugurated in 1981. After the fall of communism, it was abandoned some time in the 1990s and became increasingly dilapidated.

This derelict state of the monument in turn made it an attraction of a different sort: from the late 2000s onwards, Buzludzha became something like a holy grail for urban explorers and fans of abandoned buildings in general. For many years it was possible to slip in and explore the interior. Unfortunately, that also brought graffiti sprayers and vandalism. The mosaics of

communist leaders, including the usual triad of Marx, Engels and Lenin, but also Bulgaria's own top-dog communists, and all manner of other socialist symbolism became increasingly damaged.

The rotting roof exposed the interior to the elements more and more, and the harsh mountain winters did not help either. However, there are now plans to preserve the monument. It is guarded round the clock these days, so illegal access to the interior is no longer possible. Yet if the structure is saved and properly restored, it could become a historical pilgrimage destination of the highest order again.

Greece

This country at the southeastern-most end of Europe is mostly associated with the first high culture that developed in antiquity, including perhaps the earliest precursor of democracy (a Greek word, after all). But it has had dark chapters in twentieth-century history, including dictatorships and wars, especially with its old arch-enemy Turkey. In World War Two, Greece first came into conflict with Fascist Italy, then Nazi Germany invaded and committed numerous atrocities. Many of these are commemorated by memorials.

The Greek Jewish community was largely deported, primarily to Auschwitz, and murdered. A Holocaust Memorial Museum is currently under construction in the northern Greek city of Thessaloniki, which was once a city with a majority Jewish population, 97 per cent of whom did not survive the Holocaust. After World War Two, Greece had its own homemade dark periods, especially during the military dictatorship, which ended only in 1974. During that time political opponents were repressed, exiled or incarcerated on prison islands.

More recently, Greece has been in the headlines for other reasons, in particular for its financial crisis and the severe austerity measures introduced to tackle public debt, which in turn led to crippling unemployment. Nevertheless, Greece is a popular tourist destination and can surely do with the outside cash this brings to the country.

Gyaros & Makronisos

Cyclades islands group • Political prisons, Atrocities

★☆☆☆☆

Dark Rating: 8 ☠

These two islands were used as political prisons during the Greek Civil War that followed World War Two, and also by the subsequent military dictatorship that lasted until 1974. Communists in particular were the targeted group; many thousands were subjected to a cruel 're-education' regime on these exile islands, which often amounted to torture.

Makronisos is the northernmost of the Cyclades islands, closest to the mainland and in theory the easier one to reach. The island is mostly barren, but some ruins of the former prison camp remain along the west coast. There are no tourist facilities, but the Makronisos Political Exile Museum in Athens covers some of this history, and you can find a 'Makronissos [sic] digital museum' on the Internet.

Gyaros was already a place of exile in ancient Roman times. Located further southeast, between Kea and Syros, it is even harder to reach. It has been declared a historic monument, but is officially off limits. The buildings still stand, but are derelict. In theory you could get

a boat from neighbouring Syros, but you are technically not allowed to land or get closer than 200m (650ft) to the coastline.

The Greek Navy used the island for target practice until the year 2000, and there is allegedly unexploded ordnance lying around. However, an organization of former resistance fighters (PEAEA) holds regular commemorative meetings on the island, and one could enquire about the possibility of joining such an event in order to

get there legally. Recently, a new memorial monument has been unveiled on Gyaros. Maybe one day regular visits will become possible. This part of Greek dark history certainly deserves to be better acknowledged than it currently is.

Above
After the coup d'état in 1967 hundreds of political opponents were imprisoned on the island.

Turkey

This large country, most of which is actually in Asia, has had a momentous history, including the Ottoman period, when it was one of the dominant empires in the world. Modern Turkey was founded after World War One and the Turkish War of Independence, when the victorious Mustafa Kemal Atatürk created the Turkish Republic, abolishing the monarchy and declaring a secular state.

In the new capital city, Ankara, the Anıtkabir mausoleum of the nation's founder is testament to the reverence Atatürk has enjoyed in Turkey, even though in recent times this seems to have diminished somewhat, as Turkey has taken a more nationalistic and less secular route. Its use of its military might has also made it controversial, especially since Turkey is a member of NATO. During the Cold War period, it had a long stretch of the Iron Curtain on its eastern edge that directly bordered the USSR. Some remnants of the original Soviet-era Iron Curtain installations can still be seen on the border with Armenia (p266).

Relations between Turkey and Armenia are strained, and the border remains closed. On the Turkish side some sites of immense cultural significance for Armenia thus are out of its reach, including the ruins of the ancient former capital of Armenia, Ani, and not least the 'holy mountain' of the Armenians, Mount Ararat. The latter is also of Biblical significance as the alleged place where Noah's Ark came to rest. There is in fact a site on an adjacent mountain where some formations in the rock are claimed by especially dedicated believers to be the remnants of the Ark.

None of these places, however, are as easily accessible as they once were, owing to the ongoing tensions and conflict with the Kurds in these eastern parts of Anatolia and the countries bordering it. However, the European part of Turkey features a very accessible site of historical importance as one of the most infamous battlefields of World War One.

Gallipoli

Northwestern side of the Dardanelles Strait • WW1

★★★☆☆

Dark Rating: 5 ☢

This peninsula is of strategic importance, as it overlooks the narrow waterway separating Europe from Asia and giving access to the Bosporus and hence the Black Sea further north, and was the site of one of World War One's early bloodbaths. The Battle of Gallipoli was fought from April 1915 to January 1916 between the Ottoman Turkish military and French, British and Commonwealth forces. It turned into the kind of senseless carnage that would soon also come to characterize the battles on the Western Front (see p110–13, p116–17 and p122–25).

In total, casualties numbered about half a million, and from the Allied point of view it was all for nothing. The initial landings were successful, but in the end the battle was lost and the whole campaign failed. For Turkey it was a great victory, and a major boost for their

Above
Ottoman soldiers during the World War One campaign on the Gallipoli Peninsula (now Gelibolu, Turkey).

DARK STATS

ANZAC Day (25 April) is still commemorated in Australia and New Zealand today. At Gallipoli,

8709

Australian soldiers were killed and

19,441

wounded, while around

2779

New Zealand soldiers were killed and

5212

wounded

In total on the Allied side,

44,150

soldiers were killed and

97,397

wounded

On the Turkish/Ottoman Empire side,

86,692

soldiers were killed and

164,617

wounded

commander Mustafa Kemal, who would later rise to become the first leader of modern Turkey under the name Atatürk.

The former battlefields are now home to various memorials and monuments, including a huge Turkish one in the southern half of the peninsula commemorating the service of the Turkish soldiers who fought in the Battle of Gallipoli. British and Commonwealth monuments, memorials and war cemeteries are also dotted around the area. An especially moving spot is the Lone Pine Commonwealth war cemetery and memorial. Also significant is the ANZAC Cove memorial, especially for Australians and New Zealanders, as this is where the landing operations of these Commonwealth troops took place. Further inland, at Chunuk Bair, stands a glorifying Atatürk statue, and nearby some reconstructed trenches can be explored.

At the southern tip of the peninsula is the Helles Memorial, and some coastal fortifications can be found nearby. At the Kabatepe Museum near Eceabat, close to the entrance to Gallipoli National Park, various relics from the battle are on display: a skull with an embedded bullet is probably its most gruesome exhibit.

Above left
Çanakkale Martyrs' Memorial stands nearly 42m (137ft) high, overlooking Morto Bay at the southern end of the Gallipoli peninsula.

Cyprus

In the far southeastern corner of the Mediterranean, this island is closer to the coasts of Syria, Lebanon and the Anatolian part of Turkey, but is nevertheless classed as part of Europe. Under British administration since the late nineteenth century, Cyprus was released into independence in 1960. Soon after, conflict broke out along an ethnic divide, between Greek Cypriots and the Turkish Cypriot minority, and a UN peacekeeping mission (UNFICYP) was sent in.

In 1974, Greek Cypriot nationalists staged a coup in conjunction with the then Greek military dictatorship, a move intended to integrate Cyprus into Greece. This triggered an intervention by Turkey, which soon captured the northern part of the island. A Turkish Republic of Northern Cyprus was later declared, but is recognized only by Turkey, while de jure it remains an 'illegally occupied territory'. The UN mission was expanded and a 'buffer zone' between north and south established that still exists today.

The north remains dependent on Turkey, while the Republic of Cyprus in the south, which takes up nearly 60 per cent of the island's territory, has joined the EU. Britain still has two military bases on the south coast.

Like other Mediterranean islands, Cyprus is primarily a beach-holiday destination (in both parts), but the peculiar division offers additional dark elements. In Famagusta, a tourist beach is right next to the abandoned part of Varosha, which has since become one of the world's most fabled ghost towns. Since 1974, when its formerly Greek Cypriot inhabitants fled, Varosha has not been legally accessible; attempting to slip into any houses could result in arrest by the Turkish military. Then in late 2020, Turkey unilaterally 'opened' Varosha beach and part of the town, which attracted EU protests, as that move could endanger a 'comprehensive solution to the Cyprus problem'.

The Green Line

Nicosia • Ghost town, Fortified border

★★☆☆☆

Dark Rating: 4 ☻

Nicosia is the last divided capital city in Europe. It was already divided population-wise in the wake of confrontation between Greek and Turkish Cypriots in the 1960s, but since the Turkish invasion of the north in 1974 it has become a de facto state border. The UN-administered buffer zone is at its narrowest in Nicosia, where the demilitarized border band slices the city in two. The inside of the buffer zone, called 'The Green Line', is an uninhabited crumbling ghost town and is guarded by UN blue berets.

Access for civilians is normally impossible, but there are exceptions: for example, at the 'Home for Cooperation', which runs a café inside the Green Line and offers walking tours. You can also peek into the buffer zone from various vantage points, and apparently people have managed to sneak in. A particular attraction is the former international airport of Nicosia, which has been largely abandoned since 1974, although the UN uses part of the premises. Normally it is off limits, but it has been possible for a while to apply for a permit at the UN to visit this place and at least see the terminal building from the outside, as well as the wreck of an abandoned Trident passenger plane that still sits on the apron.

Below
In some places the 'Green Line' buffer zone is only a few metres wide.

Eastern Europe

Under this heading fall all those independent states within Europe that (re-)emerged after the dissolution of the Soviet Union at the end of 1991. Some had already declared their independence unilaterally, in particular the three Baltic states, which in fact accelerated the collapse of the USSR.

For many travellers today, especially those from the West, a key attraction of visiting these parts is precisely that Soviet legacy, and also the fact that these lands used to be inaccessible but now can be travelled more or less freely. Searching out Soviet relics is hence an important element of exploring these countries. Some of them make this easier than others, and a few, especially parts of the Baltics and western Ukraine, strive to distance themselves from their Soviet past, so that such exploration of the former 'Sovietness' is somewhat hampered but is still possible.

The Baltic states combine very easily with each other and are also the countries in this set that are best geared towards foreign visitors. Travel between the other countries in this section is less easy, as the distances get greater and the language barrier more significant – Russia also still requires most travellers to obtain visas in advance. Domestic flights help cover the longest distances within that vast country; to travel in true local style, trains are a great alternative, but can be more demanding (at least linguistically).

Estonia

Like its southern neighbours and eastern Poland, Estonia was swallowed up by the Soviet Union as part of the Molotov–Ribbentrop Pact, by which Hitler and Stalin divided these lands between themselves in the early stages of World War Two. Then Nazi Germany launched its assault on the USSR and invaded the Baltics, and with the Nazis came the Holocaust. Estonia did not have such a sizeable Jewish population, but it was wiped out entirely. There is an infamous document on display in many Holocaust-related museums that shows a map of the Baltic states with Estonia marked *judenfrei*, 'free from Jews', next to a little drawing of a coffin, meaning that the Jewish community here had been completely destroyed.

When the Red Army expelled the Nazis again, it kept hold of the Baltic states and integrated them back into the USSR. And so it remained all through the Cold War era. As the Eastern Bloc began to fall apart, Estonia began its own struggle for freedom in what became known as the 'Singing Revolution', in reference to Estonians illegally and defiantly singing traditional songs at protests across the country. Eventually Estonia became independent again in 1991.

Estonia still has a large proportion of Russians among its population, which has on occasions led to problem. For example, in 2007, in an effort to distance itself from the Soviet past, the Estonian government removed the Bronze Soldier war memorial from the centre of the capital, Tallinn, sparking violent street protests by ethnic Russians.

This monument can now be found in a military cemetery in the south of the city. Other relics of the Soviet era include the Maarjamäe memorial and museum, where a collection of communist statues can be found behind the modern history museum. The old cells in the basement of the former KGB building can now be visited.

In Estonia's second city, Tartu, the equivalent building houses a KGB Museum in its basement, complete with original cells and a historical exhibition. A monument to a post-Soviet disaster is the 'Broken Line' just outside Tallinn's Old Town; it commemorates the 852 lives lost in the MV *Estonia* ferry disaster of 1994.

Museum of Occupations & Freedom

★★★★☆

Centre of Tallinn • WW2, Communism, Repression

Dark Rating: 5 💀

The Estonian capital's take on its twentieth-century darkest times is housed in a modern, purpose-built structure. Despite limited space, it offers some intriguing artefacts, especially from the USSR times, including many everyday objects and Soviet-era consumer products. It also covers the other, briefer occupation – that by Nazi Germany in World War Two.

Among the exhibits is a whole wall made of prison cell doors, while Soviet-era propaganda posters, busts of Brezhnev and Lenin, and KGB spying equipment are banished to the basement.

Right
Busts of communist personalities are now on display in the museum's cellar.

Above
A wall of prison doors from the Soviet era in the main exhibition hall of the Occupations Museum.

Right
A vintage Estonian propaganda poster from 1942 reads 'Bolsheviks can try to make us quit – we protect our homeland until the end!'

Viru KGB Museum

Viru Hotel, Tallinn • Communism, Surveillance

★★★☆☆

Dark Rating: 4 ☠

The Viru Hotel, opened in 1972 in Tallinn, used to be a jewel in the crown of the Soviet-era Intourist hotel chain, run by the official state tourism agency of the USSR that basically all foreign visitors had to use. As such, it was also of interest to the KGB, the Soviet intelligence agency. There had always been rumours that the hotel rooms were bugged, but it was not until a few years after independence that the spying equipment left behind by the KGB on a secret floor above what was officially the top floor (the 22nd) was discovered. It turned out the hotel was bugged to the max; even restaurant tables had built-in microphones, and spy cameras were used as well. The hotel has been refurbished, and little is left these days to indicate its Soviet origins, but the secret top floor and a room full of KGB equipment can be visited on guided tours.

Right
Some of the surveillance equipment that was installed in the hotel by the KGB and left behind when the Soviets left the country in 1991.

Latvia

The 'middle one' of the three Baltic states suffered a similar fate to that of its neighbours, with Nazi atrocities and subsequent Soviet domination, but the former were especially bad here. A remarkable relic from the Cold War is the Irbene radio locator, an installation for spying on NATO communications, hidden in a remote forest. The former Soviet military garrison nearby is now a ghost town, but the biggest of the station's dishes is in use again, for civilian purposes these days, and can be visited. Another Soviet Cold War-era relic is the formerly secret government bunker underneath a health spa at Ligatne, which can also be visited on guided tours.

Riga

Central Latvia • WW2, Holocaust, Repression, Resistance

★★★★★

Dark Rating: 5 ☠

The capital city of Latvia is a true gem in many ways, not least for its fabled *Jugendstil* ('art nouveau') architecture, but also as a dark destination. When the Nazis invaded, the city's sizeable Jewish community became a target of repression and extermination. A ghetto was set up and some of the worst systematic massacres of Jews committed during the Holocaust took place on the outskirts of Riga (see p227). There were concentration camps here too. Of the one at Kaiserwald nothing remains, and only a small monument marks its location in the north of Riga. The site of the camp at Salaspils to the east of the city was given an eerie Soviet-style memorial with giant concrete statuary, but, again, nothing remains of the original camp structure.

At the end of World War Two, Latvia became a part of the Soviet Union again, and during that time Latvians suffered the typical repression, surveillance and even deportation. The former KGB building in the city is now a memorial museum. In the south of Riga across the river is a deportation memorial at Torņakalns. Nearby is a much more glorifying relic of the Soviet Union: the large Victory Monument featuring a tall needle and socialist-realist sculptures. As it is seen as a symbol of oppression (also given it was erected as late as 1985), it is understandably unloved by the locals.

The achievement of overcoming Soviet rule and regaining independence, on the other hand, is keenly celebrated in several museums, such as the People's Front Museum and the 1991 Barricades Museum, both in the Old Town.

Above
Monuments at Salaspils Memorial on the former grounds of a concentration camp.

Museum of the Occupation of Latvia

★★★☆☆

Riga city centre • WW2, Nazi and Soviet legacy, Repression, Resistance

Dark Rating: 5 ☠

Latvia's museum covering the early Soviet occupation, the subsequent Nazi era and then the long phase of being part of the USSR until 1991 does not feature the place authenticity of the equivalent in Vilnius (p214), nor the richness in artefacts of the one in Tallinn (p208), but nonetheless provides good insights into the Latvian struggle for freedom and independence.

Established in 1993 and originally housed in a Soviet-era building from the 1970s, the exhibition had to relocate to the former US embassy on Raiņa bulvāris, but it is planned that the museum will move back to the renovated and expanded original location and be given an upgraded new permanent exhibition.

Left
A Soviet propaganda poster from 1927 entreats 'Millions of workers! Join the socialist competition!'

Riga Ghetto Museum

★★★☆☆

Southeast of the Old Town • Holocaust

Dark Rating: 4 ☠

This is a small but important museum, whose exhibition is mostly in the open air, with rows of panels providing general background as well as personal stories from the Holocaust in Latvia and the deportations to and from Riga in particular. There is also a reconstructed wooden house furnished in such a way as to create an impression of what life in the ghetto was like.

In the area where the ghetto was located, the foundations of the Great Choral Synagogue on Gogol Street, which was burned down by the Nazis with hundreds of Jews inside, are a related relic. Also worth a visit is the Jews in Latvia Museum on Skolas iela in the city centre. Further out but worth the detour is the unusual Jānis Lipke Memorial in the Kurzeme district. This honours a Latvian man who, on his own initiative and at great personal risk, managed to hide over three dozen Jews in an underground shelter and thus save them from almost certain death in the Holocaust. The purpose-built museum includes an artistic recreation of the shelter and an audio guide (essential!) takes visitors through the small exhibition.

Karosta

★★★☆☆

Baltic coast, north of Liepāja • Soviet legacy, Prison, WW2, Holocaust

Dark Rating: 5 ☠

Formerly a closed garrison town and Soviet naval base, Karosta is now partly a ghost town. Some of the older buildings date back to tsarist times; others are typical Soviet-era prefab blocks, partly still lived in. Some of the ruins can be explored independently or on guided tours. This includes the visually interesting ruins of pre-World War One coastal fortifications to the north of the town (such as the aptly named Northern Forts), some of which are slowly being swallowed by the sea.

The main attraction for most, however, is the infamous Karosta Prison. This was originally built as part of the naval base at the turn of the twentieth century, and was used during the Soviet era as a navy prison. Abandoned after Latvia gained its independence, it was turned into a tourist attraction in the late 1990s. It has become notorious for the rather extreme 'show' elements on offer – you can even stay overnight behind bars here. It is all somewhat controversial. Those who can do without such elaborate 're-enactment', however, can just go on an ordinary guided tour of the prison without any theatrical add-ons (best done out of high season).

Top
One of the bunkers south of the Northern Forts that is slowly being reclaimed by the sea north of Karosta.

Above
Visitors to the old Karosta Prison can take part in role-playing tours led by actors in Soviet-era uniforms impersonating prison guards.

Lithuania

The southernmost of the three Baltic states shares a lot of modern history with its northern neighbours, but there are differences too. The Nazi era was at first welcomed as a liberation from the unloved Russians, but for the large Jewish population it was a catastrophe. Well over 90 per cent of Lithuania's Jews were murdered. The fact that many Lithuanians were complicit in this is something that is not much talked about in the country today, but it should be remembered when it comes to comparing the Holocaust with the Soviet repressions and deportations that came after World War Two.

Still, the Soviet era is the more resented part of history for Lithuanians and it shows in some of the commodification of historic places. There is also a far smaller Russian community here than in Latvia and Estonia, which may be a factor in this.

In spite of all that anti-Sovietness in large parts of the Baltics, Lithuania sports some unique places associated with that time (see below), including an intriguing Cold War relic: being on the western edge of the USSR, Lithuania was a suitable location for stationing nuclear missiles aimed at the West, especially in the early days of the development of such weapons, before ICBMs attained a global reach. Of the many mid-range missile bases in the Baltics, one has been preserved as a Cold War Museum, in Plokštinė. The underground facilities house a topical exhibition with model missiles, grim-looking dummies in uniforms, and various Soviet and Cold War-era memorabilia.

The 9th Fort

★★★★☆

Northwestern edge of Kaunas • Holocaust, Repression, Resistance

Dark Rating: 8 ☠

Left
Dominating the complex is the 33m-tall (105ft) modernist concrete monument.

Originally constructed in the early twentieth century as part of a ring of fortifications around the city of Kaunas, the 9th Fort became the site of a fierce battle between German and Russian forces in World War One. In the interwar years it served as a prison during Lithuania's brief period of independence, before the Soviet Union invaded and the NKVD (the precursor of the KGB) took over the fort. The very darkest phase followed when Nazi Germany attacked the USSR in 1941 and in the process also occupied this fort. It was then used by the Nazis as a massacre site at which at least 10,000 and possibly up to 50,000 people, mostly Jews, were murdered.

After World War Two the 9th Fort came under Soviet military administration, and a first memorial was established in the late 1950s. The gigantic concrete monument was added in 1984. After the departure of the Soviets, the complex was reworked, and now the purpose-built museum at the foot of the hill contains exhibitions about the entire history of the fort with a special section on Lithuania's struggle for independence.

The fort itself can also be visited, and the inside houses yet more exhibition elements and reconstructed cells. Outside, the Nazi massacre site is marked by a simple sign.

Vilnius

★★★★☆

Southern Lithuania • Holocaust, Soviet legacy, Repression, Resistance

Dark Rating: 4 ☗

Today's capital city of Lithuania has not always even been in Lithuania. In the interwar years it was part of Poland and called Wilno (or Wilna in German), until it was occupied together with other eastern parts of Poland and the rest of the Baltics by the Soviet Union. When the Nazis arrived during their attack on the USSR in 1941, the Holocaust started in Vilnius too. The city was once regarded as the 'Jerusalem of the North' owing to its large and thriving Jewish community of about 60,000. Only a handful of these survived the Nazis' deportations and massacres.

In Vilnius in general there is more commemoration of the repression of Lithuanians in the post-World War Two Soviet era and the struggle for independence in the late 1980s and early 90s. A key event occurred on 13 January 1991, when Soviet troops were sent in by Gorbachev (it is no wonder that he is less fondly remembered here than in Western Europe). At the TV Tower, protesters gathered to prevent the cutting off of the voice of free media by the military, and it came to a confrontation, involving tanks. Fourteen civilians were killed. A small exhibition at the base of the TV Tower is about these events. The victims are buried in Antakalnis cemetery, east of the city centre.

Relics from the Soviet era are thinner on the ground in Vilnius compared to Tallinn and Riga. An exception was the group of socialist-realist statues on the so-called Green Bridge, but these were removed in 2015, causing some controversy. A surviving architectural relic from the Soviet times can be found a little upriver: the former Concert and Sports Palace, a soaring brutalist concrete structure on the northern riverbank (controversially built in 1971 on the grounds of what was once a Jewish cemetery). It was closed in 2004 and has been derelict since, but now there are plans for refurbishing the site.

Museum of Occupations and Freedom Fights

★★★★☆

Centre of Vilnius • Soviet legacy, Repression, Holocaust

Dark Rating: 8 ☗

This used to be called the Genocide Victims' Museum, which was rightly criticized for being misleading. It has always been primarily about the Soviet era, while the Holocaust is mentioned only in passing, and calling the Soviet repression and deportations 'genocide' is at least debatable. The museum was given its new name in 2018, but is still widely referred to as the KGB Museum – because it is housed in what used to be the Vilnius headquarters of the Soviet secret police.

The main exhibition rooms upstairs mostly deal with the Soviet times and the role of the KGB. In one room, surveillance technology is still in use and on old screens you can see images of the museum and visitors walking around unaware that they're being caught on camera. The Baltic revolutions and struggle for independence are also given ample coverage. The dark chapter of the genocide that was the Holocaust, in contrast, is found in a single small room in the basement, just beyond the cell tract.

Above
The basement cells for political prisoners form part of the museum.

Grutas Park

★★★★☆

East of Druskininkai • Soviet legacy, Communism

Dark Rating: 5 ☠

Grūto parkas, as it is known in Lithuanian (also often informally and unofficially referred to as 'Stalin World' in the media) is a peculiar mix. Its main element is the open-air display of 86 statues, sculptures, busts and other works of art from the communist era. Among them are indeed a couple of Stalins, as well as several Lenins, the odd Marx and Engels and also Lithuanian former commie biggies, plus a few partisans and suchlike. In addition, the circuit around the open-air park is partly 'adorned' with loose recreations of Gulag-like watchtowers and mock electrified fences. This has at times been criticized for making light of the repressive communist times, but there are also panels at Grutas Park that counter that and put the collection into a historical perspective.

In addition to the outdoor exhibition, there are a couple of huts with exhibitions inside. Displays include propaganda posters, medals, flags, socialist-realist paintings and yet more statuary, but also some coverage of Soviet-era atrocities, so it is not just a celebration of everything Soviet. The rather odd add-on of a mini zoo within the compound of the park is also a source of controversy, mainly because of the sorry state of some of the cages, which animal rights-minded people will deplore. In general there is a certain air of incongruousness between the fun-fair-like aspect (there's a large playground too) and the serious issues of not so recent history.

Below
A monument to Soviet underground partisans – one of many such items of socialist realist statuary moved to the park after the end of the communist era.

Belarus

Of all the former Soviet republics, this is probably the one that retains more of a Soviet character than any of the others. This landlocked country between Russia and Ukraine still has a KGB and has been ruled in semi-autocratic fashion by Alexander Lukashenko since 1994. Hence Belarus has sometimes been dubbed 'the last dictatorship in Europe'. The way in which mass protests after the contested 2020 elections were brutally crushed only corroborated that assessment.

This is not North Korea, however. The cult-of-personality level is comparatively restrained and there are billboards advertising Western brands in the capital city, suggesting that at least a section of society is fairly well off. Yet there is a Soviet-like atmosphere, not least in the architecture and the omnipresence of hammer-and-sickle symbols. The most Soviet elements are relics from the USSR days, which include monuments such as the 'Mound of Glory' to the northeast of Minsk. At the so-called Stalin Line, old Soviet military glories are even more openly celebrated, not only with open-air displays of planes, missiles and artillery but also with re-enactments, helicopter and tank rides and a shooting range – a big military funfair.

It should be remembered that Belarus suffered greatly in World War Two, losing about a quarter of its population. One particular atrocity is commemorated at the Khatyn Memorial. Here the Nazis massacred an entire village's population, and burned all the houses to the ground. Many villages were wiped off the map in such a manner, but this place was picked out to represent all such tragedies in Belarus.

Brest Fortress

★★★★☆

Southwestern Belarus, on the border with Poland • WW2, Soviet legacy   **Dark Rating: 5** ☠

Originally built in the days of Imperial Russia as part of a system of fortifications to serve as a bulwark against the West, this fort at Brest was one of the first targets when Nazi Germany invaded the Soviet Union in 1941. The Germans won the battle eventually, but the defence of the fortress by the Red Army became a key ingredient in the Soviet war narrative and commemoration of what is still called the 'Great Patriotic War 1941–1945' in most of the former USSR countries. The story of the defence of Brest was underscored by the construction of one of the most over-the-top memorial complexes anywhere in the world, and (together with Volgograd, p237) is the quintessential example of Soviet sculptural monumentalism.

By the approach avenue towards the fortress is a huge five-pointed star cut out of a massive block of concrete. Beyond this gateway are several more monuments, dominated by a tall obelisk and a gargantuan sculpture of a grim-looking soldier's head. There are ruins of parts of the fortress too, the most stunning being the front of the Kholmsk Gate, which is pockmarked with bullet holes and shell scars. In addition, there are two separate museums, one more specifically about the defence of Brest Fortress and a newer one that casts the net a bit wider (also including, for example, a section about the plight of Soviet POWs in the Third Reich).

Above
The monumental stone sculpture, called 'Courage', of a heroic Red Army soldier is over 30m-high (100 ft).

Minsk

★★★☆☆

Middle of Belarus • WW2, Soviet legacy, Holocaust

Dark Rating: 4 ☣

Minsk was almost completely destroyed in World War Two, and hence rebuilt virtually from scratch after the war. The centre was given a grand Stalinist-style feast of wide boulevards and vast squares that are among the best preserved anywhere. One of the most poignant Holocaust memorials in Eastern Europe, known as the 'Pit Monument', marks the site of a massacre of some 5000 Jews at the hands of the Nazis. The main memorial space of this category, however, is found on the eastern outskirts of Minsk at the site of the former Maly Trostenets concentration and extermination camp, where most of the Jewish population of Minsk were murdered.

Among the plethora of Soviet-era sights, Independence Square stands out. Formerly known as Lenin Square in Soviet times, it still features a particularly magnificent Lenin statue in front of some imposing government buildings. Independence Avenue is the core artery featuring the grandest of the Stalinist architecture, including the ominous headquarters of the KGB.

To the east, October Square (aka Republic Square) is another very Soviet-looking place.

Victory Square further east still has a monument with World War Two bas-reliefs. The very grandest Soviet building, though, has to be the so-called Gates of Minsk ensemble opposite the main railway station, still sporting the Belorussian SSR coat of arms. Of the post-Soviet architecture, the bizarre structure that is the National Library stands out.

Top
A monument of Lenin in front of the constructivist-style Government House.

Above
A bronze sculpture at the Yama ('the Pit') memorial commemorates victims from the Minsk ghetto massacred by the Nazis in 1942.

Museum of the Great Patriotic War

★★★★☆

North of Minsk city centre
WW2, Atrocities, Holocaust, Soviet legacy

Dark Rating: 6 ☠

Left
The futuristic domed building now housing the museum in Victory Park, with a very Soviet-style statue outside.

Given a substantial makeover and a new home in a modern building by Victory Park (Park Pobedy in Russian) that opened in 2014, this now has to rank as one of the finest museums about World War Two in the former Soviet Union.

The coverage is wide, text and labelling now include English, and a plethora of artefacts are on display, including several life-size ensembles of planes and tanks from the war, both Soviet and Nazi German, as well as recreations of partisan camps, field hospitals and a deportation-train cattle car from the Holocaust. Sometimes, though, it is the smaller artefacts that are particularly poignant. One such item is the piece of bone embedded in a dented metal water flask that was apparently discovered during an archaeological dig at a mass-grave site in southern Belarus.

Despite its modernity, the museum retains a very Soviet character, for instance, in the form of a large panorama battle painting/installation. Atop the central glass dome, the Soviet red flag with its hammer-and-sickle symbol is still flying.

DARK STATS

The USSR suffered the highest number of casualties in World War Two. While exact figures are almost impossible to arrive at, it is estimated that USSR military deaths numbered approximately

11 MILLION
and civilian deaths

7 MILLION

For comparison, there were approximately

3.5 MILLION
German military deaths and

780,000
German civilian deaths

By the end of the war, the Soviet Union had lost around

10 PER CENT
of its prewar population

Transnistria

★★★☆☆

Strip of land between Ukraine and Moldova
Modern war, Soviet legacy

Dark Rating: 7 ☠

Calling itself Pridnestrovskaya Moldavskaya Respublika (PMR for short), this is a 'breakaway republic' that remains largely unrecognized. It split away from the former Moldovan SSR of the Soviet Union when it declared itself independent, and after the dissolution of the USSR a short but bloody civil war erupted in Moldova in 1992. The fault line was/is largely one of ethnicity and culture.

While the rest of Moldova is culturally and linguistically closer to neighbouring Romania and is politically looking west, the PMR on the eastern side of the Dniester River (aka Nistru, hence 'Transnistria') is Russian-speaking and looking towards the east. In fact, it was Russian peacekeeping troops that intervened and still protect the border between the two belligerents of 1992 to this day. And so Transnistria became a curiosity: a wannabe independent country, but geopolitically a kind of no man's land. It so emphasizes its allegiance to Russia and retains so much of its old Soviet character that travelling there has been called going 'Back to the USSR'.

Travelling to an unrecognized territory like this, where there are no foreign embassies and visitors are beyond the reach of consular help if they get into trouble, means there is a slight risk involved, but as long as you behave and don't break any rules it is safe. Several operators offer tours to Transnistria.

The primary attraction is the general 'Soviet-ness' of the place, which is most pronounced in the 'capital', Tiraspol. There are Soviet-era monuments, big social-ist-style propaganda posters glorifying the 'inde-pendence' of Transnistria, and plenty of Soviet-style architecture. Prime examples are the Stalinist-style *dom sovietov* ('House of Soviets') with its fierce-look-ing Lenin bust in front, and the Presidential Palace and Parliament, with a large red-marble Lenin statue and a classic Soviet-era war memorial featuring the typical T-34 tank on a plinth nearby.

Outside Tiraspol, the city of Bender on the west-ern banks of the Dniester is where the main bridge crosses the river on the route between Tiraspol and Moldova's capital, Chișinău. It was in Bender that the worst of the fighting in 1992 took place; you can still spot war scars in the form of bullet holes on some walls, and there is a small museum about the conflict.

Above
A bust of Lenin in front of the House of Soviets, Tiraspol's city hall.

Left
The T-34 Tank Monument on 25th October Street in the capital, Tiraspol.

Ukraine

This second largest country in Europe (after Russia) has been in the headlines over the past decade and a half, often for the worst of reasons, such as the violent Euromaidan clashes of 2014 in Kiev, in which hundreds were wounded and killed, with snipers aiming at peaceful protesters. It did end in the ousting of pro-Russian president Viktor Yanukovych, though, and a return to peace in the capital city, but in the southeastern parts of the country pro-Russian protests took place and eventually a civil war-like conflict between government forces and pro-Russian separatists emerged that is still unresolved.

The separatists also received military help from Russia. In March 2014 Russian forces de facto annexed Crimea, a move that was widely criticized in Ukraine and also in the West, but that in Russia has been declared a 'reunification' with the homeland. Another incident that year was the shooting down of a Malaysian passenger airliner over eastern Ukraine in July by means of a Russian anti-aircraft missile.

It is beyond the scope of this book to delve any deeper into these complicated matters; suffice it to say that while eastern parts such as the Luhansk and Donetsk regions are currently off limits to tourists and Crimea can be visited only via Russia, the western three-quarters of Ukraine are safe to travel to, and this includes the places of particular interest here.

Chernobyl ★★★★★

North of Kiev near the border with Belarus
Nuclear disaster, Ghost town, Ruins, Soviet legacy

Dark Rating: 10 ☣

The worst nuclear accident in history received a renewed high media profile thanks to the 2019 TV dramatization *Chernobyl*, which coincided with a surge in Chernobyl tourism. While the TV series was largely accurate, Chernobyl has been the subject of a lot of myths and sensationalism.

There was no 'nuclear explosion' at Chernobyl, in the sense of an atomic bomb-like detonation, so the oft-cited comparison with Hiroshima is not really helpful. What happened was a combination of human error, an ill-devised experiment, a typical Soviet combination of authority, obedience and cover-up, and, perhaps most importantly, serious design flaws in the graphite-moderated reactor type involved.

The exact details of the chain of events are complex and beyond the scope of this book. Suffice it to say that in the early hours of 26 April 1986 a test performed at Block 4 of the nuclear power plant (NPP) of Chernobyl went suddenly and disastrously wrong, causing a power surge that spiralled out of control, overheating the reactor and boiling the coolant water. This caused a steam explosion that lifted the reactor lid, which then came crashing down sideways into the reactor core. Seconds later, hydrogen gas that had accumulated from the chemical reactions inside the reactor hall also exploded, ripping the roof off the hall and ejecting debris into the open air, including blocks of graphite and reactor fuel.

More volatile by-products were then blown into the atmosphere, forming a radioactive cloud that spread northwards, polluting large tracts of land in Belarus and after two days reaching Sweden, where it was deduced that the radiation must have come from the USSR. Only then did the Soviets admit to the accident, and it became big news in the West as the radioactive cloud continued to spread. In the USSR, the news was hushed up and the May Day festivities in Kiev were allowed to take place despite the radiation risk.

At Chernobyl itself, it took the authorities more than 24 hours to evacuate Pripyat, the town purpose-built in the 1970s for the NPP staff and their families. Residents were told to pack just essential documents and an overnight bag and were carted out in convoys of buses, never to return. At the NPP, firefighters had been called in but faced an impossible task trying to extinguish the burning reactor core. Without any protective clothing, several received lethal doses of radiation.

The death toll of Chernobyl is a highly contested issue. Only 31 deaths are directly attributed to the accident (mostly firefighters) and a few hundred indirectly. But because it cannot be determined whether any subsequent cancers were caused by radiation, estimates of the casualties vary widely; those in

the range of hundreds of thousands are quite probably exaggerated.

Eventually, an army of 'liquidators' was sent in to do a massive clean-up operation. Topsoil was ploughed under, whole villages were razed, and at Block 4 a 'sarcophagus' structure was erected to shield the ruin. The operation was so costly that it has been claimed, not least by the USSR's final leader, Mikhail Gorbachev, that it was the most important factor in the collapse of the Soviet Union.

An Exclusion Zone was declared around the stricken NPP. Although some elderly residents later returned, initially illegally but later tolerated, most of the settlements and towns in the Zone have

remained depopulated ever since – of humans, that is. In humanity's absence, wildlife has thrived, including wolves, elk, wild boar and Przewalski's horses.

The town of Chernobyl that gave the whole area its name remains partly in use, being far less radioactively contaminated than other parts of the Zone, and so it is still the administrative centre. More remarkably, the NPP continued operating for years after the accident. Block 3 was the last to be shut down, in 2000. Since then, the site has been undergoing decommissioning, but thousands of people still work there. So this part of the Zone is anything but empty and is actually quite busy.

Opposite
The wreckage of the Chernobyl nuclear power plant seen from a helicopter, days after the explosion and fire.

Above
New Safe Confinement above the remains of reactor 4 and the old sarcophagus.

Left
Still intact control room at the shut-down Chernobyl nuclear power station.

A major development in recent years was the construction of a New Safe Confinement (NSC) building, a second sarcophagus that in 2016 was moved over the old sarcophagus, so that, once the NSC was properly sealed, work to dismantle the ruin and finally remove the molten reactor core could begin. Decommissioning is expected to last at least until the year 2065.

It is often claimed that tourist visits to the Zone are something new, but in fact tours have been running since the late 1990s. This was initially on a small scale, but recent years have seen significant growth in visitor numbers. Some now even complain about 'overtourism'. Indeed, being with coachloads of noisy tourists can somewhat detract from the ghost-town atmosphere, especially in Pripyat.

If you can afford it, it is recommended to invest in a private Chernobyl guide or at least join a small-group tour, and it is best to go off-season. There are now dozens of operators who can see to the paperwork required to obtain a permit and organize transport from Kiev. The official guides inside the Zone are state-appointed in any case. The standard day-return tours from Kiev by coach are quite affordable, and form the bulk of Chernobyl tourism. The more in-depth tours away from the crowds cost significantly more, but are worth it. No other place on Earth is so like time travel in both directions simultaneously – back to the Soviet past and forward to provide a glimpse of how a post-apocalyptic, post-civilization future could look in which nature slowly reclaims what humanity built.

Two questions foremost in readers' minds may be: A) is it dangerous? And B) what is there to see? As for the former, radiation levels in much of the Zone have fallen so much that parts could even be reopened. Some areas do still have elevated radiation levels, though, and there are a few 'hotspots' where one should not linger too long. But even at those, a short

moment near them won't do much harm (see over the page).

The main stops on any standard tour include a visit to some parts of the ghost town of Pripyat, in particular the funfair with its iconic Ferris wheel as well as the main town square; almost all tours also have a stop at the memorial next to Block 4 and the NSC, which now covers the old sarcophagus. Longer tours (with overnight stays) can go much beyond the standard circuit and may include visiting some of the deserted villages, meeting some 're-settlers' even, and exploring Pripyat in more depth. By special arrangement you can also visit the inside of the NPP and see one or two of the control rooms and a reactor hall.

Nominally you are no longer allowed to enter any abandoned buildings, such as Pripyat's schools and hospitals, which is a shame because they offer superb photo opportunities. Especially popular shots have always been those involving the gas masks that can be found strewn about in some

buildings (obviously these have been deliberately placed there to look atmospheric). The slowly rotting pianos found in music schools and cultural centres are another typical object in which photographers delight.

However, some buildings in Pripyat have begun to collapse, which shows that the main risk here is not radiation but unsafe structures. Some tours also visit the old harbour, a factory, or the site of Blocks 5 & 6, which were under construction at the time of the accident but never finished. Most tours these days add a stop by the Duga over-the-horizon radar array, a gigantic antenna that used to be part of the USSR's Cold War-era early-warning system. Since such installations need large amounts of energy, it made sense to put it near an NPP. They are quite a sight: the larger of the two arrays is 150m (500ft) high and together they are over 750m (2000ft) wide.

Opposite, top
Old Ferris wheel in the ghost town of Pripyat within the Chernobyl Exclusion Zone.

Opposite bottom
A view of the main square in Pripyat, showing how the forest is slowly reclaiming the town.

Top right
Socialist realist mural in the abandoned post office building.

Above right
The Chernobyl Duga radar, a Cold War-era early-warning system.

RADIATION

This is something that most people find mysterious and scary, also because you cannot see, smell or taste radiation (except at very high doses – those 'liquidators' who received such doses at Chernobyl reported sensing a 'metallic taste'). But it seems to be the case that the less you know about radiation, the scarier it appears – and vice versa. To begin with, we cannot escape radiation; it is all around us all the time. Most of it is naturally occurring, from cosmic background radiation, rocks and building materials and even food (Brazil nuts and bananas especially).

We also voluntarily expose ourselves to radiation through X-rays and CT scans and by using passenger planes (airliners' cruising altitude is closer to cosmic background radiation). Human activity, for example through the atmospheric nuclear tests of the 1950s and 60s, additionally raised global background radiation considerably. The generation of nuclear power can also add artificially produced radiation, especially of course in accidents such as Chernobyl's. But this book is not a physics primer, so let's keep things basic.

Radiation, in the form of 'ionizing radiation', and in particular gamma radiation, can cause damage to human bodies – ranging from isolated mutations in cells, which can trigger cancers, to acute radiation syndrome. While the former can occur naturally at lower levels of radiation, it takes very high levels to cause actual radiation sickness or even death. Three factors are important with regard to exposure: the strength of the source of radiation, the distance from it, and time – how long the exposure lasts. The latter factor is crucial with regard to visiting Chernobyl or Fukushima (p319); permanently living at a location with elevated radiation is not a good idea, but spending a short time there can be fine.

The unit for exposure to radiation, and the one most Geiger counters measure, is usually 'microsieverts per hour' (μSv/h). Those exposed to the open reactor at the start of the Chernobyl disaster received a lethal dose in the region of millions of μSv/h. Inside the control room, the level may have hit a few thousand μSv/h. In the open air at Chernobyl today, ambient radiation levels are typically between 0.12 and 1.3 μSv/h, but are higher at certain hotspots, such as the Red Forest or Pripyat cemetery, where topsoil was not removed and over 20 μSv/h can still be measured. There are a few even 'hotter' spots, such as the basement of the hospital in Pripyat where the highly irradiated clothes, boots and helmets of the first responding firefighters are still stored. Here levels can exceed 400 μSv/h, so it's better to stay away.

Fortunately, the heavy and extremely radioactive substances, such as uranium fuel, could largely be contained inside the reactor and its sarcophagus (next to the molten reactor core, levels are still so high as to be lethal within a quarter of an hour). Most of the dangerous contamination away from the reactor was caused by derivative fission by-products such as caesium-137 and iodine-131 that were blown into the air and spread by wind and rain. Iodine-131, which can cause thyroid cancer, has a half-life of only about a week (that is, it decays by 50 per cent within that time), and thus was only a short-term problem (and taking iodine pills can largely prevent the body from absorbing iodine-131 isotopes).

However, caesium-137 has a half-life of around 30 years and as it is highly soluble it can spread easily. This is still the main source of radiation in the Chernobyl Exclusion Zone and also the key reason why one should take care not to ingest any particles when out there (for example, by breathing in dust or eating outdoors).

National Chernobyl Museum

Podil district, Kiev • Nuclear disaster, Soviet legacy

★★★★☆

Dark Rating: 8 ☣

Left
Unsettling mannequins in rubber suits and gas masks confront visitors to the museum while atmospheric red and blue lights pulse.

Left
At the rear of the museum photographs of the children of Chernobyl are arranged in a shape echoing the reactor top.

Short of going on a tour to the real thing (see p220–23), this is the best place to learn about the Chernobyl disaster of 1986. This museum is housed in a former fire station in Ukraine's capital city, Kiev (Kyiv in Ukrainian). Outside are parked a few vehicles from Soviet times. The inside provides a good overview of the function of Chernobyl's reactors, the accident, the clean-up operation, medical effects and the aftermath, with a special focus on children affected by the radiation.

The exhibition rooms are full of intriguing artefacts, as well as models of the reactor before and after the explosion, while dummies in protective suits hang from the ceiling. The floor of the main hall is a recreation of the octagonal top of the Chernobyl type of reactor. There are also interactive elements and English-language audio guides.

Babi Yar

Northwestern outskirts of Kiev • Massacre, Holocaust

★★☆☆☆

Dark Rating: 6 ☠

Also spelled Babyn Yar, this is perhaps the best-known location of the sort of shooting massacres the Nazi German *Einsatzgruppen* (literally 'task forces', but actually 'death squads') perpetrated primarily against Jews during the invasion of the Soviet Union in 1941 (see opposite). When the Germans reached Kiev, they set about killing all the city's Jews. They were rounded up on 29 and 30 September and taken to a site just outside the city, where they were led to the edge of a ravine in batches and systematically mown down by machine-gun fire.

At the end, the perpetrators reported the official number of 33,771 victims. That made Babi Yar the largest such massacre up to that date, and one of the biggest of all time. The victims were buried in the ravine where they had

fallen, some even still alive. The site was subsequently used for further massacres, including Roma and Sinti, Soviet POWs and resistance fighters, bringing the total number of victims to somewhere between 70,000 and over 100,000. Before the Nazis had to retreat from Kiev in 1944 as the Red Army advanced westwards, *Sonderkommandos* were forced to exhume the bodies and cremate them on huge pyres, just as had been done at the death camps (p173–75).

After the war, commemoration of the Babi Yar tragedy was slow, hampered by the Soviet policy of honouring primarily anti-fascist resistance by communists, or Soviet victims in general, without acknowledging that the majority of victims at these Holocaust sites were Jewish. A typically grandiose

memorial was erected in Soviet times near the site, but a good distance away from the ravine. Only around the end of the Soviet era were more memorials added, including a menorah-shaped monument closer to the ravine (erected in 1991), as well as a 'children's memorial' (2001) at the entrance to the Babi Yar complex opposite the Dorohozhychi metro station.

More recently, the addition of a major new memorial complex and museum was announced, with construction beginning in 2021.

Above
Two of the newer memorial monuments at the Babi Yar site today.

OTHER NAZI MASSACRE SITES

The Nazis carried out mass shootings of Jews in many places, especially in the early phases of their invasion of the Soviet Union, until the so-called Final Solution was ultimately devised (p134–35). Here is a short list of examples of the larger and/or especially significant such sites:

- **Rumbula**, in a forest on the southeastern edge of Latvia's capital, Riga (p210); it is here that some 25,000 Jews, mostly from Riga, were massacred in a meticulously planned operation in just two days in late 1941. There is a small memorial at the site today.
- **Biķernieku**, also near Riga in a forest to the north-east of the city; between 1941 and 1944 some 30,000 to 50,000 Jews were massacred here. Today's memorial monument includes a field of rocks reminiscent of Treblinka (p173).

- **Šķēde**, north of Liepāja on the Baltic coast of Latvia; the site of a smaller massacre in December 1941, but one that stands out because photographic evidence of the atrocities emerged after the war. In fact, photos taken of the shootings at Šķēde are often used to stand for Babi Yar and other such massacres.
- **Ponary**, just southwest of Lithuania's capital, Vilnius (p214); at this site, called Paneriai in Lithuanian, some of the most excessive massacres were com- mitted by the Nazis between 1941 and 1944. Possibly as many as 100,000 people were murdered here. Today there is a cluster of monuments and a small museum.

Above
Biķernieku Forest Holocaust Memorial with its symbolic central altar. There are 55 marked mass graves in the forest.

Rodina Mat & war museum

Southeast of the centre of Kiev
WW2, Holocaust, Modern war, Soviet legacy

★★★★★

Dark Rating: 7 ☹

The biggest and most iconic Soviet relic and a key landmark of Kiev is this giant statue, whose Russian name translates as 'Mother Homeland'; hence she is also known as 'the Motherland Monument' (see also p237). At 62m (200ft) high, plus the 40m (130ft) plinth, this titanium-clad lady is certainly tall. Underneath her is a museum that used to be called 'Museum of the Great Patriotic War' (see also p218), but since this terminology was outlawed in Ukrainian efforts to 'de-Sovietize' the country, it was renamed National Museum of the History of Ukraine in the Second World War.

The permanent exhibition inside goes beyond just a Ukrainian perspective, however, and still has plenty of Soviet characteristics, at least in the decorative elements, especially the mosaics inside the central hall. A huge variety of artefacts are on display, including some extremely grim items in the Holocaust section. Among these is a bone-grinding machine from a Nazi concentration camp.

Outside, under the watchful eyes of Rodina Mat, are various further Soviet-era monuments in classic socialist-realist style and also an adjacent open-air museum with tanks, artillery, rockets and one really big mobile missile launcher from the Cold War era. Furthermore, there is a separate indoor exhibition called 'In Foreign Wars', with a special focus on the Soviet Afghanistan intervention of 1979–89.

Above
A mobile launcher of RSD-10 'Pioneer' intermediate-range missiles, better known in the West as 'SS-20.'

Below
The giant silver Motherland Monument.

Strategic Missile Base Pervomaisk

Between Kiev and Odessa • Cold War, Nuclear weapons, Soviet legacy

★★★☆☆

Dark Rating: 8 ☠

Left
The empty silo for an SS-24 ICBM.

Below
A strategic missile base underground launch control centre (LCC).

This is a unique Soviet relic in the middle of Ukraine: a decommissioned intercontinental ballistic missile (ICBM) silo and launch control centre. During the Cold War, both the USA and the USSR had hundreds of nuclear missiles on permanent alert in underground silos, ready to start World War Three and mutually assured destruction (MAD). This missile field alone had ten SS-24 'Scalpel' ICBMs, each with ten thermonuclear warheads all programmed for targets in the West.

After the Cold War and the dissolution of the Soviet Union, all nuclear weapons were withdrawn from the emerging independent state of Ukraine, and the bases destroyed. This one in Pervomaisk is the only exception in that at least parts have been preserved. This includes one empty ICBM silo, with its lid permanently ajar, and the base's launch control centre (LCC) deep underground.

Tours of the site include going down to the bottom of the shaft into the LCC for a simulated launch sequence. The topside of the site is now an open-air exhibition of rockets, missile carriers and associated hardware. The star piece is a decommissioned SS-18 'Satan' ICBM, the most powerful ever built in the USSR. There is also a small indoor museum about the history of the base.

As nobody at the site speaks English, foreign visitors without sufficient knowledge of Ukrainian or Russian should prearrange a tour with an English-speaking guide or interpreter. Most Chernobyl (p220–23) tour operators based in Kiev offer an excursion to the site as an add-on option.

Bottom
The largest exhibit above ground is an SS-18 'Satan' ICBM.

Russia

By far the largest country on Earth, three-quarters of Russian territory is actually in Asia, including the vastness that is Siberia, but the European part still occupies almost 40 per cent of that continent's area and is where 77 per cent of the Russian population live. But Russia is huge not only in size; its rich history is on a par, and this includes plenty of dark chapters. Many of the dark destinations associated with that history are related to World War Two, or the 'Great Patriotic War' as it is better known here.

There are also plenty of vestiges of past Soviet glories, a part of Russian history that in recent years has seen a bit of a renaissance in appreciation. Even Stalin can again be publicly regarded as a 'great Russian' (although he was Georgian by birth – see p265).

However, the darkest sides of the Stalin era do get some memorialization as well.

Update: Another consequence of Russia's invasion of Ukraine is that Russia has become largely isolated, making it very difficult for Western tourists to travel to the country for the time being.

Below
The Lomonosov Moscow State University, the largest of the 'Seven Sisters'.

Murmansk

★★☆☆☆

Kola peninsula, northwest Russia • Nuclear legacy, WW2, Cold War　　　**Dark Rating: 5** ☠

Few place names evoke associations with almost mystical remoteness like this one (except perhaps Vladivostok and Timbuktu). Murmansk is the largest city above the Arctic Circle, thanks mostly to its harbour on a fjord that is kept ice-free year-round by the final reaches of the Gulf Stream, allowing permanent access to the Barents Sea. The location is of great strategic importance; and so it became a target for Nazi attacks in World War Two, when the German Wehrmacht tried to reach and conquer the city from the west (see Kirkenes, p79).

The operation failed, though, and Murmansk remained an important port for Allied supply convoys for the remainder of World War Two. During the Cold War, the location's strategic value grew even more, and Murmansk and associated military bases further down the fjord became the home of the Soviet Arctic Fleet, including, most crucially, nuclear submarines. A significant proportion of Russia's current submarine-based nuclear deterrent is still based near Murmansk, while older subs and their reactors rust away in naval scrapyards. All those

places are naturally out of bounds to tourists, but the city itself offers glimpses into its associations with Soviet and nuclear history.

Towering high over the harbour on a barren promontory is a huge war memorial whose centrepiece is a giant soldier statue affectionately known as 'Alyosha'. From there you can sometimes see navy vessels in the shipyards to the north. A bit inland is a memorial to submariners that includes the 'conning tower' of the *Kursk*, the nuclear submarine that tragically sank in August 2000 claiming 118 lives.

The most commodified element of Murmansk's nuclear history is the icebreaker *Lenin*, the first nuclear-powered vessel of such a type, in service from 1959 to 1989. It has been turned into a museum ship and can be visited on guided tours (in Russian only), which include the chance to peek into the reactor compartment.

Above
The icebreaker *Lenin*, the first nuclear-powered vessel of this kind, in Murmansk's harbour.

Museum of Political History

★★★☆☆

St Petersburg's Petrogradsky district
Soviet legacy, Communism, Repression, War　　　**Dark Rating: 4** ☠

The main authentic 'artefact' of this museum is, as it were, the building in which it is housed. It served as the Bolsheviks' headquarters in the run-up to the 1917 October Revolution, and Lenin gave many a speech from the building's balcony. The rooms they used are a shrine-like prize exhibit.

The rest of the museum's two main exhibitions explore Russian and Soviet history from pre-revolution times to the end of the USSR and beyond, up to the beginning of the Putin era. The layout of the museum is a little confusing, but there are plenty of interesting items and stories to be

found, including about everyday life in Soviet times, war, political terror, underground resistance and much more that is quite enthralling.

Leningrad Blockade sites

Various locations in and around St Petersburg • WW2

★★☆☆☆ – ★★★★☆

Dark Rating: 3–6 ☠

DARK STATS

The siege of Leningrad lasted

872 DAYS

from 8 September 1941 to
27 January 1944

The population of Leningrad
in 1941 was just over

3 MILLION

and of these, around

600,000

were evacuated in the
early stages of the
German onslaught

Approximately

800,000

civilians died during the
siege, mostly of starvation
but also from shelling
and bombing

75,000

bombs were dropped on
Leningrad over the course of
the blockade

The Blockade of Leningrad (St Petersburg's name in Soviet times) during World War Two was one of the longest sieges in history and the costliest in terms of lives lost. After launching their attack on the Soviet Union in June 1941, the Nazi German forces arrived at the edge of the city by August but met fierce resistance. Instead of trying to take Leningrad at any cost, they decided to starve the city into submission. But that submission never came, and Leningrad never fell. This was in large part thanks to a gap in the German ring around the city through which some inhabitants could be evacuated and supplies could be brought in – not enough for all those who remained in the city, but sufficient to keep it going.

The supply route became known as the 'Road of Life', although it also consisted of train lines and boats, namely across Lake Ladoga north of the city. In early 1943 the Soviets managed to break through the German ring further east and add an additional railway link. Yet it took until January 1944 for the siege to be lifted and the Germans

to retreat, almost 900 days after the start of the Blockade.

This story of heroism and survival is commemorated in various forms in the city today. In the city centre there is a Leningrad Blockade Museum, a rather old-school affair focusing more on military aspects while covering the desperate plight of the civilian population only in passing. The grand Monument to the Defenders of Leningrad in the south of the city features some splendid examples of socialist-realist sculptures as well as a sombre underground Memorial Hall with a small exhibition.

At Piskaryovskoye cemetery on the northeastern fringes of St Petersburg, most of the victims of the siege lie buried and there is a monument and small exhibition. The course of the former 'Road of Life' towards Lake Ladoga is lined with a host of memorial monuments of various types, and on the lake's shores is a dedicated Road of Life Museum, which features large exhibits such as the sort of truck used to cross the frozen lake in winter.

Above
This grand Soviet-era monument includes a symbolization of the broken ring of the siege.

The Kremlin & Red Square

In the very heart of Moscow • Soviet legacy

★★★★☆

Dark Rating: 3 ☠

Even though the Kremlin was built for the tsars of Imperial Russia, and the iconic walls and towers were designed by Italian architects, the Kremlin became the number-one icon of the Soviet era. The red flag of the USSR may no longer be flying (replaced by the Russian tricolour), but the five-pointed red stars atop some of the towers are still in place and the whole complex retains a certain Soviet aura, despite the fact that Red Square is now tourist central in Moscow.

This square is adjacent to the Kremlin and the location for grand military parades (in Soviet times, and revived in modern Russia too). Parts of the Kremlin can be visited, though there isn't much to see in dark terms. However, the Kremlin wall facing Red Square is home to the Lenin Mausoleum (see p293), and flanking it is a row of proper graves of Soviet-era big names, including Stalin.

Below
The Spasskaya ('Saviour') Tower of the Kremlin overlooking the iconic Cathedral of Vasily the Blessed (commonly known as St Basil's Cathedral) and Red Square.

OTHER SOVIET-ERA SITES IN MOSCOW

- **The Seven Sisters**, Stalinist-style skyscrapers that dominate several parts of the city's skyline.
- **The Lubyanka**, formerly the infamous headquarters of the KGB (now FSB).
- **The Ostankino TV tower**, built in the 1960s and once the tallest structure in the world.
- **VDNKh**, an acronym of the Russian for 'Exhibition of Achievements of the National Economy', inaugurated in the Stalin era, and celebrating the USSR's industry and agriculture.
- **The Cosmonautics Museum** and the soaring Monument to the Conquerors of Space, a needle in the shape of a rocket launching into space.
- **Park Pobedy**, 'Victory Park', home to Moscow's Great Patriotic War Museum.

- **Stalin's bunker** underneath a sports stadium in the northeastern suburb of Izmailovo, visitable on guided tours.
- **Bunker 42**, a Cold War-era structure and former subterranean command post.
- **Novodevichy cemetery**, where many a big name can be found, from Khrushchev to Boris Yeltsin.
- **Muzeon sculpture park**, an open-air collection of relocated Soviet-era statues and other artwork.

Below
The imposing Lubyanka building, formerly home to the KGB and hence once the most feared edifice in the USSR.

Gulag History Museum

★★★★☆

Northern Moscow, near Dostoyevskaya • Repression, Exile, Atrocities   **Dark Rating:** 7 ☠

The brutal Gulag prison system is most notoriously associated with Stalin, but carried on after his death, albeit on a smaller scale. There were many hundreds of such camps, most infamously in Siberia, but also in European Russia and in what today is Kazakhstan (p275). Millions of people were sentenced to forced labour in these often desolate places, mainly as a means of political repression.

This museum was founded by a former Gulag prisoner and first opened in 2004, originally on a prominent site in the heart of Moscow. A decade later, however, it relocated to its present home outside the centre, prompting suspicions in the West that this may have been a politically enforced move, although the museum claims that it was to gain more space in this converted warehouse.

The exhibition, behind shuttered windows, is gloomily lit. There are not many artefacts, but some exhibits are quite poignant, such as the inmates' personal belongings, hidden letters and items of clothing (demonstrating the cold conditions in the Gulags) in rows of backlit display cases in the main hall. The exhibition is not only cleverly laid out but also bilingual, with good English – something that you cannot always take for granted in Russia.

Below
Among the exhibits in the gloomy interior of the museum are original cell doors from various Gulags.

Central Museum of the Armed Forces

★★★☆☆

Northern Moscow, near Dostoyevskaya • Soviet legacy, WW2, Modern war   **Dark Rating:** 6 ☠

The principal military museum in Russia, and in terms of unique and rare artefacts one of the richest in the world, suffers a little from a lack of English-language labels and texts. The narrative is not as balanced and objective as it could be, but nevertheless this is a must-see for anyone with at least a passing interest in military history.

The main exhibition rooms cover aspects of pre-revolution conflicts, the Russian Civil War and then the entire Soviet period, with an emphasis on World War Two and the Cold War, as well as more modern post-Soviet times, such as the conflicts in Chechnya, Georgia (p265) or even more recently Syria.

In the Cold War section, the wreck of the U-2 spy plane flown by CIA pilot Gary Powers and shot down over Russia in 1960 is one of the top-prized items in the possession of the museum. In the post-Soviet parts, stand-out artefacts include several items salvaged from the *Kursk* nuclear submarine, which sank in August 2000, as well as pieces of wreckage from a Russian military jet shot down by the Turkish Air Force over the border with Syria in 2015. In the open-air parts are various pieces of Soviet-era military hardware, including a whole upright silver nuclear missile.

Jewish Museum and Tolerance Centre

★★★★★

Northern Moscow • Holocaust, WW2, Persecution

Dark Rating: 7 ☠

One of the newer sizeable museums in Moscow, this hi-tech, state-of-the-art institution, financed in large part by Jewish Russian oligarchs, opened in 2012 and has probably the most in-depth coverage of the Holocaust in the former Soviet Union and the role of Jews in Russia in general. In addition to the extensive focus on the plight of Jews before and during World War Two, it covers the postwar persecution of Jews and lingering anti-Semitism in the USSR. While the dark aspects of the topic get the widest coverage, there are also sections celebrating Jewish cultural contributions, such as those by the singer-songwriter Vladimir Vysotsky.

Above
The museum makes ample use of the most modern interactive display technology and is visually highly engaging.

OTHER JEWISH MUSEUMS

- **The Jewish Museum**, Berlin, is possibly the most celebrated such institution worldwide, housed in an extravagantly modern building. The vast permanent exhibition covers Jewish culture through the centuries in great depth, but the darker sides are much less of a focus here and the Holocaust is mainly presented in symbolic ways.
- **The POLIN Museum of the History of Polish Jews**, Warsaw (p167), is an award-winning institution that opened in 2014. It is in part similar to its Berlin equivalent, but has some coverage of the Holocaust that is graphic rather than symbolic.
- **The Shoah Museum**, Paris, is specifically about the Holocaust, especially from a French perspective.
- **The Holocaust Memorial Center**, Budapest, focuses mainly on the tragic fate of the Hungarian Jews in the Holocaust.

- **Norwegian Center for Holocaust and Minority Studies**, Oslo. This is housed in the Villa Grande, which used to be the residence of Norway's leader of the collaborationist puppet regime during that time. (His name, Quisling, has even acquired a generic meaning.)
- **Shoah Memorial**, Milan (p184), is rather unusual, and more a highly visual memorial site than a museum proper. It is located at the main railway station and incorporates a four-carriage deportation train.

Many more cities in Europe also have Jewish museums and/or Holocaust memorial sites, for example Prague (p176), Skopje (p198), Riga (p210) and Bucharest (p200). There are plenty in other parts of the world too, not least the USA (see p34).

Mamayev Hill & Rodina Mat

In the north of Volgograd • WW2, Soviet legacy   **Dark Rating:** ☠

Volgograd in southern Russia is the former Stalingrad – a name of more significance in the context of World War Two than most others. In the course of de-Stalinization, the city was renamed in 1961 after the Volga River, on the banks of which it stands. During the war, Stalingrad was an important target for the invading Nazi German army, desperate to capture this industrial city with its significant name. But instead the battle became the turning point of the war, a major defeat for the Germans and a great victory for the USSR, although that came at a terrible price.

The battle lasted from August 1942 to February 1943 and cost over a million lives. Almost the entire city was destroyed. When the encircled German 6th Army finally capitulated, some 100,000 German soldiers were taken prisoner. Only about 5000 POWs would survive and eventually return home in 1955.

The importance of the victory at Stalingrad prompted the Soviet authorities to have a memorial complex constructed in the rebuilt city that can arguably be considered the grandest and most monumental such site in the world. Its centrepiece, the gigantic Rodina Mat statue, is certainly the most iconic of all Soviet war monuments. The name is short for *Rodina-mat zavyot*, meaning 'the Motherland calls'. When the monument was completed in 1967, it was the tallest statue in the world – and it still holds the record of largest female figure. She towers over the city atop a hill and is thus its premier landmark.

Also part of the memorial complex are more statues of a similar style but smaller in scale, as well as bas-reliefs, a reflecting pool and a circular 'Hall of Glory' around a central eternal flame held by a giant hand like a torch.

Below
From the base to the tip of the sword the statue is 85m (280ft) tall, of which the (hollow) female figure alone is 52m (170ft).

Panorama Museum & Old Mill

Between Volgograd city centre and Mamayev Hill • WW2, Soviet legacy

★★★☆☆

Dark Rating: 6 ☠

After the Battle of Stalingrad, virtually the entire city lay in ruins. One particularly large shell of a building, a former grain mill, was preserved as a memorial while the rest of the city was rebuilt. This is a stunning sight today. It was joined in the 1980s by a large cylindrical building containing a giant panorama depicting the battle.

There are additional monuments too, as well as open-air exhibits such as tanks, planes and artillery pieces.

Beneath all this is a proper museum about the battle. The permanent exhibition is quite old-school and very Soviet, with flags, uniforms, medals and weapons dominating the displays alongside photos, documents and battle charts. There is plenty to keep war history buffs entertained, but what is largely missing is an account of the human aspects of the battle, especially on the German side. Instead, it is all overwhelmingly glorifying.

Above left
Inside the museum is a giant panorama in classic Soviet style, mixing 3D objects and soldier figures with a huge circular 2D painting.

Above right
The Old Mill is a five-storey structure of red-brick and concrete, preserved in its ruined state as a memorial.

Museum Pamyat

Centre of Volgograd • WW2

★★★★☆

Dark Rating: 7 ☠

Pamyat means 'memory', here that of the Battle of Stalingrad. The museum's location has great place authenticity: the basement of a former department store where the German 6th Army's commander General Paulus had his headquarters, and where he was captured. His office has been reconstructed and features a dummy Paulus looking suitably dejected as he is taken prisoner. Other life-size reconstructions include a field hospital and

an improvised wartime German Christmas celebration scene.

There are plenty of artefacts, photos and documents. What sets this museum apart from its bigger and grander counterpart (above) is the fact that the German side gets more attention, in particular the desperation of the ordinary soldiers and their increasingly dire situation towards the end of the battle. This is especially reflected in the countless letters on display, written

by German soldiers, but that the German army postal service could no longer send. You obviously need the requisite language skills to read them, but these documents provide unparalleled insights, including not only resignation and final good-byes but also unfaltering loyalty to Hitler, even in the face of impending defeat.

Perm-36 Gulag memorial

Northeast of Perm, Urals region • Repression, Prison, Soviet legacy

Dark Rating: 9 ☠

The Gulag system (p235) is mostly associated with Stalin's purges in the 1930s and beyond, and most of the hard labour camps of that era have long since vanished without much of a trace, but this place is an exception in more than one way. It was set up comparatively late, in 1946, and unlike most other camps it was not closed down after the end of Stalin's rule but continued as a 'correctional labour colony'; from 1972 it also became a camp for political prisoners. It was not until 1987 that it ceased that function, and a year later it was closed down altogether. Remarkably, it was not torn down but preserved, and today is the only original Gulag site turned into a memorial for visitors.

The memorial was originally run by an independent organization, which got into trouble when Putin tightened up legislation and NGOs of this kind were declared 'foreign agents'. The site had long been listed as 'endangered', and in 2015 it had to close down after

water and electricity were cut off. However, it did not remain closed for long but was taken over by the state and is now officially the State Independent Cultural Institution of Perm Region. Instead of that mouthful, though, it is still better known as 'Perm-36', the code name this remote place was given in Soviet times, even though it is some 120km (75 miles) from that city just west of the Ural Mountains.

After the takeover in 2015 there was much criticism in the West and among the Russian opposition that this was a political move to 'sanitize' the dark history of the Gulag. Indeed, in the current exhibitions there is a stronger emphasis on 'criminals' and 'nationalists' (Ukrainians, say), but the fact that this was part of the Soviet system of political repression is by no means swept under the rug.

The original independent exhibition has not been completely replaced but augmented by additional ones, including one

on banned books and the reasons political prisoners were sent here. The site's main attraction is the buildings themselves, including the cells, as well as the watchtowers and many fences around the two compounds – one the 'strict' camp, the other the 'special' (i.e. even stricter) camp.

Above
The bleak site oozes place authenticity. It is a solitary monument to the millions of political prisoners who suffered and died under communist repression.

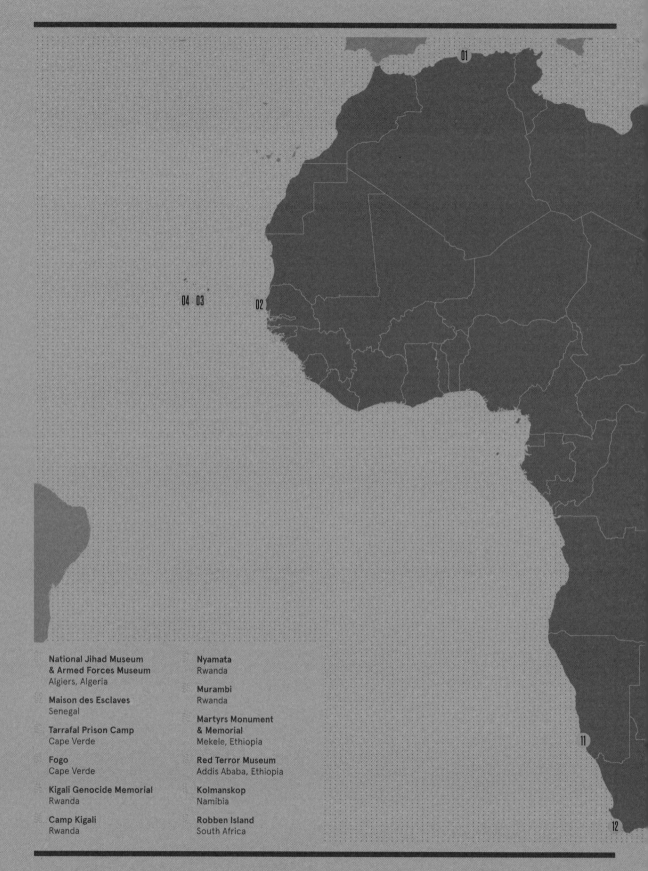

**National Jihad Museum
& Armed Forces Museum**
Algiers, Algeria

Maison des Esclaves
Senegal

Tarrafal Prison Camp
Cape Verde

Fogo
Cape Verde

Kigali Genocide Memorial
Rwanda

Camp Kigali
Rwanda

Nyamata
Rwanda

Murambi
Rwanda

**Martyrs Monument
& Memorial**
Mekele, Ethiopia

Red Terror Museum
Addis Ababa, Ethiopia

Kolmanskop
Namibia

Robben Island
South Africa

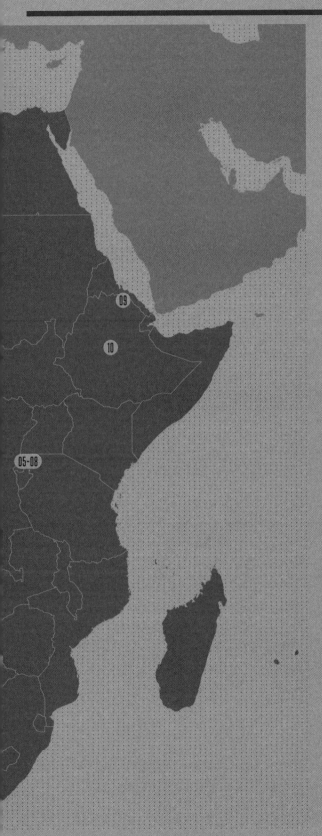

Africa

This is the continent that is least on most travellers' radars, except for a handful of classic destinations such as Morocco and South Africa. There is no shortage of dark history all over Africa, what with colonialism, the slave trade, civil war, famine, dictatorships and even genocide. So it's certainly of interest in dark terms. But it cannot be denied that parts of Africa are 'difficult'. Quite a few areas are positively dangerous and can be regarded as no-go zones. Many governments have warnings in place against any or at least all but essential travel to such regions (e.g. Libya, Chad, Somalia and the Central African Republic); and let's face it, travelling as a tourist is great, but never essential.

However, the countries featured here are largely more manageable for foreign (and in particular Western) travellers. But the security situation can change, and it has in the past, from extremely dangerous to perfectly safe, even in the case of some of the countries listed here (e.g. Algeria, Ethiopia and Rwanda). Checking ahead is always advisable.

It is often easier to fly into one specific African country from outside the continent than it is to travel from one African country to a neighbouring one overland. Border bureaucracy is something many African countries excel at.

Algeria

This North African country is the largest on the continent by area. Most of it is desert, namely the famous Sahara, and hence sparsely populated, owing to the harsh climate and a near-total absence of rainfall. Only the thin strip along the Mediterranean coast is fertile. It is here that the larger settlements are, including the capital city, Algiers.

From 1830 to 1962 Algeria was a French colony, and from the mid-1950s a bloody War of Independence was fought. The brutal approach France took in this war did damage not only to Algeria but also to France's reputation internationally. After pressure from the UN, France eventually released Algeria into independence. However, France continued to use some remote spots in the south Algerian desert for testing its early nuclear weapons, namely at In Ekker and Reggane, thus leaving behind not only hard feelings but also radiation. The last test took place as late as 1966.

National Jihad Museum & Armed Forces Museum

Algiers • Algerian War of Independence

★★☆☆☆

Dark Rating: 5 ☢

These two institutions form part of an extensive memorial complex in Algeria's large and challenging capital city, Algiers. The complex is located atop the El Madania hill. Its dominant feature is the giant Martyrs' Monument, erected on the 20th anniversary of the country gaining independence. It is a soaring 92m-high (300ft) concrete structure towering over the city and visible from almost everywhere. Underneath it is the National Jihad Museum, aka *Musée National du Moudjahid*.

This museum is not, as you might think, about any recent Islamic-extremist warriors (such as the Mujahedin of Afghanistan) but about the Algerian War of Independence against France in 1954–62. The same applies to the neighbouring Musée central de l'Armée (Armed Forces Museum). This is a huge affair spread over several floors, plus an open-air part with larger exhibits such as missiles and planes.

Left
Three concrete palm leaves, each with a statue of an Algerian soldier at the bottom, surround the central 'eternal flame' of the *Mémorial du Martyr*.

Senegal

This westernmost country of West Africa is a former French colony and is still largely francophone. Since gaining its independence in 1960, the country has had its share of troubles, especially the conflict with the separatist movement of the southern province of Casamance. But the reason Senegal is included here has to do with a dark chapter in history that goes back much further: the transatlantic slave trade (see p244–45).

Senegal is quite varied, landscape-wise, from desert-like areas in the northern regions bordering Mauritania to wetlands and savannah further south.

Its capital city, Dakar, is a large metropolis plagued by pollution, but is the principal entry point for most foreign visitors. The city itself has a few points of dark interest: for instance, the memorial dedicated to the victims of the MV *Le Joola* ferry disaster of September 2002, which claimed the lives of nearly 2000 people.

A peculiar landmark of Dakar is the 50m-tall (164ft) sculptural group of a man, woman and child called the African Renaissance Monument. Its enormous cost and the fact that it was built by sculptors from North Korea (p314) make it highly controversial.

Maison des Esclaves

Dakar • Slavery

★★☆☆☆

Dark Rating: 7 ☠

Top
The 'House of Slaves', with its doorway of no return between the two flights of stairs.

Above
A view of the old fortifications on Île de Gorée.

This was one of the slave-trading posts in West Africa, on the small island of Gorée just outside Senegal's capital city, Dakar. The Portuguese used Gorée for this purpose from the fifteenth century. Later came Dutch traders, until the region fell into the hands of France, another big player in the transatlantic slave trade.

The current structure was built in 1776 and served as an embarkation point for slave ships sailing to the 'New World'. How big a role it played in this dark business is contested, and similar trading posts (see page 245) may have had greater importance. However, the Maison des Esclaves ('house of slaves' in French) has been a national memorial since the 1970s and is now one of the top sights of Dakar, from where there are regular boat excursions to Gorée.

The building is not particularly big, and there is only a small exhibition on the first floor (the former slave-trader quarters), but the ground-floor dungeons for the slaves and the 'doorway of no return' are grim reminders of this dark chapter of world history.

THE TRANSATLANTIC SLAVE TRADE

Slavery is as old as civilization, and was common in the Roman Empire, ancient Egypt and the pre-Columbian cultures of the Americas. However, the colonial trans-atlantic slave trade between the sixteenth and nineteenth centuries reached new dimensions and must rank as one of the worst crimes against humanity in history.

Portugal, the pioneering explorer nation in the fifteenth century, initially almost monopolized this business. Later, the other major colonizing world powers – Spain, Holland, Britain and France – competed too. The slave trade was at its peak in the eighteenth century. Enslaved people were mainly captured, or procured from local slave traders, in West Africa, West Central Africa and to a lesser extent East Africa. There were dedicated, purpose-built slave-trading posts on the coast and outlying islands for 'warehousing' the captives (see opposite). From here, the soon-to-be slaves were then dispatched – packed like sardines under the decks of the slave ships. Many did not survive the journey.

Enslaved Africans were sold in the European colonies in the Americas, in particular Brazil, the Caribbean and in southern and eastern parts of North America, where they were set to work in the plantations. The goods from these plantations, such as sugar, coffee, tobacco and cotton, were mostly shipped to Europe. The trade routes thus formed a triangle: from Europe to the African coasts, from there to the Americas, and from there back to Europe.

Somewhere between 10 and 15 million Africans were thus uprooted and transplanted to the 'New World'. Many Caribbean nations are still ethnically characterized by the descendants of these enslaved Africans – as is the USA, with its large African-American population.

Despite the big profits made in the slave trade, its obvious immorality led to a movement that condemned slavery as a shameful practice for enlightened nations. There were calls for abolition in Britain and elsewhere from about the mid-eighteenth century onwards. France abolished slavery towards the end of the century, and in Britain it took until 1807 for the slave trade to be declared illegal.

However, slavery as forced labour continued. In the British Empire, it was not outlawed altogether until 1833. In addition, the British Navy formed an Anti-Slavery Squadron targeting slave ships that were still operating, and managed to liberate many thousands from their fate as slaves (see p70). In the USA, there was a sharp divide between the abolitionist northern states and the southern states, which kept on exploiting slaves in the vast plantations of the Deep South. Eventually, this division led to the American Civil War from 1861 to 1865. Slavery officially ended in North America with the defeat of the Confederate states.

More countries followed suit, but slavery continued in several pockets around the world. The last country to abolish slavery officially was Mauritania – as late as 1981. Yet slavery is far from over. There is no longer any open slave trade, but illegal forced labour, human trafficking, child labour and extreme forms of exploitation of workers and domestic servants (with deprivation of freedom and no pay) are still significant problems today.

Above
An American poster from 1857 advertises a slave auction.

Opposite
Cape Coast Castle, one of around 40 'slave forts' built on West Africa's coast by European traders.

OTHER SITES RELATED TO THE SLAVE TRADE

In West Africa there are several former slave-trading posts that can be visited along what was once known as the 'Slave Coast'.

- **Ghana**: this is a prime destination for such sites, with Cape Coast Castle and Elmina Castle being the largest and best-known ones.
- **Sierra Leone**: Bunce Island was a British slave-trading post from where slaves were shipped primarily to North America, especially South Carolina.
- **Gambia**: Albreda was another pivotal slave-trading post and is associated with Alex Haley's novel, *Roots*, and the TV series. A nearby island takes its name from the main character: Kunta Kinte.
- **Benin**: this small country's port of Quidah was a major slave-trading post for more than 300 years. More black Africans may have been dispatched from here than from anywhere else.
- **Nigeria**: the ancient town of Badagry was also a slave-trading post, operated by Africans trading with Europeans and Brazilians. There are now three slavery-related museums here.

At the other end, the destinations of the slaves, there are also places of commemoration, e.g. the Slavery Museum in Willemstad on the Dutch Antilles island Curaçao. In Liverpool, UK, the International Slavery Museum is the most significant European institution on this topic.

DARK STATS

An estimated

10-15 MILLION

Africans were shipped to the 'New World' between 1525 and 1866, and around

15 PER CENT

of these did not survive the journey

Britain and Portugal dominated the trade, transporting

70 PER CENT

of all enslaved Africans

3.1 MILLION

Africans were transported by Britain between 1640 and 1807, and around

3,204,313

enslaved people in the US in 1850 (according to the Census; total population was 23,191,876). Most enslaved Africans were sent to the Caribbean and Brazil

Cape Verde

This is a group of islands in the Atlantic named after the westernmost point on the African mainland, Cap Vert in Dakar, Senegal (p243). The archipelago is of volcanic origin, caused by a hotspot in the Earth's crust (see p51). There is still an active volcano on the island of Fogo, whereas the northern island of Sal has eroded to an almost flat sand, rock and salt desert and is today a popular beach-holiday destination.

Portuguese explorers discovered the then uninhabited islands in the mid-fifteenth century and turned Cape Verde into a strategic trading post, especially in the transatlantic slave trade (p244–45). The first slaves, however, were brought here to develop the islands, and so the islands' inhabitants constitute one of the oldest Creole populations in the world.

The slave trade eventually ended and Cabo Verde, as the name goes in Portuguese, lost much of its strategic importance. The land is hard to work because of the scarcity of water and the general topography,

and drought remains a major problem. Yet the islands' isolated location proved useful again during the years of the dictatorship of António de Oliveira Salazar in Portugal (p98), when political prisoners and especially freedom-fighter rebels from its other African colonies were banished to Cape Verde. However, the independence movements in these colonies proved stronger, and little Portugal had overstretched its global imperial ambitions.

At home, the dictatorship finally fell in April 1974. Most colonies declared their independence (Guinea-Bissau already had in 1973), although Cape Verde took a little longer, until the summer of 1975. The islands escaped post-independence civil wars like those in other former Portuguese colonies such as Angola and Mozambique (see also East Timor, p304), but its economic hardships meant that many islanders emigrated. Today, the Cape Verdean diaspora is actually larger than the population still on the islands.

Tarrafal Prison Camp

★★☆☆☆

In the north of Santiago • Political prison, Concentration camp

Dark Rating: 7 ☠

The prime dark destination on the Cape Verde Islands is this former prison camp at Tarrafal on the archipelago's main island. Set up shortly after the right-wing regime under dictator António de Oliveira Salazar came to power in Portugal (p98) in 1933, this remote spot was chosen to incarcerate political opponents.

By the mid-1950s the practice of sending prisoners so far from the homeland had come in for international criticism, so the camp closed in 1954. However, it reopened in the 1960s to house captured freedom fighters from the Portuguese African colonies where the resistance movements against colonial rule were getting stronger, such as in Guinea-Bissau and Angola.

The camp closed for good shortly after the so-called Carnation Revolution in Portugal in 1974, which ended the dictatorship, and

one by one the old colonies became independent. The buildings of the former camp were abandoned or used for other purposes, until the site was finally turned into a memorial in about 2010.

Exhibition elements have been added to some of the cell blocks, but in Portuguese only. The signs outside the buildings have English and French translations, so at

least some information is provided for those international visitors who make it here.

Above
Visitors can wander the eerily empty and silent compound and explore the former cell blocks.

Fogo

Southern Cape Verde • Natural disaster (volcano)

★★☆☆☆

Dark Rating: 6 ☠

This is the island currently above the volcanic hotspot that created the whole Cape Verdean archipelago. As such, it is also the youngest of these islands, estimated as only around 100,000 years old. In that time Fogo's stratovolcano (see p51), which is simply called Pico do Fogo ('Peak of Fire'), has grown to almost 3000m (10,000ft) in height.

The volcano sits in a massive caldera several kilometres across, bounded on three sides by a near-vertical escarpment, but open to the sea on the east. The summit crater of the steep cone last erupted more than 200 years ago, but more recent eruptions have occurred through fissures on the flanks of the main cone.

Amazingly, a small Creole community lived right inside the caldera and eked out a living from growing grapes and other fruit in small plots of volcanic soil. The community, called Chã das Caldeiras, consisted of some 700 people in the twin villages of Portela and Bangaeira. In 1995 a new eruption threatened the settlement; the lava flow narrowly missed the villages, but destroyed parts of the agricultural co-operative.

However, the community was less lucky during the eruption of December 2014 to February 2015. Gradually the houses were engulfed by lava and the only road into the caldera was destroyed. Fortunately, the flow was so slow that nobody was hurt, and the villagers were able to rescue their most important possessions before watching their homes slowly being eaten up by the lava.

The evacuated population had to find new accommodation outside the caldera. In the meantime, a few resilient caldera inhabitants have returned, and some of the guest houses have reopened, sitting atop the still-warm lava that now covers the predecessor buildings.

The wine-making co-operative was destroyed, so the only source of income now is from tourism, including those keen to climb Pico do Fogo. There are mountaineering guides to arrange such climbs.

As a dark destination, it is not just the dramatic volcano and surrounding otherworldly lava

Above and below
A print shows the volcanic eruption on the Island of Fuego, ca. 1745; Pico do Fogo today.

landscape that are an attraction. The destroyed villages, some of the roofs of which still poke out of the new lava, add a tragic ghost-town element.

Rwanda

One of the smallest but most densely populated nations in Africa, present-day Rwanda is primarily defined by two big dark Gs: gorillas and genocide. Mountain gorillas are the most endangered ape species, famously depicted in the movie *Gorillas in the Mist* (1988). Trekking to see these gentle giants in their natural habitat in the Virunga Mountains brings the largest proportion of visitors to Rwanda, despite the steep cost of a gorilla trekking permit.

There is something dark in the more figurative sense related to the gorillas too: the violent murder in 1985 of Dian Fossey, the famous conservationist and researcher (also depicted in *Gorillas in the Mist*). In addition to gorilla trekking, you can hike to the ruins of her research station at Karisoke, high up on Mount Bisoke, which is in the Virunga National Park. Fossey and several of 'her' gorillas are buried at the site, so it is a veritable pilgrimage (you need to arrange a park ranger, guards and porters for this).

The darkest chapter of Rwanda's modern history is concerned with violent death on a much greater scale: the genocide in 1994 (see p250). In addition to the genocide memorials featured here separately, there are three other major memorials: Ntarama, just south of Kigali; Bisesero in the west, near Lake Kivu; and Nyarubuye in the southeastern corner of the country, near the border with Tanzania. Furthermore, there are countless unofficial memorial sites all over the country.

Other sites associated with the genocide include a hotel in Kigali made famous by the movie *Hotel Rwanda* (2004), even though this was shot in South Africa and the building featured in the film looks nothing like the real thing. This also has a different name in real life: Hôtel des Mille Collines. But its dramatic story is genuine. The hotel's manager (a Hutu) sheltered over a thousand Tutsis and moderate Hutus who had sought refuge here, and through a combination of clever negotiating and bribery prevented the Interahamwe from entering the compound and killing its occupants.

The hotel's swimming pool became the main water supply for those sheltering here. Today, the refurbished hotel is still in operation and is one of the more upscale accommodation options in Kigali – and the swimming pool fulfils its original purpose again.

Kigali Genocide Memorial

Gisozi district, Kigali • Genocide, Mass graves

★★★★☆

Dark Rating: 8 ☠

Above
Family photographs of victims hang on display in an exhibition at the memorial centre.

Rwanda's capital city is the usual point of entry for visitors to this country. It is also where the most accessible of its genocide memorials is located – and in most cases it will be the only such memorial visitors will see. It is hence the one most geared towards international visitors. The permanent exhibition (curated by a British NGO) is modern, multilingual and illuminating without being as shocking as some of the more rural memorials in Rwanda.

Nevertheless, some of the images are very graphic and the skulls of victims are on display, so it is by no means an 'easy' museum to visit. Yet in a city with few mainstream tourist attractions, the

Kigali Genocide Memorial has established itself as one of the mustsee places for visitors. It is also a good introduction for those not yet familiar with the topic. Outside the main building are several mass graves, set in a landscaped garden-like park, and a wall of victims' names. The graves are said to contain the remains of a quarter of a million victims.

Right
The Wall of Names is an ongoing project to record victims' names, and is a poignant record of the scale of the atrocity.

Camp Kigali

Central Kigali • Murder, Assassination

★★☆☆☆

Dark Rating: 5 ☠

Probably the most historically significant genocide-related site in Rwanda's capital city is the compound where, on 7 April 1994, the second day of the genocide, Hutu extremists killed ten Belgian UN soldiers. This was a deliberate and calculated assassination that triggered the withdrawal of all Belgian soldiers and large parts of the UN staff in general (see p250).

Today, the site is a Belgian memorial. A building pockmarked with holes from gunfire and grenades contains a small exhibition, which is, unsurprisingly, rather critical of the UN.

Above
The bullet-sprayed building has been preserved as a memorial to the slain Belgian soldiers.

THE RWANDAN GENOCIDE

One of the worst genocides in history, this was a mass slaughter of some 800,000, perhaps up to one million, people in just 100 days between April and July 1994. At the time it was under-reported in the West, especially in Europe, where the media focus then was more on the Balkan conflicts. Hence some background information is needed here.

The roots of the genocide lie partly in the ethnic divide between Hutu and Tutsi. The former have long lived in this part of the world and have traditionally been farmers. The Tutsi migrated in from the north a few centuries ago as cattle herders and over time established themselves as an economic and political elite. However, intermarrying increasingly blurred the ethnic distinction, which became more one of class than ethnicity. Still, during the time when Rwanda was a Belgian colony (like the Congo), the ethnic divide was institutionalized, through ID cards on which membership of one of the two groups had to be marked.

Tensions between Hutus and Tutsis had already developed before Rwanda was released into independence in 1962. Outbreaks of violence led to many Tutsis fleeing into exile, especially to neighbouring Uganda. Moreover, the outgoing colonial rulers put Hutus in power instead of Tutsis, but without any adjustment to the political structures or democratic reforms. Disillusioned Tutsis meanwhile became rebels, and a small-scale civil war was emerging. As tension grew, the United Nations brokered negotiations and sent a peacekeeping force: UNAMIR (United Nations Assistance Mission for Rwanda). However, it was underfunded and under-equipped and so could not prevent what would happen in 1994.

The genocide was not just a tribal war, as was wrongly perceived by some in the West. It was a planned, systematic attempt at exterminating the Tutsis in Rwanda. Weapons caches had been set up and 'death lists' of names drawn up. Hate-filled propaganda spread through mass media (predominantly radio) incited the Hutu population. One incident, the shooting down of the president's plane (by whom is still unknown), was enough to trigger the starting gun. 'Hutu Power' extremists established a 'crisis government' and militias started going from house to house in Kigali to round up Tutsis and politically moderate Hutus. Then the mass slaughtering began all across the country.

After a group of Belgian UN soldiers was deliberately targeted and killed (see p249), instead of reinforcing their troops, the Western military evacuated all foreigners and large parts of their military personnel, just as the Hutus had hoped, leaving behind a hopelessly inadequate rump force.

Ordinary Hutus were called upon to 'do the work' – that is, butcher 'the enemy', who had often been their neighbours. But the driving forces were the military and in particular a militia group called the Interahamwe, who manned the roadblocks and led the massacres. Since firearms and ammunition were scarce, the principal murder weapon was the machete. The victims were hacked to death with unparalleled brutality.

The residual UNAMIR troops were largely helpless in the face of the scale of the atrocities. Meanwhile, at the UN headquarters in New York, lengthy debate as to whether or not what was happening in Rwanda constituted 'genocidal acts' delayed matters further, as no one wanted to bear the cost of, or assume the responsibility for, a decisive intervention.

In the end it was a Tutsi rebel army, the Rwandan Patriotic Front, led by Paul Kagame that invaded from their base in Uganda and pushed through Rwanda to put a stop to the genocide. Well-organized and disciplined, they achieved a military victory and brought the slaughter to an end. The Hutus, now fearing reprisals, fled in their hundreds of thousands into neighbouring Congo (then called Zaire). At the same time France suddenly launched a 'humanitarian' mission of its own and French troops created a 'safe zone' in the west of Rwanda – thus controversially providing safe passage for many of the genocide's perpetrators (the genocidaires). The large displacement of people and the squalor of the Hutu refugee camps eventually came to the attention of the world – although it probably fostered the false impression that these were the victims – and foreign aid began to be channelled towards this part of Africa. In the end the cost was far higher than a proper investment in preventing the genocide would have been.

Within Rwanda, Kagame established himself as a solid, even authoritarian, ruler and successfully saw through a programme of reconstruction, reconciliation and commemoration.

Opposite
The bloodstained clothes of genocide victims on display at the Murambi Genocide Memorial in Gikongoro.

Nyamata

★★★☆☆

Bugesera district • Genocide, Atrocity

Dark Rating: 10 💀

This is one of the most significant of Rwanda's official genocide memorials. Here, a church in which thousands had taken refuge came under attack from the *genocidaires*. They used hand grenades to gain entry to the church and then machetes to slaughter those hiding inside. As part of today's memorial, hundreds of pieces of bloodstained clothing of the victims lie strewn all over the pews. Next to the church is a mass grave. You can enter this and literally walk among the dead, or rather their bones and skulls.

Left
The skulls and bones of victims are piled high on shelves on both sides of the dark corridors.

Murambi

★★★☆☆

Gikongoro • Genocide, Mummified bodies

Dark Rating: 10 💀

This genocide memorial in the south of Rwanda is one of the darkest destinations there is. It is actually two sites in one. There is a museum exhibition, designed and curated by the same NGO that runs the Kigali Genocide Memorial (see p248), and is hence fairly 'Westernized'. However, the rest of the Murambi site features something that is deeply disturbing.

Here, at this former school complex, it is not only skulls and bones that are on display, but semi-mummified bodies, victims of the massacres who were later exhumed from the mass graves. Preserved with lime, the bodies are now white and displayed on wooden table-like structures within a series of bungalows.

A peculiar smell permeates the rooms and it takes a while to get used to it. But what you see is impossible to get used to: contorted bodies, some with facial expressions that seem to be silently screaming in agony. Some hands still clutch rosaries. You see smashed-in skulls; you see missing limbs – hacked off by machete. Probably worst of all, some of the bodies are tiny. Even infants were not safe from being butchered.

The amassed evidence of humanity violated on such a scale is truly shocking, thoroughly heartbreaking and possibly the most emotionally taxing memorial in the world. You may ask yourself why such a drastic approach was chosen. The answer is partly political. The idea is that with these graphic displays there can be no chance of genocide denial. You have to remember that this rural memorial is aimed more at the local population (more than half of whom are too young to have any memories of the genocide), and only secondarily at foreign visitors.

Ethiopia

This large, multi-ethnic East African country has had a number of very dark chapters in its modern history. It was the only country in Africa never to have been colonized by European powers, instead remaining a feudal monarchy. Then in 1936 Fascist Italy invaded and briefly created Italian East Africa, which also included neighbouring territories such as Eritrea. That was a short episode, though: the Allies forced the Italians out again by 1941, but left Eritrea as part of Ethiopia and reinstated the monarchy.

Revolutionary resistance grew from the 1960s onwards, and in 1974 the Derg, a paramilitary social-ist-inspired organization, toppled the monarchy and assumed power. The subsequent period of violence and repression became known as the 'Red Terror'.

Among the many atrocities committed by the Derg was the aerial bombing of a market in Hawzen in 1988, which killed some 2500 civilians. Hawzen is in the northern region of Tigray, where resistance against the Derg regime was strongest. However, it took until the early 1990s for the Derg regime to collapse, partly because outside support was waning in the wake of the end of the communist Eastern Bloc. At the same time Eritrea broke away again, declaring independ-ence, which it formally gained in 1993. Yet border dis-putes between the two countries soon led to military conflict. A UN-brokered ceasefire put an end to the war in 2000, but relations remained tense and have only recently calmed down.

The idea, which many in the West hold, that all of Ethiopia is a famine-ridden desert is quite incorrect. The country's highland landmass is quite verdant, and economically Ethiopia has become a veritable pow-erhouse within Africa. The main tourist attractions are of the ancient cultural sort, but also include sites of the recent, dark political and military past. Moreover, Ethiopia features the Danakil Depression, the hottest region on planet Earth, an extreme land of desert, salt pans and active volcanoes, including Erta Ale with its lava lake. The old city of Harar has an alto-gether different and unique attraction, the nightly feeding of hyenas in which tourists are invited to take part. Here, hyenas are not vilified as elsewhere, but revered, and play an important role in local traditions, beliefs and customs.

Below
A bas-relief at the Tiglachin Monument in Addis Ababa. Also known as the Derg Monument, its statuary was donated by North Korea.

Martyrs Monument & Memorial

★★★☆☆

Mekele, Tigray • Civil war

Dark Rating: 6 ☠

This is a memorial complex in the capital city of the Tigray region, in the north of Ethiopia, and the area where the resistance against the Derg regime was strongest. The monument and adjacent museum opened in 2001 on the tenth anniversary of the overthrow of the regime. The museum exhibition mainly consists of black-and-white photos of Tigrayan resistance fighters in battle, in training, at leisure or in political meetings, plus display cases with artefacts such as guns and communications equipment. What will become of this place in the wake of the renewed civil war that broke out in late 2020 remains to be seen. As government forces focused their attack on the Tigrayan leadership, that leadership's memorial complex could well be threatened too.

Left
Flanking the tall main monument with its golden globe at the top are fine sculptures depicting armed fighters as well as civilians.

Red Terror Museum

★★★☆☆

Addis Ababa • Atrocities, Civil war

Dark Rating: 8 ☠

This museum in Ethiopia's capital city is the main place commemorating the dark period of the Derg regime, the military junta that ruled Ethiopia between 1974 and 1991. There is very little descriptive/interpretative text at the museum to provide background information, so it's best to read up on the history before visiting. The displays include some very grim items such as instruments of torture, while whole walls are covered with little portrait photographs of victims of the regime. The very darkest part of the exhibition is a small side room where display cabinets are filled with the skulls and bones of victims exhumed from mass graves, and glass cases contain the clothes they had been wearing.

Above
Skulls of some of those killed during the Red Terror on display at the museum.

Namibia

This large and thinly populated country in the south-west of Africa has had a turbulent modern history with many dark chapters. The area became a colony of Imperial Germany in the late nineteenth century, and in 1904 a rebellion against German colonial rule by the Herero people led to a campaign of punishment that is widely regarded as the first genocide of the twentieth century; the majority of the Herero were wiped out by 1908. Most died after they were forcibly driven into the desert, where they succumbed to dehydration and starvation. A significant number were also put in concentration camps. This then new concept was adopted by the German rulers from the British model established in South Africa during the Boer Wars.

Some camps, such as the one on Shark Island, a rocky promontory in the coastal town of Lüderitz, had death rates in excess of 90 per cent. Moreover, medical experiments were undertaken on prisoners and skulls of dead inmates were sent for 'scientific examination' back in Germany, where the subject of eugenics was all the rage (that is, pseudo-scientific attempts at 'proving' the superiority of the European white race). All this can be seen as a sinister precursor to what would later happen on a larger scale under the Nazis in the Third Reich.

In World War One, Namibia was taken over by the then British colony of South Africa. From the 1960s, the decades-long Namibian War of Independence ensued, also known as the South African Border War. This ended only in 1990, at the time when South Africa began its transition from apartheid (p258–59) to democracy, and Namibia was subsequently granted independence.

In contemporary Namibia, commemoration of the dark past was slow to develop, but there is now an Independence Memorial Museum, which also covers the 1904–7 genocide. Apart from this museum in the capital, the main dark attractions have more to do with Namibia's stark landscapes. The northern stretch of desert by the Atlantic Ocean is known as the Skeleton Coast, after the countless shipwrecks along its beaches. Otherwise, there are remnants of the German colonial period, as well as relics of a German POW camp and a war cemetery near the small town of Aus in southern Namibia.

Kolmanskop

Near Lüderitz • Ghost town, Desert
★★★☆☆
Dark Rating: 4 ☠

In spite of all Namibia's history of war and genocide, its most famous dark destination is not quite so dark in historical terms, but is a hugely atmospheric ghost town. Kolmanskop started out with a bright future as a diamond-mining town after abundant deposits of these gems were found in this remote desert spot in 1908. By 1912 the place was supplying more than 10 per cent of the world's diamonds. Accordingly, it grew incredibly rich, and this was reflected in the infrastructure and nature of the buildings. Despite its isolated position in the desert near the coastal town of Lüderitz, the inhabitants enjoyed every modern Western luxury as well as state-of-the-art medical care.

Above
An old sign at the abandoned, former German mining settlement.

Left
The sand-covered ruins of what was once a thriving town with a wealth of amenities including a bowling alley and swimming pool.

After the German colonial era came to an end, mining operations resumed following the end of World War One, but now under the aegis of the mighty South African De Beers corporation. However, the diamond deposits were being depleted, and the town began to decline from the 1930s onwards. Eventually, the whole place was given up altogether. The last inhabitants left Kolmanskop in the late 1950s, and since then it has been abandoned.

Desert sand is slowly filling the empty houses, and several structures have become dilapidated beyond repair. A few other buildings, however, have seen some refurbishment and can be visited on guided tours. You can explore the ghost town independently, but you have to obtain a permit in advance. This is advisable for photography enthusiasts, for whom Kolmanskop is a dream site.

Right
Encroaching sand dunes are gradually swallowing up the buildings.

South Africa

Occupying the southern tip of the African continent, this large, multi-ethnic nation was first colonized by the Dutch in the seventeenth and eighteenth centuries. Starting from the initial outpost at what today is Cape Town, Dutch-descendant whites moved inland long before the Scramble for Africa by other European colonial powers began.

The British took over first the Cape Colony and then other parts of present-day South Africa from the turn of the nineteenth century onwards. This led to conflict with the earlier settlers, who moved further northeast to form the Boer Republics. 'Boer' literally means 'farmer' in Afrikaans, the language that developed in South Africa from Dutch. Discontent with British rule sparked the Anglo-Boer Wars of the late nineteenth and early twentieth centuries, in which the British fully established their grip on the country.

South Africa became nominally a quasi-independent state in 1910, but was not granted full sovereignty until 1931. By then, the disenfranchisement and repression of the native black population was already well established, but it became formally institutionalized with the introduction of 'apartheid' in 1948 (see p258–59).

When the decades-long struggle against apartheid was finally successful and the system was formally abolished in 1994, this also ended the political isolation that South Africa had manoeuvred itself into. In turn, this opened up the country to international visitors too. Today South Africa is among the world's top tourist destinations and is the most visited sub-Saharan African nation, famous in particular for its wildlife.

Robben Island

★★★★☆

Outside Cape Town • Prison island, Apartheid

Dark Rating: 8

This island in the bay outside Cape Town was used as a prison during the apartheid era (see p258–59). From 1961 onwards, the South African regime systematically sent leaders of the black resistance to the maximum-security facility for political prisoners that had been established on the island (alongside a regular prison). The most famous person to serve time here was Nelson Mandela, who spent 18 out of his total of 27 years in prison here. He was moved to another facility in 1982, but the one on Robben Island was not closed down until the 1990s, during the transition from apartheid to democracy.

Today, Robben Island is a memorial and a popular destination for tours from Cape Town. Boats depart from the Victoria & Alfred Waterfront in Cape Town. On arrival at the island, visitors are taken on a tour by bus around the historic sites, including the lime quarry where prisoners had to work, World War Two-era fortifications and gun emplacements, administrative blocks and finally the former maximum-security prison. A highlight of the tour is viewing Mandela's cell. Some tour guides are former prisoners and so can add their personal stories to the general history.

Right
The cell on Robben Island in which prisoner 466/64, Nelson Mandela, was held for 18 years.

APARTHEID

This term in Afrikaans means 'separateness' and stands for the state policy of racial segregation and oppression in South Africa until the early 1990s. After the National Party won the general election in 1948, a series of laws were passed (by the all-white government, voted in by an all-white electorate) that increasingly separated blacks from whites, both physically and in terms of education and the availability of amenities and services. Millions were forcibly removed from their homes and sent to so-called Bantustans, rural 'homelands'.

In the cities, special 'townships' were created for blacks. The architects of apartheid ensured that the blacks would not unite against the white elite by dividing the black population into subgroups, mainly along linguistic lines, in order to pit them against each other.

Among the whites, there were basically just two subgroups – Boer-descendant Afrikaans-speakers and British-descendant English-speakers – but these were called upon to unite as one white class. With increasing decolonization in the 1960s and 70s all over Africa, whites in South Africa believed they were threatened if they did not uphold and reinforce their privileged status.

There was naturally resistance to such an unjust system, both within the country and from abroad. South Africa was widely condemned internationally at the time and increasingly faced sanctions and boycotts. The best-known resistance organization within South Africa was the African National Congress (ANC), associated mostly with the name Nelson Mandela. Spontaneous mass protests frequently ended up being violently crushed by police. One of the most infamous cases was the Soweto uprising of 1976, when students protested against the introduction of Afrikaans as the sole language of instruction in schools. The police eventually opened fire on the peaceful protesters, killing dozens of them.

By the early 1980s black protest movements were pooling their efforts under the banner of the United Democratic Front (UDF), with support from such prominent figures as Mandela and Archbishop Desmond Tutu. Faced with increasing opposition, the government then under P.W. Botha declared a 'state of emergency' in 1985. This gave the security police even greater leeway for censorship, suppression, arrests and torture.

Meanwhile, however, ideas of reform were being floated, and there were even initial meetings between Botha and Mandela. Yet it was only after Botha had been succeeded by Frederik Willem de Klerk that things really moved forward. De Klerk basically paved the way for the

Top
An English and Afrikaans sign to enforce racial segregation in apartheid-era South Africa.

Above
Former street signs of the bulldozed District Six of Cape Town, now on display at a museum.

abolition of apartheid and full democracy (with universal suffrage). Eventually this earned him and Mandela a joint Nobel Peace Prize in 1993.

De Klerk had released Mandela from prison in 1990. In South Africa's first fully democratic election, in 1994, the ANC won an absolute majority and Mandela became the country's first black president. Meanwhile, a Truth and Reconciliation Commission, under the chairmanship of Tutu, was created to facilitate coming to terms with the crimes committed during apartheid (although this has faced substantial difficulties).

The transition from apartheid to democracy was anything but peaceful. Infighting and clashes between different black ethnic groups in the early 1990s actually caused more deaths than the police violence during apartheid had. To this day, South Africa still faces many troubles: crime, inequality and unemployment are major problems, even though a new black middle class has also established itself.

Above
Nelson Mandela being released from prison, Cape Town, February 1990.

Above
An apartheid-era prison, now part of the Constitution Hill heritage complex, in Johannesburg.

OTHER APARTHEID-RELATED SITES

Cape Town
The District Six Museum is a worthwhile addition to a tour of Robben Island. It recounts the destruction during apartheid of one of the city's districts and the forced removal of the mixed-race community that lived there.

Johannesburg
This city has several apartheid-related sites: first and foremost the large, state-of-the-art Apartheid Museum, which is the best place to learn about the topic. Constitution Hill is a heritage complex in the city centre that incorporates an apartheid-era ex-prison. Then there's the Workers' Museum, which chronicles the plight of black labourers and the trade unions' role in the struggle against apartheid. In Soweto (South-Western Townships) Nelson Mandela's former house is now also a small museum. Further places related to the topic are the Central Police Station, Chancellor House and the Central Magistrates' Court.

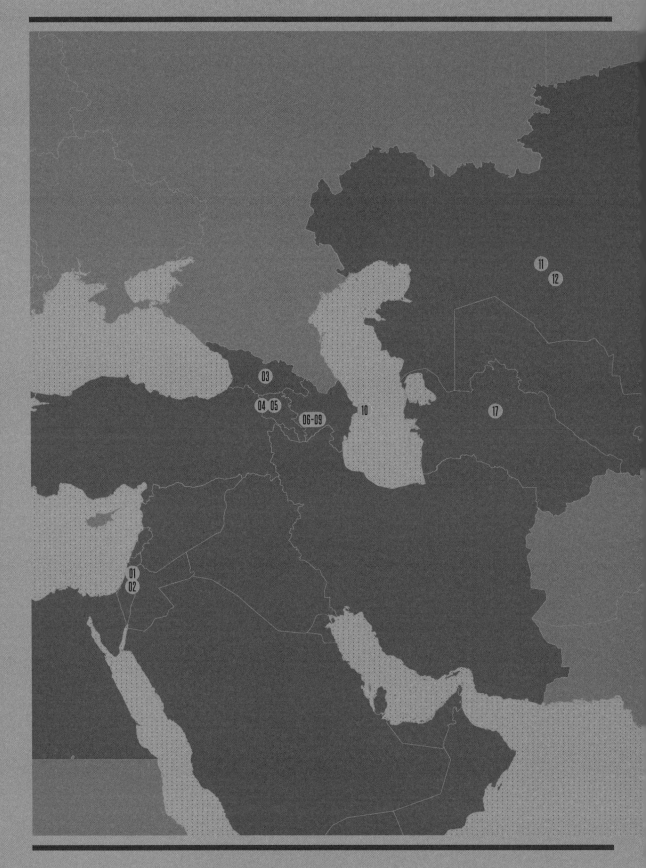

Middle East, Caucasus & Central Asia

The Middle East contains some of the most perennially troubled regions on Earth, with the ongoing conflicts of Israel with its neighbours and the uncertain status of Palestine, as well as the recent and current wars and insurgencies in Iraq and Syria. Much of the region is therefore out of bounds for most tourism, although there are exceptions, including Israel. Things can change, however, so one should always check ahead for the current security situation. It may also be that areas currently not recommended as travel destinations will calm down sufficiently and open up again to foreign tourists in the future. There is certainly plenty of potential.

The countries of the Caucasus and Central Asia were previously part of the Soviet Union, and have fared very differently after its dissolution. In the Caucasus, regional animosity between some of the countries remains, while others get along fine, although the frozen conflict over Nagorno-Karabakh seems as unsolvable as the Palestinian issue. It is a complex but highly rewarding region.

The large countries of Central Asia (the 'Stans') offer unique dark destinations of types not encountered anywhere else on Earth and thus deserve special attention in this book. Travel in those countries can be a bit demanding, but it is doable with some investment in time and money, adaptability and solid preparation.

Israel

Steeped in controversy and historical complexities, modern Israel, although built on millennia of history, is a fairly young nation state politically speaking. It came about in the wake of World War Two and the Holocaust, although the Jewish claims on these lands go back to antiquity.

Jewish people have almost always been persecuted nearly everywhere and were hence scattered around the world in a global diaspora. The original Israeli lands were occupied by a long string of conquerors from the Babylonian, Ancient Roman and Byzantine empires to the Arabs, the Crusaders and eventually the British.

In the first half of the twentieth century moves were made to provide a homeland for Jews in this territory; many settlers preceded the founding of a Jewish state. This came with a UN plan in 1947 that Jewish representatives accepted but Arabs did not. Following a short war in 1948, the Jewish state of Israel formally declared its independence. The Six-Day War of 1967 further consolidated Israel's position and gained it extra territory. This includes Jerusalem as well as lands that had originally been earmarked for Palestine, such as the Gaza Strip and the West Bank.

Against international law and countless UN resolutions, Israel has held on to large parts of these occupied territories, although some were handed over to quasi-autonomous rule by Palestinians. Yet there is no Palestinian state as such. All this remains unsolved and a source of political controversies that have proved insurmountable. Palestinians complain about repression, Israel about terrorist attacks by Palestinians, and generally it feels threatened in its existence by many of its Arab neighbours. The situation could not be more complicated, and no real solution is in sight.

As a travel destination, however, Israel is comparatively easy for most international visitors. Security is noticeably tight, and immigration procedures can be intimidating, especially for holders of passports containing stamps from Islamic countries such as Iran. Conversely, an Israeli stamp in your passport will automatically disqualify you from entry into a number of Arab states (people who travel between these countries a lot need to have two passports). Once in the country, however, you're more or less free to move around and do what you like.

Arguably, Israel qualifies as a 'dark' destination for all the reasons indicated and more, but unless there is a specific crisis or war on, it is surprisingly easy-going and relaxed (although some underlying tension is always palpable). The dark places covered here are more or less independent of the contemporary political situation anyway.

Yad Vashem

Jerusalem • Holocaust

★★★★★

Dark Rating: 8 ☸

This national memorial site was first established in the 1950s, shortly after the founding of the modern state of Israel. It has since been expanded significantly and has become one of the most eminent museums on the subject of the Shoah, as the Holocaust is often referred to in Hebrew (the official language of Israel, in which it means 'catastrophe'). Yad Vashem now proclaims itself the 'World Holocaust Remembrance Center'.

Core elements are the original Hall of Remembrance, the low, square, bungalow-like structure that contains an eternal flame and the names of death camps and concentration camps (p134–35) set into the floor. It is here that state guests solemnly lay down wreaths and write in the guest book. For ordinary visitors, the core part of Yad Vashem is the Holocaust History Museum. This was opened in 2005, after a decade of planning and construction, to replace a smaller, earlier incarnation.

The new museum is mostly subterranean and arranged in ten thematic sections branching off a central corridor that slices through Mount Herzl in an architecturally spectacular fashion. Only the triangular skylight pokes out above ground for most of its length before the corridor ends in a wide opening, with a balcony that hovers over the valley.

The thematic galleries of the exhibition cover the complete history of the repression of Jews prior to the Holocaust, the systematic ghettoization of Jews under the Nazis and the subsequent industrialized murder of some six million Jews. But the exhibitions also cover resistance (e.g. the Warsaw Ghetto

Right
The Hall of Names at Yad Vashem represents
a historic mission to memorialize every Jew
murdered in the Holocaust.

Right
The Hall of Names at Yad Vashem represents
a historic mission to memorialize every Jew
murdered in the Holocaust.

Uprising, p167) and the postwar
'return to life'.

Outside there are further elements, such as monuments, a cattle
wagon signifying the deportation
trains, and the Garden of the Right-
eous Among the Nations. The latter
is dedicated to those non-Jews who
saved Jews during the Holocaust,
often at great risk to themselves,
such as the well-known Raoul Wal-
lenberg and Oskar Schindler (see
p169).

Yad Vashem is to the west of the
Old Town of Jerusalem, the city that
is the self-proclaimed (although

not widely recognized internationally) capital of Israel and an
ancient place at the heart of all the
complex layers of history. Because
Jerusalem is a holy site for all three
of the large monotheistic religions,
security is a particular problem
here. But walking the cobbled
streets and seeing the ancient sights
can give you a sense of millennia
of history like few other places
on Earth.

Above
The stark lines of the museum open up to a
platform that gives views over the lands below
and beyond.

The Dead Sea & Masada

★★★☆☆

Judaean desert

Extreme landscape, Environmental disaster, Mass suicide

Dark Rating: 5 ☠

Located in the lowest depression on Earth, more than 400m (1300ft) below sea level, the Dead Sea is one of the world's saltiest lakes, ten times saltier than the oceans. It is indeed quite dead, as no fish or plant could survive in this brine, except in a small zone in the north where the Jordan River flows into the lake.

However, not enough water flows into the lake these days owing to extensive diversion of water for irrigation on both the Israeli and the Jordanian banks of the river. And so the Dead Sea is shrinking. Its surface area has halved over the past century, and the receding water levels now constitute an environmental disaster. The dropping of the groundwater level has caused sinkholes to appear along the shores, so the unstable ground has become dangerous to walk on too.

The salty waters have made the Dead Sea a peculiar tourist attraction. Many people visit to experience the bizarre buoyancy of the briny water: you can simply sit down in the water and float like a cork. It's fun but also carries risks; the main one is accidentally swallowing some salt lake water, in which case you should seek medical attention immediately.

Other than the harsh environment, there is also a dark historical spot here: Masada, a former stronghold atop a table mountain-like rock on the southern shores of the Dead Sea, where a siege by Roman troops ended in the mass suicide of the Jewish Zealot group that had taken refuge there. As defeat was looming, they chose to die by their own hands rather than end up as slaves in the Roman Empire. This collective act is still glorified in contemporary Israel, and so the rock of Masada has been made accessible to visitors.

Georgia

Not to be confused with the US state of the same name, this Caucasus country offers dramatic scenery, ancient culture, a unique language and highly distinctive cuisine and viticulture.

For most of the twentieth century Georgia was part of the USSR, and several Georgians played a crucial role in it, not least Joseph Stalin. The end of the Soviet era was difficult for the country, and after its declaration of independence in 1991 it descended into chaos. Some stability returned in the 1990s but continued disillusionment with the government of former Soviet foreign minister Eduard Shevardnadze led to his ousting in 2003 in the so-called Rose Revolution.

Georgia has long had a difficult relationship with Russia and went to war with its mighty neighbour in 2008 over the breakaway republics South Ossetia and Abkhazia. Although geographically on the Asian side of the Great Caucasus, contemporary Georgia is mostly looking towards Europe, politically and culturally, and has recently emerged as a much-lauded travel destination too. The capital, Tbilisi, is an ideal base for exploring the country, and also has a few dark sites, such as the Museum of Soviet Occupation.

Stalin Museum

★★★☆☆

Gori, Georgia · Cult of personality, Repression, War

Dark Rating: 5 ☠

In 1878 Iosif Jughashvili was born in Gori in central Georgia. He would later become known as Stalin, meaning 'man of steel'. The epithet was certainly fitting when Stalin, one of the most ruthless dictators in history, led the USSR in the wake of Lenin's death, through the country's industrialization and eventually World War Two. It's thus little wonder that his home town would celebrate its famous son and make his birth house a cult-of-personality destination.

What is surprising is that this shrine-like site survived de-Stalinization in the USSR under Khrushchev after Stalin's death in 1953. Even after the USSR's collapse and Georgia becoming independent, it still survives to this day. It is a unique relic.

In the museum's main exhibition time has basically stood still since 1953 and Stalin is still celebrated as a genius and hero. Displays include some of his clothes, furniture, gifts from other leaders and a Stalin death mask in a hall that is as sombre and over the top as can be.

Unsurprisingly the bias at this museum has caused controversy. And so an extra section has been added more recently that points out the darker sides of Stalin too: the purges, show trials and deportations to Gulags. Outside are Stalin statues, his personal railway carriage and his preserved birth house.

Left
A temple-like superstructure was built around and above Stalin's birth house.

Above
Stalin's death mask on display.

Armenia

This smallest of the three recognized ex-Soviet nations in the Caucasus was once much larger and has a history full of tragedy. The worst was what most historians agree to have been genocide: from 1915, Ottoman Turkey massacred some Armenians and drove others en masse into the Syrian desert. An estimated 1.5 million perished. In present-day Turkey this is still vehemently denied, but many countries officially recognize the genocide.

What used to be Western Armenia is in Turkish hands, including the 'holy mountain' of the Armenians, Mount Ararat, which is clearly visible from Armenia but unreachable across the border in eastern Anatolia. That border remains closed, and Turkish–Armenian relations are complicated. As regards Armenia's eastern neighbour, Azerbaijan, things are even more difficult, owing to the unresolved frozen conflict over Nagorno-Karabakh (p268).

On the other hand, Armenia has the unique distinction of being on good terms with both the USA and Russia as well as with its southern neighbour, Iran. Russia maintains a military presence in Armenia, and guards its western border. Given that this border was once between the USSR and Turkey, a NATO member, you could claim that it constitutes a surviving stretch of the Iron Curtain. Some original Soviet-era border fences can still be seen here.

For travellers, all this means that overland access is only easily possible via Armenia's northern neighbour Georgia (p265), or by flying into the capital, Yerevan's, international airport. The city is also a good base for various excursions; a well-oiled tourism industry caters for this. Most tourism within Armenia takes the form of cultural heritage tourism; Armenia's distinctive churches and monasteries dominate that area. In terms of dark destinations, Soviet-era relics are an attraction, such as the giant Mother Armenia statue overlooking Yerevan (with a war museum underneath).

Gyumri & Spitak

Shirak Province • Natural disaster (earthquake)

★★★☆☆

Dark Rating: 6 ☠

Gyumri has had this name since the early 1990s. It was known as Alexandropol in tsarist times and then Leninakan in Soviet times, when it was the second largest city and an important industrial centre within the Armenian SSR. Then came the Spitak earthquake of 7 December 1988 which devastated the region. Some 25,000 to 50,000 people were killed, and countless more injured and made homeless in the winter cold. In this desperate situation, the USSR asked for aid and an international appeal was launched.

The death toll of the disaster was exacerbated by the fact that the prefabricated apartment blocks typical of the Brezhnev era had been totally inadequate for such an earthquake-prone region. Buildings from the Stalinist era suffered less damage overall, and the sturdy stone structures from the tsarist times fared even better. Gyumri still has earthquake ruins, even though reconstruction has made much progress. For example, the Holy Saviour Church, destroyed in the quake, has since been rebuilt.

The epicentre of the 1988 earthquake was close to the small town of Spitak, which was completely levelled and lost a third of its population in the disaster. In its cemetery, full of disaster victims, a makeshift sheet metal-clad chapel still stands as a reminder of the tragedy.

Left
Earthquake damage in 1988. The poorly constructed prefab blocks collapsed like a house of cards.

Tsitsernakaberd

Yerevan • Genocide

★ ★ ★ ★ ☆

Dark Rating: 7 ☠

Located on a hill just west of the centre of Armenia's capital city, Yerevan, this is the main official site commemorating the Armenian genocide. The monument itself was constructed in Soviet times, partly in response to mass demonstrations in Yerevan in 1965 on the occasion of the 50th anniversary of the beginning of the genocide. Marking the genocide also had propaganda value against neighbouring NATO member Turkey.

The monument consists of a 44m-tall (145ft) stele (allegedly symbolizing the 'rebirth' of Armenia) and a ring of basalt stone slabs (standing for the 12 'lost provinces' of Western Armenia) surrounding a central eternal flame. In more recent years, smaller additional memorials have appeared at the site. Even more importantly, since 1995 there has been a proper museum about the genocide adjacent to the memorial.

The multilingual (Armenian, English, French and Russian) exhibition covers the prehistory of the genocide, Armenian culture at the time, and of course the genocide itself. There aren't many original artefacts on display but plenty of documents, photographs, charts, maps and suchlike are, as well as large paintings depicting the atrocities graphically. Particularly memorable are the displays of pleas by Western diplomats and journalists for the world to take notice of what was happening in those dark days.

Nagorno-Karabakh/Artsakh

★★☆☆☆

De facto Armenia, de jure Azerbaijan • Modern war, Frozen conflict   **Dark Rating: 8** ☣

This is the disputed territory in the South Caucasus that Armenia and Azerbaijan went to war over in the 1990s, and again in 2020, and that remains volatile. The root of the conflict is an ethnic divide. In the Soviet era Nagorno-Karabakh was made a semi-autonomous region ('oblast') within Azerbaijan, but the majority of inhabitants were of Armenian descent. It didn't matter quite so much as long as the Soviet Union existed. After its dissolution, however, Nagorno-Karabakh found itself part of a newly independent Azerbaijan, and the Armenian population took to arms. Nagorno-Karabakh declared its independence in late 1991 (and now calls itself the Republic of Artsakh), although no UN members have ever recognized it.

In the ensuing war, Azeri forces initially gained the upper hand, also with the help of outside mercenaries (including Russians), yet the tables were turned with Armenian support, and with the supply of heavy Russian weaponry. After a few tens of thousands of people had lost their lives in the conflict, a ceasefire was brokered by Russia that Azerbaijan's pro-Russian new ruler Heydar Aliyev signed with Armenia and Nagorno-Karabakh in 1994. However, all Azeris had fled the contested territory (and Armenia)

and thus became internally displaced persons within Azerbaijan. Some 15–20 per cent of Azeri territory came de facto under Armenian control, not just the old Nagorno-Karabakh region itself but also the strip of Azeri land between this enclave and Armenia, plus a 'buffer zone' to the east and north.

This led to the strange situation that despite Armenia holding on to these lands, de jure it remained part of Azerbaijan. Nominally negotiations continued under the aegis of the Minsk Group of the OSCE (Organization for Security and Co-operation in Europe) to find a solution to the problem, but internationally it was more or less accepted that the Nagorno-Karabakh issue has the status of a 'frozen conflict', like that of Transnistria (p219). For travellers this meant that no embassy could assist if any problems arose, but otherwise it was relatively unproblematic to make it there, overland from Armenia. The renewed conflict of 2020 complicated things again.

Below
Abandoned military vehicle in the de facto
independent Nagorno-Karabakh Republic.

Karabakh War Museums

★★☆☆☆

Stepanakert · Modern war

Dark Rating: 5 ☠

This nominal capital city of Nagorno-Karabakh/Artsakh boasts three museums about the conflict and its aftermath. One is the very sombre Museum of Fallen Soldiers, a competing one a stone's throw away is the Museum of Missing Soldiers, and the general Artsakh History Museum has a section about the war too. Just north of the city by the road heading northeast stands the iconic 'We are our Mountains' monument, although the couple of stone heads, a veiled woman and a bearded man, are better known as Papik Tatik (grandpa and grandma).

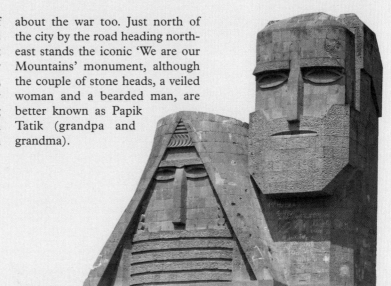

Right
The large monument is a symbol of the Armenian heritage of Nagorno-Karabakh and appears on the coat of arms of Artsakh.

Ağdam

★☆☆☆☆

In the former 'buffer zone' between Nagorno-Karabakh and Azerbaijan
Ghost town, Conflict zone

Dark Rating: 9 ☠

This Azeri city gained the title of the world's largest ghost town after the war of the 1990s because it ended up in the Armenian-controlled, largely depopulated 'buffer zone' to the east of Karabakh proper. Looters have stripped Ağdam bare, so it's just an expanse of broken ruins, although an old mosque remains semi-intact. It used to be possible, though not without risk, for intrepid travellers to venture there from Stepanakert, even though it was not covered by the Artsakh visa and one had to take care not to be caught by the military. Since Azerbaijan recaptured territory in the renewed war in the autumn of 2020, Ağdam fell back into Azeri hands. Whether it can still be visited from Nagorno-Karabakh now seems unlikely, nor will it be easy to get there from within Azerbaijan any time soon.

Left
Ağdam became one of the largest ghost towns on Earth after the 1990s Karabakh war.

Shushi

South Caucasus • War ruins, Monument

★ ★

Dark Rating: 4 ☠

This second biggest town in Nagorno-Karabakh was captured by Armenian forces in 1992 after a devastating battle that has left several buildings in ruins ever since, including entire multi-storey apartment blocks that are just empty shells.

Shushi (or Şuşa in Azeri) once had a disproportionately high Muslim Azeri population, and just before the Karabakh war it was almost entirely Azeri/Azerbaijani, a stronghold within the otherwise predominantly Armenian enclave. This, together with the town's position high on a hill overlooking the plains and Karabakh's capital city, Stepanakert, gave it prime strategic importance during the war. From here, Azeri forces indiscriminately fired missiles on Stepanakert. On 8 May 1992 Armenian forces launched a daring night-time attack up the steep hillside towards Shushi, and within a day they had conquered the city and forced out the Azeri military as well as the population.

In the latest outbreak of the conflict in 2020 Shushi was recaptured by Azerbaijan – and a subsequent Russian-brokered peace deal cemented that territorial change. So whether it will still be possible at some point to visit this place from the rest of Nagorno-Karabakh seems doubtful. One also has to wonder what will happen to the tank monument by the road up the hill to the town, which served as a memorial to the 1992 battle, or to the recently renovated Armenian cathedral, which also suffered damage from shelling during the latest confrontation.

Azerbaijan

This easternmost of the Caucasus countries is predominantly Muslim, but religion does not permeate Azerbaijan as much as it does other Islamic countries. This secular atmosphere can partly be explained by the fact that the country used to be part of the Soviet Union. But its integration was not a happy one: in 1920 the Bolshevik Red Army invaded the country, and it became part of the USSR in 1922.

The country suffered badly during Stalin's purges, and some 120,000 Azerbaijanis were deported to Gulags or executed. Azeri nationalism and religion continued to be repressed after Stalin's death. Then, in 1969, Moscow made the only Azeri member of the politburo, Heydar Aliyev, head of the Azerbaijan SSR. He remained in power until he was unseated in 1987 during Perestroika. The final years of the USSR were especially bitter, with Soviet troops being sent in amid escalating clashes between different ethnicities.

Azerbaijan declared its independence in 1991 and the subsequent few years were chaotic. The war in Nagorno-Karabakh (see p268) was taking its toll too. In 1993 the ageing Aliyev returned to power, signed a ceasefire deal over Nagorno-Karabakh and restored some stability. After he died in 2003, his son Ilham succeeded him. While the Heydar Aliyev cult of personality has continued, his son steered the country towards economic success. However, accusations of corruption and nepotism, coupled with authoritarian rule and suppression of the freedom of the media, mar Azerbaijan's international reputation.

As a travel destination, Azerbaijan is a bit more challenging than its western neighbours. But with good planning and by investing in local guided tours (not cheap), it can be rewarding. The capital, Baku, has a few dark places of its own, such as the grand Martyrs' Lane memorial complex with monuments and graves of those killed in the 1990 Soviet intervention and the Nagorno-Karabakh conflict. The Azeri side of the conflict is also covered in the Museum of Independence.

Absheron peninsula

Northeast of Baku, on the Caspian Sea • Industrial wastelands

★☆☆☆☆

Dark Rating: 7 ☠

Baku's and Azerbaijan's wealth is based primarily on oil. It's one of the places where the oil industry was born, and by 1905 it was supplying half of the world's oil. The industry is still key to the country, but extraction comes at the price of environmental pollution. All around Baku you can see evidence of oil-industry detritus.

The most legendary of Azerbaijan's oil installations is Neft Daşları ('Oil Rocks'), which famously featured in the 1999 James Bond movie *The World Is Not Enough*. This is a whole city on stilts (and partly landfills), with almost 300km (200 miles) of road and buildings housing a population of 2000. Sadly the place is off limits to most people. However, you can, theoretically, get closer to similar offshore structures at the northern end of Pirallahi Island, just off the Absheron peninsula, provided you have a guide/driver willing to take you. The oil industry is secretive and camera-toting tourists are not welcome, so you have to be discreet.

At Lökbatan, just south of Baku, there's an oil-rig 'graveyard' close to the shore, which is quite a dramatic sight. The Absheron peninsula also features mud volcanoes, a Zoroastrian fire temple and the Yanar Dağ flaming hillside where natural gas seeping from the ground is permanently on fire (quite a sight after dark). Finally, at the northwestern end of the peninsula, at Sumqayit, the land is blighted by the industrial wastelands of Soviet-era chemical industry plants.

Below
Offshore oil rigs stud the Caspian Sea, many connected by roads on stilts in the water.

Kazakhstan

This is the world's ninth largest country and the largest landlocked one. It was once part of the Soviet Union, and all the dark sides of the USSR came together here: Gulags, environmental disasters, rocket-launching sites and nuclear testing grounds. Kazakhstan was the last Soviet republic to declare independence, just days before the USSR was officially dissolved in 1991.

The country's last communist leader, Nursultan Nazarbayev, simply took over after independence to become the first president. He continued to rule in a quasi-authoritarian style for the next 28 years until his surprise resignation as president (he did not resign from his other influential posts) in March 2019.

The capital city had in 1997 been moved from Almaty, the largest city in Kazakhstan. Until then Astana was just a small town called Akmola, but once declared capital ('Astana' simply means 'capital' in Kazakh), it saw a construction boom and massive expansion. The mostly planned city now boasts some mind-boggling modernist architecture.

Outside the cities, Kazakhstan consists largely of endless steppe, giving way to desert towards the shores of the Caspian Sea (the world's largest lake) and mountain ranges in the north, south and east. The steppe is interspersed with Soviet-era industrial centres, including the world's largest opencast coal mine, Bogatyr near Ekibastuz, and the tallest power-station chimney stacks.

For the traveller, Kazakhstan is a bit demanding, not least because of the vast distances between places. Logistically it is not easy, especially for those lacking the requisite language skills (Russian is still widely spoken; English is not). Guided tours can be expensive, but the country has plenty to offer. In addition to those covered below, there are other Gulag-related sites; for example, the ALZHIR memorial in Malinovka not far from Astana. And near Ekibastuz, east of Astana, is the gigantic apocalyptic-looking open-cast coal mine of Bogatyr.

Aralsk & the Aral Sea

★☆☆☆☆

Kyzylorda Region • Environmental disaster, Extreme landscape

Dark Rating: 7 ☠

The desiccation of the Aral Sea, once the world's fourth largest lake, is a textbook example of a man-made environmental disaster. From the 1960s, the rivers that feed the Aral Sea were diverted to obtain water for large-scale irrigation projects, in particular to grow cotton (which is a very thirsty plant). In the short term, it seemed successful, but for the Aral Sea the fact that less water arrived at the lake meant that it began to shrink.

A knock-on effect was the increasing salinity of the remaining water, which resulted in the fish dying off; this was the death knell for the Aral Sea's once thriving fishing industry. It would, however, be wrong simply to blame Soviet incompetence. The drying up of the Aral Sea actually accelerated after the dissolution of the USSR,

Above
A stranded ship at a former port on the Aral Sea, a reminder of its once vibrant fishing past.

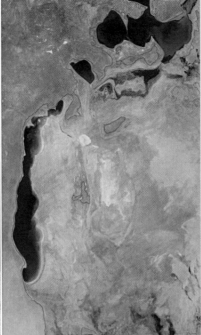

DARK STATS

68,000 SQ KM (26,300 SQ MILES)
surface area of the
Aral Sea in 1960

33,800 SQ KM (13,000 SQ MILES)
surface area of the
Aral Sea in 1992

17,160 SQ KM (6630 SQ MILES)
surface area of the
Aral Sea in 2004

By 2010 the Aral Sea had
shrunk to around

10 PER CENT
of its original size and has
remained roughly around this
size to the present day

as even more water was diverted for irrigation. By 2014 the Southern Aral Sea had dried up completely except for a thin, crescent-shaped body of water in the west, cut off from any water inflow.

Not only has the desiccation of the lake brought economic devastation to the area, but also the resultant dry former seabed, now a desert called Aralkum, is heavily polluted – salt and agricultural chemicals are blown across the lands by the wind. Potentially worse still is remote Vozrozhdeniya Island, where in Soviet times there was a biological weapons research centre. Now no longer surrounded by water, remnants of whatever agents were developed here and that escaped the insufficient decontamination efforts after the closure of the site could be carried further afield by wildlife.

While the Southern Aral Sea is now lost for good, the North Aral Sea in Kazakhstan is slowly returning thanks to a dam holding back water from the Syr Darya (the river that is still reaching the Aral Sea). Water levels have been rising and fish have reappeared, so the fishing industry is being revived to a degree.

The main centre for fishing in the north was (and may be again) Aralsk, a small city on what used to be the northern shore of the lake. At the time of writing, the waters of the North Aral Sea have not yet reached the old harbour of Aralsk again, but fishermen drive to the rising waters and bring back the catch to new fish-processing plants in Aralsk. So here there is some hope for the once proud and thriving harbour city that had turned into a desolate, dusty, hopeless place characterized by unemployment, poverty and health problems caused by the pollution.

As a travel destination, Aralsk remains extreme. It can be reached by way of the main train line running from Almaty to Ekaterinburg that passes through the town, but Aralsk has hardly any tourism infrastructure. Yet some specialist travel agents can arrange tours for hard-core, adventurously minded travellers.

Around Aralsk, desolation and dereliction still dominate, from the rusting cranes in the ex-harbour to the stranded shipwrecks. A couple have been turned into memorials; others can still be found out in the desert. But these rusting hulks are disappearing, cut up and sold as scrap metal.

Above
Satellite images taken in 1990 and 2014. The sea, once the size of Ireland, today covers a fraction of its previous expanse.

Baikonur

Near Tyuratam, southern Kazakhstan
Rocket launch site, Cold War, Soviet legacy

★★★★☆

Dark Rating: 4 ☠

This remote site in the middle of the steppe is the fabled Soviet 'Cosmodrome', or space port, where Sputnik (the first satellite in space) and Yuri Gagarin (the first human in space) were launched. It is still the most active rocket-launching site on Earth, leased by the Kazakh government to Russia (until 2050, for now), so it is administratively outside Kazakhstan. Baikonur is mostly associated with the glorious successes of the early Soviet space programme, but it also has its dark sides.

The rockets developed and launched here initially were not for civilian purposes but the world's first intercontinental ballistic missile (ICBM), the R-7, designed to carry nuclear warheads to the other end of the world (i.e. America). So it is a significant place in terms of Cold War legacy too. The rockets that carried Sputnik and Gagarin into space were adapted from the R-7, which later was given the designation *Soyuz*. It is still in production and is the most used and most reliable type of rocket in history. Yet there have been accidents too

at Baikonur, including some catastrophic ones, such as the explosion of an R-16 test missile on the launch pad in 1960, which killed around a hundred people, the worst such accident in history.

Although less deadly, the explosion of an N-1 rocket at Baikonur in 1969 was the biggest such event ever. The N-1, intended for Soviet manned Moon missions, was subsequently cancelled.

Visits to Baikonur are possible from within Kazakhstan or by direct flight into the site's airport from Moscow. The latter tours are very expensive, especially if they are to involve watching a launch. However, many people make the investment to experience such a fiery and noisy spectacle. Usually also included are visits to various historic sites and the on-site museum, and, if there is a manned launch, attendance at the pre-launch press conference with the cosmonauts. Of course, such tours emphasize the non-dark aspects of space exploration, but you can also visit the monument to the R-16 disaster in Baikonur City.

Below
It is possible to arrange a tour of the Baikonur Cosmodrome that includes watching a real live rocket launch.

KarLag

★★★★☆

Dolinka, Karaganda Region • Gulag, Torture

Dark Rating: 7 ☠

This is the largest and most important Gulag memorial in Kazakhstan, located not far from the city of Karaganda, hence the 'Kar' in the name. The 'Lag' is short for 'lager', meaning 'camp'. A few of the original camp barracks survive to this day, as does an old cemetery. But the main focus is on the former administrative building, which now houses an extensive exhibition. This includes mock-Gulag sleeping quarters, mock-torture chambers, mock-KGB offices and plenty of documents, photos and artefacts.

Top
The classical façade of the former administrative building of the KarLag Gulag complex belies its dark nature.

Above
Interior of the Museum for the Victims of Political Repression, with reconstruction of an interrogation cell.

Left
Life-size exhibits in the museum depict what life in the camps was like.

The Polygon

★★ ★ ★ ★

East Kazakhstan steppes • Nuclear testing, Cold War, Soviet legacy

Dark Rating: 10 ☣

This desolate area was the Soviet Union's main proving ground for nuclear tests. It is better known internationally as the Semipalatinsk Test Site (STS). It contains the Opytnoye Pole site where the USSR tested its first ever atomic device, RDS-1, in 1949 (in the West it was soon nicknamed 'Joe One', in reference to Joseph Stalin).

More than 450 nuclear explosions followed over the next 40 years. More than 100 of these tests were atmospheric (above ground), while from the 1960s onwards further tests were conducted underground. One was conducted in 1965 to see whether atomic bombs could be used for large-scale earth-movement operations. For this test, called Chagan, a device was buried shallowly in the ground. Its detonation did indeed create a giant crater, some 400m (1300ft) in diameter and 100m (320ft) deep.

A similar test had been conducted at the equivalent US site (the NTS, see p25), but in both instances it was found that the problem of radioactively contaminated material spewing into the air more than outweighed any engineering benefits, so no further such experiments were undertaken. Today the Chagan crater is partly filled with water, forming the so-called Atomic Lake.

With the dissolution of the USSR in 1991, independent Kazakhstan inherited the irradiated territory of the Polygon, and most of the problems it had created for the local population. The test site was closed for good and Central Asia declared itself a nuclear-weapons-free zone. That doesn't mean the grim legacy of the tests is no longer haunting this part of the world; to this day, birth defects occur that are attributed to radiation.

In the past it was quite easy to drive into the Polygon; the site was not fenced nor guarded much. Hence you could encounter scavengers pulling out irradiated electric cables from the ground between the former test installations. These days, however, access to the Polygon is regulated. For visits, a permit and guide are required, so you cannot go there independently. Residual ambient radiation levels (see p224) in most of the area are not worryingly high these days, but one has to be careful not to ingest or breathe in any particles, so wearing a face mask is advisable at certain hotspots.

What is left to see inside the Polygon may not seem that dramatic at first glance. There is the nondescript bunker from where the first test was triggered, and some structures built specifically for the test to study the effects of atomic blasts, such as a former concrete bridge, but most characteristically there are rows of concrete towers of different shapes fanning out from the original 'ground zero' of Opytnoye Pole. The equipment is all gone, so these measuring towers just stand like forlorn shark teeth piercing the sky above the endless steppe. The Polygon and its silent relics of the Atomic Age are unique and among the most exotic and fascinating dark places on Earth.

Kurchatov

★★☆☆☆

East Kazakhstan • Nuclear testing, Ghost town

Dark Rating: 7 ☠

Left
An aerial view of a nuclear reactor facility in Kurchatov, once the centre of nuclear weapons development.

Named after the 'father' of the Soviet A-bomb, Igor Kurchatov, this was the Los Alamos (p25) of the USSR, as it were: a secret, closed city built specifically for the development of the Soviet nuclear weapons programme. It was the nerve centre of the STS (Semipalatinsk Test Site).

It is still home to the National Nuclear Centre of Kazakhstan, but today large parts of the city are practically a ghost town. However, there are rudimentary facilities for visitors, making Kurchatov the best base for excursions to the Polygon.

Museum of the STS

★★★☆☆

Ulitsa Krasnoarmeyskaya, Kurchatov • Nuclear testing

Dark Rating: 9 ☠

Kurchatov is home to a remarkable museum about the Polygon's legacy. On display are operating consoles, high-speed cameras for filming nuclear explosions, dioramas of the test arrangements and underground tunnels, plenty of photos of mushroom clouds, and various other items related to the history of nuclear testing, such as a jar with a scorched pig's head (from animal testing to study the effects of the blasts on skin – apparently pig skin is similar to human skin). Visits to this museum must be prearranged.

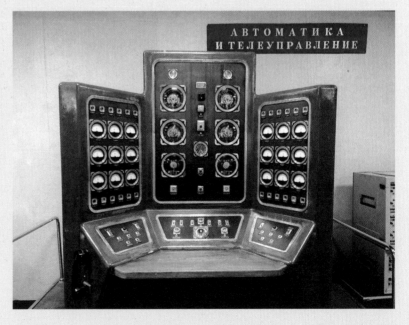

Right
A control console from the 1950s is one of the star exhibits at the museum.

Turkmenistan

This desert country used to be the southernmost constituent part of the Soviet Union from 1925 until 1991. Unlike many other Soviet republics, it didn't particularly fight for independence but was more or less released into it by default at the dissolution of the USSR. The last communist leader of Turkmenistan simply carried on as ruler after independence. He had himself elected once (as the only candidate), in 1992, but was later declared president for life. His real name was Saparmurat Niyazov, but he adopted the name 'Turkmenbashi', meaning 'head of all Turkmen'. His penchant for renaming things didn't stop there. He later renamed a whole city after himself and even gave months new names after members of his family.

Moreover, he developed one of the most autocratic and repressive regimes, coupled with a bizarre level of cult of personality. He had countless gold statues of himself erected, including one atop a giant monument that rotates so as to always face the sun. The list of eccentricities could go on.

In December 2006 the eternal president suddenly died. His place was taken by Gurbanguly Berdimukhamedov, who continued the style of autocratic rule and cult of personality. The country has remained almost closed to foreigners and certainly to outside scrutiny. It has been likened to a Central Asian North Korea, with one significant difference: Turkmenistan has rich reserves of natural gas. The wealth gleaned from this fuelled the construction of countless monuments, parks with over-the-top water features (in a desert country!) and numerous white marble-clad palaces and residential buildings for the privileged elite.

As a travel destination, Turkmenistan is predictably not easy. Independent travel is prohibited outside the capital, Ashgabat. To see the country, all foreign visitors must be on a state-sanctioned guided tour. For this reason it is one of the least-visited countries in Asia.

Darvaza

Karakum Desert • Industrial accident, Extreme landscape

★ ★ ★ ★ ★

Dark Rating: 8 ☠

Informally known as the 'Door to Hell', this is a unique anomaly: a huge crater in the middle of the Karakum Desert that has been alight with natural gas flames since at least 1971. It is now Turkmenistan's principal claim to 'dark' fame. Exactly how it came into being is not easy to ascertain, as sources vary wildly, but what seems clear is that the crater, which is some 75m (250ft) in diameter and around 20m (65ft) deep, is the result of an accident that happened when Soviet prospectors drilled for natural gas or oil and hit a hollow cavern that then collapsed (presumably taking some of the prospectors and their equipment with it).

The natural gas that was emitted from the ground then either ignited naturally or was deliberately set alight in the hope that it would burn off quickly. But this hasn't happened, and the flames show no sign of abating.

It is possible to join tours that include an excursion to this ultra-remote place, with camping overnight, which makes sense, as the flame-filled crater looks its best in the dark. It is one of the most amazing and mesmerizing sights anywhere on planet Earth.

Below
The legendary flaming crater has recently been fenced in for safety, which unfortunately detracts from the dramatic sight.

01 **Wagah border**
India

02 **Jallianwala Bagh**
Amritsar, India

03 **Bhopal**
India

04 **Cellular Jail**
Port Blair, Andaman

05 **Yala tsunami memorial**
Sri Lanka

India &
Indochina

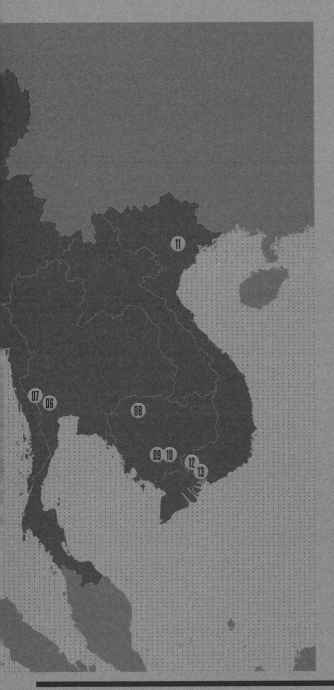

Grouped in this Asia section are countries that are diverse in nature but also have things in common, apart from just geographic proximity. The Indian influence is obvious, not least in culinary terms. Buddhism is also an export from India; the Buddha is believed to have come from and lived in northeastern India. Today, Buddhism is more dominant in Sri Lanka, Thailand and Cambodia, whereas in India it is now a minority religion.

These countries also show similarities in economy and social strata. Poverty is widespread, especially in India and Cambodia, whereas the economies of at least India and Thailand are classed as 'newly industrialized' with a middle class and a wealthy upper-class elite.

Vietnam is something of an anomaly here: it is nominally still communist but, like China, has embraced capitalism in economic terms while remaining a socialist republic politically. Thailand and Cambodia, in contrast, are nominally kingdoms, although in both countries the king, while widely revered, does not have much direct political power.

As travel destinations, all of these countries are extremely rewarding, and increasingly popular. All feature dark sites too, with Cambodia taking the top place for the most tragic of reasons (genocide).

India

This huge yet densely populated country (one in five people on Earth is Indian) takes up most of a landmass classed as the Indian subcontinent between the Arabian Sea and the Indian Ocean. It features great diversity in terms of culture as well as landscape, and its history is very complex.

Colonialism played a significant role in the modern era, in particular the British Empire's. This is also one aspect that makes India a dark destination, since colonialism came with repression and exploitation, and the British perpetrated several massacres in India during their time here. It was only after a long and disciplined, yet largely non-violent struggle led by the legendary Mahatma Gandhi that India became independent in 1947. However, the new country almost immediately broke apart, largely along religious fault lines, with Pakistan and Bangladesh eventually becoming separate Muslim countries. The process was chaotic and violent and involved mass migration.

To this day, India and Pakistan are arch-enemies and the contested northern territory of Kashmir, claimed by both countries, has frequently led to military conflict. Both nations are also nuclear powers, which only makes the friction between the two countries more worrying.

The dark places in India are often linked to the struggle against colonial rule, in particular the rebellion of 1857, which in British parlance is mostly still referred to as a 'mutiny'. There are significant memorial sites commemorating the rebellion and its brutal crushing by the British, especially in Lucknow (The Residence) and in and around Kanpur, but also in the capital, Delhi. The latter city also has various colonial relics as well as places of Gandhi worship, in particular his former residence (Gandhi Smriti), where he was assassinated in 1948.

Wagah border ★★★☆☆

Road from Amritsar to Lahore, Pakistan • Fortified border, Modern conflict   **Dark Rating: 5** :☻:

The border between India and its arch-rival Pakistan is one of the most heavily guarded fortified borders on Earth. The Indian Border Security Force claims to be the largest in the world. Of the few border-crossing points between the two nations, Wagah has often been the only one that remained 'open'. Since 1959 the two sides have been performing an increasingly elaborate 'border-closing ceremony' here at sunset every day.

Above
The colourful daily border-closing ceremony expresses the two nations' rivalry in ritualized symbolic form.

This has become a tourist attraction, in particular on the Indian side, although you can also watch it on the other side, where the crowds are smaller.

In 2014 there was a suicide-bomber terrorist attack on the Pakistani side, and the border may be closed at times of increased tension. But on normal days the ceremony attracts large numbers of visitors – mostly domestic, but also some foreigners. It is a highly ritualized spectacle, when border soldiers in exuberant uniforms try to outdo each other in goose-stepping and saluting and even waving angry fists at each other. It is expertly choreographed and only symbolic – but it still represents the lasting animosity between the two countries.

It is not unusual to see the audiences also displaying forceful demonstrations of patriotism, with plenty of flag-waving and shouting. It is more bizarre and entertaining than truly dark, but one should not forget the very real political-military confrontation that all this stands for.

Jallianwala Bagh

Amritsar, Punjab • Massacre site

★★★☆☆

Dark Rating: 6 ☠

Left
Markings highlight the bullet holes left on a wall from when the British troops opened fire on the peaceful crowd.

Below
Topiary hedge figures depicting British soldiers firing rifles.

This is where British colonial forces committed one of the worst atrocities in India in the twentieth century. In April 1919, at a time of political unrest, crowds gathered in Amritsar for a harvest festival but the British colonial governor feared a political rally or even a rebellion. Armed forces were sent to the venue at Jallianwala Bagh, a walled-in park in the city centre. The commanding colonel positioned his soldiers at the sole entrance to the complex, trapping the crowd, and had his men open fire on the defenceless civilians.

Hundreds (possibly as many as 1500) were shot dead in this bloodbath, and many victims tried to seek shelter in a large well inside the park, where they were then crushed to death by more people jumping in. News of the atrocity soon spread and reached the British homeland, where it led to strong public condemnation, including in the House of Commons (by Winston Churchill, among others). An inquiry commission was set up and the commander cross-examined, but nobody ever faced prosecution.

Jallianwala Bagh soon came to stand as a symbol for resistance in India and the site was turned into a memorial after independence.

There is a small, rather rudimentary, museum, but the main elements are the well and a wall on which you can still see bullet holes. In addition, hedges and bushes have been trimmed into shapes like soldiers taking aim with rifles. It's a little bizarre, and the supposed solemnity of the memorial is also undermined by the behaviour of many domestic visitors incessantly taking selfies.

Above
The historical 'Martyrs' Well', where victims tried to seek shelter.

Bhopal

★★☆☆☆

Madhya Pradesh • Industrial disaster

Dark Rating: 9 ☠

Left
The rusting former chemical plant.

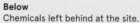

Below
Chemicals left behind at the site.

The name of this city is synonymous with the worst chemical industrial accident in history. It happened during the night of 2–3 December 1984, when a tank containing methyl isocyanate (a component in pesticides) leaked at the ageing and poorly maintained Union Carbide plant. Its location in the middle of a residential area meant that people were caught by the toxic clouds in their sleep.

Once they realized something was wrong, panic ensued and people ran into the streets trying to flee (they would probably have been safer indoors). In the stampede, people breathed in even more of the substance. Some were trampled to death. Children were particularly affected because the poisonous fumes, being denser than air, clung low to the ground. The effects of the gas were gruesome, affecting the respiratory tract, causing burns to the eyes, vomiting, convulsions, and eventually collapse of the kidneys, lungs and brain. Hospitals soon became overwhelmed by thousands of patients whose symptoms the staff could not identify; they would not have had the means to treat the victims anyway.

The death toll was massive. The official figure was 3800, but other sources suggest that as many as 25,000 may have died. About half a million people who were exposed to the gas but survived have had to cope with long-lasting after-effects. To this day, many birth defects in Bhopal are attributed to the disaster.

The legal battles began soon afterwards – and are not over. Union Carbide alleged that sabotage might have caused the leak and refused to take responsibility. The company was later acquired by another chemical industry corporation, which then claimed that it wasn't their responsibility either because the disaster had happened before their time. Several charities and victims' associations, both in India and abroad, carry on the fight for proper compensation. The Remember Bhopal Trust runs a small museum about the disaster, but there is no official memorial. However, a sculpture has been erected outside the plant and the walls feature murals and graffiti calling for justice.

The abandoned Union Carbide plant is a rusting industrial ruin. It has never been properly decontaminated so it still stands, ominous and brooding, while slums encroach on the perimeter. Locals slip into the compound through holes in the wall, or simply climb over. Children play in the grounds.

As an international visitor, however, you are not allowed to go in, unless you have an official permit, which is tricky to obtain given India's levels of bureaucracy. Apparently there are also guards patrolling the plant, and it's been said that these days you cannot bribe them any more to turn a blind eye. Gaining access to the plant is thus difficult for foreigners. However, you can get some decent views of the overgrown plant from outside, in particular from a bridge that crosses the railway line to the north of the complex.

Andaman

The Andaman and Nicobar Islands are politically a possession of India far in the east of the Bay of Bengal, close to Thailand and Myanmar, and geologically constitute the northern end of the Indonesian archipelago. Culturally and ethnically, the islands were originally distinct too, although by now a lot of 'Indianization' has taken place.

The best known of the Andamans' indigenous tribes are the Sentinelese, who number only about 300 and have to this day refused contact with the outside world. Whenever anybody gets near their island, North Sentinel, they are ready to attack with bows and arrows. A couple of fishermen who landed on the island's shore in 2006 were killed, as was a wannabe US missionary in 2018. So obviously North Sentinel is out of bounds to tourists.

However, there are other dark places here, mostly related to colonial times, when the British Empire used Andaman as a penal colony from the mid-nineteenth century onwards. The predecessor of the Cellular Jail (see below) on Viper Island, for instance, can be visited on boat tours. Another dark aspect in the more recent history of the Andamans is the Indian Ocean tsunami of 2004, which badly affected this archipelago. A monument by the harbour of Port Blair commemorates this disaster.

Cellular Jail

★★★★☆

Port Blair • Prison, Colonial atrocities

Dark Rating: 8 ☠

This former prison is the premier attraction in Port Blair. It was constructed from 1896 onwards to replace earlier, smaller facilities, and was primarily intended to house political prisoners – that is, Indians who rebelled against British colonial rule. The prison regime was brutal, with forced labour, severe punishments, force-feeding of hunger strikers and even torture and medical experiments. With Indian independence in 1947, the Andamans were integrated into the Indian Union and the grim old prison became redundant.

Four of the cell blocks were demolished in the 1960s to make way for a new hospital, but the remaining complex was declared a National Memorial. Today you can wander the cell blocks, visit the museum exhibition parts and also see the former execution chamber. In the evenings there is a sound and light show portraying, with much pathos, the Indian struggle for independence and the hardship endured in this prison.

Below
Two of the remaining cell blocks radiating out from the central observation tower, and a dummy torture victim on display on the right.

Sri Lanka

This island nation, formerly known as Ceylon, south of India, shares some aspects with its larger neighbour – for instance, it was also a British colony – but in other ways is quite different. For one thing, Sri Lanka is predominantly Buddhist, and ancient Buddhist historical sites dominate the mainstream cultural tourism sector.

In terms of dark history, there is the legacy of the decades-long civil war between the 'Tamil Tigers'– a militant separatist organization that fought for an independent state for the Tamil ethnic minority – and the government representing mainly the Sinhalese majority. The power of the state military eventually gained the upper hand and brutally crushed the last resistance in 2009. Until then, the Tamil stronghold areas in the north and east had been more or less off limits to tourists, but they have opened up meanwhile. The war is commemorated in various places in the north and east, but the victor's prerogative of one-sidedness is palpable in many of these.

In the 2004 tsunami Sri Lanka suffered the second worst death toll of all countries affected (after Indonesia, p299). This included the tragedy of the *Queen of the Sea*, a train that ran on a coastal rail line in the south and was swept away by the tsunami waves, killing some 1700 passengers – which makes it the single worst train disaster in history. For a while the wrecked carriages were left in place, but most have now been removed. Only a single carriage remains and was put upright back on the tracks at a station siding. There are a couple of monuments nearby commemorating the tsunami tragedy, and a Tsunami Museum opened in Hikkaduwa. It displays mainly photos of the disaster and its aftermath.

Yala tsunami memorial

Southern Sri Lanka • Natural disaster (tsunami)

★★★★★

Dark Rating: 4 ☠

Left
The tiled partial remains of a bathroom of the ruined Rest House.

Yala is said to be the best spot for wildlife watching in Sri Lanka, and that is indeed the main attraction here. In fact, you can only visit the park on a jeep safari. These safaris usually include a stop at a very sobering site: the ruins of the former Patanangala Rest House, right by the beach. When the tsunami of 2004 hit Sri Lanka, Yala was also inundated.

According to the National Park website, no animals were killed (how could that be possible?), but 250 people died: 47 at this site, 29 of them locals, the rest Japanese and German tourists. Of the house very little remains – basically just the foundations and some tiled bathroom-floor remnants. Most of the building was swept away by the force of the water. Adjacent to it is a memorial stone dedicated to the victims, plus a metal monument resembling a series of waves.

Thailand

This country was also hit by the tsunami in 2004, although only in the southern parts on the west coast of the Malay Peninsula, such as the popular Phuket. Even though the death toll was not as high as in Indonesia, Sri Lanka or India, the majority of video footage associated with the disaster was taken here. There are a few tsunami memorials in the region, but Thailand is included here as a dark destination for a different reason.

Unlike all its neighbours in Indochina, Thailand (formerly Siam) was never colonized by Western powers. In World War Two, it sided with the Axis Powers, and granted Japan 'free passage'. The Japanese built a railway line to Burma (today's Myanmar), the British colony that Imperial Japan occupied between 1942 and 1945. The hard labour was mainly done by POWs, many of them British, Dutch, Australians and Americans, although Burmese and Malayan forced labourers were also used. Since the working conditions were so harsh, and Japanese brutality so ruthless, many thousands did not survive and the train line became known as the Death Railway (see below).

Kanchanaburi & Bridge on the River Kwai

Western Thailand • War crimes, POWs

★★★★★ – ★★★★★

Dark Rating: 7 ☠

Left
The real bridge on the River Kwai in Kanchanaburi.

The abuse of POWs in the building of the Death Railway is one of the best known of Japan's many war crimes of World War Two. It was famously depicted in the movie *The Bridge on the River Kwai* – a rather glamorized account, shot on location in Sri Lanka rather than Thailand, and the bridge featured in the film looked nothing like the real thing. The actual bridge across the river still exists, namely in Kanchanaburi, where the story of the Death Railway is also told in a whole set of museums of variable quality.

Of those, the modern Thailand-Burma Railway Centre is the best by a huge margin. The others include a disorganized and truly weird one right by the railway bridge. This real Bridge on the River Kwai has become a visitor attraction itself. Little tourist trains travel back and forth, but you can also walk across (watch out for trains!). Proper trains even travel the entire surviving stretch of the line all the way to Nam Tok, where it now ends; it no longer connects with Burma/Myanmar.

Hellfire Pass

Sai Yok District • War crimes, POWs

★★★★★

Dark Rating: 6 ☢

Left
The main part of Hellfire Pass, where POWs, many of them Australians, were forced to work under the harshest conditions.

While Kanchanaburi can feel rather too touristy, the memorial complex at Hellfire Pass is more sombre and hence probably the best place commemorating the Death Railway. There is a small but excellent modern museum that focuses on the Australian POWs' plight (it is run by the Australian government), but is also representative of the other victim groups.

From the museum a trail leads down to the railway line itself. Here you find what is called 'Hellfire Pass'; it was actually called Konyu Cutting, but assumed its nickname because the POWs had to work at night by torchlight. Except for a short reconstructed stretch, the tracks of the railway have long since disappeared, but you can hike a 6km (4-mile) stretch of its course leading through more cuttings and other reminders of the railway. Eventually you come to the point where the former line has not been cleared of the jungle that has reclaimed most of it. The hike is quite serene, thus combining the dark with the pleasant, and few tourists come this far.

Cambodia

Like its neighbours Laos and Vietnam (p292), Cambodia was part of the French colony of Indochina, with a short interruption during the Japanese occupation between 1941 and 1945, until it gained its independence in 1953. During the Vietnam War, Cambodia declared itself neutral, but it got dragged into the conflict and was attacked by the USA because the Vietcong were using parts of Cambodia's territory for some of their operations.

Following a military coup in 1970, the new government sided with the USA. This in turn fostered the strengthening of the rebel forces of the Khmer Rouge. In 1975 the Khmer Rouge reached the capital city, Phnom Penh, and seized power. What came next was the Cambodian genocide (see p290). The country is still struggling to come to terms with its grim past, but has made tremendous progress in many ways. In the process it has also become a popular travel destination.

Many tourists visit the world-famous temple complex of Angkor Wat and maybe a few other temples, but some of the dark places have also become part of the standard tourist itineraries, especially in the capital.

Landmine Museum

Near Siem Reap and Angkor Wat • Modern war, Atrocities

★★★☆☆

Dark Rating: 8 ☠

This private museum was founded by a former Khmer Rouge child soldier who was made to lay thousands of anti-personnel landmines. Later he defected to the Vietnamese, then started de-mining for a UN peacekeeping force.

The museum was set up in 1999. On display are specimens of landmines and other military hardware, but also rather graphic artistic impressions of the mutilation that landmines cause. In the courtyard is a 'mine garden' where you can try your hand at de-mining (safely: none of the exhibits contains explosives). The museum is near Siem Reap, the base for tours to Angkor Wat.

Tuol Sleng

Phnom Penh • Prison, Torture, Genocide

★★★★☆

Dark Rating: 10 ☠

One of the many special prisons of the Khmer Rouge during their reign of terror between 1975 and 1979, Tuol Sleng, also known as S-21, was a former school-turned-prison in the heart of Cambodia's capital. This 'security prison' became the principal interrogation and torture centre of the city.

Between 14,000 and 20,000 people passed through Tuol Sleng; most victims ended up in the killing fields of Choeung Ek (see p291). Very few prisoners – about seven – survived this hell, and only because they were 'useful' (e.g. painting Pol Pot portraits). Initially the victims were the usual suspects: intellectuals or those associated with the previous government. Following internal purges, even members of the Khmer Rouge, accused of being 'traitors of the revolution', later ended up here too. The motto was: 'better kill ten innocent people than let one enemy go free.'

The compound consists of four three-storey buildings and a central single-storey one, around two courtyards. In the southernmost building, visitors can see the torture rooms where the final victims were found dead by the Vietnamese liberators in 1979. Graphic photos on the wall show the state these victims were found in.

In the next block you can see small cells, and shackles and torture instruments are on display, as are hundreds of the registration photos the Khmer Rouge took of their victims (just like the Nazis, they were quite bureaucratic about their crimes). There are lots of frightened faces, some of them young children. Upstairs in one of the blocks is a historical exhibition that chronicles the regime of the Khmer Rouge. In the courtyards you can see the gallows, more torture facilities and a couple of monuments.

Left
Bare metal bed frame on which victims were tortured to death by the Khmer Rouge.

THE CAMBODIAN GENOCIDE

Unlike other genocides, in which the group of victims is defined as 'a people' on ethnic and/or religious grounds, the Cambodian case is unique in that it was an 'auto-genocide': mostly Cambodians slaughtering fellow Cambodians. It started when the radical Marxist-Leninist organization Khmer Rouge ('red Cambodians') under their French-educated leader, Pol Pot, seized power in Cambodia in 1975 – which they renamed Democratic Kampuchea (although, as usual in extreme communist states, there was no democracy at all). The takeover was referred to as Year Zero.

Society was completely changed as the Khmer Rouge installed their idea of a de-industrialized agrarian utopia. This also meant an anti-urban anti-intellectualism of unprecedented proportions. The cities were emptied and everybody was forced into the countryside, where they had to work in collective farming labour camps. Intellectuals were regarded as enemies and systematically killed (simply wearing glasses could be enough reason for being singled out) along with anyone considered a 'traitor' for whatever reason. Owing to widespread malnutrition and the fact that the medical profession had been practically eradicated, many died from the terrible conditions in the collectives. But worst was the mass slaughter.

Given a lack of weapons and ammunition, victims were mostly bludgeoned to death in what have become known as 'killing fields'. There were more than 100 special prisons too, where torture was commonplace. In total, at least 1.5 million, and possibly as many as twice that, were killed in the Cambodian genocide, between a fifth and well over a quarter of the entire population. In relative terms this makes it the deadliest genocide in modern times.

This nightmare only ended in 1979, when neighbouring Vietnam, recently victorious in the war against the USA, invaded Cambodia and drove the Khmer Rouge leadership towards the Thai border. However, because the USA opposed the invasion by Vietnam, and China continued its support for the Khmer Rouge, these were still regarded as the representatives of Cambodia and even held on to their seat in the United Nations.

Meanwhile, a new government of Cambodia, installed by the Vietnamese, began trials and sentenced Pol Pot in absentia to death. Yet he only died in 1998, under mysterious circumstances, in the northern Khmer Rouge stronghold of Anlong Veng. In 1993 elections were held and Cambodia was released into a shaky democratic independence. In 2001 a national tribunal was set up and over the years a handful of Khmer Rouge have been tried. The chief of the Tuol Sleng prison (p289), called Comrade Duch (real name Kaing Guek Eav), was tracked down in 1999, became the first high-ranking Khmer Rouge official to be tried for crimes against humanity and in 2012 was sentenced to life in prison. He died in September 2020.

Left
Leaders of the Khmer Rouge in 1977, with Pol Pot on the far left.

Choeung Ek

Outside Phnom Penh • Genocide, Massacres, Mass graves

★★★☆☆

Dark Rating: 9 ☠

Sometimes referred to simply as the 'Killing Fields', this is actually only one of thousands of such places all over Cambodia, but it has become the most visited by foreign tourists and is the one most integrated into the country's tourism industry. It is practically part of the mainstream 'things to do when in Phnom Penh' sightseeing attractions. This has a downside; the way some visitors act at the site leaves a lot to be desired, and signs have been put up that warn people to behave respectfully.

At the centre of the site is a stupa filled with skulls; behind this are the actual mass graves from which these skulls were dug up. Today the mass graves are just empty hollows in the ground, but allegedly bits of bones can still be found there, especially after heavy rain. Some graves are marked by plaques explaining what sorts of victim were found there. One tree is labelled as one 'against which executioners beat children'.

Above
A Buddhist stupa at the Choeung Ek memorial. It contains more than 5000 human skulls of victims of the Khmer Rouge regime.

Vietnam

The country occupies the eastern coast and southern tip of the Indochina peninsula. Its name is still associated with one of the longest and nastiest wars of the second half of the twentieth century. The Vietnam War is known in the country as the 'American War', since it was preceded by a war against the French, known as the First Indochina War. France had taken Vietnam as a colony in the second half of the nineteenth century, and the rise of communism and nationalism in Vietnam was mainly a reaction to this colonialism. Under their charismatic leader Ho Chi Minh, the revolutionaries defeated the French and established the Democratic Republic of Vietnam, better known simply as North Vietnam. South Vietnam meanwhile remained anti-communist and thus enjoyed the support of the US. So it came that in the 1960s a 'proxy war' developed between the two sides, with the Soviet Union arming the North and the US the South.

The US was also taking part increasingly actively with its own troops and massive air raids.

The Americans lost nearly 60,000 soldiers in the war – although the losses, in particular of civilian lives, were significantly higher on the Vietnamese side. Chemical warfare was employed, especially the defoliant 'Agent Orange', as well as carpet-bombing of regions of countryside.

The carnage reported in the Western media led to increasing protests in the USA and Europe. In the end, the resilience of the North Vietnamese and the escalating costs of the war led to the USA's withdrawal in 1975 – essentially a defeat. The North Vietnamese conquered the South and reunited the country under communist rule. Ho Chi Minh did not live to see his side's victory; he died in 1969, but is still revered as the founding father of modern Vietnam.

In more recent decades, Vietnam has followed a path similar to China's: nominally holding on to communism politically, but embracing a fully capitalist economic approach. This has led to a thawing of US-Vietnamese relations and a massive boom in tourism.

Ho Chi Minh Mausoleum

Hanoi • Dead on display, Communism, Cult of personality

★★★☆☆

Dark Rating: 7 ☠

Left
The grand mausoleum of Vietnam's communist leader Ho opened in 1975, the year of the country's victory against the Americans.

This is the holy of holies of Vietnamese communism: the grand mausoleum where the former leader of North Vietnam, Ho Chi Minh, has been lying in state since he was embalmed following his death in 1969. 'Uncle Ho', as he is affectionately referred to, had actually requested to be cremated, but his political successors saw the need to honour him in the same way as the Soviets did with Lenin (see below). In fact, the Vietnamese received assistance in the preservation of Ho's body from the Soviets.

Visiting is a very solemn affair. You have to stand in line and, when it's your turn, you pass Ho Chi Minh's open crystal coffin in a matter of minutes, but it's still a pilgrimage that many Vietnamese go on, and foreigners join too. The mausoleum is in the country's capital, Hanoi, which also has a Ho Chi Minh Museum. Furthermore you can visit his humble house in the garden outside the Presidential Palace (a colonial building that he deemed too grand for a revolutionary leader).

OTHER COMMUNIST LEADERS' MAUSOLEUMS

Ho Chi Minh's mausoleum is one of the 'Big Four' of such places. These are the other three:

- **The Lenin Mausoleum** on Red Square in Moscow (p233) is the original. Here the leader of the Russian Revolution has been lying in state since his death in 1924 (the requisite embalming technique was developed for him, and the body still has to be regularly re-embalmed).
- **The Mao Mausoleum** on Tiananmen Square (p310) in Beijing was the second place, after Ho Chi Minh's, where this embalming process was copied. In this case, it was the Vietnamese who lent their Chinese allies a hand in 1976–77.

- **The Kim Mausoleum**, Pyongyang, North Korea (p315), is the latest such place, these days a double bill. The founder of the DPRK, Kim Il-sung, was put on display after his death in 1994, and he was joined by his son and successor, Kim Jong-il, after his demise in 2011. Will there be a trio of Kims one day?

Other communist leaders were originally put on display in mausoleums too, such as those of Bulgaria and the ČSSR, but these did not survive the course of history. Nor did Stalin; originally having joined Lenin in his mausoleum after his death in 1953, he was interred beside the Kremlin wall in 1961 in the course of the country's de-Stalinization.

Cu Chi Tunnels

Outside Ho Chi Minh City • Modern war

★★★☆☆

Dark Rating: 6 ☠

This system of narrow underground tunnels was used by the North Vietnamese Vietcong for guerrilla warfare within South Vietnam. By night, they would launch attacks on their adversaries in the area, then retreat to their tunnels during the day. The tunnel entrances were tiny and well camouflaged; the Americans often walked just overhead without noticing them. The Vietcong had an ingenious system of keeping other evidence of their presence hidden too, such as diverting smoke from cooking and keeping toilets 'odourless'.

Their ingenuity extended to the kind of improvised weapons and booby traps they laid for the enemy. The communist victors were understandably proud of all this, so parts of the Cu Chi complex were preserved after the war. Since the opening up of the country to international tourism, the site has become a major attraction, usually done as a half-day excursion from the southern metropolis of Ho Chi Minh City (the former Saigon). And it really is quite touristy, with souvenir stalls and guides demonstrating the various reconstructions of booby traps with glee. Some visitors are encouraged to try crawling through a claustrophobic stretch of tunnel (even though some of these have been widened so that bodies larger than those of the lithe and petite Vietnamese can fit through).

Above
Inside the Vinh Moc tunnels, in which North Vietnamese civilians took shelter from US carpet bombing.

OTHER VIETNAM WAR-RELATED SITES

- **Vinh Moc tunnels.** These are much less touristy than those at Cu Chi. They were not for combat but for retreating to during the heavy American carpet-bombing of the area, not far from the former North–South Vietnam border.
- **Hien Luong Bridge.** This crosses the Ben Hai border river, and serves as a memorial. There is also a war museum, a modern Reunification Monument and a giant flagpole on a pedestal adorned with glorifying socialist-realist mosaics. Huge loudspeaker systems that once blared propaganda across to the other side can still be seen, now thankfully silent.
- **My Lai Massacre site.** This infamous site (aka Son My), where US soldiers burned down an entire village and killed all inhabitants, is now a sombre memorial and museum between Dalat and Hoi An.

- **The DMZ.** This is the most significant cluster of Vietnam War sites, in an inland area of central Vietnam referred to at the time as a 'demilitarized zone' (hence DMZ), even though it was anything but (see also p317). Some of the heaviest fighting took place here, and infamous names of battle sites include Hamburger Hill, the Rockpile and Camp Carroll. The most significant site to visit is Khe Sanh, where there used to be a US base with an airstrip until its evacuation. There is now a museum and an open-air display of US helicopters, tanks and other hardware.

War Remnants Museum

Ho Chi Minh City • Modern war, Atrocities

★★★★☆

Dark Rating: 10 ☠

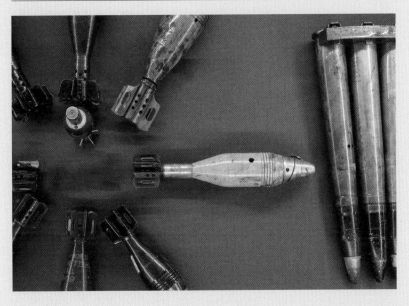

DARK STATS

2 MILLION

estimated civilian deaths in Vietnam (North and South) over the course of the Vietnam War

200,000-250,000

estimated South Vietnamese soldiers killed

1.1 MILLION

estimated North Vietnamese and Viet Cong fighters killed

Almost

60,000

US military personnel killed

Over

7 MILLION TONS

of bombs dropped by the US during the Vietnam War

Formerly known as the Museum of American War Crimes, but renamed in the wake of the thaw in US–Vietnamese relations, this large site is perhaps the most significant of all places in the country commemorating the Vietnam War. There are sections concentrating on war crimes, but the coverage is much broader than that, spanning everything from the run-up to the war to its aftermath. Some of the photos on display, showing the effects of napalm on human bodies or dead Vietnamese decapitated by US soldiers, are extremely graphic.

The section on birth defects caused by America's use of chemical warfare is drastically illustrated too, including the display of grotesquely deformed dead babies preserved in formaldehyde. The cold facts are sobering; for example, statistics showing that the USA dropped three times the tonnage of bombs on Vietnam than they did during the whole of World War Two.

In the courtyard, various US tanks, planes and pieces of artillery are on open-air display. There is also a section about a prison that used to be here, and you can see so-called 'tiger cage' cells and a French guillotine from the colonial era that was allegedly used in South Vietnam until as late as 1960.

Above
A display of ammunitions at the museum.

Left
The guillotine is a lasting and grisly reminder of the French occupation of Vietnam.

| Changi | Trunyan Burial Site | Chega! Exhibition |
| Singapore | Bali, Indonesia | Dili, East Timor |

| Banda Aceh | Balibo | Xanana Reading Room |
| Sumatra, Indonesia | East Timor | Dili, East Timor |

| Sidoarjo | Dili | Santa Cruz Cemetery |
| Java, Indonesia | East Timor | Dili, East Timor |

Ijen	Timorese Resistance
Java, Indonesia	Museum
	Dili, East Timor

Maritime Southeast Asia

Maritime Southeast Asia is the term for those parts of Southeast Asia beyond the Indochina peninsula, spread over numerous islands, of which the Indonesian archipelago forms the largest part. The other two countries covered here are comparatively tiny: Singapore and East Timor. The former had a significant role in World War Two; the latter's dark history is much more recent.

For the traveller, the contrasts couldn't be greater. Singapore is a highly developed, rich city-state with exceptional standards of safety, infrastructure and tourism facilities. The other destinations covered here, on the other hand, all are more of an adventure. In Banda Aceh or East Timor you're unlikely to encounter any other tourists; transport and accommodation options are limited, and it's best to go with a guide to make the necessary arrangements.

The destinations selected for Java and Bali are similarly off the usual tourism tracks, except to a degree Ijen. That mountain however requires a physical adventure to get there. In general, getting around in this huge archipelago often comes with certain risks in the form of dodgy airlines or not fully seaworthy boats. But the rewards are immense. All Indonesian destinations featured here are unique in the world and profoundly impressive visually.

Singapore

This modern city-state on an island off the southern tip of the Malay Peninsula used to be a British colony at a significant strategic position (hence the epithet 'Gibraltar of the East'), controlling the Strait of Malacca. This was why it was a target of the Japanese Empire's expansion in World War Two. In fact, Japan's landings on the Malay Peninsula preceded its attack on Pearl Harbor (p339) by more than an hour, but because Hawaii is on the other side of the international date line it was still 7 December there but already the 8th in Singapore.

The Battle of Singapore raged for the next two months. Eventually, the British and their Australian, Malayan and Indian allies had to surrender. What followed was a brutal Japanese occupation regime that lasted three and a half years. POWs were mistreated, some sent to work on the construction of the Death Railway in Thailand (p287-88). Of the civilian population, the ethnic Chinese had it worst. Thousands were killed in March 1942 in the so-called Sook Ching massacres, which amounted to 'ethnic cleansing'.

British rule was re-established after the war, but since 1965 Singapore has been an independent state and has become an economic powerhouse. Politically it has a strict regime, and the many rules and penalties for transgressions have earned it the sarcastic title 'fine city'. Yet it is relatively easy to handle for Western visitors. It is officially an English-speaking country, and the cleanliness and service standards have earned Singapore the epithet 'Asia light'. However, it is also quite expensive.

From a dark perspective, the sites commemorating the war and the Japanese occupation are of particular interest, such as Bukit Chandu (site of a decisive battle) or the exhibition at the Former Ford Factory (where the British surrender was signed in February 1942). The National Museum also has a section about the occupation years. More war-related sites are Fort Canning, the Kranji War Memorial, Labrador Park and Fort Siloso.

Changi

★★★★☆

Eastern Singapore • POWs, Atrocities, WW2

Dark Rating: 6 💀

This is probably the most infamous place associated with the Japanese occupation of Singapore. Changi is actually the name of the whole district at the eastern end of the island, and is also the designation of the international airport and adjacent Air Force base. In dark terms, it is mainly known for Changi prison. The original, built in 1936, was one of the places where the Japanese incarcerated their POWs from 1942 onwards. Designed for 600 prisoners, it eventually had some 5000 inmates crammed into it.

In 1944 Australian POWs constructed a simple chapel at the prison; after the war this was moved

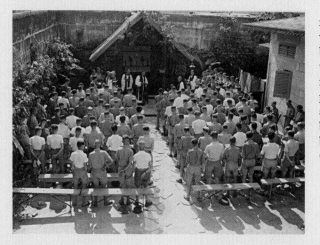

to Australia, but a replica was set up at the original site in 1988. When the old prison was demolished (preserving just the gate and two corner watchtowers), the chapel replica was moved to a new site and an informative museum created

next to it. This can be visited independently, but there are also guided tours that include the museum, chapel, a drive past the current prison and stops at a coastal gun battery and at Changi beach, one of the 'Sook Ching' massacres sites.

Above
A replica of the chapel that was originally created by Australian POWs can be visited at the Changi museum.

Indonesia

This large nation of some 20,000 islands and a population of over 250 million (the largest Muslim nation on Earth) is also rich in diverse dark destinations. Indonesia has more active volcanoes than any other country, and these regularly create natural disasters. Moreover, northern Indonesia was worst hit by the tsunami of 2004. As if all this weren't enough, Indonesia has also added man-made disasters, and its slash-and-burn approach, replacing rainforest with large monoculture palm-oil plantations, has earned it a bad reputation in environmental terms.

Historically there have been plenty of dark chapters too. The once heavily exploited Dutch colony was occupied by Japan during World War Two, and from 1965 to 1998 came the long dictatorship under General Suharto. This began with an unprecedented systematic murder of up to a million alleged communists (described in the movie *The Act of Killing*). Remarkably, even more than two decades after he was deposed there are still celebratory monuments and exhibitions about Suharto's regime, especially the bizarre Pancasila Sakti site in Jakarta. Even wildlife watching can be regarded as dark in Indonesia, such as seeing the scary Komodo dragons on the island of that name, or the last endangered orangutans.

Banda Aceh
★★★☆☆

Northern Sumatra • Natural disaster (tsunami)

Dark Rating: 7 ☠

Aceh, the northernmost province in Indonesia, has long been a troubled region. It was off limits to tourism for many years owing to a conflict between separatist militias and government forces. Then came the earthquake and tsunami of 2004. Banda Aceh, the region's capital, was hit worst of any location by this largest ever natural disaster in modern history. About 150,000 people perished in this region alone, and large parts of the city were levelled.

Reconstruction has made enormous progress in the subsequent years, and the disaster facilitated a political solution to the previous military conflict. A truce was reached, the army withdrawn and the region given a certain level of autonomy. With this came sharia law, although this isn't a huge problem for visitors today (except that no alcohol is sold). In fact, foreign tourists are still so rare that the friendly welcome and concomitant requests for group selfies with the locals can be overwhelming at times, although the atmosphere is certainly anything but threatening.

Above
A number of boats that ended up stranded inland after being deposited there by the wave can still be seen.

The disaster of 2004 is commemorated in a Tsunami Museum as well as by the memorial park around the PLTD Apung 1, a former floating power station that ended up far inland after the flood waves. From the Tsunami & Disaster Mitigation Research Centre, several tsunami ruins can still be seen. And the Thanks to the World Park's monuments pay tribute to various countries that provided relief funds after the disaster.

Sidoarjo

★★ ☆ ☆ ☆

South of Surabaya, Java • Man-made/natural disaster, Ghost town

Dark Rating: 8 ☠

In May 2006 an oil and gas company was exploring this region when one of its drilling operations accidentally triggered a massive mud volcano. Soon several villages around the borehole that kept spouting mud had been swallowed up by a thick layer of grey muck. Over the years, tens of thousands of people were displaced, infrastructure was destroyed and there were fatalities too.

The whole situation is a mess, not just literally but also socially and legally. The company's claims that this was a natural disaster linked to an earthquake at Yogyakarta, 250km (160 miles) away, are dismissed by the locals who hold the company accountable. In any case, this man-made and/or natural disaster is one of the most unusual dark sights in Indonesia.

You might think that foreigners visiting the site could be considered voyeuristic, but locals actually encourage people to come and see for themselves what has happened. There are viewing points by the dykes that have been constructed in an attempt to contain the muddy floods, and you can pay for a motorcycle ride across the hardened mud flow and around it (that way at least a little money comes into the region).

At the southeastern end of the mud field, an abandoned mosque and surrounding ghost-town ruins with a mud-drenched cemetery are one of the most captivating sights to behold. It is a unique place worth the excursion from Surabaya, the nearest city.

Above
A marooned former mosque and abandoned village at the edge of the mud fields.

Below
Houses completely drowned in and destroyed by mud. The steam cloud in the distance indicates the source of all this sludge.

Ijen

★★★

Eastern Java • Volcano, Infernal sulphur mine, Acid lake

Dark Rating: 9 ☠

This may not be Indonesia's most active volcano – the last proper eruption was 200 years ago – but it is arguably the most unusual and visually appealing. A legendary aspect is the blue flames that are visible when it's dark, forming a most captivating sight. These blue fires are from ignited sulphur, which is liquidized and collected and then mined by locals who make a living from selling the sulphur. It is hard work, given the toxic sulphurous fumes emitted by the volcano and the heavy loads (up to 90kg/200lb) that the workers carry on their shoulders up a steep path to the crater rim and down to the foot of the mountain.

The crater also contains the world's largest and most acidic sulphurous lake – which is deadly. This was sadly proven a few years ago when an unwary tourist fell in and was killed by the acid. The hike up to the crater rim, and especially the steep climb down to the lakeshore and the sulphur mine, is not without hazards either, so great care should be taken.

Many tours only go to Ijen at sunrise to see the eerie lake from the crater rim, but to see those blue flames you have to go at night and clamber down. Ideally you need a respirator mask, because the sulphurous fumes emitted by the fumaroles at the crater bottom are extremely acrid. However, it is worth the effort and risk as walking into this otherworldly infernal scenery is incomparable; it's like being on another planet.

OTHER VOLCANOES WORTH VISITING

– **Krakatoa**, in the Sundra Strait between western Java and southeastern Sumatra, is the most infamous volcano in Indonesia. Its cataclysmic eruption in 1883 not only caused massive destruction locally but also had knock-on effects globally because of the ash that spread throughout the atmosphere. The original volcano was blown to smithereens in the explosion, but a new cone, called Anak Krakatau, literally 'child of Krakatoa', has grown in its stead. You can go on boat tours to this island volcano, provided there isn't another phase of volcanic activity – because, even as a mere 'child', the new young Krakatoa is still quite unruly.

– **Merapi**, central Java, is Indonesia's most dangerous volcano these days. It is very explosive, known for its massive pyroclastic flows and lahars (see p51). Its frequent eruptions threaten the densely populated region around it. Yet since volcanic deposits make for fertile land, and the lahar ash is even mined for producing high-quality building materials, people are reluctant to move to safer distances from the cone. At its foot you can go on jeep tours into the destruction zone of recent eruptions (especially 2010); there is also a Merapi Volcano Museum.

– **Bromo**, East Java. This is the most visited volcano in Indonesia, famous for its scenic setting and photogenic sunrises. It too is still active, so at times visiting is not recommended; even at quieter periods the sulphurous fumes emitted from the crater can be overpowering when you are at the rim.

Indonesia has countless other volcanoes, far too many to list here. The same is true of the entire Pacific Ring of Fire, which includes the volcanoes of New Zealand (p335), the Philippines, Japan (p318), Kamchatka and the entire Pacific side of the Americas (see Mount St Helens, p14), in particular in Guatemala, Nicaragua, El Salvador, Costa Rica, Mexico, Ecuador, Peru and Chile.

Other parts of the world have volcanoes too, especially the Caribbean (see Montserrat, p49) and the Atlantic (see Iceland, p77, and Fogo, p247). The world's most active hotspot volcano is found in the middle of the Pacific, on Hawaii (p343–44). Africa has some noteworthy volcanoes too, including the rather temperamental Nyiragongo in the DR Congo, which features the world's largest lava lake, and Erta Ale in Ethiopia (p253).

In Europe it is Italy (p184) that has some of the world's best-known volcanoes, in particular Vesuvius near Naples, which infamously destroyed Pompeii in the year 79 CE, as well as the constantly active island volcano of Stromboli and the massive Mount Etna in Sicily.

Above
An early-morning view of the Tengger massif, with the smoke-emitting Bromo crater bottom left and the also active Mt Semeru looming in the background.

Trunyan Burial Site

By Lake Batur, northeastern Bali • Dead on display

★★☆☆☆

Dark Rating: 9 ☠

This is a unique dark place related rather directly to death. It is a burial site of sorts, except that here the local Trunyan tribe of Bali don't actually bury their dead underground, nor do they cremate them; instead they put them in basket- or cage-like bamboo structures and leave them to rot in the open. Only after decomposition is complete are the bones scattered in the forest, except for the skulls, which are lined up neatly on a rocky ledge nearby.

Visiting this site is possible; local guides can arrange boats to take you across Lake Batur to the burial site, which is in an otherwise inaccessible place on the lake's forested shores. What awaits you there will vary – sometimes there are fresh corpses, only just placed in their baskets, complete with mementos and select personal belongings of the deceased. Sometimes the encounter will rather be with semi-decomposed bodies, or just bones.

This is obviously not for the faint of heart. However, it is not at all a 'horror site', but rather an exceptionally serene and peaceful experience. There is even a welcome sign in English by the pier and entrance. Remarkably, the decomposition of bodies does not fill the air with the stench normally associated with this. Nor is the place swarming with flies or other insects. Legend attributes this to a type of 'fragrant' tree next to the site.

Top
Bamboo burial cages contain decomposing bodies, while mementos and offerings to the deceased are placed beside them.

Above
Skulls from previous burials are collected and stacked in rows on a nearby stone wall.

East Timor

This small and remote country, occupying one half of an island of the Indonesian archipelago north of Australia, was the first new nation to become independent and join the United Nations in this millennium. The years leading up to this were tumultuous.

Until 1975 the country was a colony of Portugal (p98). In the wake of the Carnation Revolution in Portugal in 1974 which ended the dictatorship and freed several of the country's colonies, a revolutionary movement in East Timor seized power and declared independence too. Before the year was out, mighty Indonesia, with the approval of the USA, had invaded and annexed little East Timor and put an end to its left-leaning self-governance. What followed was decades of brutal repression that at times took on genocidal proportions. Yet the Timorese underground resistance movement never gave up.

Representatives went abroad to campaign internationally. In 1991 video footage of the Santa Cruz Massacre (see p307) was smuggled out to raise international awareness of the plight of the Timorese. Eventually the end of the Cold War, coupled with a change of atmosphere towards peaceful co-operation and the end of the Suharto dictatorship in Indonesia in 1998, helped to pave the way towards a resolution of the situation in East Timor.

A referendum was held in 1999 under the protection of a UN peacekeeping force, which resulted in the vast majority of Timorese voting for independence, despite a campaign of intimidation and violence on the part of the Indonesians. After the announcement of the result, pro-Indonesian militias went on the rampage. For once, however, the UN gave a resolute response, possibly because then Secretary-General Kofi Annan did not want a repeat of the failure of the UN that had occurred a few years earlier in Rwanda (see p250). UN forces, in particularly Australians, put an end to the violence and disarmed the militias, many of whom fled to West Timor (still part of Indonesia).

East Timor officially became independent in 2002. The devastation left behind by the Indonesians took a long time to repair, and the political situation internally was still volatile, yet overall the country more or less stabilized. Economically it is still struggling and remains one of the poorest countries in Asia.

As a travel destination, East Timor is exotic and the tourism infrastructure minimal, especially outside the capital, Dili. But tours of the country are available and provide great insights. The fact that you will encounter hardly any other tourists is in a way part of the attraction.

Balibo

★★☆☆☆

Western edge of East Timor • Murder, Modern war

Dark Rating: 5 💀

Probably the most significant memorial outside Dili, this place near the border with West Timor commemorates the 'Balibo Five': a group of journalists working for Australian TV who were in the country to monitor the volatile situation in 1975 and who witnessed the Indonesian invasion. The military, not keen on allowing footage of their aggression to reach the outside world, murdered the five on the spot when they discovered them – and that despite the fact that the journalists were unarmed and, in order to indicate that they were from the foreign media, had painted the word

'Australia' and a crude rendition of its flag on the house they were staying in.

The Indonesians subsequently tried to cover up the incident, and Australia, which sided politically with Indonesia at the time, went along with the cover-up for decades. Only when Australia changed its stance on East Timor did it allow an inquest.

Right
Today's memorial for the Balibo Five is housed in the original building they had used; inside is a small exhibition.

Dili

★★★☆☆

Central north coast • Repression, Atrocities

Dark Rating: 5 ☠

The capital of East Timor is the only sizeable conurbation in the country and its sole political, economic and transport hub – and also the place where the turmoil of the 1999 post-referendum violence mainly played out. You can still spot the odd ruin of houses destroyed back then, but overall the city has recovered and is quite functional. Dili is also the principal point of entry for visitors and home to most of the places of interest here.

Left
Ruins in the city recall the nation's violent struggles for independence.

Timorese Resistance Museum

★★★★☆

Centre of Dili • Repression, Atrocities, Resistance

Dark Rating: 5 ☠

This memorial museum, archive, research institution and cultural centre in the heart of the city is the main place where the country's momentous modern history, and the dark chapters of repression by Indonesia, are commemorated.

Its permanent exhibition is state of the art, sleek and informative. It is trilingual (in local Tetum as well as Portuguese and English) and has many multimedia and audiovisual elements in addition to more conventional museum designs. The narrative runs from colonial times to the final achievement of independence, and details the Indonesian invasion, the complicit roles the USA and Australia played in it, and the atrocities committed by Indonesia. The organizational structures of the resistance movement are presented in detail too.

Above
East Timor spokesperson and later president José Ramos-Horta with East Timorese freedom fighters in 1975.

Chega! Exhibition

★★★☆☆

Southern edge of Dili • Prison, Atrocities, Repression

Dark Rating: 5 ☠

This is another memorial space about the Indonesian occupation of East Timor, all the violence it came with, and how it was overcome. 'Chega', incidentally, is Portuguese for 'enough'. The exhibition is lower-key and cruder than that in its bigger and more modern sister institution in the city centre. However, it has the bonus of place authenticity, being housed in a former prison. This was built in colonial times, but during the occupation it became an overcrowded political prison and torture centre operated by the Indonesian regime.

Above
One of the isolation cells, with prisoners' graffiti in evidence.

Xanana Reading Room

★★☆☆☆

Northeast of central Dili • Resistance, Assassination attempt

Dark Rating: 2 ☠

A kind of cultural centre, named after Xanana Gusmão, the charismatic former leader of the resistance and first president of East Timor after independence, the reading room is just that: a local library. The main building of the compound, a colonial-era villa, is worth seeing for the various paintings, photos and objects related to the country's national hero. A more sobering sight is the open-air display of the car in which the president narrowly escaped an assassination attempt in 2008. It serves as a reminder of the fragility of the new nation in its first decade or so after gaining independence.

Above
The Toyota Land Cruiser in which Xanana Gusmão was travelling when the assassination attempt was made.

Santa Cruz Cemetery

★★☆☆☆

Southern Dili • Massacre site, Cemetery

Dark Rating: 5 💀

The Santa Cruz Massacre occurred in 1991, when the Indonesian army mowed down hundreds of peaceful civilians in a funeral procession for a protester, Sebastião Gomes, who had been killed by Indonesian security forces the previous day. As panicked protesters fled deep into the cemetery, the trigger-happy Indonesian soldiers pursued them; in the end, some 250 Timorese were shot dead.

Scenes of the massacre were filmed by the Western journalist Max Stahl. The footage was later smuggled out of the country and used in an award-winning documentary. This was instrumental in raising international awareness of the plight of the Timorese and exposed the Indonesian brutality. In light of the footage, Indonesia could no longer uphold claims that it was merely 'restoring order'. In that sense, the Santa Cruz Massacre became a turning point for the Timorese freedom movement.

At the cemetery today, the grave of Gomes is obviously the main pilgrimage spot. The Santa Cruz Massacre is also commemorated by a dramatic monument outside Motael Church, which is where he was killed. The sculpture is a recreation of one of the iconic still images from the video footage taken during the massacre.

Above
Sebastião Gomes's grave in Santa Cruz cemetery.

Left
A sculpture of a dying man cradled by a shocked and frightened co-protester recalls a scene from the Santa Cruz massacre.

East Asia

Like the previous section, this one is dominated by one large, powerful country – in this case, China. The People's Republic of China has become one of the world's superpowers, second only to the USA. Some of the other countries covered here, on the other hand, have an 'unresolved' status, in particular Taiwan.

The Korean peninsula has been split into two states since the Korean War of 1950–53 (see p316). Officially, both countries pursue the distant prospect of reunification, but realistically that seems unlikely in the foreseeable future. Politically the two countries could not be more different: South Korea is a modern, capitalist member of the world community, whereas North Korea, with its dynastic version of an ultra-Stalinist dictatorship, is regarded by most as a 'rogue state'.

Japan and its tropical outpost Okinawa (once an independent kingdom) are open and, like Taiwan and South Korea, partly Westernized, partly steeped in enigmatic old traditions.

The dark destinations in these countries vary a lot, from sites related to past wars to ongoing confrontations and from natural disaster areas to nuclear sites. And while Taiwan, South Korea and Japan can largely be travelled in freely, China and especially North Korea are more restricted.

China

This huge and populous country was once one of the greatest empires on Earth, but by the twentieth century had lost much of that role. It suffered from internal divisions, colonialism, civil war and then a ruthless invasion and occupation by Japan from 1937 to 1945. During that time various war crimes were committed by the Japanese. After that conflict, civil war continued within China until the mainland became the communist People's Republic of China (PRC) in 1949, while Taiwan split from the rest of China (p312).

The communist leader of the PRC, Chairman Mao Zedong, steered the huge country through a series of reforms, although the so-called Great Leap Forward resulted in mass starvation. Yet China became an industrial nation and eventually a nuclear power too. The Cultural Revolution during Mao's final decade was another grim phase in communist China's history – a period of political repression and persecution of unprecedented proportions. Following Mao's death in 1976, the country began to change as his successor, Deng Xiaoping, initiated economic reforms and slowly opened up the country to the outside world.

China has meanwhile become a key superpower in both economic and military terms. Nominally the government is communist, and freedom of speech is still suppressed. But economically the country has embraced turbo-capitalism. Many Chinese have benefited from the economic growth of recent decades, and the face of China has changed a lot.

In terms of dark travel destinations, China is relatively restricted. The many dark aspects of the PRC's own domestic history do not feature much within tourism, and usually cannot be talked about openly. However, previous dark episodes in which China was the victim are commemorated, in particular the Nanjing Massacre (p311). Other than that, the cult of personality surrounding the legendary Mao continues to some extent today, and his birthplace and locations related to the revolution he led are still revered. Most tourism, however, is about ancient Imperial relics, including the famous Great Wall of China.

Tiananmen Square

★★★☆☆

Central Beijing • Massacre, Repression, Communism, Cult of personality   **Dark Rating: 7** ☠

This vast expanse in the heart of China's capital city is primarily known in the outside world for the massacre in June 1989, when the military crushed large-scale student protests with brutal force. How many lost their lives is still unknown: maybe a few hundred, possibly thousands. That tragedy can still hardly be mentioned within China itself, and it is not commemorated at the site in any way. The show of force by the government has had a lasting effect. No protests on such a collective scale have been seen in China since 1989. Repression and surveillance are complete. When visiting the square, you can perhaps spare a few thoughts about all this, but it is best to do so quietly.

The square is ringed by government buildings. To the north is the world-famous Forbidden City (the former Imperial palace complex), which is Beijing's principal tourist attraction. The main gate of this sprawling compound of traditional imperial architecture still features a large portrait of Chairman Mao. His revolutionary spirit may no longer be prevalent, but his cult of personality lives on.

The man himself – or rather his embalmed body – lies in the large purpose-built Mao Mausoleum right on Tiananmen Square (see p293). Large numbers of visitors continue to make the pilgrimage to get a brief glimpse of Mao in his crystal coffin.

Below
The mausoleum with the embalmed body of 'the Great Helmsman' Mao Zedong stands in the centre of Tiananmen Square.

Nanjing Massacre Memorial

★★★★☆

In the southwest of Nanjing, Jiangsu Province • War crimes, Atrocities

Dark Rating: 9 ☹

The city of Nanjing has been one of the most important cities in Chinese history, sometimes serving as the nation's capital. It had that function from 1927 to 1937 in the Republic of China under nationalist leader Chiang Kai-shek before he fled to Taiwan (see p312). In the Second Sino–Japanese War from 1937, the then capital was a target for the invading army of Imperial Japan. After fierce battles, the city fell on 13 December 1937.

There followed a wave of retaliation and murderous violence by the Japanese. It has been called the Nanjing Massacre and the 'Rape of Nanjing'. Indeed, mass rape was part of the atrocities, along with widespread looting and arson. But it was the random slaughtering of civilians that took on unprecedented proportions. According to Chinese figures, as many as 300,000 may have been killed.

In Japan this figure is often contested, if the fact that the Nanjing Massacre happened at all is even acknowledged (at the Yushukan in Tokyo – see p320 – for instance, it is not). To this day, the issue strains Sino–Japanese relations. The 300,000 figure, however, features repeatedly at the official Nanjing Massacre Memorial Hall and Museum established in the city in 1985 and expanded in 1995. The original main hall was constructed atop a mass grave of victims on Jiangdongmen Square.

Below left
Ceremony at the Memorial Hall of the Victims of the Nanjing Massacre.

Below
Inside the museum is a gruesome exhibition including many graphic photographs of the atrocities.

Taiwan

Formerly known as Formosa, this island state officially calls itself the Republic of China (ROC), since it was here that its government under Generalissimo Chiang Kai-shek fled after it lost against the Chinese communist revolution under Mao Zedong in 1949. Until the end of World War Two, the island had been occupied by Japan. It remained a contested territory, with Taiwan claiming to represent all of China while The People's Republic of China (PRC) still refuses to recognize the ROC or even to co-operate with states that do officially recognize it (many countries do so only unofficially). Hence Taiwan is also the largest country, both by its population and by the size of its economy, that is not a member of the United Nations.

Taiwan was ruled dictatorially under Chiang until his death in 1975, yet rapidly industrialized into an economic powerhouse. From the late 1980s onwards there have also been democratic reforms. Relations with the PRC remain difficult, and the rhetoric by the PRC's leadership has at times been threatening, but in practical terms things have improved and travel connections between the two were opened.

Politics and war aside, the country is frequently battered by natural forces: earthquakes and typhoons. While the former are unpredictable, the typhoon season is usually from July to September, so that's a time for tourists to avoid. Otherwise, Taiwan is welcoming towards travellers, has modern infrastructure and is a comparatively easy Asian destination.

In addition to the places covered below, there are intriguing military history sites, in particular in the outlying islands of Taiwan closer to the PRC mainland, such as Kinmen and Matsu. Here you can visit underground tunnels originally dug as shelters during the decades up to the 1970s in which both sides kept shelling each other. Various other military installations have been commodified for tourism too, such as Green Island (see below).

Green Island

To the southeast of Taiwan • Repression, Prison

★★★☆☆

Dark Rating: 7 ☠

This small volcanic outcrop off Taiwan's coast was used as a place of exile and incarceration for thousands of political prisoners, who had to do forced labour and faced frequent torture. Executions were common too. This carried on up to the late 1980s. Today there is a Human Rights Memorial Park, and the four cell blocks that made up the prison with the Orwellian name 'Oasis Villa' are now open to the public. Green Island is connected to Taitung/Fugang on the main island by ferry as well as light aircraft services.

2-28 Memorial Museum

Central Taipei • Atrocity, Massacre, Repression

★★☆☆☆

Dark Rating: 4 ☠

This museum's name is a reference to a specific date, 28 February 1947 (in US format). On that day violent clashes, triggered by the confiscation of contraband cigarettes by Chiang Kai-shek's Nationalist Chinese Kuomintang Army, escalated into mass killings. Estimates of the death toll lie between 10,000 and 30,000. The martial law declared afterwards essentially continued for the next 40 years and is commonly referred to as the 'White Terror'. It lasted until Taiwan began a process of liberalization in the 1980s. The museum opened on the 50th anniversary of the killings in 1997. The White Terror is also commemorated at the Jing-Mei White Terror Memorial Park at a former military detention centre in the south of Taipei.

9·21 Earthquake Museum

Wufeng District, Taichung, central Taiwan • Natural disaster (earthquake)   **Dark Rating: 8** ☠

★★★★☆

This is another place using a date abbreviation in the American format to refer to a tragic event: in this case, 21 September 1999, when an earthquake of around 7.5 magnitude struck the centre of Taiwan. It caused large-scale damage, almost 2500 people were killed, more than 11,000 were injured and more than 100,000 were made homeless. Along the fault line a surface rupture some 100km (60 miles) long formed and land along this line was raised by up to 7m (22ft). The effect is clearly visible at what used to be Guangfu Junior High School in Wufeng District. The school stood directly on the fault line and was largely destroyed.

The site was subsequently turned into a museum. It incorporates the semi-collapsed ruins of the school and a preserved part of the section of its sports field and running tracks that was ruptured and raised by the fault. Inside are recreations of the internal damage to the buildings, plus several large blow-ups of photos of residential high-rise buildings that collapsed in the quake. There are informative text panels (also in English), plus a machine that demonstrates the different shake modes of earthquakes. Given how rarely earthquakes are commemorated in such a dramatic way, this is a highly unusual and significant dark destination.

Below
The devastation wreaked by the earthquake is evident from the fortified ruins of the school, which forms part of the museum site.

North Korea

Often seen from the outside as the ultimate 'pariah state', the Democratic People's Republic of Korea (DPRK), aka North Korea, occupies the northern half of the Korean peninsula. It is the final stronghold of communist rule, with collectivization, a planned economy, suppression of freedom of expression, surveillance and a huge cult of personality around the nation's leaders. In fact, the DPRK is unique as a communist state in that its regime is dynastic at the very top.

Power was handed from the state's founder, the 'Great Leader' Kim Il-sung, to his son Kim Jong-il, known as 'Dear Leader' after his father's demise in 1994 (Kim Il-sung continued to carry the title of 'Eternal President'). In 2011, upon Kim Jong-il's death, his youngest son, Kim Jong-un, was made 'Supreme Leader', aged only 28. After initial doubts about his suitability for the post, he has asserted himself as just as ruthless a leader as his predecessors.

Following the Korean War (see p316), the North initially made more rapid progress and outdid the South in economic terms. Politically, however, it was not just a single-party communist state but a one-man show under the increasingly god-like Kim Il-sung. The cult of personality around Kim eventually outshone even Stalin's in the Soviet Union.

After the dissolution of the USSR things became increasingly difficult for the DPRK without the support of that key former ally, with droughts and subsequent famines adding to the dire situation. At the same time, South Korea left the North far behind economically. However, the North set about developing nuclear weapons. The DPRK had understood clearly what had happened in Iraq and Libya and was adamant that not giving up its nuclear programme was the best lifeline it had to maintain independence and sovereignty. So far this strategy has worked remarkably well. How it will continue remains to be seen.

As a travel destination today North Korea is undeniably exotic. But it is possible to go there and, contrary to what many in the West may think, it is safe to do so – provided you follow the rules. To begin with, you cannot go independently, but must always be accompanied by two state 'guides' who are also 'minders'. Of course, you will be shown only what the DPRK wants you to see. Labour camps, obvious poverty and suchlike will not feature, and their existence will be denied. But if you are willing to go along with the propaganda-soaked narratives and the expected rules of conduct (see opposite), you can still gain insights into a country that is totally different from the rest of the planet. That alone makes it worth it.

There are specialist tour operators that offer packages of different lengths, from short breaks in Pyongyang to weeks-long comprehensive tours.

Below
A military parade with ballistic missiles on display at Kim Il Sung Square in the capital, Pyongyang.

Pyongyang

In the southwest of the DPRK • Communism, Cult of personality, War

★★★★☆

Dark Rating: 7 ☠

Left
Two over 20m-high (66 ft) statues of Kim Il-sung and Kim Jong-il on Mansu Hill.

The capital city of North Korea is a strange place. It was bombed flat by the USA in the Korean War, so virtually all buildings today have been built since then. The architecture is prototypically socialist: large high-rise apartment blocks interspersed with grand monuments and oversized sports facilities. The latter includes the largest of its kind: the 150,000-seat May Day Stadium. This is where the famous Mass Games are performed when they take place (they are not consistently held). The games are a spectacle second to none: the largest mass choreography, gymnastics and all-out propaganda show on Earth, as breathtaking as it is bizarre.

Of the permanent attractions, an especially important one is the Mansudae Grand Monument: towering bronze statues of Kim Il-sung and, since 2012, Kim Jong-il. A visit here is mandatory for all tourists, and every group is expected to lay down a bunch of flowers by the Kims' feet and bow. This ritual is the biggest stumbling block for many when contemplating a trip to North Korea. If you cannot handle the idea, don't go.

The Kim Mausoleum (p293) is now a double act where both the first and the second Kim lie in state, embalmed, in crystal coffins. It is the holy of holies of the DPRK. Again, visitors must be on their best behaviour (and in best attire) and bow as they pass the coffins.

Easier to handle are the many grand monuments, such as the Workers' Party Monument, a giant depiction of its symbol: a hammer (representing workers), a sickle (peasants) and a calligraphy paintbrush (intellectuals). Not far from it on the banks of the Taedong River stands the Juche Tower, a tall stone edifice with a stylized red torch-flame sculpture at the top. 'Juche' is the Korean name for the state ideology of self-sufficiency.

On the other side of the river is the wide expanse of Kim Il-sung Square, which is frequently used for big propaganda shows and military parades. Other imposing monuments include the Arch of Triumph, which is modelled on the iconic equivalent in Paris, but, as the guides are keen to emphasize, is 10m (33ft) higher. Finally, the title of most over-the-top monument in Pyongyang probably goes to the flamboyant Reunification Monument, dedicated to a wishful thinking idea rather than any actual event.

Another regular stop on a tour of Pyongyang is a visit to Kim Il-sung's birth house on the outskirts of the city. But a visit to the Victorious Fatherland Liberation War Museum provides a full-on dose of martial propaganda. Here you are told the North Korean version of the historical events known elsewhere as the Korean War, e.g. that it was started by American 'imperialist aggression'.

Now part of the museum is the USS *Pueblo*, an alleged American spy ship that the North Koreans captured in 1968 to great propagandistic effect and subsequently put the crew on a show trial. You can enter the boat and marvel at all the electronic espionage equipment inside.

THE KOREAN WAR AND ITS AFTERMATH

The Korean peninsula had been under Japanese rule since the early twentieth century, but after Japan's defeat in World War Two, the USA and the Soviet Union agreed to 'share' rebuilding Korea and split the country into two zones along the latitude of the 38th parallel. Soon the Cold War developed and the two sides pursued different goals. The Soviets wanted a communist ally on their border; the Americans took a strict anti-communist stance.

Kim Il-sung, who had fought for the Red Army in Manchuria, formed the Korean Workers' Party. Tough and charismatic, he emerged as the political leader in the north, with Soviet respect and support. By 1948 two independent Koreas had been established – the Republic of Korea (ROK) in the south and the DPRK in the north – recognized only by their respective sides of the Cold War divide.

Both the Americans and the Soviets left, as had been agreed, after their five years of 'shared' administration. Yet both Koreas whipped up propaganda calling for reunification. In the north, given the supplies of Soviet weapons (and weapon factories), it was assumed that this could best be achieved through swift military action – and so the Korean War began.

North Korean forces stormed southwards and conquered nearly all of the ROK, which held only a final bastion around Pusan on the southern tip of the peninsula. Then the Americans, with the support of several allied countries, intervened and reversed the North's advance, pushing them back across the 38th parallel and further towards the Chinese border.

At that point the Chinese, who had also just established a communist state, came to the DPRK's assistance; with sheer manpower (around a million soldiers), they pushed the Americans back to the dividing line at the 38th parallel. Both sides dug in there and continued bloody but futile battles, with neither side gaining the upper hand despite heavy aerial bombing by the US (dropping a higher tonnage on the North than on either Nazi Germany or Japan in World War Two). It was a stalemate.

In June 1953 the US, China and the DPRK signed an armistice at Panmunjom (see opposite) and the first proxy war of the Cold War era was over – or not quite, as the case may be. The armistice was no more than a truce, and no peace treaty has ever been signed, so technically speaking the DPRK and ROK are still at war with each other. However, repeated border skirmishes notwithstanding, all-out war has since been avoided.

Left
US bomber scores a direct hit on warehouses and docks at Wonsan harbour on the east coast of Korea.

South Korea

The Korean peninsula's southern half is called the Republic of Korea (ROK) and has been the DPRK's arch-enemy for over seven decades. It could hardly be more different culturally, politically and economically from its estranged communist cousin in the north. South Korea has developed into a more or less stable democracy, is a major export-driven player in the world economy and shows a noticeable degree of westernization. It's also much easier to travel to for foreign visitors than to the DPRK.

From a dark perspective, the DMZ (see below) is a key attraction. But the ROK also has dark places all of its own. These include the Korean war museum in the glitzy capital city, Seoul, a prison history museum (Seodaemun) and the April 3 Peace Memorial on Jeju Island, which commemorates a bloodily crushed uprising that started on that date in 1948.

Panmunjom & DMZ

★★★☆☆

Border between North and South Korea • Fortified border, War

Dark Rating: 8

Left
South Korean soldiers standing guard at the DMZ border at Panmunjom, looking towards the north.

The border strip between the DPRK and the ROK is officially called the 'Demilitarized Zone' (DMZ; see also p294). Actually, it is one of the most militarized areas on the planet. It's like a stretch of the Iron Curtain, between communism and capitalism. The only point of contact is at Panmunjom, where the armistice of 1953 was signed (see opposite).

Actually straddling the borderline is the 'Joint Security Area', although following a bloody border incident in the 1970s it has also been divided into north and south. Right on the border stand some UN blue huts, still in use for negotiations. Soldiers from both sides guard the site.

Excursions to the DMZ are part of many state-sanctioned DPRK tours. Visits from the ROK side are also offered, by several competing operators, usually as full-day or half-day guided excursions out of Seoul. Independent trips to this high-security area are not possible. Tours that include Panmunjom can allow visitors to briefly enter the central blue hut, where a table stands right in the middle straddling the borderline. If you circle the table you've technically speaking walked on a bit of DPRK territory. Many DMZ tours from Seoul also include stops at some viewpoints as well as at one of the 'infiltration tunnels' dug under the border.

Japan

This island nation is an enigmatic country for most foreigners, and full of contradictions. Hyper-modern in many ways, but very conservative and traditional in others, its culture is unique, and that partly makes travelling in this country so rewarding. Japan has plenty in terms of dark chapters in its history. Some are unique in the world, in particular the only two cities to have ever been the target of atomic bombs (see p25): Hiroshima and Nagasaki.

There are also places associated with the much more recent triple disaster of 11 March 2011 ('3/11' for short, and in allusion to '9/11'): firstly, the second largest earthquake ever measured, which, secondly, triggered a monster tsunami that killed nearly 20,000 people and caused the costliest damage to infrastructure of any natural disaster in history; thirdly, the tsunami led to the nuclear disaster at Fukushima-Daiichi NPP (see opposite).

Travelling around Japan is greatly facilitated by its excellent rail network featuring super-fast bullet trains that cover large distances almost as fast as domestic flights. Moreover, Japan's trains boast an unparalleled punctuality and are very comfortable. The language barrier can be a problem, but Japanese people are generally friendly and willing to help.

Okawa Elementary School

★★☆☆☆

Miyagi Prefecture, northern Honshu • Natural disaster (tsunami)

Dark Rating: 8 ☠

Left
The toppled concrete foot bridge at the Okawa school memorial is a powerful illustration of the physical forces that were at play in the 2011 tsunami.

This has to be one of the most tragic places associated with the '3/11' tsunami that devastated large parts of the northeastern coast of Honshu, Japan's main island, in 2011. What makes this spot especially tragic is the fact that, out of the 75 schoolchildren who perished in the tsunami while in the care of their teachers, 74 lost their lives here. This disproportionate number has been the subject of lengthy investigations and a court case. Apparently it was caused by a combination of inadequate regulations, confusion and hesitation on the part of the teachers as to when and where to evacuate to, and a culture of deference to authority.

Eventually, the children were led to an unsuitable 'evacuation area': a traffic island by a bridge across the river. This meant that they walked towards the tsunami that was funnelling up the river, instead of climbing the hill directly behind the school, which would have provided safe higher ground. Only a couple of children, who disobeyed and turned around to make a dash for the hill, survived. The rest were washed away and perished – together with 10 out of the 11 teachers. One of the surviving children later successfully campaigned for the school ruins to be preserved as a memorial, so it is possible for visitors to make a pilgrimage to this sombre place.

For foreign visitors, it is not logistically easy to get there unless you have a car, because there is no public transport to the location. Otherwise, the best way is to get a train to the nearest large town, Ishinomaki (itself the conurbation worst hit by the tsunami), and arrange a taxi from the Ishinomaki Community and Information Center.

Fukushima

★★★★☆

East coast of northern Honshu
Natural disaster (tsunami), Nuclear disaster

Dark Rating: 10 ☠

Left
An aerial photo shows the stricken Fukushima Daiichi nuclear plant following the disaster.

This is the name of both a city and the prefecture – and it became infamous after the '3/11' earthquake and tsunami that led to the worst nuclear disaster since Chernobyl (p220–23), at the Fukushima-Daiichi nuclear power plant (NPP) on the Pacific coast of Tohoku. The plant used to generate electricity for the Tokyo Electric Power Company (TEPCO), supplying the capital city, not the local area. Four of the plant's six reactors were damaged in the wake of the tsunami when the emergency generators, located underneath the reactors, failed after they were flooded.

The subsequent loss of power for cooling the reactors led to a triple core meltdown, and three of four reactor buildings were damaged in gas explosions; as a result, the region was exposed to large amounts of radiation. Tens of thousands of people were evacuated and an exclusion zone was set up around the stricken plant. Extensive

clean-up operations started, but the decommissioning of the plant is expected to take decades. However, much progress has been made in the recovery efforts and in recent years a few of the evacuated areas outside the innermost 'Red Zone' have been reopened.

Some evacuees have returned, but only a relatively small proportion of the previous population. The Red Zone, also known as the 'difficult to return to zone', remains off limits except for one road that leads through it and that normal cars are allowed to use; stopping and getting out is prohibited, however. Access to the villages around it is strictly controlled, and there are plenty of guards along the road and at intersections to enforce these restrictions. However, it is possible to go on guided tours here. There are a small number of operators, including a local one based in the recently reopened settlement of Odaka.

Tours include a brief visit, with an official permit (prearrangement

and carrying passports on the day are required), to some parts of the Red Zone, such as a street in the ghost town of Okuma, as well as some abandoned places on the coast not far from the NPP. Tourists cannot go to the plant itself, but you get a view of it from a nearby hill.

A visit to the flashy new TEPCO information centre is also part of the tour – and despite a certain (predictable) PR atmosphere it does illustrate the unfolding of the disaster and the subsequent decommissioning efforts well. Tours also go to some tsunami-stricken areas north of the NPP, where regeneration and construction work are ongoing. Radiation exposure during these tours is well within safe limits.

Yasukuni Shrine & Yushukan

Central Tokyo • WW2, Imperialism, War crimes, Revisionism

★★★★☆

Dark Rating: 5 💀

The most important dark site in Tokyo is the controversial Yushukan war museum. It is controversial for its portrayal of Imperial Japan's campaigns in China and Korea, which is rather glorifying and fails to adequately cover the topic of Japanese war crimes (such as the Nanjing Massacre, p311).

The one-sidedness is also evident in the display of a steam engine from the Thailand–Burma Railway, aka 'Death Railway' (p287), without mention of forced labour by POWs. The kamikaze missions in the Pacific War are given a similarly glorifying treatment.

Despite the rather revisionist narrative, this is nonetheless a must-see place to get a feeling for Japanese militarism. The Yasukuni Shrine outside is where the Japanese, including politicians, worship their war dead, whether they are 'heroes' or war criminals. All this has repeatedly led to protests by China and Korea.

Above
The Yasukuni Shrine in Chiyoda district, Tokyo was founded by Emperor Meiji in 1869.

Left
This Japanese steam locomotive was the first one used on the Thailand–Burma railway line, known as 'Death Railway'.

Centre of the Tokyo Raids & War Damage

Kitasuna, Koto district, Tokyo • WW2, Aerial bombing

★★☆☆☆

Dark Rating: 6 💀

This is a small museum about the fire-bombing of the Japanese capital by the USA towards the end of World War Two. The attacks on 9 and 10 March 1945 went down in history as the deadliest air raid ever, surpassing the A-bombings of Hiroshima (p322–23) and Nagasaki (p326) in their total death toll: an estimated 100,000 people,

overwhelmingly civilians. Another one million inhabitants were made homeless as 270,000 buildings were destroyed in an area of 40 sq km (16 sq miles).

Unlike at Hiroshima and Nagasaki, there is no national memorial commemorating this horror; a private initiative opened this museum in 2002, having collected artefacts,

records and documents. It is aimed primarily at Tokyoites rather than foreign visitors, but the staff are welcoming and appreciative of any outside recognition.

Daigo Fukuryu Maru

★★★☆☆

Yumenoshima Park, southeastern Tokyo • Nuclear testing, Cold War   **Dark Rating: 6** ☠

On 1 March 1954 the USA conducted the Castle Bravo thermonuclear test at Bikini Atoll (p338). It was expected to be in the six-megaton (MT) region, but the actual yield turned out to be 15MT – the biggest of all American tests. With the explosion being so much more powerful than expected, so too was the fallout, going beyond the officially declared 'danger zone' of 250km (160 miles).

A Japanese fishing boat was just outside that zone. For three hours white powder rained down on it – the fallout from the bomb, consisting of highly irradiated pulverized coral. Soon the crew were suffering from acute radiation syndrome, and all were hospitalized; one, radio operator Aikichi Kuboyama, later died. The affair was a PR disaster for the USA and severely soured Japanese–American relations for a while. The boat was later saved from being scrapped and was put on display in a purpose-built exhibition hall. Also displayed is a sample jar of 'ash of death', the pulverized coral that irradiated the crew. The place is thus a unique piece of Cold War-era legacy.

Above
Daigo Fukuryu Maru ('Lucky Dragon 5'), the very unlucky fishing boat that was in the wrong place at the wrong time and had radiation rained down on it.

Okunoshima

★★★★☆

Hiroshima Prefecture, southwestern Honshu • Chemical warfare   **Dark Rating: 6** ☠

Above
The abandoned shell of the power plant that supplied electricity to the secret chemical weapons factory on this island.

This small island in the Seto Inland Sea just 3km (2 miles) off the coast is primarily known as 'Rabbit Island' due to the population of around 700 feral rabbits that live there. Seeing and feeding these cute animals is hence the main attraction for the visitors who come in droves, especially domestic tourists, although foreigners are welcome too. Yet the island harbours a dark secret: in World War Two, a production facility for chemical weapons was located here.

It was a top-secret site then, and it was not until the 1980s that the story was brought to light. Today there is a Poison Gas Museum right by the path between the ferry pier and the island's tourist hotel. Dotted around the island are remnants of the old production and storage facilities. The largest relic is the empty shell of the site's former power plant. So Okunoshima offers a unique juxtaposition of dark tourism, plus a bit of urban exploration, and the overwhelmingly endearing mass of bunnies. What a contrast!

Hiroshima

Southwestern Honshu • Atomic bombing, WW2

★★★★★

Dark Rating: 10 ☠

The name of this city stands for one of the darkest chapters in world history: the first use of an atomic bomb 'in anger' (as they say in the military) as a weapon of mass destruction. About 70 per cent of the city was destroyed. All traditional wooden houses were incinerated. Only the burnt-out shells of sturdier reinforced-concrete buildings were left standing; everything else was flattened.

The bomb had been developed by the Manhattan Project (p23) in the USA. It was a gun-type uranium bomb (see p25) and was untested. The first test explosion of an A-bomb, at Trinity (p22), was of the Nagasaki bomb design (p326). Yet the Hiroshima bomb worked as expected when it was dropped on the city at 8:15 a.m. on 6 August 1945.

The decision to drop the bomb on Japan was controversial, even among the scientists of the Manhattan Project, some of whom had argued that a demonstration over uninhabited territory would have sufficed to convince the Japanese that they had to surrender. Others argued that using it for real over a city was required to achieve the necessary shock effect – also with a view to the beginning of the Cold War with the Soviet Union. In the end it was also a human experiment on a mass scale. The effects of the bomb on the city but also on the citizens could thus be studied. Despite those 'benefits' and arguments, the A-bombings remain controversial; some consider them to have been a war crime.

Prior to the A-bombing, Hiroshima was deliberately spared any conventional air raids. It was also chosen for its size, the densely built-up cityscape and the fact that there were no known POWs there. The bomber carrying the device to its target was named *Enola Gay* by its pilot (after his mother), and that name too has become notorious (see p36). The bomb itself was euphemistically nicknamed 'Little Boy'. The plane took off from the Pacific island of Tinian and was accompanied by two other planes carrying measuring devices and photographic equipment. The bomb was dropped from a high altitude, to give the aircraft time to get away from the blast, and detonated about 600m (2000ft) above the ground.

The fireball above the hypocentre pushed downwards and reached further than a ground explosion

DARK STATS

4000KG (9000LB)

approximate weight of the 'Little Boy' atomic bomb

70,000-80,000

killed by the bomb according to an early US estimate

140,000

killed overall, according to a later independent estimate

13 SQ KM (5 SQ MILES)

of the city destroyed by the A-bomb

The bomb had a yield of approximately

15 KILOTONS

equivalent of TNT

would have. The inferno it created was beyond the imaginable. Besides the immediate horrors, the long-term effects of exposure to radiation lasted for decades – even to this day. After the war, Hiroshima was rebuilt and it is now a modern, thriving city again, but the association with the A-bombing remains its defining characteristic.

Opposite
Hiroshima in the aftermath of the atomic bomb attack on 6 August 1945.

Above
Shadow left by a man vaporized in the bomb's heat as he was sitting on a bank's entrance steps, which are now on display in the Peace Museum (p325).

Right
The 'Little Boy' nuclear weapon, dropped on Hiroshima by the US bomber *Enola Gay*.

A-Bomb Dome

Central Hiroshima, opposite the Peace Park • Atomic bombing

★★★☆☆

Dark Rating: 10 ☠

Above
A deceptively serene image of the iconic A-Bomb Dome in evening light, with cherry blossoms in the foreground.

This is the most iconic landmark of Hiroshima, and a symbol of the horrors brought by the atomic bomb that is recognized worldwide. It is the gutted ruin of what was the Hiroshima Prefectural Industrial Promotion Hall, built in 1915. It stood just 150m (450ft) from the hypocentre of the atomic bomb explosion; everybody inside was incinerated instantly.

Its solid construction meant that the building did not collapse altogether; it remained partly standing amid a sea of smouldering rubble. The only other surviving structures in this zone of devastation were similar reinforced-concrete buildings. The ruin is surrounded by a fence, so you cannot go inside, but it still emanates a sinister atmosphere when you stand by it. A few information panels around the site provide some background.

Above
A grim historical image of the ruined building amid a sea of devastation after the A-bombing.

Hiroshima Peace Memorial Museum

★★★★★

Central Hiroshima • Atomic bombing, WW2, Nuclear weapons

Dark Rating: 10 ☠

The main centre of commemoration of the atomic bombing in the city is the Hiroshima Peace Memorial Park, where a plethora of monuments can be found. Also in the park is this museum. It is the principal visitor attraction of Hiroshima and one of the world's top dark-themed museums.

Following a complete makeover, it reopened in 2019 with an all-new exhibition. The new design is visually gloomier than before but technologically state of the art, featuring multimedia and interactive elements. Artefacts on display include the stone steps of a bank on which the shadow of a person who was vaporized in the blast is still visible (see p323), and a wall showing traces of 'black rain', the fallout that rained down from the mushroom cloud and that many injured people desperate for water drank, making their exposure to radionuclides even worse (see p224).

Also on display are melted bottles, roof tiles and other A-bombed objects. The historical, technological and medical contexts are explained in depth too.

Left
An especially poignant exhibit is this scorched tricycle and helmet of a 4-year-old victim of the Hiroshima bombing.

OTHER HIROSHIMA SITES ASSOCIATED WITH THE A-BOMBING

- **Honkawa Elementary School**, just across the river to the northwest of the Peace Park. Set within the school's grounds is a preserved ruin of part of the old school building damaged in the A-bombing. In the basement is a small exhibition with artefacts and a diorama of Hiroshima after the bombing.
- **Fukuro-Machi Elementary School** also features a part of the damaged original building and a small exhibition. The focal point here is a section of the staircase wall on to which survivors scribbled messages, mostly enquiring about the whereabouts of relatives, when the shell of the school served as a relief station immediately after the bombing.
- **Hiroshima Castle**, largely reconstructed after the war, a bunker ruin that was part of a Japanese Army HQ can still be seen. From here the first messages reporting what had happened to the city were sent.
- **Bank buildings** that partly survived the blast include the former Bank of Japan Hiroshima Branch on Rijo-dori and the Imperial Bank building on a corner of the now pedestrianized Hondori shopping street.
- The former **Army Clothing Depot** is a particularly remarkable set of buildings almost 3km (2 miles) from the hypocentre: the bent-in iron window shutters are still testimony to the force of the blast even this far away.

Nagasaki

On the west coast of Kyushu • Atomic bombing, WW2

★★★★★

Dark Rating: 10 💀

Just three days after the Hiroshima bombing, at 11:02 a.m. on 9 August 1945, the port city of Nagasaki became the target of the second atomic bomb ever dropped in war. In a way, this was even more tragic and controversial than Hiroshima. Originally, a different city had been selected as the target of the second bomb: Kokura. But because the crew of the bomber (the *Bockscar* – see p29) were under instructions to drop the bomb in good visibility conditions and they found the sky overcast, they turned towards Nagasaki as the secondary target.

On arrival there the sky was initially overcast too, but then the cloud layer broke enough and the bomb was released over the suburb of Urakami. The scale of devastation was similar to that in Hiroshima, although the death toll was lower because the bomb was dropped away from the city centre. Still, an estimated 75,000 people were killed by the bomb and its after-effects.

It has often been claimed that the second A-bombing brought the Japanese to the point of surrender and thus ended the war without the need for a US invasion of the main islands, which might have cost even more lives. However, the Japanese did not surrender straight after Nagasaki, but rather about a week later. Even though it was not mentioned in the Emperor's surrender speech, the more decisive reason for the surrender may well have been the fact that the USSR had entered the war against Japan and had made great headway in then Japanese-occupied parts of China.

In any case, the three days between the two bombings would not have given the Japanese enough time to fully comprehend what sort of new weapon they were dealing with. The second bomb was more for the sake of it, dropped because it was there – and perhaps to justify the enormous costs of its development. Fortunately, the Nagasaki bomb was the last one used in war up to the present date.

The bomb dropped on Nagasaki, nicknamed 'Fat Man' because of its bulky shape, was of the same type as that tested at Trinity (p22) with a yield of about 20 kilotons. Today Nagasaki is a thriving city again. It is perhaps the most multicultural one in the country, architecturally but also religiously (there are more churches here than anywhere else in Japan).

Left
The mushroom cloud that formed over Nagasaki, photographed from one of the accompanying USAF planes.

Atomic Bomb Museum

★★★★★

In Urakami District, northern Nagasaki • Atomic bombing, WW2, Cold War   **Dark Rating: 10** ☠

As in Hiroshima, there is a dedicated museum about the A-bombing in Nagasaki. Although smaller than its counterpart, the exhibition in Nagasaki covers wider related aspects such as nuclear testing in the Cold War. It also has a section about POWs. That's because, unlike Hiroshima, Nagasaki had POW camps, whose inmates were used for forced labour in the city's industrial plants, including some Dutch, Australian and American citizens. They also became victims of the A-bombing, and the museum has testimonies from a few survivors. The physics of the bomb, details of the destruction, and a substantial medical section are also part of the museum.

Above
A replica of the 'Fat Man' A-bomb that was dropped on Nagasaki.

Left
The museum's displays include tattered clothes as well as images of the effects of heat and radiation on the victims.

OTHER NAGASAKI SITES ASSOCIATED WITH THE A-BOMBING

- **Peace Park**, north of the A-Bomb Museum. It features several monuments donated by numerous countries around the globe. Within the grounds you can see the outline of the foundations of what used to be Urakami Prison, which was flattened in the blast, the inmates and staff inside killed.
- **Hypocentre Park**, just west of the museum. The hypocentre is marked by a black pillar ringed by concentric circles set into the pavement to symbolize the shock wave of the blast.
- **Urakami Cathedral**, on a hillside east of the park and museum, was largely destroyed in the bombing but rebuilt after the war. Original pieces of the ruin, such as the toppled belfry top, can still be seen at the site.

- **Shiroyama Elementary School**. Some 500m (1500ft) to the west of the hypocentre, this school still shows charred scars from the inferno inside the staircase. It now features a small exhibition.
- **Torii gate**, 750m (2460ft) south of the hypocentre, was partially toppled by the blast. This iconic one-legged relic of the A-bombing has its broken bits lying next to the still standing part.
- **Sumiyoshi World War Two Tunnels**. A more obscure site, well off the beaten path, these were dug into the mountainside in a northern suburb of Nagasaki as an underground production facility for torpedoes; in the wake of the A-bombing it became a shelter for injured survivors, as a plaque by the tunnel entrance explains.

Oka Masaharu Memorial Peace Museum

★★★☆☆

Near Nagasaki railway station • POWs, WW2, War crimes

Dark Rating: 8 ☠

This offbeat institution takes its name from an activist who championed efforts to raise awareness of the Korean victims of the Nagasaki A-bombing and the plight of Koreans 'mobilized' for slave labour in Japan during World War Two in general. The museum was created in his memory after he died in 1994. It is a rare exception in Japan in that it addresses the uncomfortable topic of Japanese war crimes – not just the treatment of Koreans and POWs in general, but other aspects too, such as the experiments with human 'guinea pigs' at the infamous biological weapons research facility 'Unit 731' operated in occupied Manchuria.

Such topics are generally unacknowledged in contemporary Japan, so it is not surprising that this museum does not enjoy state support and remains a private initiative going against the national grain. But it is an important counterbalance to the rather sanitized narrative given on the tours to Hashima (see opposite) or at the corresponding museum in Nagasaki (the Gunkanjima Digital Museum), neither of which acknowledge this dark side of the famous island.

International visitors should ideally make arrangements in advance to get a guided tour in English, since in the exhibition most of the labels and texts are in Japanese only. It consists mainly of documents, charts, maps and photos. There are few artefacts, although there is a life-size recreation of a small section of a coal-mining tunnel.

Above
The exterior of the museum, in a side street behind the 26 Martyrs Monument.

Left
Although smaller and lower key than the Atomic Bomb Museum, this private institution fills an important gap in the commemoration narrative in Nagasaki and Japan in general.

Hashima

★★★☆☆

Outside Nagasaki Bay • Ghost town, POWs, Forced labour

Dark Rating: 8

Originally just a rock in the sea, this island 16km (10 miles) south of Nagasaki was gradually expanded to its present size. At its peak it was home to more than 5000 inhabitants, which made it the most densely populated place on Earth. But why would anybody build a town on a small rocky island, and why would people choose to live there? Because of coal.

The island allowed access to undersea coal seams. From the late nineteenth century onwards, the coal was extracted to fuel the rapid industrialization of Japan. Not all workers went there voluntarily, though. From the 1930s until the end of World War Two, Korean and Chinese forced labourers, including POWs, were sent there, and many died as a result of the harsh living conditions and accidents in the mines. This dark aspect is not much talked about by the Japanese today, except at a small dedicated museum in Nagasaki (see opposite).

The island was abandoned after the coal mines closed down in 1974. It has since fallen into ruin, frequently being battered by typhoons. However, it has acquired a legendary status as one of the most photogenic ghost towns on the planet, which was boosted by it featuring in the James Bond movie *Skyfall*. Boat tours for tourists started in 2009 and have been thriving since the island was granted UNESCO World Heritage Status in 2015. However, there is no access beyond three viewing points a safe distance from the by now dangerously crumbling buildings.

Access to the more densely built-up parts and their interior has been granted only sporadically to historians and industrial archaeologists, as well as some film crews and photographers (there are some impressive photo collection books available).

The island is better known in Japan as 'Gunkanjima', meaning 'battleship island', because its silhouette resembles that of a warship. Hashima's association with forced labour and POWs is not mentioned on the boat tours. Instead, the island is celebrated for its role in the Meiji Industrial Revolution, the community spirit that allegedly once characterized the island, and of course for the architecture, including Japan's first seven-storey reinforced-concrete apartment block.

Below
Ghostly shells of the abandoned buildings on the once thriving Hashima island.

Okinawa

★★★☆☆

Between Japan and Taiwan • WW2, Modern war

Dark Rating: 5 ☻

This group of tropical islands is part of the Ryukyu archipelago, which was an independent kingdom for centuries until Japan annexed the islands in the second half of the nineteenth century during the Meiji period. In World War Two, the islands became the battleground for the heaviest fighting in the entire Pacific 'theatre' and its largest amphibious operation. It was the final part of Japan that the USA captured before they would have had to face an invasion of the main islands.

The extent of the bloody fighting and fierce Japanese resistance is often given as one of the motivations for dropping the A-bombs on Hiroshima (p322–23) and Nagasaki (p326): namely, in order to push Japan into surrendering so that no land invasion would be necessary. The Americans lost 14,000 troops in the 82-day Battle of Okinawa between April and June

1945. While the US losses were severe, those on the Japanese side were far larger. Worse, some 150,000 Okinawan civilians (almost half the population) also lost their lives, many through committing suicide.

This was partly the result of Japanese propaganda that tried to convince people that US soldiers were savages coming to enslave them, and that it would be more 'honourable' to take one's own life. They even distributed hand grenades for that purpose, although many people simply jumped off the coastal cliffs. After the war Okinawa remained in American hands until it was officially returned to Japanese rule in 1972, although the US still maintains military bases on the main island. These were heavily used during the Vietnam War for B-52s taking off on carpet-bombing sorties. To this day the American presence on Okinawa is controversial locally.

Former Japanese Navy Underground HQ

★★★☆☆

Tomigusuku, on the edge of Naha • WW2, Suicide

Dark Rating: 5 ☻

Left
Steps leading deep underground to the tunnels where the Japanese Navy had their main command post on Okinawa.

This subterranean site outside Okinawa's capital city, Naha, has a more military focus than the other memorials here. It is a tunnel system that was used by the Japanese Navy as their headquarters during the Battle of Okinawa. Here the commander and other officers eventually 'died an honourable death' – that is, committed suicide rather than being captured. In one cavern, a sign claims that the pockmarks all over the wall are from a hand-grenade explosion used in such a suicide.

Okinawa Prefectural Peace Memorial Museum

Southern coast of Okinawa Island • WW2, Atrocities, Suicide

★★★★☆

Dark Rating: 8 ☠

Left
Rusty old torpedoes and gun relics on display outside the main museum building.

The largest and most significant place where the Battle of Okinawa is commemorated is the vast Okinawa Prefectural Peace Memorial Park not far from the southernmost tip of the island. Apart from a plethora of war-related monuments, it is also the home of this large museum. Its main permanent exhibition is state of the art and caters well for international visitors.

Occasionally there is a somewhat revisionist labelling (such as calling the Japanese invasions of Indonesia and the Philippines 'liberation from colonization'), but otherwise the presentation is excellent, with artefacts and modern interactive elements. The main focus is on the battle, but the fate of Okinawan civilians is covered too, illustrated with some quite gruesome photographs. The postwar period gets a lot of space as well, in particular the topic of the controversial continued military presence of American forces and the associated cultural friction with the locals.

Just to the west of the memorial complex is the Kenji monument and cave, where hundreds of schoolboys, who had been recruited into military service just before the battle, took refuge. Most died here, many as a result of American bombs, while others committed suicide. More caves with similar stories can be found in the area, such as the more obscure Todoroki cave. A much more commodified site, where there was once a Japanese army field hospital staffed largely by schoolgirls, is the much-visited Himeyuri Monument & Peace Museum.

Right
A torchlit small memorial stele at the hard-to-find Todoroki cave in southern Okinawa.

Port Arthur
Tasmania, Australia

Rainbow Warrior
North Island, New Zealand

Te Wairoa buried village
North Island, New Zealand

Quake City
Christchurch, New Zealand

Nauru
Micronesia

Pearl Harbor
O'ahu, Hawaii

USS Missouri
Pearl Harbor, Hawaii

Pearl Harbor Aviation Museum
O'ahu, Hawaii

The Punchbowl
Honolulu, Hawaii

Kalaupapa
Molokai, Hawaii

Mauna Loa & Mauna Kea
Big Island, Hawaii

Pacific Tsunami Museum
Hilo, Big Island, Hawaii

Kilauea
Big Island, Hawaii

Easter Island
South Pacific

01

05

06-09   10

11 12
    13

Australia
& Oceania,
Pacific

14

02

03

04

This final section may be shorter but it covers the vastest area of them all, namely from Australia and its neighbour New Zealand to the various islands in the Pacific, the largest body of water on planet Earth. Those many small island nations and overseas possessions of bigger powers are often subsumed under the collective term Oceania. Within this area are also a few dots in the ocean that are of particular importance as dark destinations, ranging from World War Two heritage sites to natural and man-made disasters. Some are in flux, as especially the recent changes in Volcanoes National Park on Hawaii have shown in dramatic fashion.

Given the enormous distances, flying in by plane is generally the only means of getting to those faraway islands. Ironically some of those long-haul flights, namely those to Hawaii and Easter Island from the American mainland (the USA and Chile, respectively), are still classed as domestic flights. With regard to tourist facilities, these islands vary a lot, from excellent (such as Hawaii) to rather limited (Nauru).

Australia

The only nation state to cover an entire continent (albeit the smallest one), this is a large and for the most part thinly populated country that was a dark destination from the arrival of colonialism, namely as a British penal colony.

Before convicts were sent there, the lands 'down under' had long been inhabited by indigenous tribes now referred to as Aboriginals. The way these people were treated by British colonialists and settlers is an especially dark aspect of the history of Australia. Tens of thousands of Aboriginals were murdered; others were pushed out of view into 'reservations'. Children were taken from their families and forcibly sent to be 'Europeanized' by whites. The repression lasts to this day in many ways, and commemoration of this dark legacy is sparse.

Britain also used Australia's remoteness to conduct nuclear tests. These sites were at an inland Aboriginal area called Maralinga and on the Montebello Islands off the northwest coast. At the former there are now tours, and the latter can be visited by sailing boats.

Australia's roots in penal colonies and prisons, as well as the nation's military role in both world wars, are much more openly commemorated at specific sites and museums, including the Australian War Memorial near the capital, Canberra, as well as at further military museums, such as those in Darwin and Brisbane. Several penal sites and prisons have become museums too, such as in Fremantle in Western Australia or the well-known Old Melbourne Gaol. For this book, however, only one such site has been picked out, because it has an additional, much more recent, dark aspect.

Port Arthur

★★★★☆

Southeastern Tasmania • Prison, Mass shooting

Dark Rating: 4 ☻

This is one of Australia's historic sites of a former penal colony and penitentiary, located not on the mainland but on the island of Tasmania to the south. The whole historic site (part of Tasmania's 'Convict Trail') is heavily commodified for tourists, including guided tours and 'ghost hunts'. There is, however, a much more real, and contemporary, extra element of horror here.

In 1996 a gunman went on the rampage and, using three semi-automatic weapons, randomly killed 35 people. Unlike in so many such incidents, the killer did not turn his gun on himself, nor was he shot dead by the police. He was captured, put on trial and sentenced to life imprisonment. At the Port Arthur Historic Site, a memorial garden and cross have been added to commemorate the victims of the shootings.

The incident triggered a discussion about gun ownership laws, and legislation was tightened up. Since the introduction of these stricter rules, no similar incidents on such a scale have occurred in Australia. This success is often cited as an example when there has been another mass shooting incident in the USA, where similar calls for stricter laws are still regularly met with resistance from the gun lobbies.

Left
The Port Arthur Historic Site includes the ruins of the old cell blocks, the convict church and cemetery, and a memorial garden dedicated to the victims of the mass shooting in 1996.

New Zealand

Australia's dual-island smaller neighbour New Zealand is known for its grand and varied scenery and is also a highly developed country, including for tourism. The powers of nature that have shaped the often spectacular landscapes, however, can also be destructive. There's a constant risk of natural disaster, especially volcanic eruptions and earthquakes, because New Zealand is part of the Pacific 'Ring of Fire' (see p51). Volcanic activity can be dangerous to observe too: in December 2019 a number of tourists were killed in a sudden eruption on White Island. Earthquakes have likewise caused tragedy on the South Island.

Rainbow Warrior
★☆☆☆☆

Off the coast of Matauri Bay, North Island • Sinking, Shipwreck, Terrorism   **Dark Rating: 3** ☠

Above
The partially submerged wreck of the *Rainbow Warrior* after its sinking by French agents in Auckland harbour.

A political earthquake in 1985 severely soured New Zealand's relations with France, namely when the Greenpeace boat *Rainbow Warrior*, which had been on a mission protesting against French nuclear testing in the Pacific, was sunk (killing one person on board) right in Auckland harbour after explosives were planted by French secret service agents (who were later arrested and tried).

The wreck was removed and turned into an artificial reef for divers. It lies at a depth of 26m (85ft) off the north coast. Seeing it requires proper diving skills and equipment. On land there's a memorial involving the boat's salvaged propeller, while the masts ended up at a museum in Dargaville.

Te Wairoa buried village
★★★☆☆

Near Rotorua • Natural disaster (volcano)   **Dark Rating: 4** ☠

Of the two main islands of New Zealand, North Island is the one with more volcanic activity. It is here that you can visit geothermal fields with geysers, fumaroles, bubbling mud pools and so forth. Of actual volcano eruptions the one of Mount Tarawera in 1886 was one of the largest natural disasters in the country's recorded history. It completely destroyed the famous sight of the 'Pink and White Terraces' (a large and picturesque system of sinter terraces similar to Pamukkale in Turkey).

Moreover, the hot ash ejected from the volcano and the mud that formed subsequently buried Te Wairoa village and several other smaller communities in the area. Some 120 people lost their lives, 17 of them at Te Wairoa. The destroyed village was later partly excavated; today the site is a tourist attraction, complemented by a small museum.

Above
A historic photo shows the ruined McRae's Hotel and Terrace Hotel in Te Wairoa, 1886.

Quake City

★★★★☆

Christchurch • Natural disaster (earthquakes)

Dark Rating: 5 ☠

The largest city of New Zealand's South Island has been struck by tragedy repeatedly in recent years. Between 2010 and 2012 the city was hit by a series of earthquakes, the worst of which occurred in February 2011. This killed almost 200 people and destroyed scores of buildings or rendered them so unstable that they had to be demolished. Among the most iconic casualties was Christ Church Cathedral, whose spire and upper part of the tower collapsed in the quake.

The exhibition at 'Quake City' features parts of the collapsed cathedral and two clocks from the railway station, which had to be demolished following the quakes. Perhaps the most unique part of the museum is the hands-on liquefaction simulator exhibit. Soil liquefaction is one of the spookiest geological phenomena that can be brought about by earthquakes: it is when the vibrations from the shaking loosen sandy and/or water-saturated soil, turning it into a liquid-like quicksand. This can cause houses to collapse and cars to sink into the ground; it can also make buried objects such as sewers gain buoyancy and rise up.

Above
Christ Church Cathedral in ruins after the earthquake; it is set to be reinstated.

Below
The severely damaged former Catholic Cathedral of the Blessed Sacrament after the February 2011 earthquake.

Nauru

★☆☆☆☆

Micronesia • Overexploitation, Environmental disaster

Dark Rating: 7 ☠

The third smallest nation state, and the very smallest independent island country, Nauru was once one of the richest places on Earth; now it is one of the poorest. The reason is phosphate deposits (a raw material prized in agriculture and industry), which had accumulated in the island's interior from millennia of seabirds' nesting. Phosphate rock is basically fossilized bird droppings. Yet these deposits were finite.

Nauru had long been settled by a Polynesian/Micronesian people but, like so many other Pacific islands, was colonized, first by Germany, later by the UK and Australia, and for a brief period by Japan during World War Two. After the war it was UN-administered, but it gained independence in the late 1960s. The formerly British-Australian phosphate mines were nationalized, and for the next few decades Nauru's small population benefited from the huge profits. They lived a tax-free life of luxury, until the phosphate was depleted by the end of the 1990s.

The economy collapsed, unemployment went through the roof, and so did poverty. Financial preparations for a post-phosphate era had been squandered through corruption and mismanagement. Eighty per cent of the island is a strip-mined moonscape in the interior, while the thin coastal belt offers little in the way of alternative sources of income.

For a time the desperate country became a haven for money laundering; then the Australian government made an offer: in return for aid, they would use Nauru to set up detention camps for refugees who were seeking asylum in Australia. The appalling conditions in these camps, and the whole policy of moving the refugee issue offshore, dubbed the 'Pacific Solution', was widely criticized by human-rights organizations and in the international media. The scheme began in 2001, was suspended in 2007, but resumed a few years later and was still going on at the time of writing.

Even without such asylum-seeker camps, Nauru would be an extreme travel destination. It is far from a tropical holiday island. The infrastructure for visitors is limited, there are power cuts and drinking water is scarce. Yet on a very small scale tourism does exist here. There is an airport with a few connections (mostly to Brisbane, Australia), as well as two hotels and a couple of restaurants.

A Nauru tourism website advertises the interior moonscape as one of the attractions alongside the remains of Japanese bunkers and coastal gun emplacements that you can explore. Vestiges of the phosphate-mining industry include an old conveyor-belt system that used to transport the material to ships for loading, now rusting and crumbling away.

Below
The moonscape that the phosphate mining left behind in the interior of Nauru.

OTHER PACIFIC ISLANDS OF DARK SIGNIFICANCE

There are several Pacific islands that also hold dark secrets, some related to World War Two, others to nuclear testing, yet others for natural forces at play.

For the latter, the island state of Vanuatu includes Ambrym, a volcano island whose crater is home to the world's most violently boiling lava lake, probably the most infernal sight on Earth. On the island of New Britain, now part of Papua New Guinea, the former regional capital of Rabaul, once a jewel of the Pacific, was partly destroyed by a volcanic eruption in its bay in 1994.

The remote island of Tinian in the Northern Marianas was the place from where the B-29 bombers took off to carry the two atom bombs to Hiroshima (p322–23) and Nagasaki (p326). The 'atomic bomb pit', from where the bombs were loaded on to the planes at the remains of the airbase, is now a local visitor attraction.

An island associated more than any other with the post-World War Two nuclear testing of atomic weaponry is Bikini Atoll in the Marshall Islands. It was the site of the most iconic nuclear explosion ever recorded, namely the Baker shot of Operation Crossroads in 1946. It was also where the USA's largest ever hydrogen bomb explosion, the Castle Bravo test, took place in 1954 (and irradiated a Japanese fishing boat; see p321).

The island is still contaminated, but can occasionally be visited – mainly by divers keen on exploring the unique cluster of wrecks from the Baker test, including an aircraft carrier. Other former nuclear test sites in the Pacific remain completely out of bounds (such as Enewetak Atoll, Kwajalein and the French nuclear proving ground on Moruroa).

Countless islands still sport notable relics from the 'Pacific Theatre' of World War Two, be it fortifications and coastal guns or wrecks of ships and shot-down planes. Among the most important islands in that regard are Saipan, Guam, Tarawa, the Solomon Islands and Peleliu (Palau). Moreover, the Philippines has a wide range of war-related sites too, especially on Corregidor, Leyte and the Bataan peninsula.

Above
Probably the most iconic image of the Atomic Age is this photo of the Baker shot nuclear test at Bikini Atoll in 1946.

Hawaii

This chain of islands was created by a volcanic hotspot on the Earth's crust in the middle of the Pacific tectonic plate (see p51). As this moves northwards, new islands build up over the hotspot while the older ones slowly erode away. The most recent volcanic activity is on the archipelago's youngest and biggest island, Hawai'i, or simply 'Big Island'; O'ahu, with the capital Honolulu, is the most densely populated island and the archipelago's economic, financial, transport and tourism hub.

The islands were first settled by Polynesians. Hawaii was an independent state until the late nineteenth century, when the king was overthrown. After a short period as a republic, the islands were de facto annexed by the USA, although it wasn't until 1959 that Hawaii officially became its 50th state. Hawaii played an important role in World War Two. It was here that, through the Japanese attack on the US naval base of Pearl Harbor, the USA was dragged into the war. Other than war and volcanism, Hawaii is threatened by other potentially destructive forces, in particular tsunamis, which have battered it repeatedly in the past and probably will again.

Pearl Harbor

Northwest of Honolulu, O'ahu, Hawaii • WW2, Shipwreck, Mass grave

★★★★★

Dark Rating: 5 ☠

The US military base at Pearl Harbor on Hawaii was the target of a surprise attack by Imperial Japan on 7 December 1941. It was a carefully orchestrated aerial attack, and within just a couple of hours hundreds of American planes were destroyed on the ground and five battleships and various smaller vessels sunk. The single worst death toll was in the sinking of the USS *Arizona*. She received a direct hit to a munitions magazine and sank instantly, taking more than 1000 sailors with her.

The Japanese goal had been to deliver a crippling blow to the US, and it partly did. However, the three US aircraft carriers stationed at Pearl Harbor were out at sea at the time of the attack and so survived. It soon became clear in the unfolding Pacific War that carriers were a much more crucial weapons system than old-fashioned battleships. The USA was able to compensate quickly for its losses, and only six months after Pearl Harbor its victory in the Battle of Midway set the scene for the last few years of the war, ending in the total defeat of Imperial Japan.

Pearl Harbor is still an active US naval base, but part of it has become a memorial and tourist magnet. In fact, it is one of the most visited dark places on Earth. The substantial visitor centre features two exhibitions plus outdoor exhibits and is the starting point for tours, by ferry, to the USS *Arizona* Memorial, a structure built directly over the sunken wreck, of which only a few bits poke out above the water's surface. It is a sombre site and rules for behaviour are strict, because the wreck is also a mass grave.

DARK STATS

The Japanese attack force included

6 AIRCRAFT CARRIERS

and about

400 PLANES

The strike was launched from a staging area

370KM (230 MILES) OFF O'AHU

The attack lasted for nearly

TWO HOURS

US casualties comprised

2403 PERSONNEL KILLED

and over

1000 INJURED

USS Missouri

Ford Island, Pearl Harbor • WW2, Modern war

★★★★★

Dark Rating: 4 💀

Above
Finally decommissioned in 1992, the USS *Missouri* was donated to the public and opened as a museum.

Moored opposite the main visitor centre and museums, and just south of the USS *Arizona* memorial, is another big old battleship, afloat and in perfect condition. It complements the other parts of Pearl Harbor in historic terms, as it was aboard this ship that the official instrument of surrender by the Japanese was signed. Seeing the spot where the ceremony that ended World War Two took place in 1945 is a key element of a visit today.

The USS *Missouri* is a comparatively recent addition, since the vessel remained in service for many years. Having fought in Iwo Jima, Okinawa and Korea, she was modernized and even took part in the Gulf War of 1990–91.

Pearl Harbor Aviation Museum

Ford Island, Pearl Harbor • WW2, Modern war

★★★★☆

Dark Rating: 4 💀

Above
The wreck of the Boeing B-17E Flying Fortress bomber *Swamp Ghost* on display at the museum.

This institution, formerly known as the Pacific Aviation Museum, includes some original buildings where you can still see bullet holes from the 1941 attacks. Inside the hangars, as well as on open-air display, are a large number of aircraft, not only from World War Two but also many more modern types used, for example, in the Korean and Vietnam wars (see p292 and p316).

Perhaps the most remarkable exhibit is the *Swamp Ghost*, a B-17E bomber that in 1942 crash-landed in a swamp in Papua New Guinea, where the semi-submerged but relatively intact plane lay for more than half a century before being salvaged and brought here.

The Punchbowl

Puowaina Drive, Honolulu • WW2, Cemetery

★★☆☆☆

Dark Rating: 2 ☠

Mainly known by this informal name is what's officially called the National Memorial Cemetery of the Pacific, located in a former volcanic crater high above Honolulu's cityscape. Here many thousands of Americans who were killed in the war in the Pacific of 1941–45 are buried. Later they were joined by more US soldiers who had fallen in the Korean and Vietnam wars (p316 and p292). It is still an active military cemetery.

One notable grave is that of Hawaiian astronaut Ellison Onizuka, who perished in the *Challenger* space shuttle disaster in 1986. The site is also home to the central Honolulu Memorial featuring a large Lady Columbia statue.

Above
On marble blocks flanking the stairs of the main memorial are engraved the names of ca. 30,000 soldiers missing in action or lost at sea.

Kalaupapa

On the north coast of Molokai • Leper colony, Extreme landscape

★★★☆☆

Dark Rating: 5 ☠

Above
The cemetery at the Kalaupapa colony to which sufferers of leprosy (now 'Hansen's disease') were forcibly moved from 1866 onwards.

The island of Molokai features a rather special place: the leper colony on an isolated, flat peninsula called Kalaupapa, now a National Historical Park. It's reachable only by a long mule ride on steep tracks down a cliff, or by small plane from Honolulu. Visits are by mandatory guided tour and you are asked to be discreet, since some of the ex-leper colony's inhabitants still live there. A bus takes visitors to the key locations around the peninsula as you learn about its history. Apart from its association with the infamous (but now curable) disease leprosy, this is also a superbly scenic spot.

Mauna Loa & Mauna Kea

★★★☆☆

Centre of Big Island, Hawaii • Extreme landscape, Volcanoes

Dark Rating: 3 ☠

Right
Observatories at Mauna Kea near the summit in what is known as the 'Astronomy Precinct'.

Below
View from Mauna Kea towards Mauna Loa, the world's largest active volcano.

Big Island's massive twin peaks, Mauna Loa and Mauna Kea, form the planet's largest volcanic massif, indeed the very highest mountains on Earth if measured from their base on the ocean floor, easily outshining Mount Everest. Above water, both peaks reach over 4000m (13,000ft). Mauna Loa is regarded as still active; its last eruption was in 1984, with lava flows nearly reaching the town of Hilo. It does not look dramatic – no steep cone, just a brooding typical shield volcano (p51). Climbing to the summit is possible, but registration with the National Park is required.

The slightly higher Mauna Kea in contrast is dormant, although the scenery shows plenty of evidence of earlier activity in the form of various cinder cones. However, it is interesting for other reasons. Owing to its unique position far away from any light pollution, and its peak being high enough to be usually above the clouds that frequently form around the southeast of Big Island, it has become one of the key locations for astronomical observatories. A cluster of these has been constructed, and they are a very sci-fi-like sight.

Guided tours to the peak, especially at sunset, are popular and are offered from Kona and Hilo. After dark, you can engage in amateur stargazing. The professional observatories are mostly off limits, yet provide an intriguing backdrop. As you're coming all the way from sea level, a half-hour stop at the Visitor Information Station at ca. 3000m (10,000 feet) is mandatory for acclimatization to avoid altitude sickness.

Pacific Tsunami Museum

Hilo bayfront • Natural disaster (tsunami)

★★★☆☆

Dark Rating: 4 💀

Not only does the Hawaii geology cause tsunamis of its own, but also even far-off earthquakes along the Pacific 'Ring of Fire' bring waves to these islands' shores. Hilo, the capital of Big Island, was hit by especially destructive tsunamis twice in the twentieth century. The first, in 1946, was caused by an undersea earthquake off the Aleutian Islands of Alaska. It washed away the entire bayfront in Hilo and killed 153 people.

In 1960 the biggest ever measured earthquake, a magnitude 9.5 monster off the coast of Chile, caused a mega-tsunami that eventually hit Hilo, again sweeping away the bayfront, this time killing 61 people. After that, the bayfront row of houses was not rebuilt and the city partly moved inland and to

higher ground. On what is now the ocean-facing first street, the Pacific Tsunami Museum recounts these events, explains tsunamis in general, and also covers the two big ones of the twenty-first century in the Indian Ocean in 2004 (see p286 and p299) and in Japan in 2011 (p319).

Above
A former bank building now houses the museum dedicated to the various tsunamis that have hit Hilo and Hawaii.

Kilauea

In the south of Big Island • Natural disaster (volcano)

★★★★☆

Dark Rating: 5 💀

This is one of the most active volcano on Earth and the centrepiece of the Volcanoes National Park on Big Island, Hawaii. Kilauea may not look like much as a mountain, being rather flat and lacking a noticeable peak, but it had been putting on one of the most spectacular volcanic shows for much of the twentieth century and beyond. At times there are bubbling lava lakes in its summit caldera; at other times fissures spew out lava fountains over 300m (1000ft) high.

There was continuous activity from 1952, with only a brief break between 1982 and 1983. After that most of the action moved away from the main caldera and its Halema'uma'u crater

and shifted to the Eastern Rift Zone, where new vents, in particular the Pu'u O'o cone, and temporary fissures appeared, emitting lava in the lower-lying lands of the southeast coastal area, frequently blocking roads and swallowing up houses. Especially dramatic were lava flows that reached the ocean, making a spectacular show as the red-hot lava drained into the cold ocean waters.

After 2008 a new lava lake formed in a vent inside Halema'uma'u crater, which at times even overflowed on to the crater floor. At other times, when the lava was lower, it just emitted an orange glow after dark, and plumes of sulphurous gases.

Activity peaked from May 2018, when new fissures spewed out lava and destroyed numerous houses, forcing the evacuation of some 2000 residents. The lava flows drained the lava lake at Halema'uma'u, which then fell in on itself in a major collapse-explosion event. This completely changed the appearance of the crater. Volcanoes National Park had to be closed, and could only be partially reopened when the eruption stopped in August 2018. This ended the longest ever recorded phase of activity: a solid 35 years.

Recovery efforts are ongoing, but most of the roads and trails through the park have been reopened. However, some elements

Left
The glow of the former lava lake inside
Halema'uma'u at dawn in 2015.

either remain out of bounds (such as the caldera floor) or have been lost forever. This may include the former Jaggar Museum at the Hawaii Volcano Observatory right on the caldera rim, where there was a splendid Halema'uma'u lookout. Since the 2018 events, however, the ground has been found to be unstable, and the museum has been evacuated. Its contents were saved, so there is a good chance that some new incarnation of the museum will be reconstructed somewhere else, but at the time of writing it is unclear when that might be.

One attraction that has re-opened is the Thurston lava tube, a former underground liquid lava channel that drained out and left a solidified natural tunnel behind, this one so big it could be a road tunnel.

The National Park is full of further interesting features, from solidified craters and lava flows to the areas where lava created new land along the coastline. There are numerous hiking trails of different difficulty levels too. In the past Kilauea was one of the places on Earth where lava flows could be approached relatively safely, being mostly slow-flowing, non-explosive, non-splattering flows. But since August 2018 all this has ceased. Magma has been found to be refilling the drained cavern below Kilauea, however, and indeed in late December 2020 activity resumed at Halema'uma'u and a new lava lake formed. In any case, it is always a good idea to consult the National Park Service website before going there, to get the latest updates and info on closures and general developments.

A particular attraction in this volcanic land in the south of Big Island is flying over it by chopper from outside the National Park. Various companies offer such scenic helicopter flights, including at least one that uses a type of craft that can fly with the doors off, so you can take photos without having to deal with reflections on the glass, and also get to feel the air. You can see the latest lava flows and changed landscapes from above, and perhaps even spot some orange glow from lava, for example inside the Pu'u O'o cone, should activity resume there too.

Right
Following the 2018 eruptions, lava flows
destroyed housing and cut off streets in the
Puna district of Big Island, as seen here.

Easter Island

★★★★☆

Middle of the South Pacific • Societal collapse

Dark Rating: 3 ☠

This small dot in the Pacific Ocean, also known by its Polynesian name, Rapa Nui, is famously the most remote inhabited spot on Earth. The nearest other inhabited islands are Pitcairn, nearly 2000km (1300 miles) away to the west; the nearest mainland, Chile (p60), is well over 3500km (2000 miles) away to the east. Despite this extreme isolation, Easter Island is these days easily reached by daily scheduled flights from Santiago de Chile, and there is a decent tourism infrastructure.

Almost all visitors come to Easter Island in order to see the world-famous *moai*, those mysterious statues with their distinctive shapes that are the cultural heritage of the old society of Rapa Nui. Yet they are all reconstructions, or at least re-erections, because all were toppled when that old Easter Island society collapsed. And it is that collapse – and the lessons to be learned from it – that make this island a very dark place, symbolically.

Rapa Nui was first settled by Polynesians about 1000 years ago. They developed a very intricate hierarchical culture. The famous *moai* were probably quasi-religious symbols of power. The fate of the Rapa Nui is assumed to have been this: as they became more numerous they started overexploiting their small land of only 170 sq km (66 sq miles). It was once covered in trees, but gradually these were all cut down (so no more fishing boats could be built), all land mammals were hunted to extinction, and intensive agriculture depleted the soil.

The old societal 'contract' based on the assumption that the power elite's special relationship with the deities assured everybody's well-being, and hence kept the majority of commoners in their place, eventually no longer held. When challenged, the clan chiefs tried to reinforce their position by ordering even bigger *moai*. But as resources started running out, the increasingly desperate population toppled the old system – along with their symbols, the *moai*. Only some unfinished ones at the Rano Raraku quarry, where the *moai* were hewn from volcanic rock, remained upright, but these are by now partly sunken into the soil.

Civil war, famine and possibly even cannibalism ensued some time in the seventeenth century; when the island was 'discovered' by Western explorers, they found a dwindled, poverty-stricken population. This was further reduced in the subsequent exposure to new diseases and through abduction into slavery. At one point, just over 100 native Rapa Nui survived. The island was annexed by Chile in the late nineteenth century, and its unique archaeology eventually attracted the attention of researchers. It is thanks to them that numerous *moai* were re-erected and restored.

While the Rapa Nui were not completely wiped out (today about 3000 islanders identify as native), its history has given the world the term 'Easter Island Paradigm': societal collapse as a consequence of overpopulation, overexploitation and environmental destruction, plus an inability to adapt in time. This was a model in miniature, as it were, of what is currently happening on a global scale, so Easter Island can be seen as a warning. The Rapa Nui had to learn the hard way that there was no other island they could evacuate to, just as the people of planet Earth must learn – to quote an often-used slogan at climate-change demonstrations – that there is no planet B.

Above
Re-erected *moai* at Ahu Tongariki. These solemn stone statues are the iconic symbols of the collapsed former Rapa Nui society, the 'Easter Island Paradigm'.

Index

Picture credits

The author and publisher would like to thank the following institutions and individuals for permission to reproduce images in this book. In all cases, every effort has been made to credit the copyright holders, but should there be any omissions or errors the publisher would be pleased to insert the appropriate acknowledgement in any subsequent edition of this book.

14 (top) © Jassen Todorov/Solent News/Shutterstock **14** (bottom) © Kenneth C. Zirkel/Getty Images; **15** (top) Nikolay Tchaouchev/Unsplash **15** (bottom) © Eliza Snow/Getty Images **16** Rita Morais/Unsplash **18 &19** Courtesy Titan Missile Museum **20** Nick Fewings/Unsplash **21** 2021 Maxar Technologies, US Geological Survey, USDA Farm Service Agency, Map data © 2021 Google Earth **22** (left) © Marilyn Haddrill/Getty Images **22** (right) Samat Jain, CC **23** (top) Jack Aeby **23** (bottom) National Archives and Records Administration **24** © Peter Hohenhaus **26** Trager & Kuhn, Chadron, Nebr. the U.S Library of Congress's Prints and Photographs division **27** © Peter Hohenhaus **28** © Gunnar Rathbun/Shutterstock **30** (top) Rhonda Humphreys, CC **30** (bottom) © Amy Cicconi/Alamy Stock Photo **31** (top) Carol M Highsmith, CC **31** (bottom) Mariano deMiguel, CC **32** Brian W Schaller, CC **33** (top) © Peter Hohenhaus **33** (bottom) U.S. Navy photo by Brien Aho **34 & 35** © Giuseppe Crimeni/Shutterstock **36** (top) Photo by James E. Weichers **36** (bottom) ClassicStock/Alamy Stock Photo **37** (top) © Felix Mizioznikov/Shutterstock **37** (bottom) Ashim D'Silva/Unsplash **38** José Sánchez/Unsplash **39** Pit Stock/Shutterstock **42** (top)© Kobby Dagan/Shutterstock **42** (bottom) José Guadalupe Posada illustration **43** Mario Armas/AP/Shutterstock **44** AP © 1960 Shutterstock **45** Photo © 1950 Everett/Shutterstock **46–48** © Peter Hohenhaus **49** © Christopher Pillitz/Getty Images **50** Photo by Wayne Fenton/AP © Shutterstock **51** ilbusca/Getty Images **54** © 1978 AP/Shutterstock **55** (top) © Ken Hawkins/Alamy Stock Photo **55 & 56** © Peter Hohenhaus **57** (top) © Peter Hohenhaus **57** (bottom) Chatsam, CC **58** © Peter Hohenhaus **59** (top) © Mark Green **59** (bottom) © Peter Hohenhaus **60–62** © Peter Hohenhaus **63** (top) Dmitriy Serafin/Unsplash **64** (bottom) Antonella865 | Dreamstime.com **66** (top) © Global Warming Images/Shutterstock **66** (bottom) © Peter Hohenhaus **67** (top) © Peter Hohenhaus **67** (bottom) © Paul Grover/Shutterstock **68** © Peter Hohenhaus **69** (top) © Vadim Sidoruk/Getty Images **69** (bottom) © Alexey Seafarer/Shutterstock **70** Rama, CC **71** © Marc Lavaud/Shutterstock **72** James Eades/Unsplash **73** (top) Herbert Ponting, CC **73** (bottom) Sandwichgirl, CC **76** © Peter Hohenhaus **77** © Dirk Bleyer/Shutterstock 2011 **78** (top) Diego Delso, CC **78** (bottom) ARCTIC IMAGE/Alamy Stock Photo **79** © Peter Hohenhaus **81** ©A.Film/Shutterstock **82** (top) Johan Elisson, CC **82** (bottom) Andreas Lakso, CC **83** Ian Dagnall/Alamy Stock Photo **84** © 1972 Daily Mail/Shutterstock **85** (top) Joaquin Ossorio Castillo/Shutterstock **85** (bottom) Diego Cue, CC **86** George Sweeney/Alamy Stock Photo **87** © 2017 Shutterstock **88** AlBa344, CC **89** (top) Yoav Aziz/Unsplash **89** (bottom) Giuseppe Milo, CC **90** © Terry Kettlewell/Shutterstock **91** Avalon/Photoshot License/Alamy Stock Photo **92** Horton (Capt), War Office official photographer, Library of Congress's Prints and Photographs division **93** (top) EQRoy/Shutterstock **93** (left) Slavomir Freso, CC **93** (right) © Peter Hohenhaus **94** (top) © Mario De Biasi per Mondadori Portfolio/Getty Images **94** (bottom) © Peter Hohenhaus **95** (top) Have Camera Will Travel | Europe / Alamy Stock Photo **95** (bottom) Sergio Thor Miernik/Unsplash **98** © Gunter Hoffmann | Dreamstime.com **99** Hemis/Alamy Stock Photo **100** (top) © imageBROKER/Shutterstock **100** (bottom) © Everett Collection/Shutterstock **101–103** © Peter Hohenhaus **104** Danrok, CC **105** © Peter Hohenhaus **106** (top) Jebulon, CC **106** (bottom) Conseil Régional de Basse-Normandie/National Archives USA **107** (top) mauritius images GmbH/Alamy Stock Photo **107** (bottom) Bert Kaufmann, CC **108** (top) Helfaut Wizernes, CC **108** (bottom) openroads.com, CC **109** © Peter Hohenhaus **110** Ernest Brooks, CC **111** (top) Poudou99, CC **111** (bottom) © Peter Hohenhaus **112** (top) BRYANT Nicolas/SAGAPHOTO.COM/Alamy Stock Photo **112** (bottom) Tetris L, CC **113** (top) © Kev Gregory/Shutterstock **113** (bottom) Wernervc, CC **114** (background) Dale Cruse, CC **114** (foreground) Fred Pixlab/Unsplash **115** Jerome Cid/123RF **116** © Ossuaire de Douaumont **117** Isopix/Shutterstock **118** Photo by Anne Frank Fonds – Basel via Getty Images **119** (left) 2018 Joe deSousa, CC **119** (right) Robin Utrecht/Shutterstock **119** (bottom) Cezary P, CC **120** (top) JoJan, CC **120** (bottom)Trougnouf (Benoit Brummer), CC **121** (top) Michel van der Burg, CC **121** (bottom left) Katrien Hendrickx **121** (bottom right) JMDV – Fonds Kummer **122** F.J. Lamphere. Everett Collection/Shutterstock **123** (top) © Peter Hohenhaus **123** (bottom) Tim Bekaert, CC **124** (top) © Peter Hohenhaus **124** (bottom) ThruTheseLines, CC **125** (top) Henry Armytage Sanders. National Library NZ on The Commons **125** (bottom) Jamain, CC **128** Gift of the USHMM, from the Collections of The National World War II Museum **129** (top) Jens Lingenau, CC **129** (bottom) Carmelo Paulo R. Bayarcal, CC **130** (top) Photo: KZ-Gedenkstätte Neuengamme (ÖA) **130** (bottom) Patrick Piel/Getty Images **131** United States Army Signal Corps, photographer, U.S. National Archives and Records Administration **132** Hohl/Getty Images **133** (top) imageBROKER/Shutterstock **133** (bottom) Rennett Stowe, CC **134** Victor Malyushev/Unsplash **135** Prisma by Dukas Presseagentur GmbH/Alamy Stock Photo **136** (top) © Peter Hohenhaus **136** (bottom) imageBROKER/Shutterstock **137** (top) Chron-Paul, CC **137** (bottom) Dietmar Rabich, CC **138** ©2007 Jürgen Matern **139** (top) Pim Menkveld/Unsplash **139** (bottom) CC **140** (top) Einaz80, CC **140** (bottom) Slaunger, CC **141** (top) © 1981 Shutterstock **141** (middle) Central Intelligence Agency **142** (top) Stephanie Pilick/EPA/Shutterstock **142** (bottom) Dennis Jarvis, CC **143** © Peter Hohenhaus **144** Michael Sohn/AP **145** (top) Adrià Ariste, CC **145** (bottom) Courtesy Spy Museum Berlin **146** Courtesy Stasi Museum **147** © Peter Hohenhaus **148** Gero Camp/Unsplash **149** (top) Andreas Daniel Teutsch, CC **149** (bottom) U.S. Army Lt. Moore, National Archives and Records Administration **150** (top) Rainer Halama, CC **150** (bottom) Anne Seubert/Unsplash **151** © Peter Hohenhaus **152** (top) Sockenhorst, CC **152** (bottom) Michiel2005 **153** Julie Woodhouse/imageBROKER/Shutterstock **154 & 155** © Peter Hohenhaus **156** (top) Deutsches Bundesarchiv **156** (bottom) Dnalor 01, CC **157** Stefan Just, CC **158** Alexander Godulla **159** © Peter Hohenhaus **160** (left) Gryffindor, CC **160** (right) CC **161** (top) Peter Haas, CC **161** (bottom) Ronald Zak/AP/Shutterstock **162** (top) Thomas Ledl, CC **162** (bottom) Alexander Klein/Getty Images **163** © Peter Hohenhaus **164** (top) © Krzysztof Nahlik | Dreamstime.com **164** (bottom) Wojciech Pędzich, CC **165** Andrzej Otrębski, CC **166** Dr. Avishai Teiche, CC **167** CC **168** (top) Endless Travel/Alamy Stock Photo **168** (bottom) Adrian Grycuk, CC **169** Adrian Grycuk, CC **170** (top) Robert Hoetink/Shutterstock **170** (bottom) imageBROKER/Alamy Stock Photo **171** (top) © Peter Hohenhaus **171** (bottom) anonymous, possibly SS photographers E. Hoffmann & B. Walter. Collection at Yad Vashem **172** (top) © Bernard Bialorucki | Dreamstime.com **172** (bottom) © Peter Hohenhaus **173** © Peter Hohenhaus **174** (top) Gysembergh Benoit/Getty Images **174** (bottom) Azymut (Rafał M. Socha), CC **175** Christian Faludi/Shutterstock **176** Ashley Pomeroy, CC **177** LI SEN/Shutterstock **178** Hamza Makhchoune/Shutterstock **179** Keystone/Getty Images **180** (top) Tito Slack/Shutterstock **180** (bottom) Wilson44691, CC **181** (top) Darren Donahue, CC **181** (bottom) Alizada Studios/Shutterstock **185** Davide Ederle/Getty Images **186** (top) © Peter Hohenhaus **186** (bottom) courtesy Museo per la Memoria di Ustica **187** (top) © Enzolisi84 | Dreamstime.com **187** (bottom) © Izanbar | Dreamstime.com **188** (top) Wellcome Collection. Attribution 4.0 International (CC BY 4.0) **188** (bottom) geogphotos/Alamy Stock Photo **189 & 191** © Peter Hohenhaus **192** (top) Sasa Stojanovic Sapa/Getty Images **192** (bottom) Stepo/Getty Images **193** © Peter Hohenhaus **194** © Fotokon | Dreamstime.com **195** (top) © Andrey Shevchenko | Dreamstime.com **195** (bottom) © Tatsiana Hendzel | Dreamstime.com **196** © Krutenyuk | Dreamstime.com **197** © Svglass | Dreamstime.com **198** Robert Mullan/Shutterstock **199** © Tomasz Wozniak | Dreamstime.com **200** © Mihai Olaru | Dreamstime.com **201** © Peter Hohenhaus **202** Jean Tesseyre/Getty Images **203** George Grantham Bain Collection, Library of Congress Prints and Photographs Division **204** © Tarik Gok | Dreamstime.com **205** © Mariohagen | Dreamstime.com **208** Chris Lewington/Alamy Stock Photo **209** (left) Ann Randall **209** (right) Shawshots/Alamy Stock Photo **209** (bottom) Geoff Moore/Shutterstock **210** © Romans Klevcovs | Dreamstime.com **211** Heritage Images/Getty Images **212** (top) © Peter Hohenhaus **212** (bottom) Courtesy Karosta Prison **213 & 214** © Peter Hohenhaus **215** © Robert Harding/Alamy Stock Photo **216** © Peter Hohenhaus **217** (top) © Mariusz Prusaczyk | Dreamstime.com **217** (bottom) © Kateryna Levchenko | Dreamstime.com **218** © Ryhor Bruyeu | Dreamstime.com **219** © Peter Hohenhaus **220** © 1986 Shutterstock **221** (top) Mick dePaola/Unsplash **221** (bottom) © Peter Hohenhaus **222** (top) © Tetyana Kochneva | Dreamstime.com **222** (bottom) © Peter Hohenhaus **223** © Peter Hohenhaus **224** CC **225** © Vladyslav Musiienko | Dreamstime.com **226** © Peter Hohenhaus **227** Dorling Kindersley Ltd/Alamy Stock Photo **228** (top) 8H/Shutterstock **228** (bottom) M101Studio/Shutterstock **229** (left) © Sergeyussr | Dreamstime.com **229** (right) © Peter Hohenhaus **229** (bottom) © Sergeyussr | Dreamstime.com **230** Daniel Klein/Unsplash **231** © Igor Dolgov | Dreamstime.com **232** © Anna Krivitskaia | Dreamstime.com **233** Michael Parulava/Unsplash **234** © Markwaters | Dreamstime.com **235** Maxim Shipenkov/EPA/Shutterstock **236** © Alexander Tolstykh | Dreamstime.com **237** Dmitry Antropov/Unsplash **238 & 239** © Peter Hohenhaus **242** © Leonid Andronov | Dreamstime.com **243** (top) Salvador Aznar/Getty Images **243** (bottom) © Smandy | Dreamstime.com **244** Collection of the Smithsonian National Museum of African American History and Culture, Gift of the Liljenquist Family **245** Michael Agbenyegah/Shutterstock **246** © Peter Hohenhaus **247** (top) Digital Commonwealth/Boston Public Library **247** (bottom) © Peter Hohenhaus **248** Ben Curtis/AP/Shutterstock **249** (top) © Peter Hohenhaus **249** (bottom) © Antonella865 | Dreamstime.com **251** Susie Bennett/Alamy Stock Photo **252** Chip Somodevilla/Getty Images **253** Joerg Boethling/Alamy Stock Photo **254** (top) panoglobe/Shutterstock **254** (bottom) © Peter Hohenhaus **255** renelo/Getty Images **256** (top) SkyPixels, CC **256** (bottom) Justin Reznick/Getty Images **257** © Ariadna22822 | Dreamstime.com **258** Naeblys/Shutterstock **259** (top) Sipa/Shutterstock **259** (bottom) Robert Harding/Alamy Stock Photo **263** (top) Avishai Teicher via the PikiWiki, CC **263** (bottom) © Rrodrickbeiler | Dreamstime.com **264** Dave Herring/Unsplash **265** (left) © Turfantastik | Dreamstime.com **265** (right) © Atosan | Dreamstime.com **266** Morten Hvaal/AP/Shutterstock **267** Aravind Patnaik/Unsplash **268** Ondřej Žváček, CC **269** (top) © Peter Hohenhaus **269** (bottom) KennyOMG, CC **270** Joel Carillet/Getty Images **271** © Peter Hohenhaus **272** © imageBROKER/Shutterstock **273** NASA Photo **274** NASA Photo/Alamy Stock Photo **275** (top and middle) Nina Alizada/Shutterstock **275** bottom) Bert de Ruiter/Alamy Stock Photo **276** John van Hasselt/Corbis Historical/Getty Images **277** (top) Alexander Zemlianichenko/AP/Shutterstock **277** (bottom) John van Hasselt/Corbis Historical/Getty Images **278** Freda Bouskoutas/Getty Images **282** © Smandy | Dreamstime.com **283** (top)© Sisirbanga | Dreamstime.com **283** (bottom left) Narinder Nanu/Getty Images **283** (bottom right) cornfield/Shutterstock **284** (left) chris0241/Shutterstock **284** (right) © Arindam Banerjee | Dreamstime.com **285–289** © Peter Hohenhaus **290** CPA Media Pte Ltd/Alamy Stock Photo **291** Mak Remissa/EPA-EFE © 2020 Shutterstock **292** © 1960 Shutterstock **293 & 294** © Peter Hohenhaus **295** (top) © Gougnaf16 | Dreamstime.com **295** (bottom) © Dndavis | Dreamstime.com **298** Northcliffe Collection/ANL © 1945 Shutterstock **299** © Peter Hohenhaus **300** (top) © Peter Hohenhaus **300** (bottom) © Yudhistira Dharma | Dreamstime.com **301** (main image) Maksym Ivashchenko/Unsplash **301** (inset image) Moritz Wolf/imageBROKER/Shutterstock **302 & 303** © Peter Hohenhaus **304** James D Morgan/Getty Images **305** (top) © Torsten Pursche | Dreamstime.com **305** (bottom) Penny Tweedie/Getty Images **306** (top) CC **306** (bottom) KC Hunter/Alamy Stock Photo **307** (top) © Peter Hohenhaus **307** (bottom) © Torsten Pursche | Dreamstime.com **310** Kevincho Photography/Getty Images **311** (left) Chine Nouvelle/SIPA © 2019 Shutterstock **311** (right) Hap/Quirky China News © 2014 Shutterstock **313** agefotostock/Alamy Stock Photo **314** Kcna/EPA-EFE © 2014 Shutterstock **315** Bjørn Christian Tørrissen, CC **316** United States Navy **317** © Artaporn Puthikampol | Dreamstime.com **318** © Peter Hohenhaus **319** Air Photo Service/AFP **320** (top) winhorse/iStock/Getty Images **320** (bottom) © Bennnn | Dreamstime.com **321** (top) yoshi0511/Shutterstock **321** (bottom) © Peter Hohenhaus **322** Air Photo Service/AFP **323** (top) World History Archive/Alamy Stock Photo **323** (bottom) Glasshouse Images © 1945 Shutterstock **324** (top) © Peter Hohenhaus **324** (bottom) AP/Shutterstock **325** © Nuvisage | Dreamstime.com **326** GBM Historical Images © 1945 Shutterstock **327** (left) pang_oasis/Shutterstock **327** (right) Michael Gordon/Shutterstock **328** Courtesy Oka Masaharu Memorial Peace Museum **329** Aflo Co. Ltd./Alamy Stock Photo **330** PassionPhotography/Shutterstock **331** © Peter Hohenhaus **334** Keith Davey/UnSplash **335** (top) Sipa © 1985 Shutterstock **335** (bottom) Album/Alamy Stock Photo **336** (top) yenwen/iStock/Getty Images **336** (bottom) © Nigel Spiers | Dreamstime.com **337** Frilet © 1988 Shutterstock **338** U.S. Dept of Defense, Library of Congress **340** (top) © Peter Hohenhaus **340** (bottom) © Jordan Tan | Dreamstime.com **341& 342** © Peter Hohenhaus **343** © Vacclav | Dreamstime.com **344** (top) © Peter Hohenhaus **344** (bottom) U.S .Geological Survey **345** © Peter Hohenhaus

Dark statistics resources

While it is rarely possible to provide definitive statistics for almost any subject, with facts and figures relating to wars and atrocities in particular it is especially difficult to give information with any great degree of assurance. The statistics provided in the boxes throughout this book should be seen as a guide only. Any omissions or errors are the responsibility of the publisher and not the author. These have been largely researched from the following sources and cross-checked against other reliable sources in order to be as accurate as possible. Please note that links were correct at the time of writing in March 2021.

p16 Alcatraz
alcatrazhistory.com: https://bit.ly/3rtQab8

p39 9/11 Memorial
National 9/11 Memorial & Museum (911memorial.org):
https://bit.ly/2OeS5SH
CNN.com: https://cnn.it/3ekpF4s

p50 Soufrière Hills
Encyclopedia Britannica (britannica.com):
https://bit.ly/3kVp4Hr

p61 Villa Grimaldi
Reuters (reuters.com): https://reut.rs/2MX9UFf
The Valech Report (officially The National Commission on Political Imprisonment and Torture Report) November 29, 2004 and June 1, 2005

p86 The Troubles
reuters.com: https://reut.rs/3qxKg7S
britannica.com: https://bit.ly/3bqQxOj
Lost Lives by David McKittrick, Seamus Kelters, Brian Feeney, Chris Thornton and David McVea (Edinburgh: Mainstream Publishing, 2007.

p110 The Somme
Imperial War Museum (iwm.org.uk):
https://bit.ly/3emZ9aq
National Army Museum (nam.ac.uk):
https://bit.ly/2MVrsRZ

p114 Paris Catacombs
Catacombes de Paris (catacombs.paris.fr):
https://bit.ly/3bow24z
Smithsonian Magazine: https://bit.ly/38C7Vhl

p131 Nuremberg Trials
britannica.com: https://bit.ly/3cfvAFd
United States Holocaust Memorial Museum
(encyclopedia.ushmm.org): https://bit.ly/38jVVAW

p135 The Holocaust
encyclopedia.ushmm.org: https://bit.ly/3ejZMBy

p146 The Stasi
britannica.com:
https://bit.ly/2MZAOwc
https://bit.ly/3bqsEX1

p153 Dresden Bombings
britannica.com: https://bit.ly/3v7nhUi
bbc.co.uk: https://bbc.in/3c6ayJ2

p196 Bosnian War
ushmm.org: https://bit.ly/3OmWBkr
britannica.com: https://bit.ly/3OluKkP

p204 Gallipoli
History Group of the New Zealand Ministry for Culture and Heritage (NZHistory.net.nz): https://bit.ly/3kV3Ucw

p218 Great Patriotic War
The caveat relating to these statistics in Encyclopedia Britannica bears repeating here:
'The statistics on World War II casualties are inexact. Only for the United States and the British Commonwealth can official figures showing killed, wounded, prisoners or missing for the armed forces be cited with any degree of assurance. For most other nations, only estimates of varying reliability exist. Statistical accounting broke down in both Allied and Axis nations when whole armies were surrendered or dispersed. Guerrilla warfare, changes in international boundaries, and mass shifts in population vastly complicated postwar efforts to arrive at accurate figures even for the total dead from all causes.'
britannica.com: https://bit.ly/3cawcvH

p232 Leningrad Blockade
history.com (A+E Networks® UK, a joint venture between Hearst and Sky): https://bit.ly/3ek53Jm
The Guardian: https://bit.ly/3ek7gVm
britannica.com: https://bit.ly/3qA9vGF

p245 The Slave Trade
The National Archives (nationalarchives.govt.uk):
https://bit.ly/3kUTE44
The New York Times: https://nyti.ms/3rEKFqt

p273 Aral Sea
britannica.com: https://bit.ly/3cavy1f
sciencedirect.com: https://bit.ly/3eliSHI

p295 The Vietnam War
britannica.com: https://bit.ly/3bopUcC

p323 Hiroshima
atomicarchive.com: https://bit.ly/3cdZyZZ
San Diego Tribune: https://bit.ly/30qbi6e

p339 Pearl Harbor
history.com: https://bit.ly/3eiYNlb

Acknowledgements

First of all I'd like to thank senior editor Gaynor Sermon at Laurence King Publishing for her tireless work and seeing the book through to the final stages of the editing process. My thanks also go to Laurence King's commissioning editor Zara Larcombe, who first contacted me about the idea for this book and with whom the initial plans were laid out and who also accompanied the project through its most critical early stage. My thanks additionally go to the book's designer, Charlie Smith.

Furthermore there have been various people who I'm indebted to for advice, hints, comments, support or organizational assistance with regard to particular destinations (especially those that are trickier to get to). In no particular order these people include the following: Darmon Richter, Rachelle Meilleur, Evan Panagopoulos, Sam Clark, Tom Coote, Tony Johnston, Jan-Peter Abraham, Katharine Eyre, Christian Wagner, Salvador de Caires, Hideto Kimura, Cheryl Robbins, John Turner, Dylan Harris, Michael Klenner, Tsvetelina Tsankova, Simon Cockerell, Pete Ford, Simon White, Robin Hilliard, Ian Vasey, Lucas Klamert, David Robinson, Tom Brosnahan, Howard Sawyer, Chuck Penson, Derek Pettersson, Patrick Watts, Karin Taira, Richard Halberstadt, Andrew Meek, Mykhailo Teslenko, Brano Chrenka, Alan Warren, Richard Weber, Alexander Shchepetkov, and all those many excellent guides I had at particular sites, too many to list in full. If I've forgotten anybody important, then I apologize.

Most significantly, I'd like to express my infinite gratitude to my beloved wife, Sally McMullen, for all her moral and practical support and active involvement in the editing process. Without all of that, this book would never have been possible!

About the author

Dr. Peter Hohenhaus was born in Hamburg, north Germany. It's also where he studied and took his PhD in English linguistics. He worked as a lecturer in a number of British and German universities and now lives in Vienna, Austria. He's been studying dark tourism since 2007, has written about it in both academia and the media, and has been compiling the largest online resource about dark destinations worldwide, dark-tourism.com, since 2009. As an active traveller, and keen photography enthusiast, he's been to some 900 dark destinations in almost 100 countries.